the Drunken Sailor

THE LIFE OF THE POET

Arthur Rimbaud

IN HIS OWN WORDS

the Drunken Sailor
THE LIFE OF THE POET
Arthur Rimbaud
IN HIS OWN WORDS

by nick hayes

JONATHAN CAPE
LONDON

1 3 5 7 9 10 8 6 4 2

Jonathan Cape, an imprint of Vintage Publishing,
20 Vauxhall Bridge Road,
London SW1V 2SA

Jonathan Cape is part of the Penguin Random House group of companies
whose addresses can be found at global.penguinrandomhouse.com.

Copyright © Nick Hayes 2018

First published in the United Kingdom by Jonathan Cape in 2018

penguin.co.uk/vintage

A CIP catalogue record for this book is available from the British Library

ISBN 9781910702062

Printed and bound in China
by C & C Offset Printing Co., Ltd

for all those
setting out...

"Watchman,
what of the night?"
he asked.
It was
Rimbaud
who was to reply
to that.

—JOHN BERGER

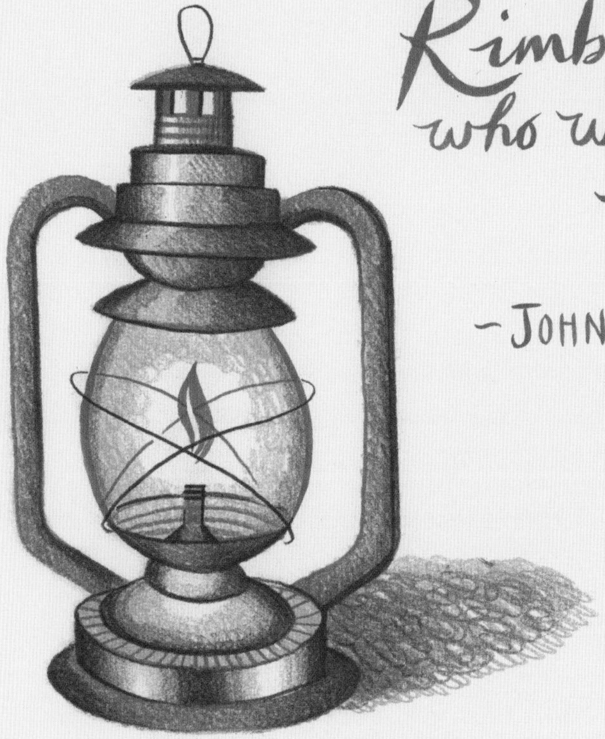

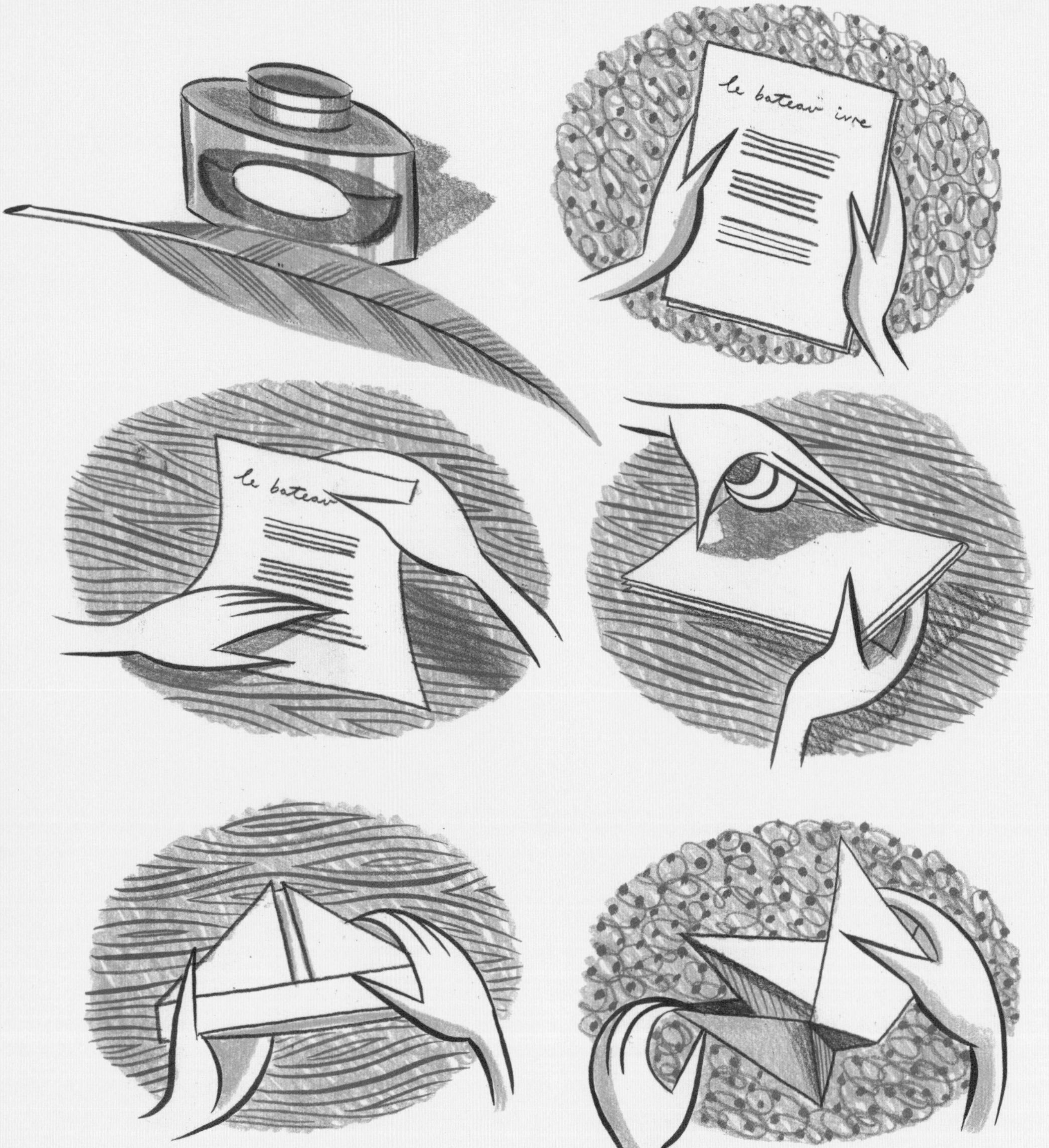
le bateau ivre
le bateau

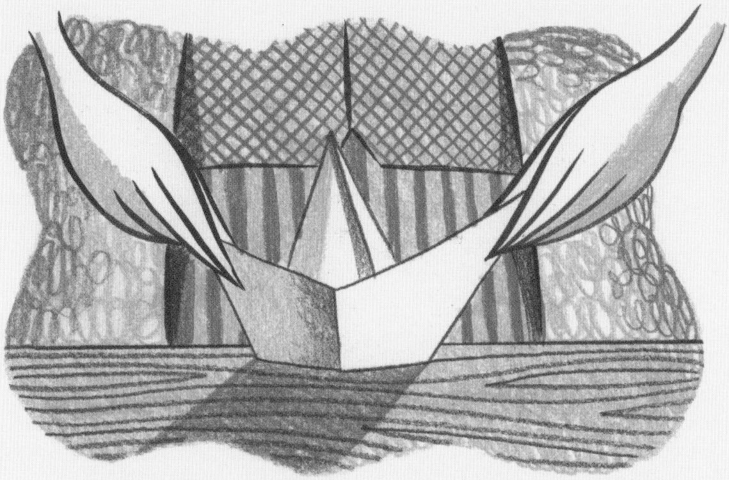
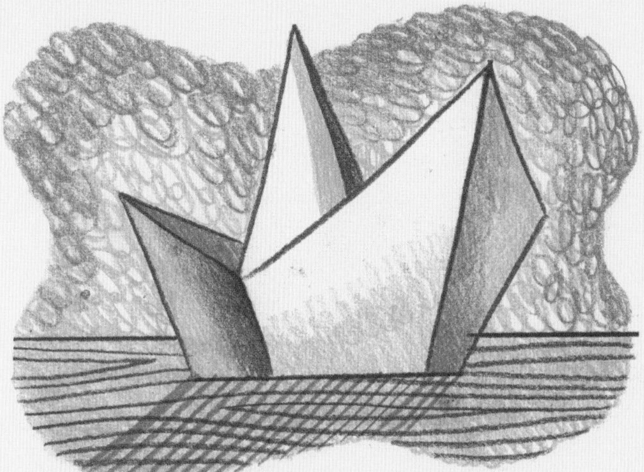
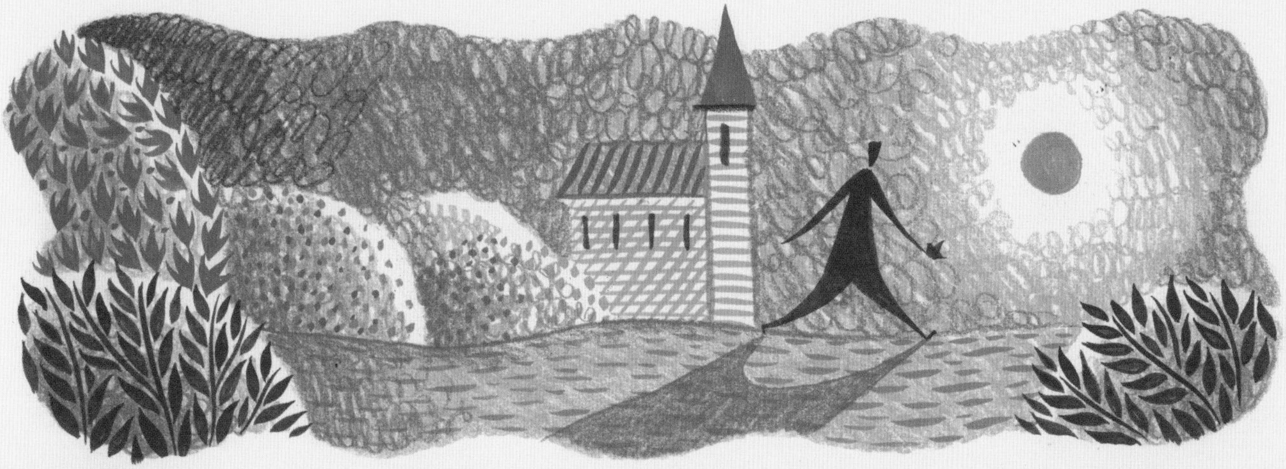
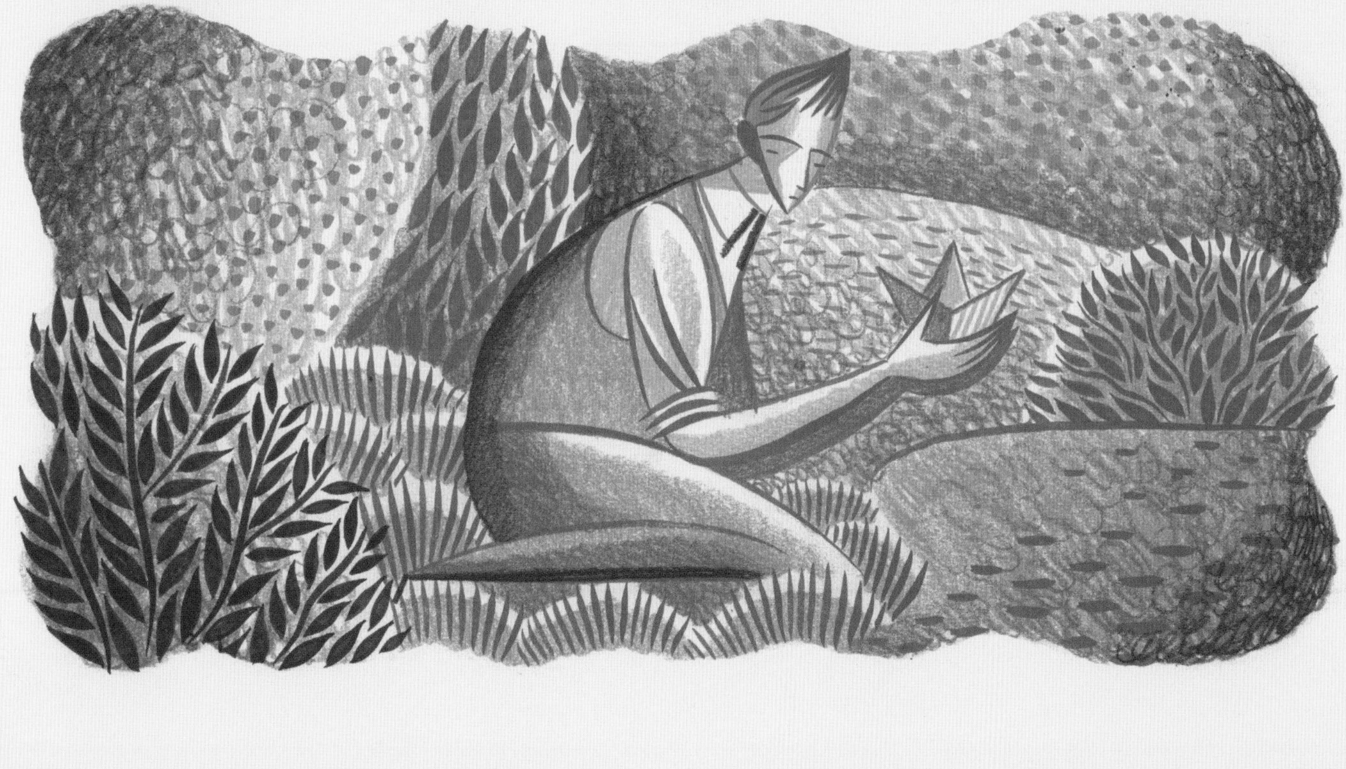

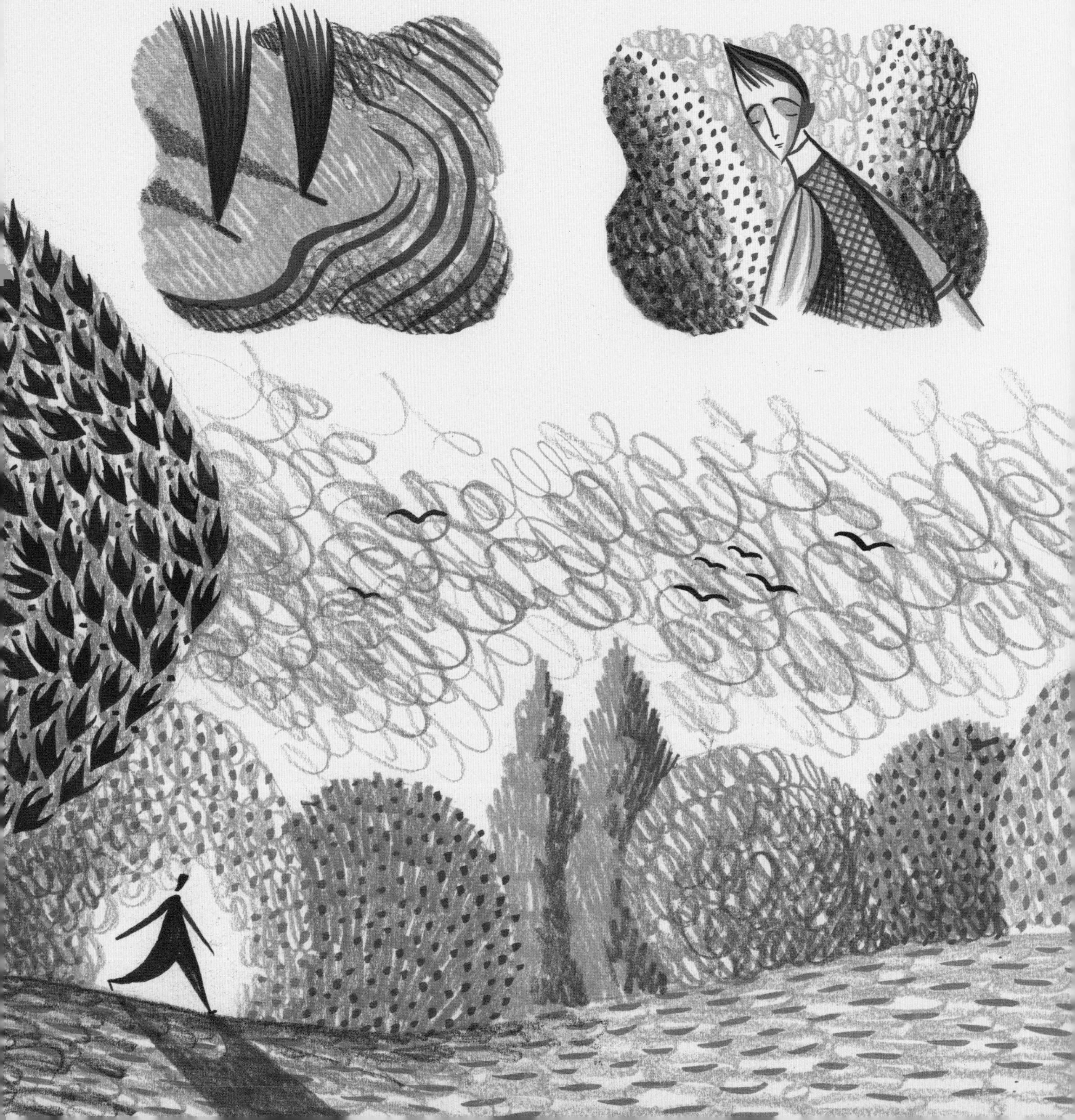

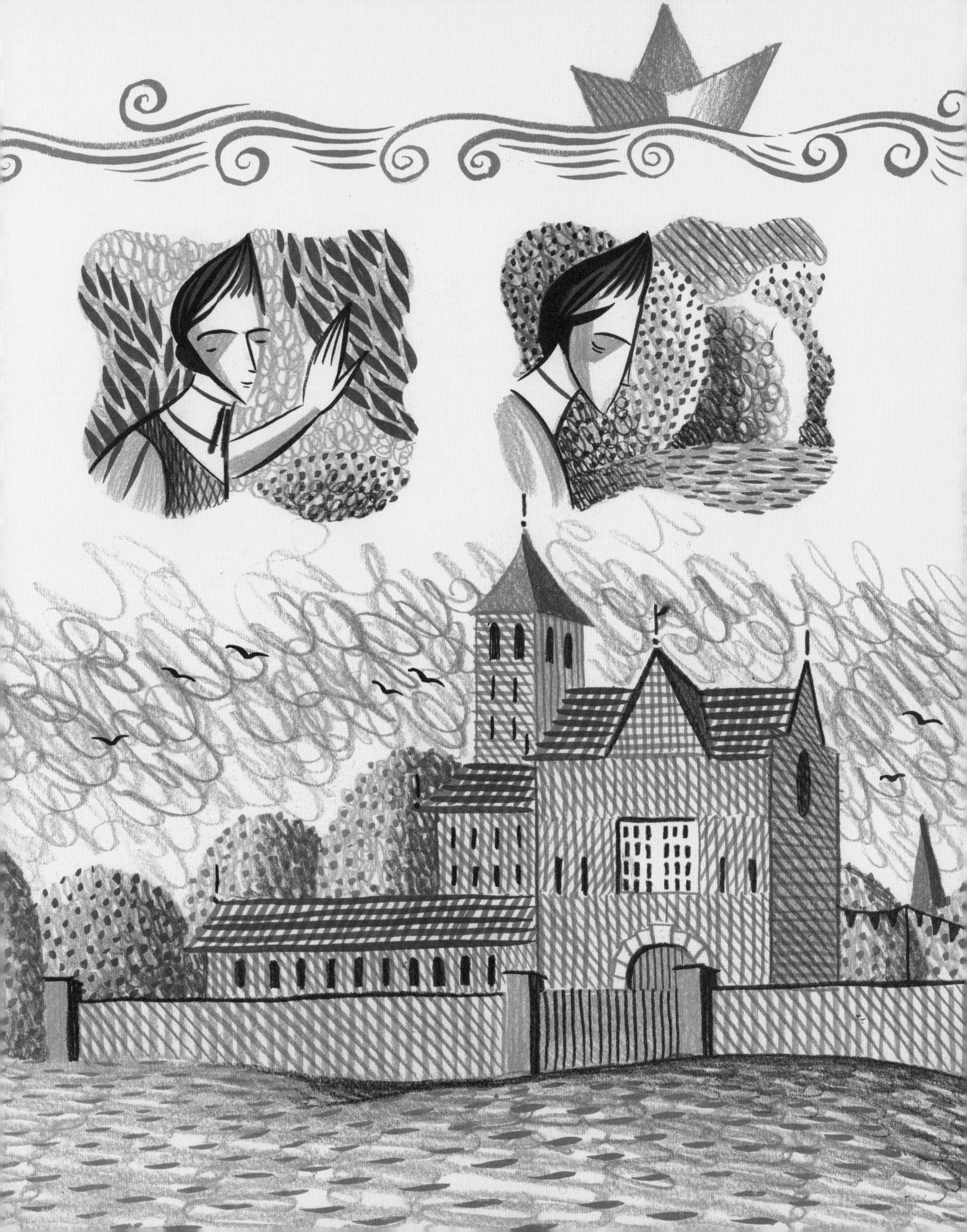

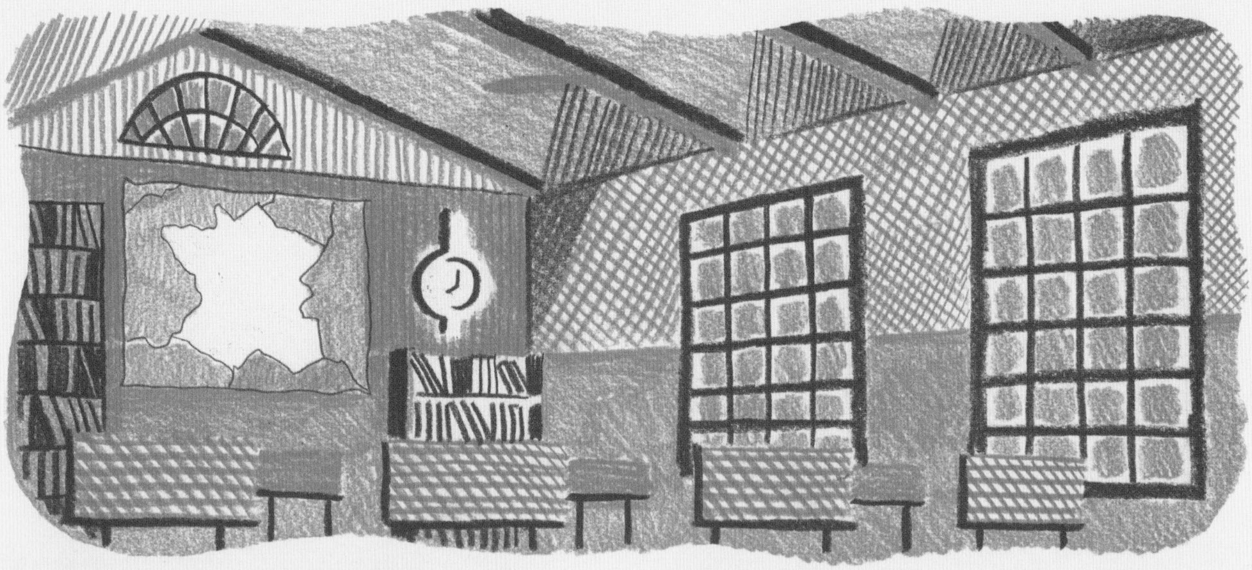

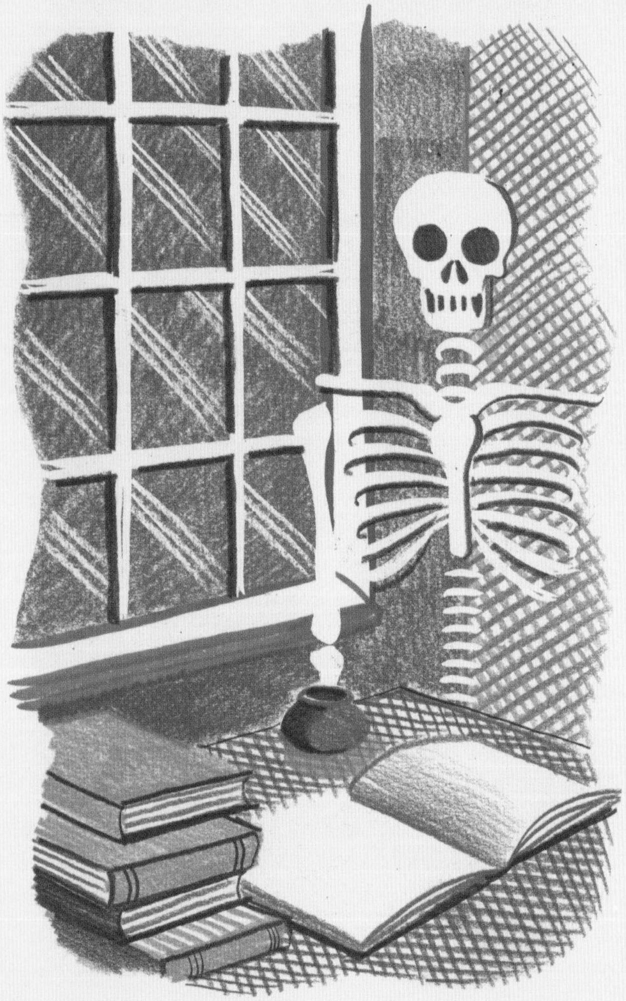

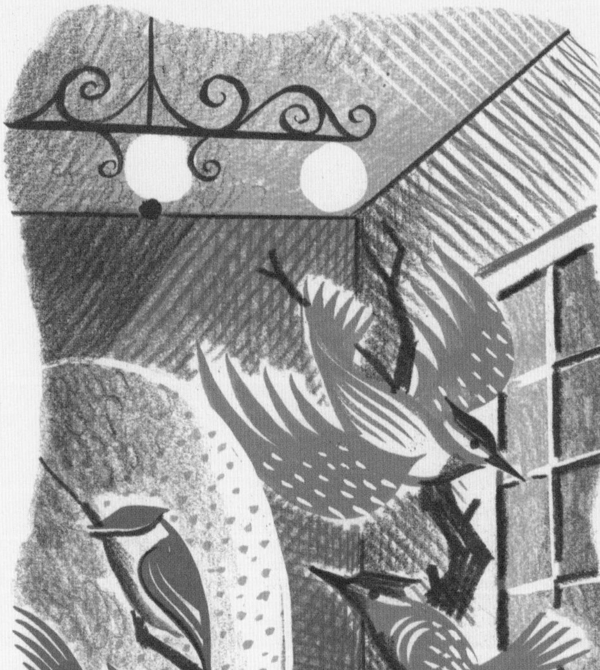

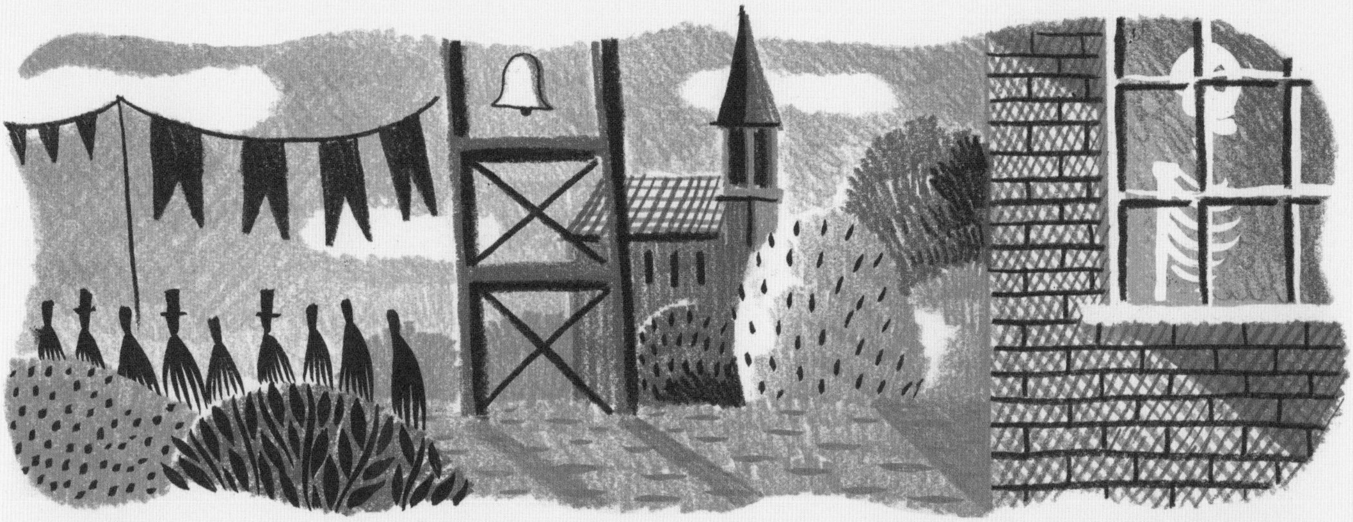

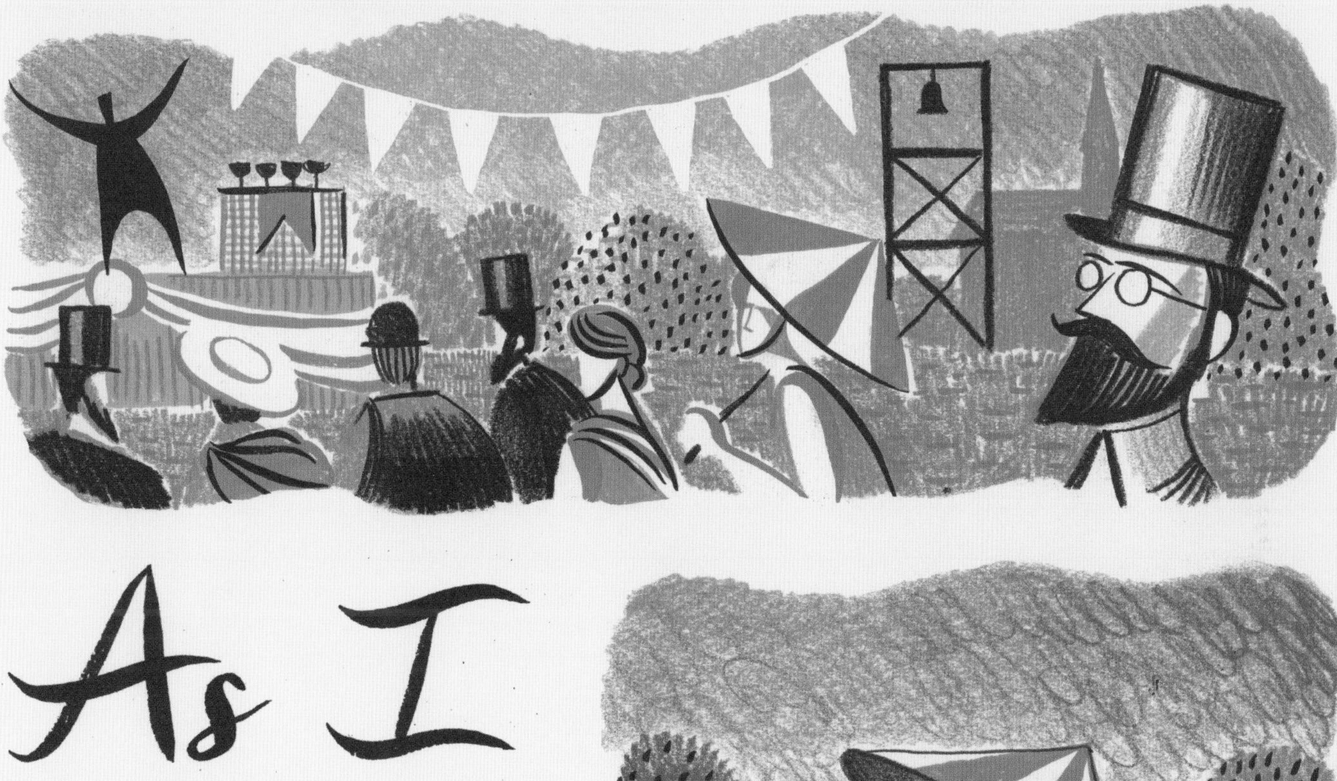

As I

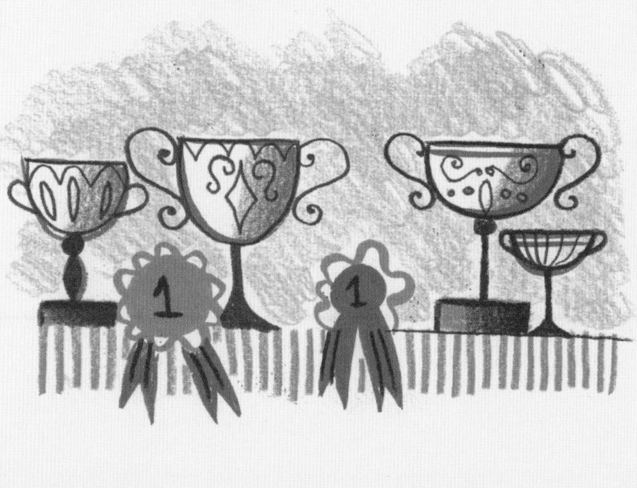

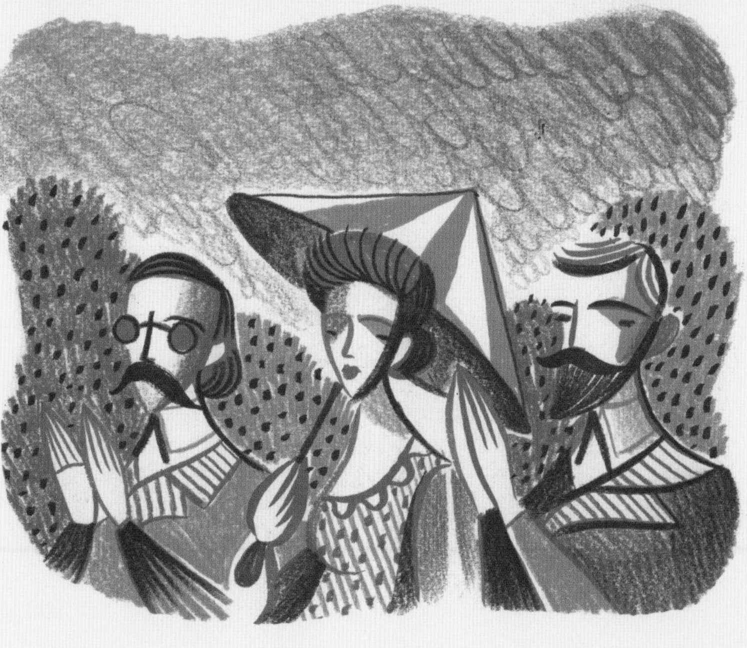

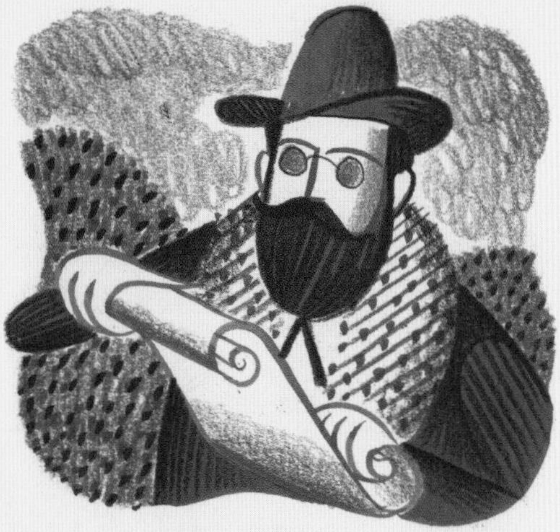

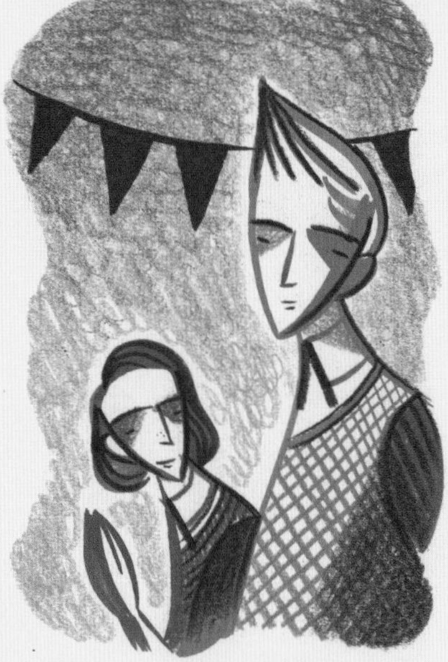

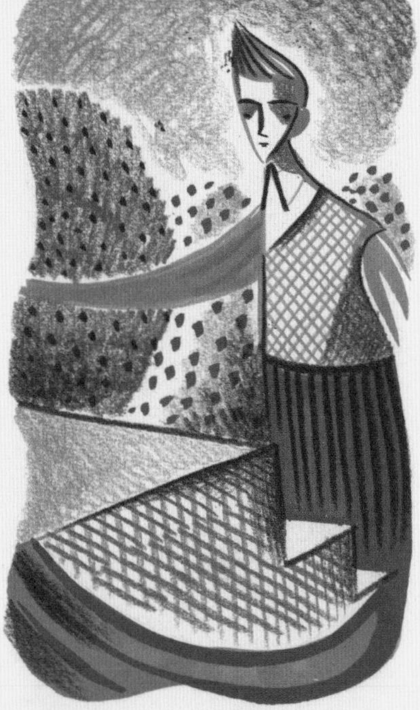

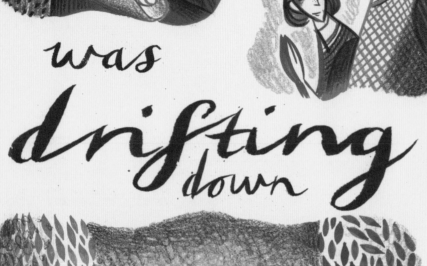

was
drifting
down

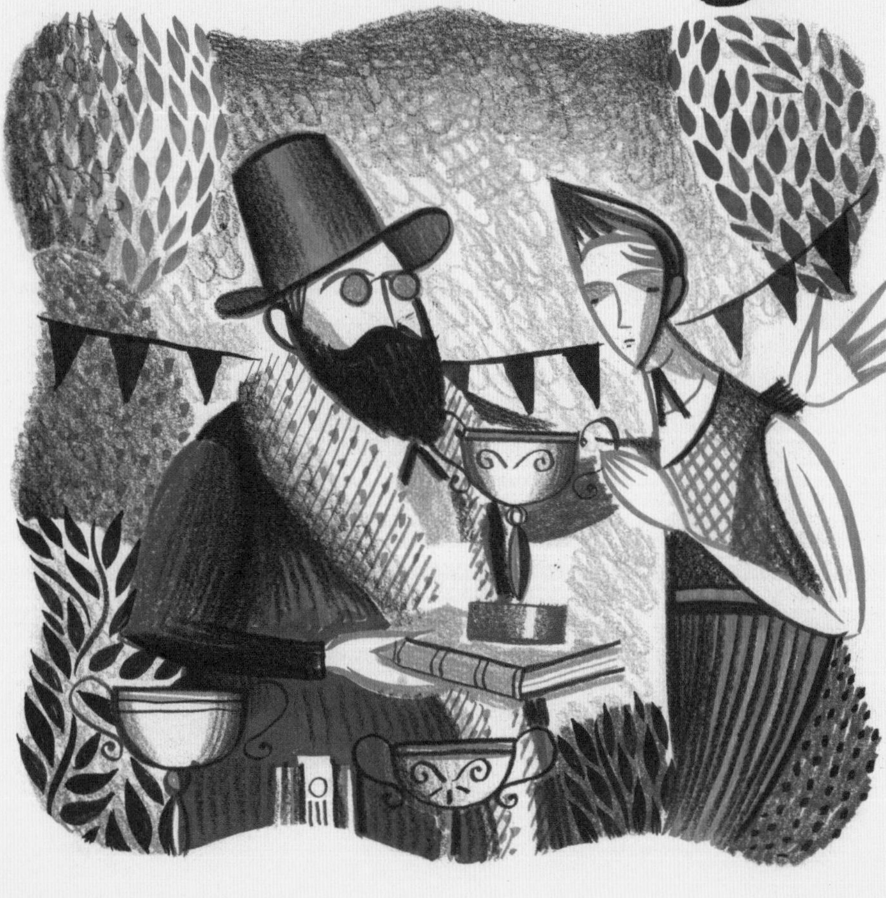

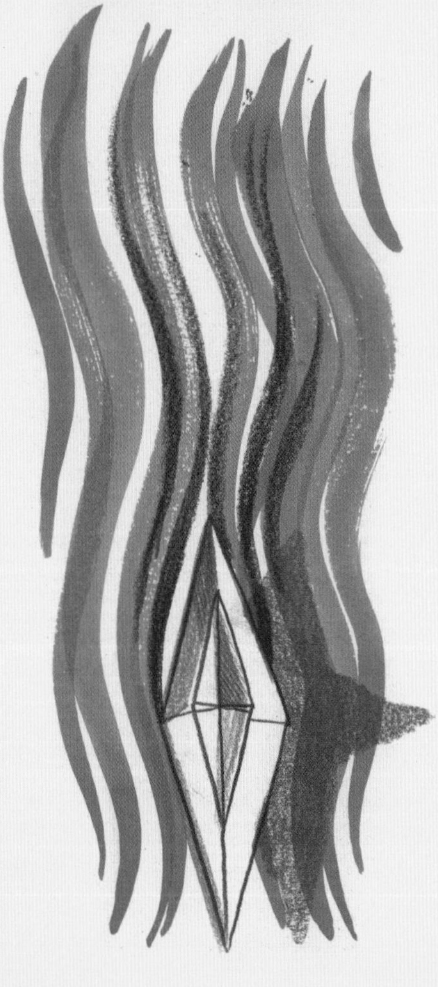

INDIFFERENT

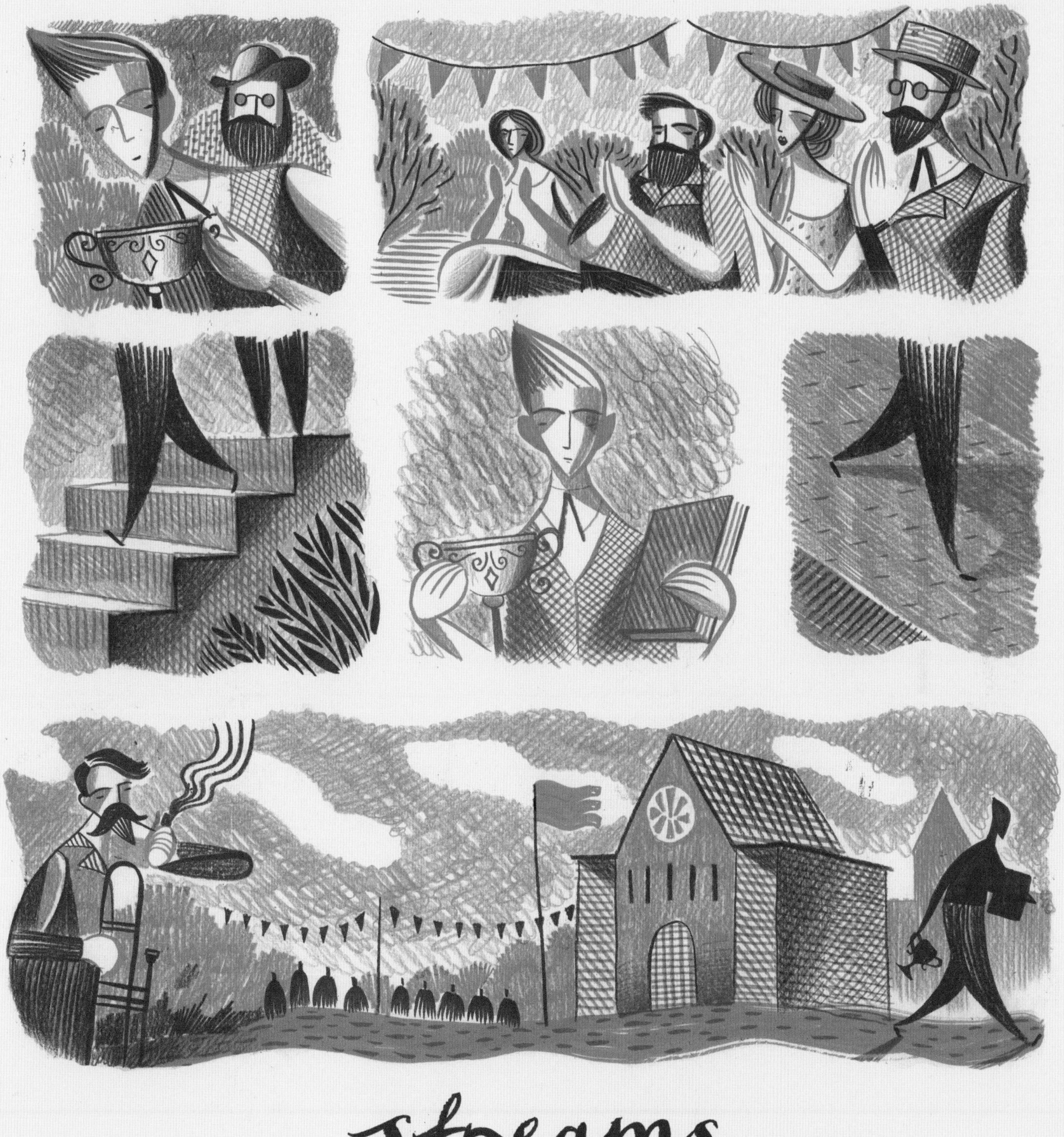

streams,

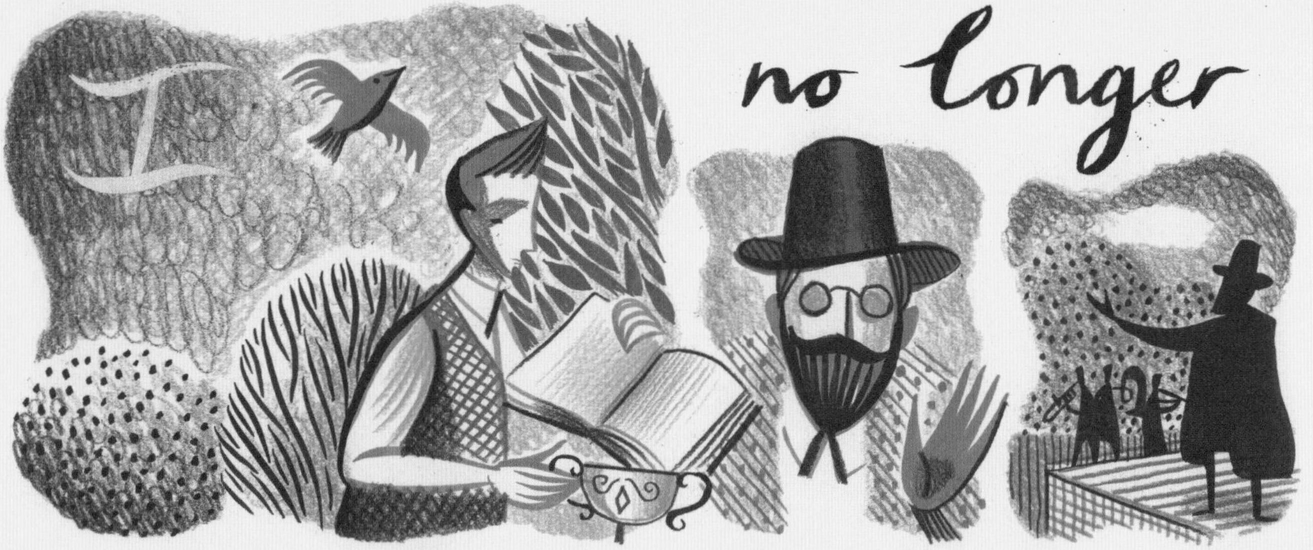
I

no longer

heeded

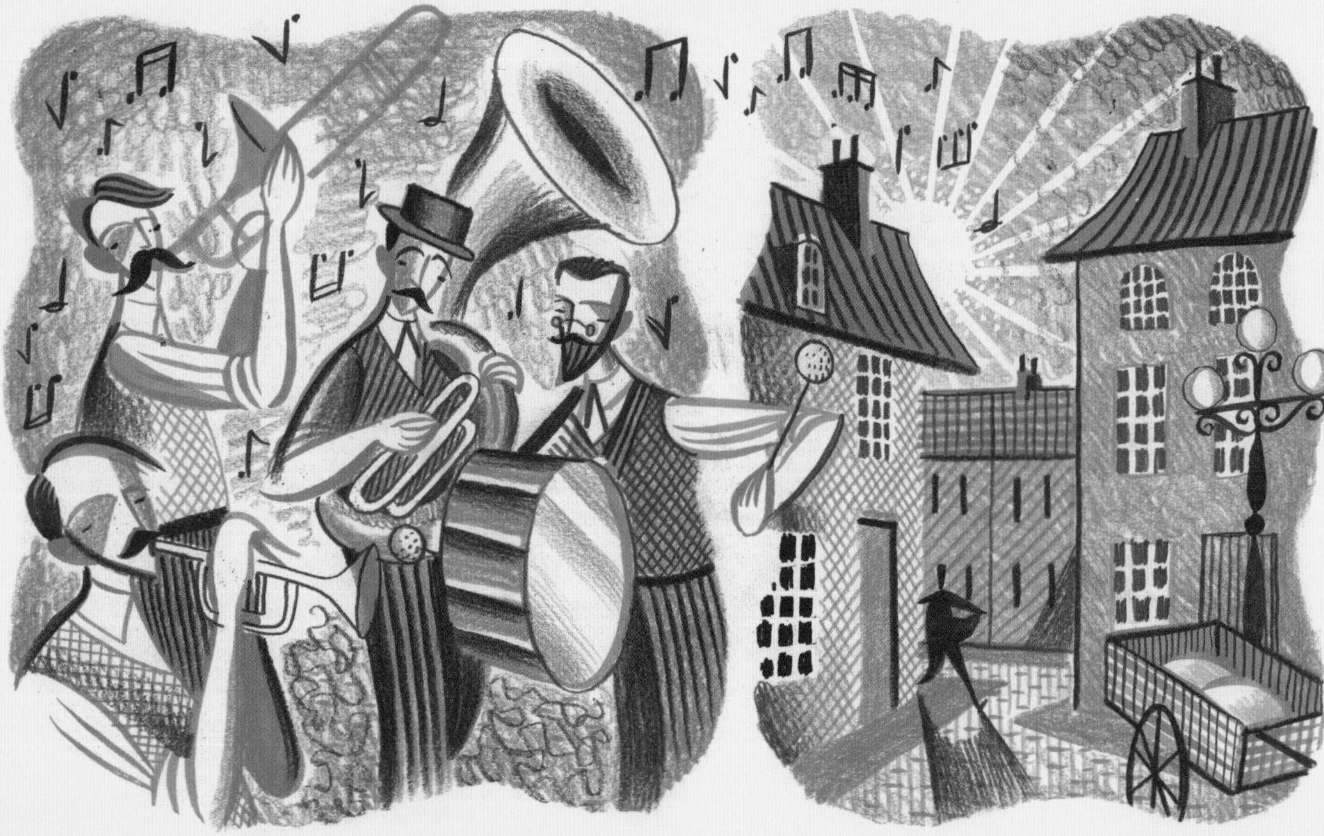

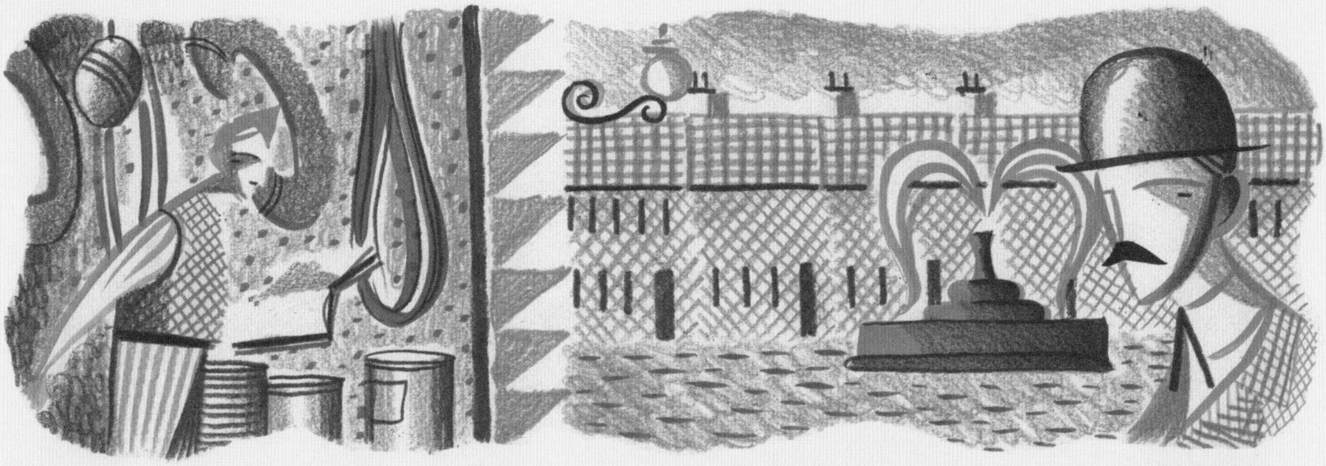

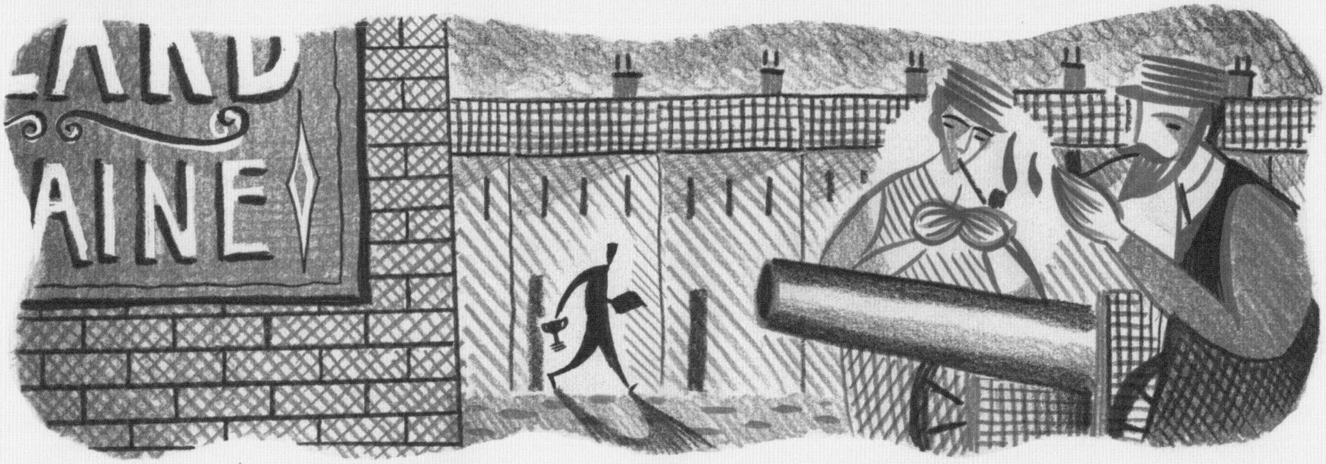
ARD
AINE

the haulers,

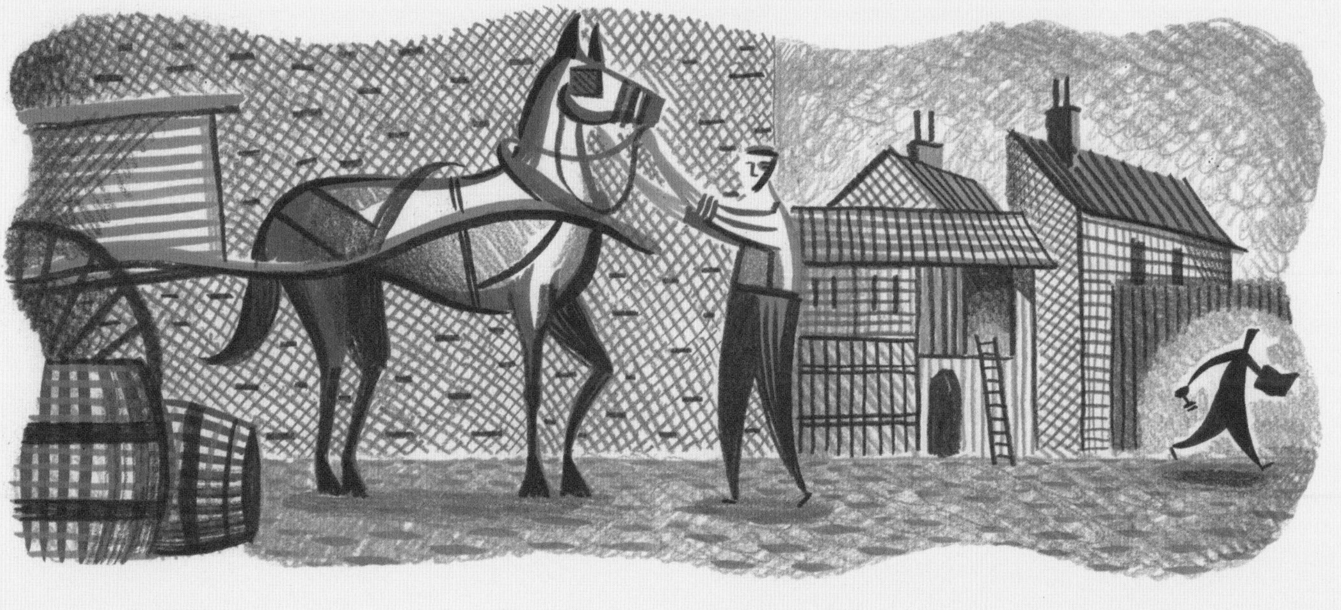

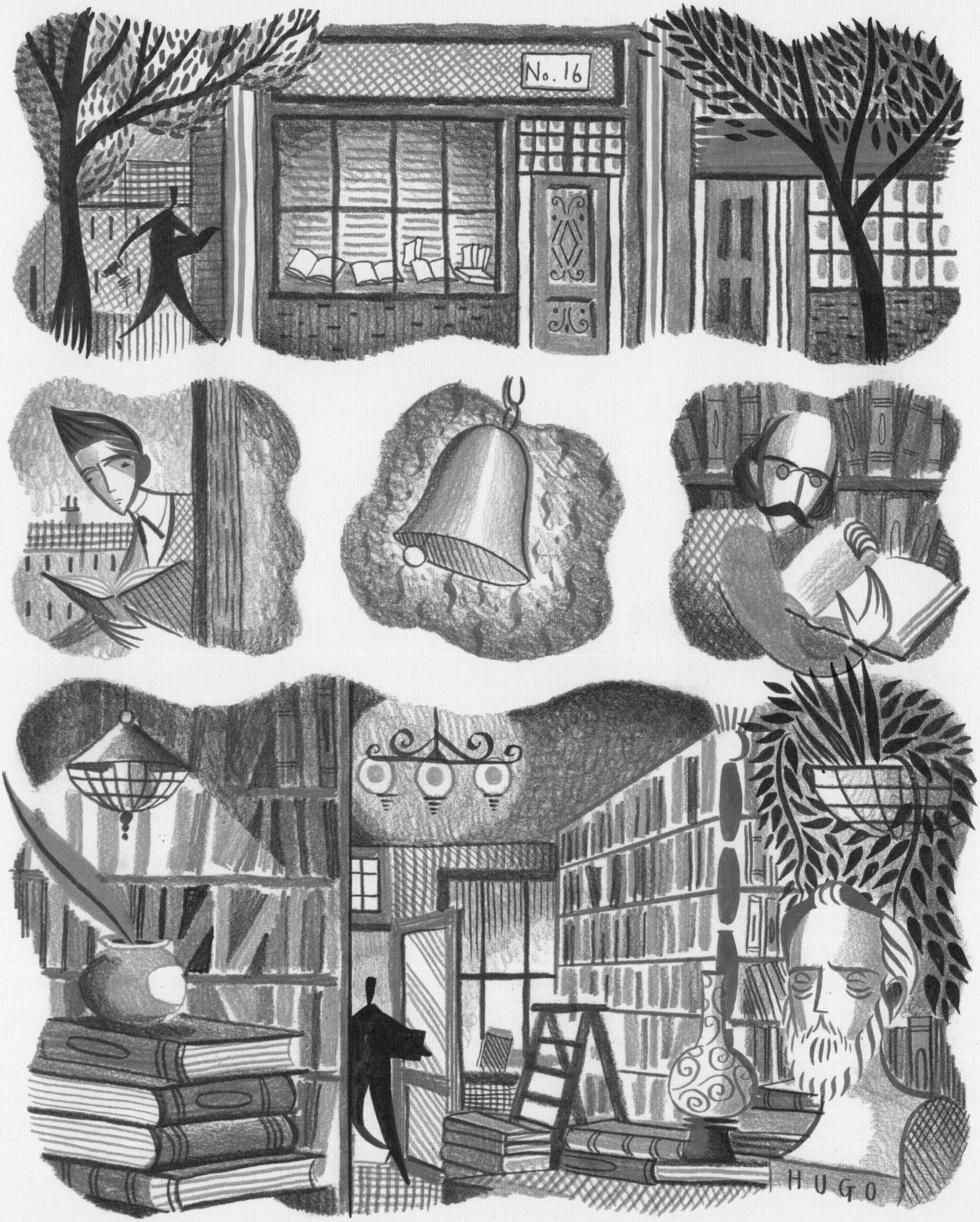
No. 16
HUGO

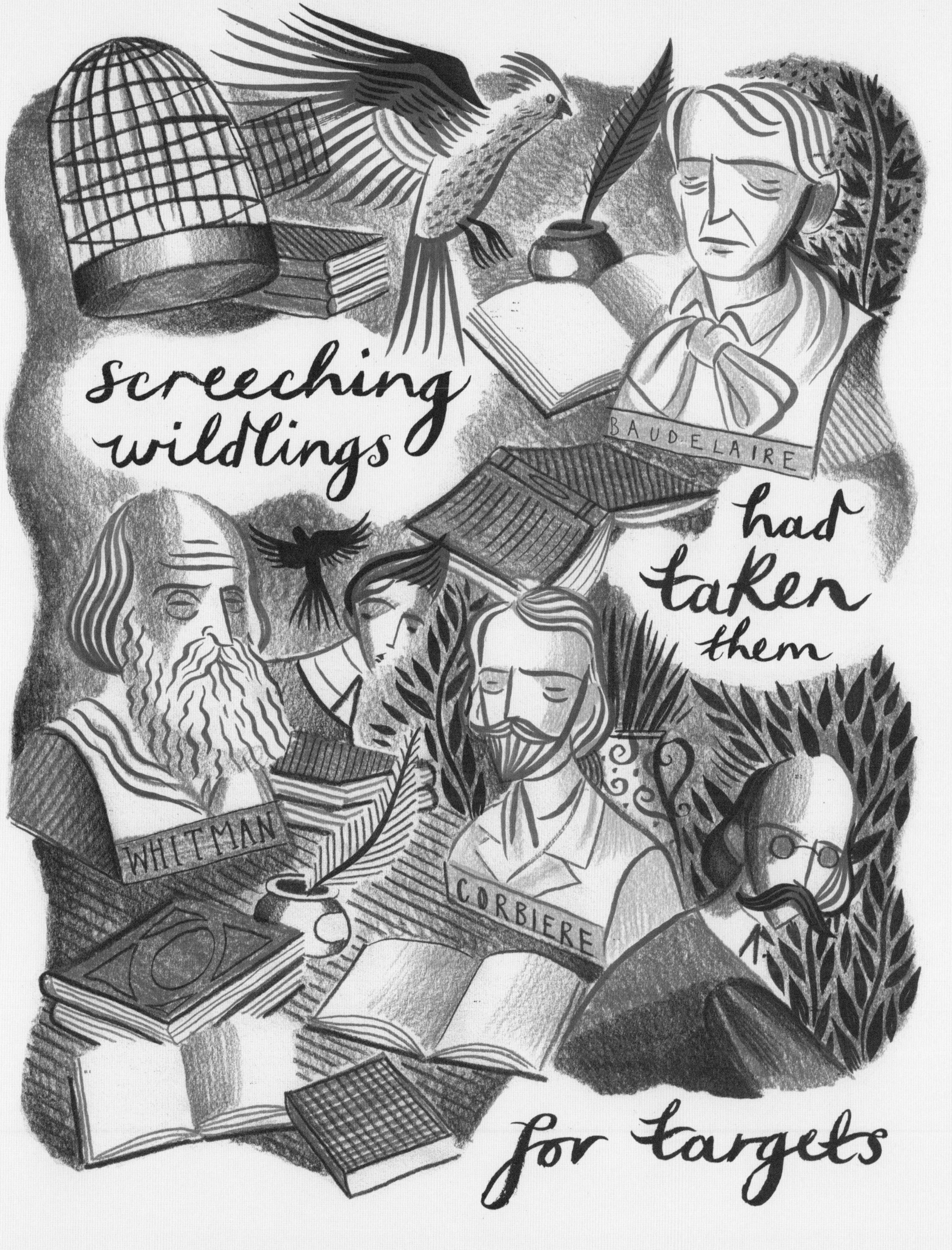
screeching wildlings
BAUDELAIRE
had taken them
WHITMAN
CORBIERE
for targets

and nailed them,

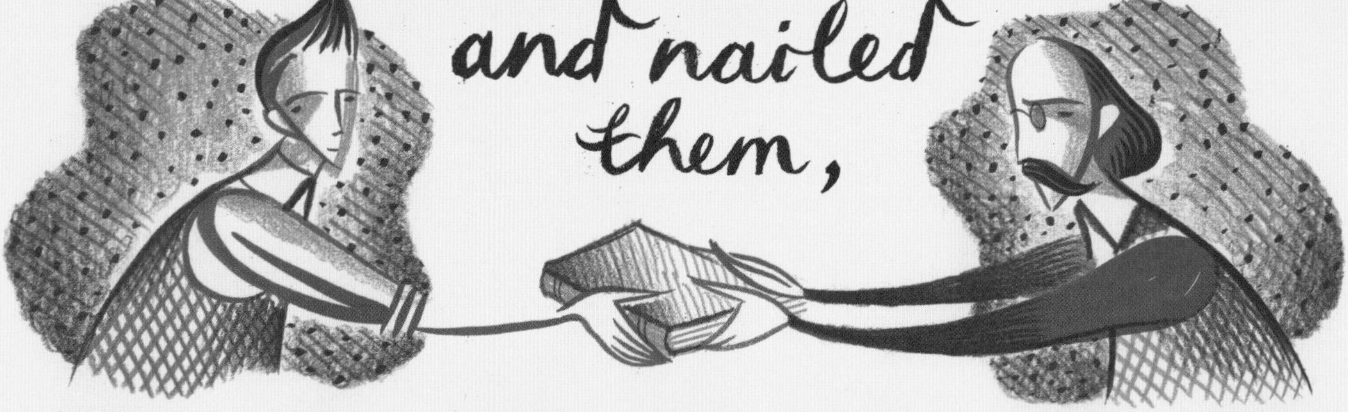

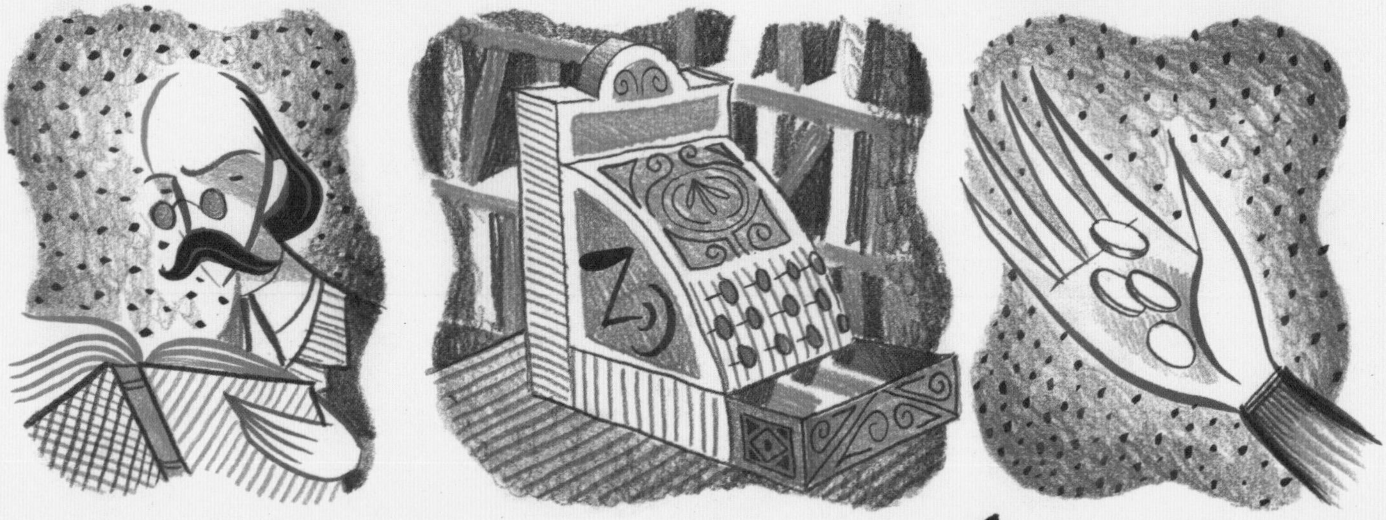

naked,

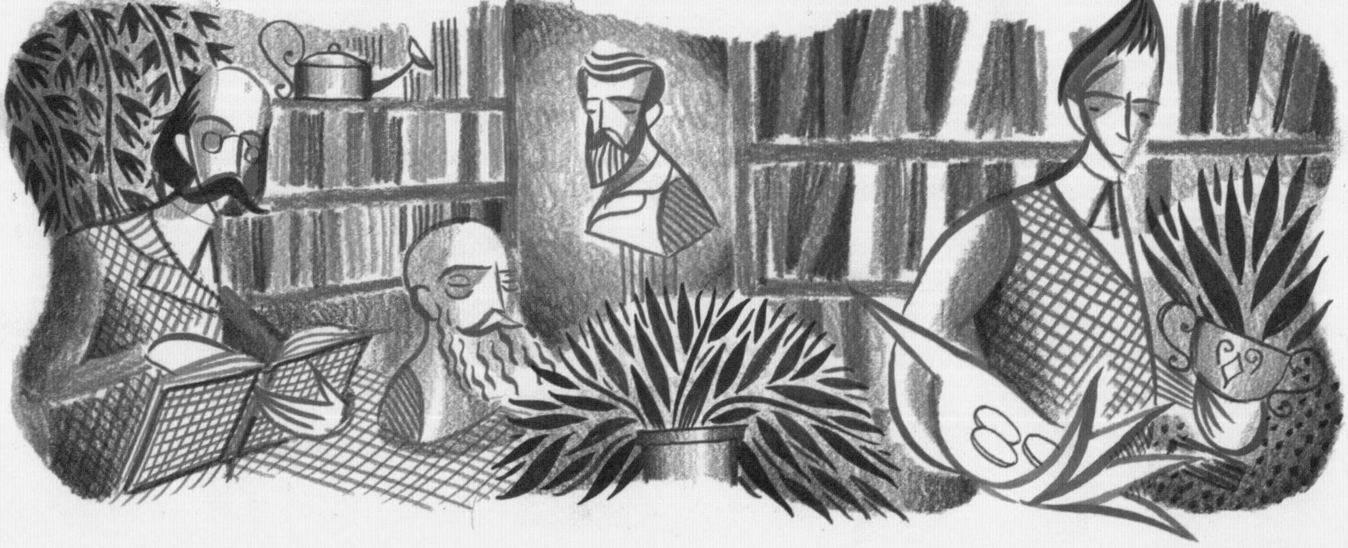

Z

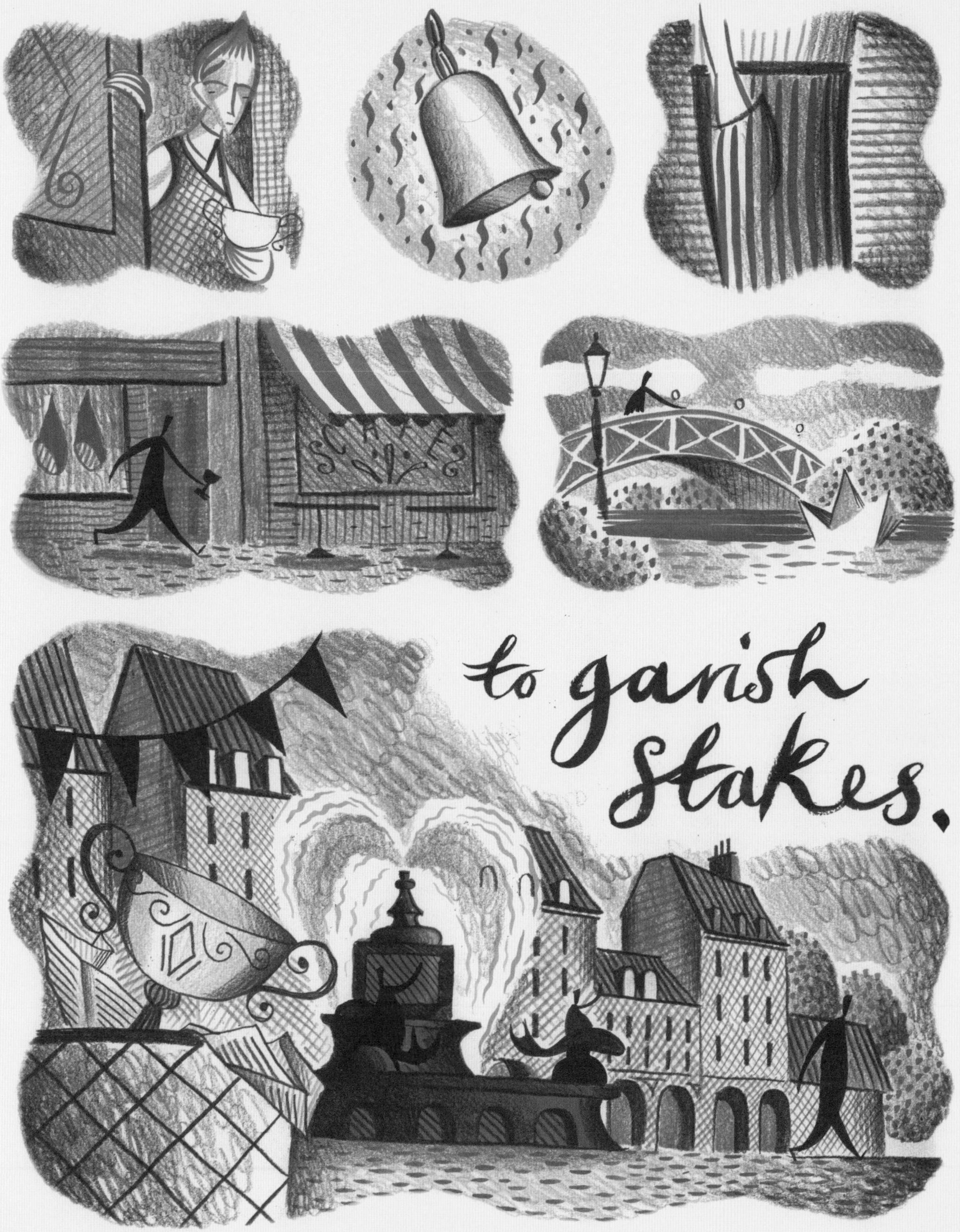
to garish stakes.

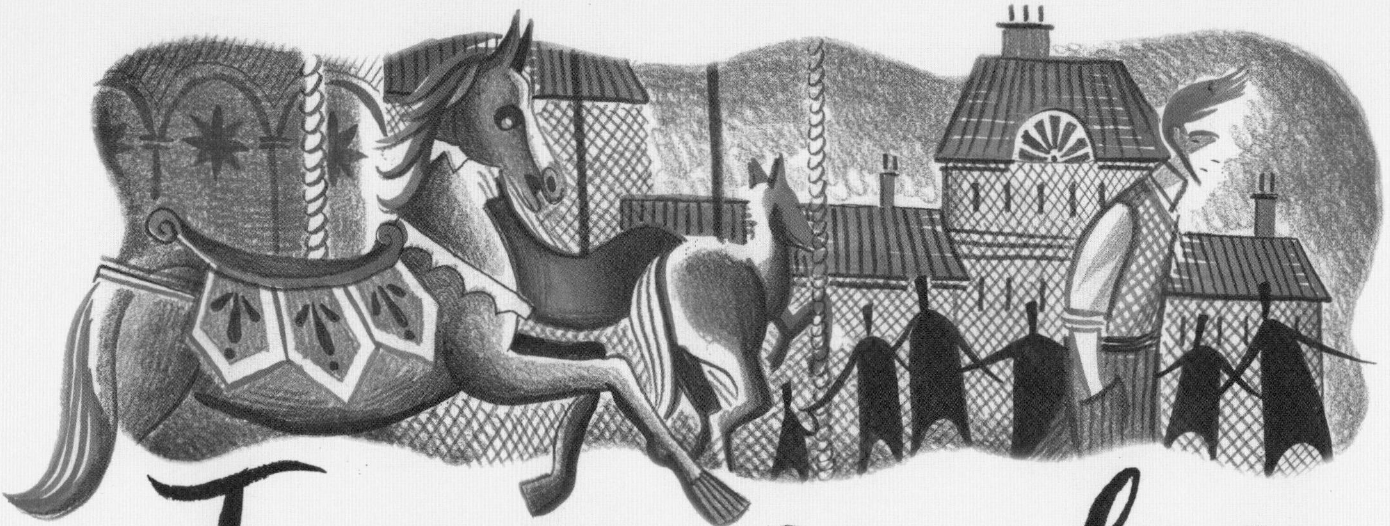

I was careless of all crews,

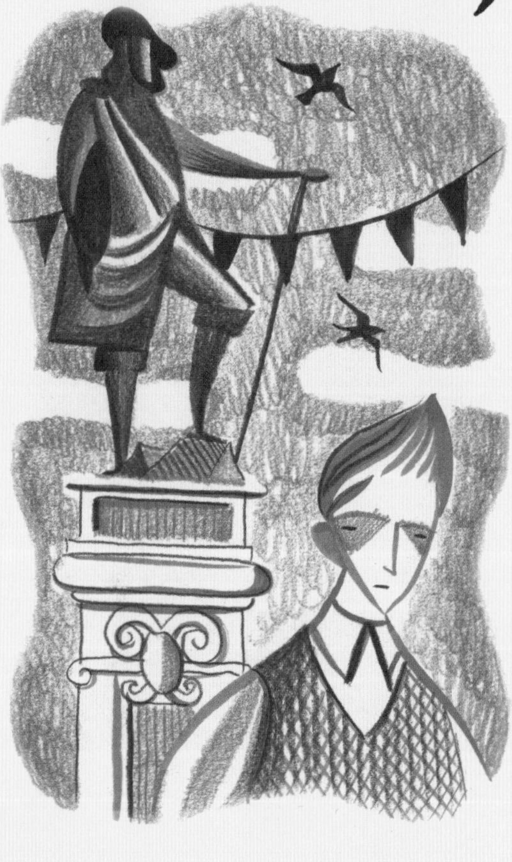

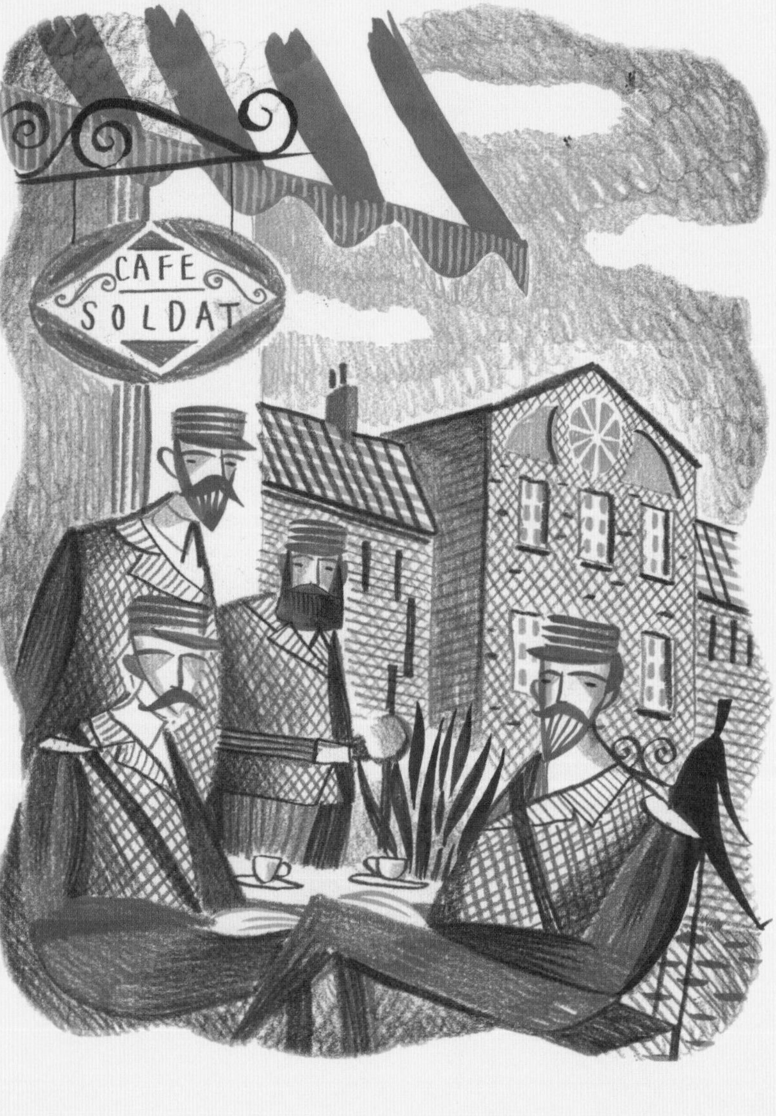
CAFE
SOLDAT

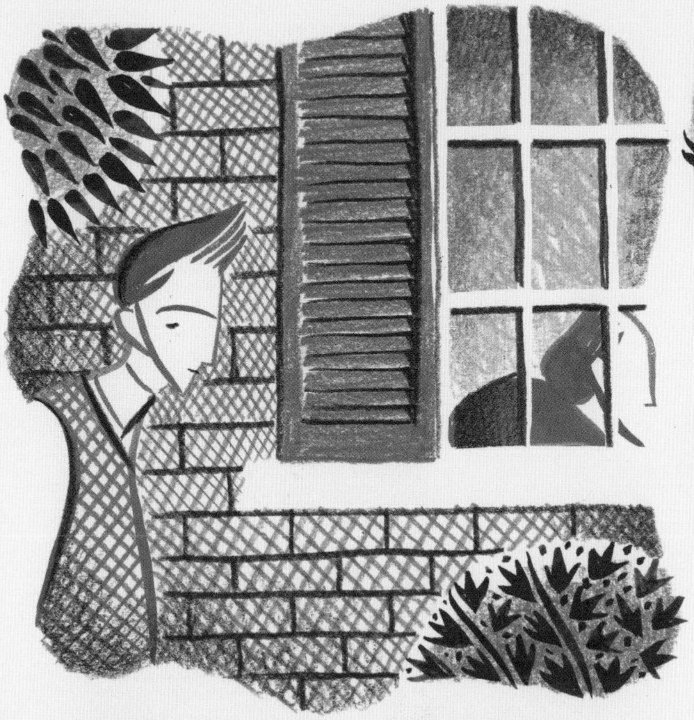

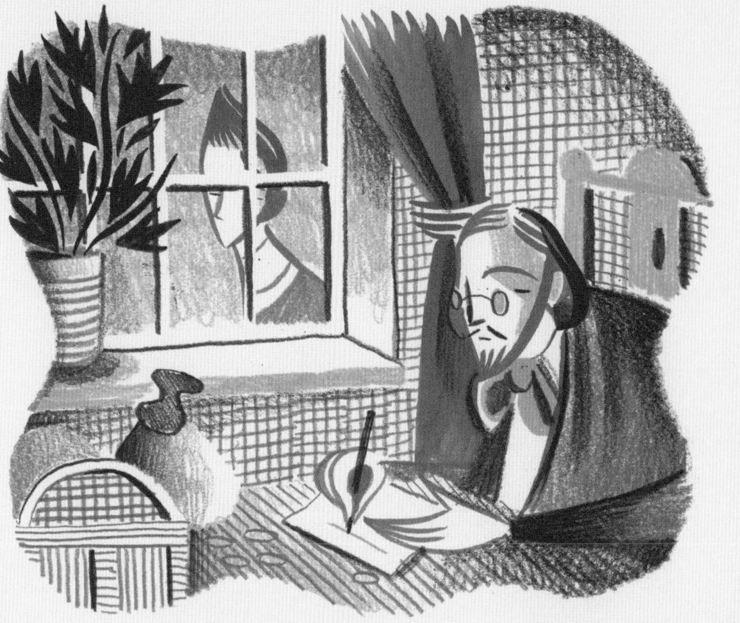

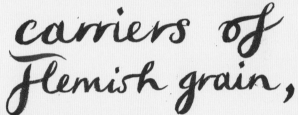

carriers of Flemish grain,

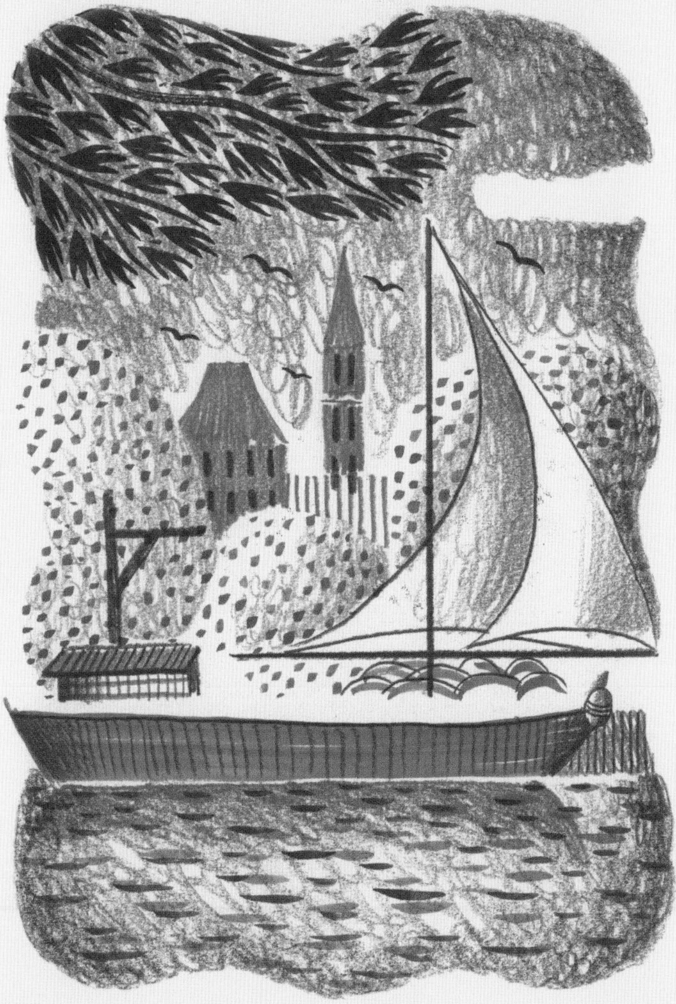

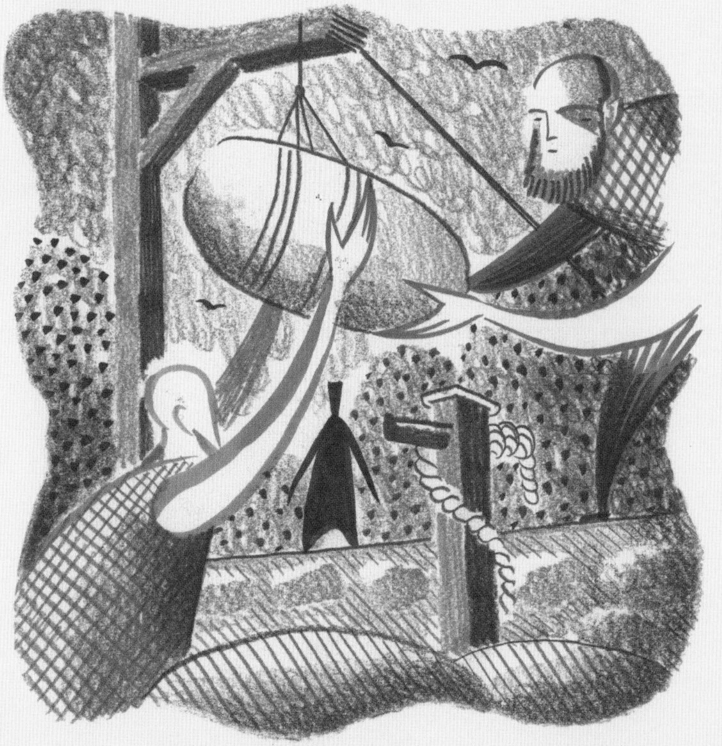

or English cotton,

When,

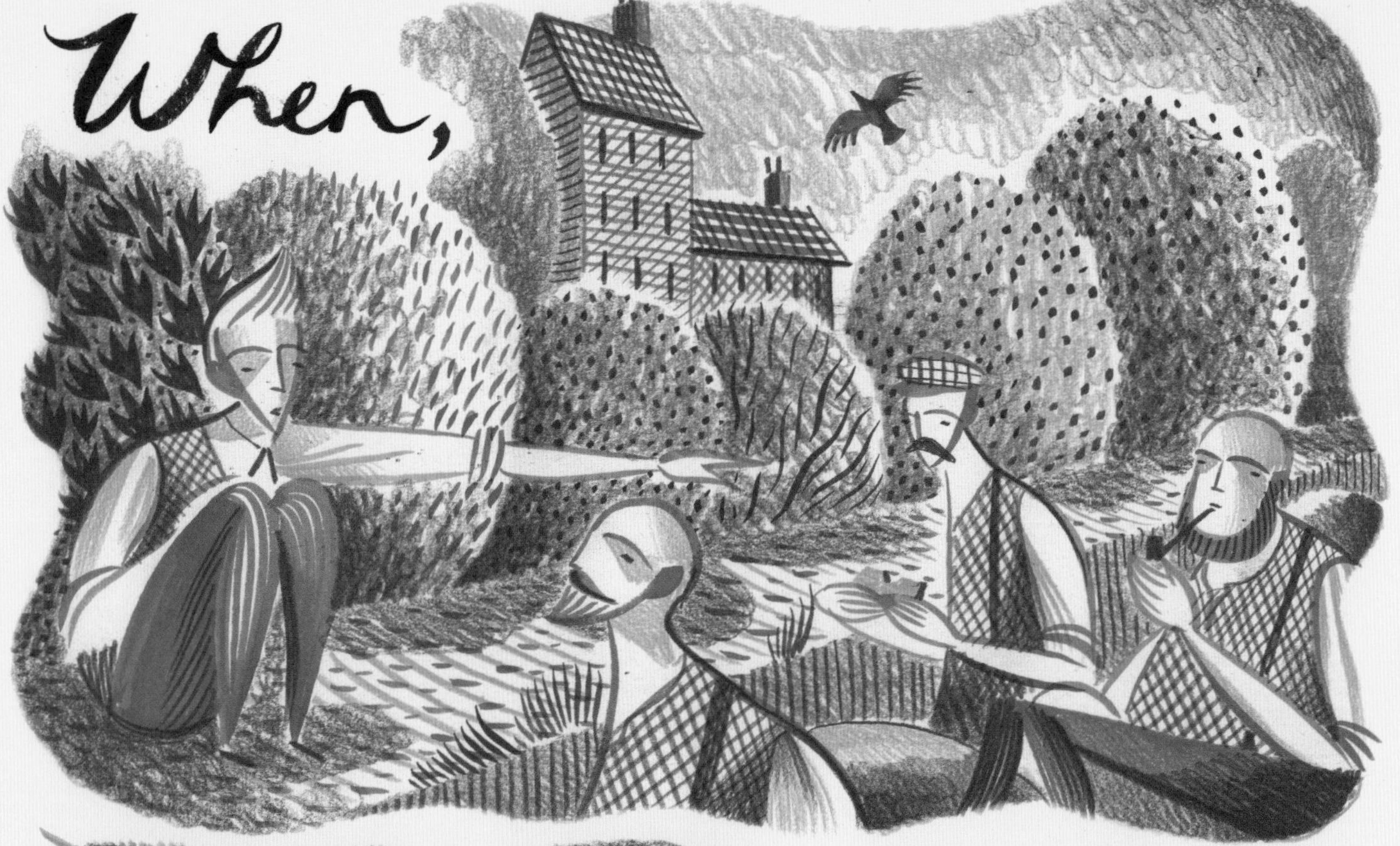

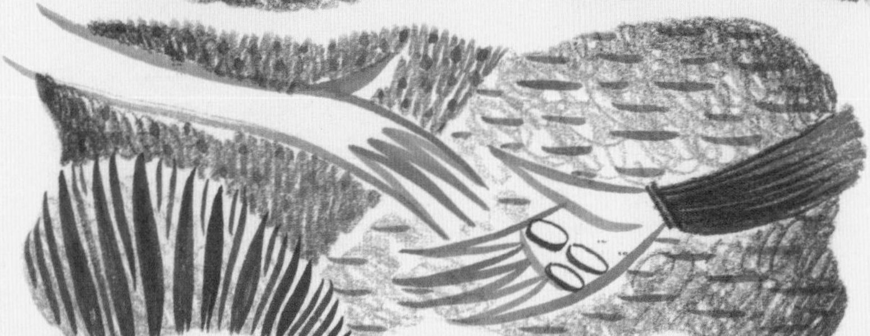

with my haulers,

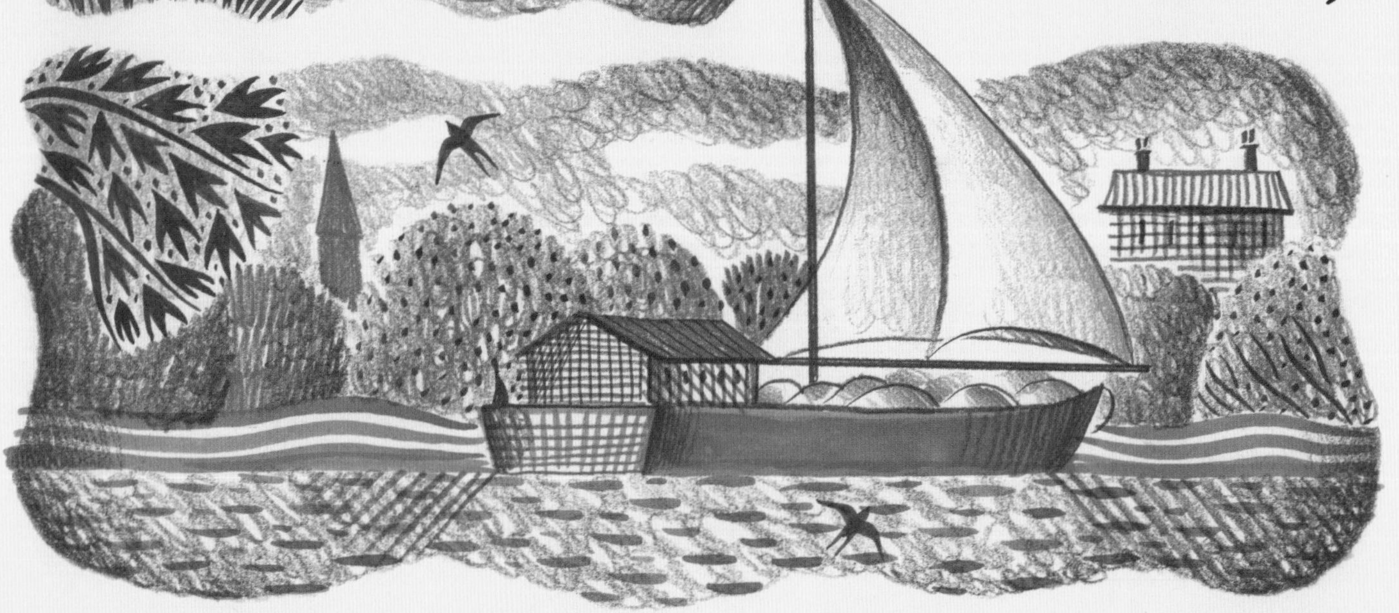

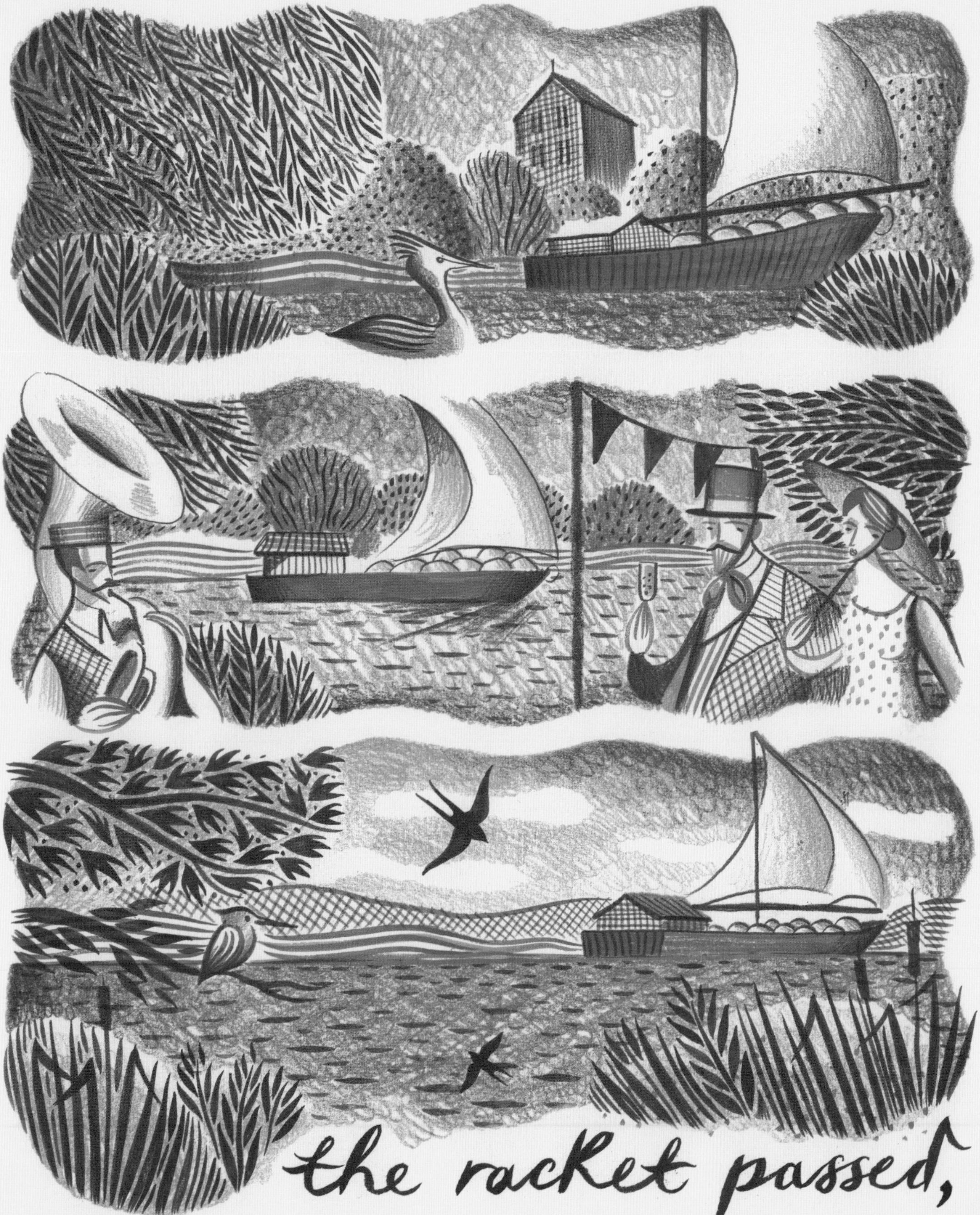

the racket passed,

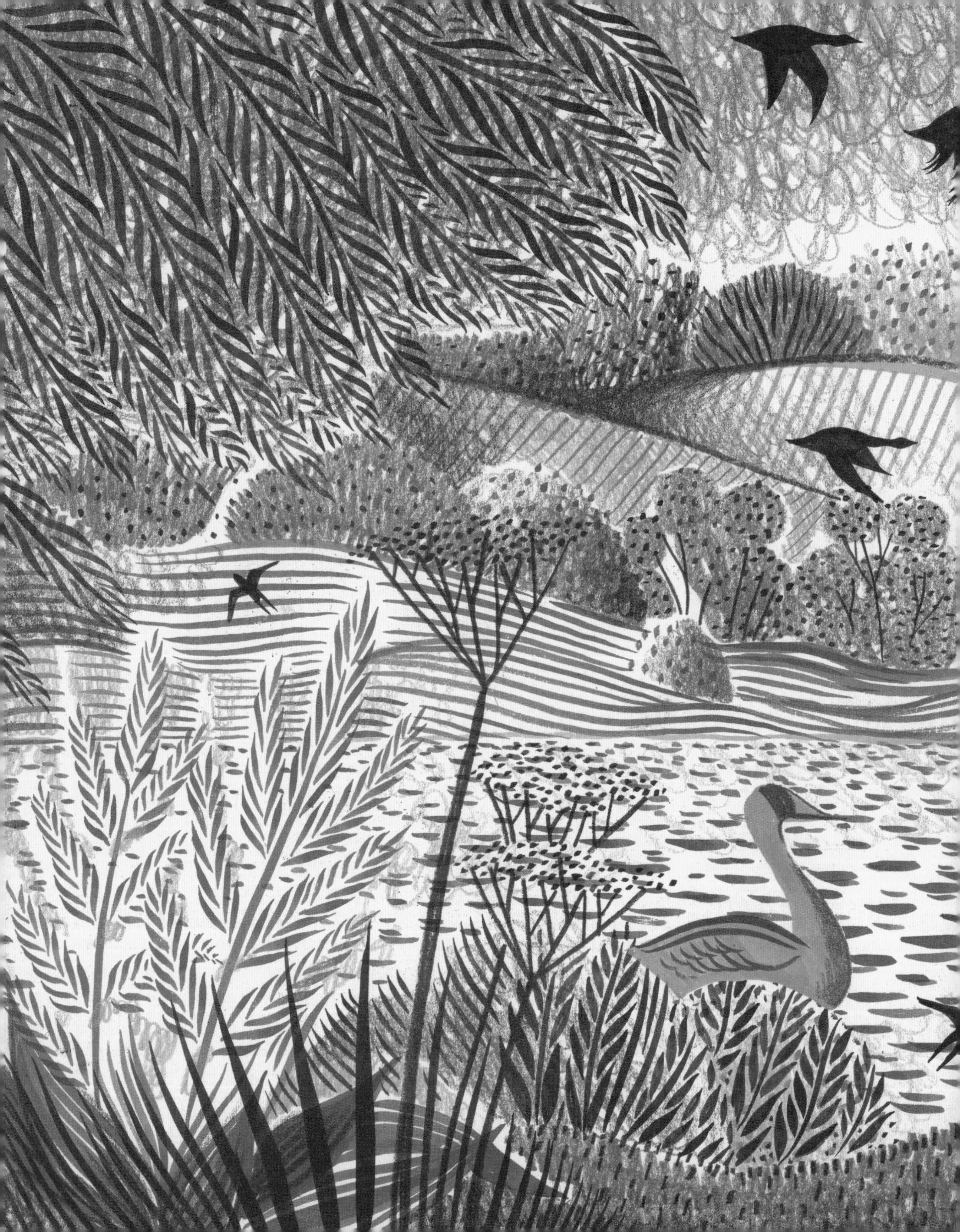

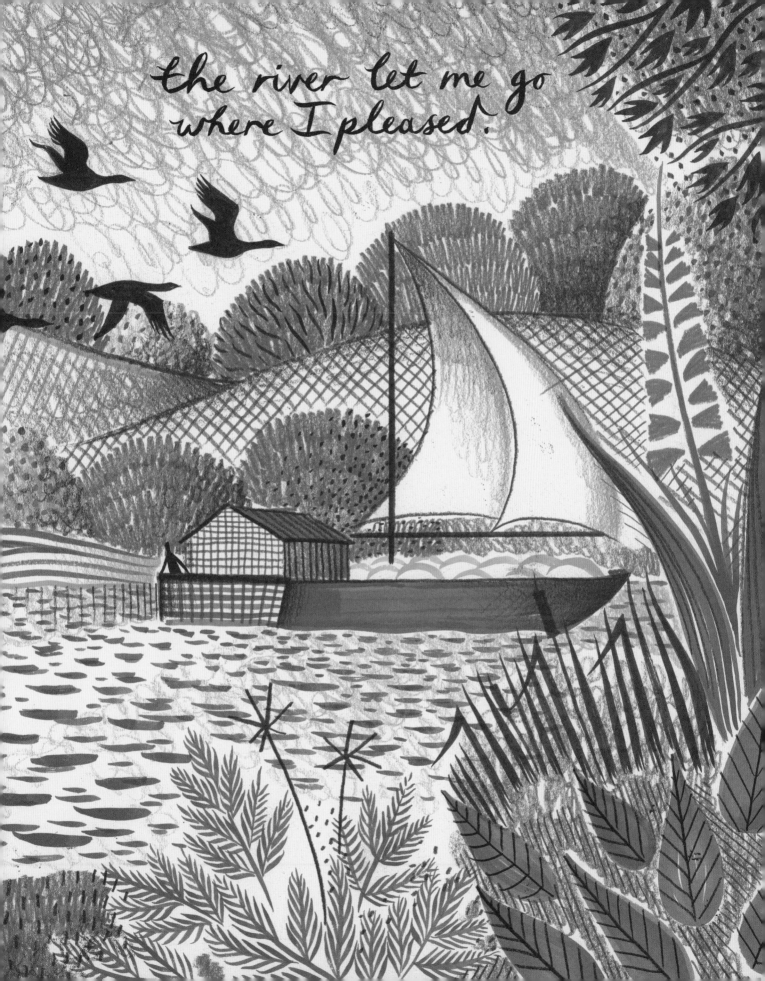

the river let me go
where I pleased.

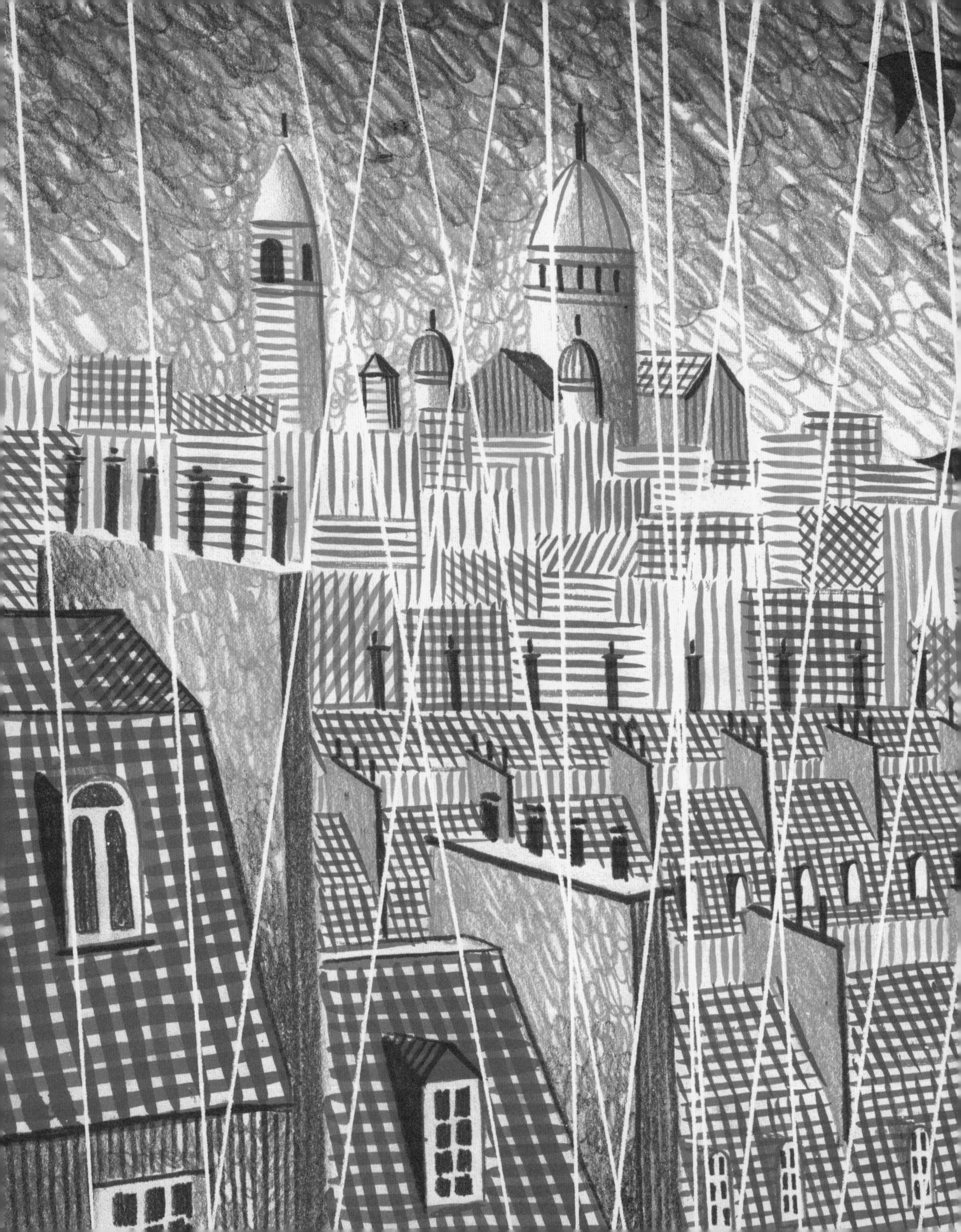

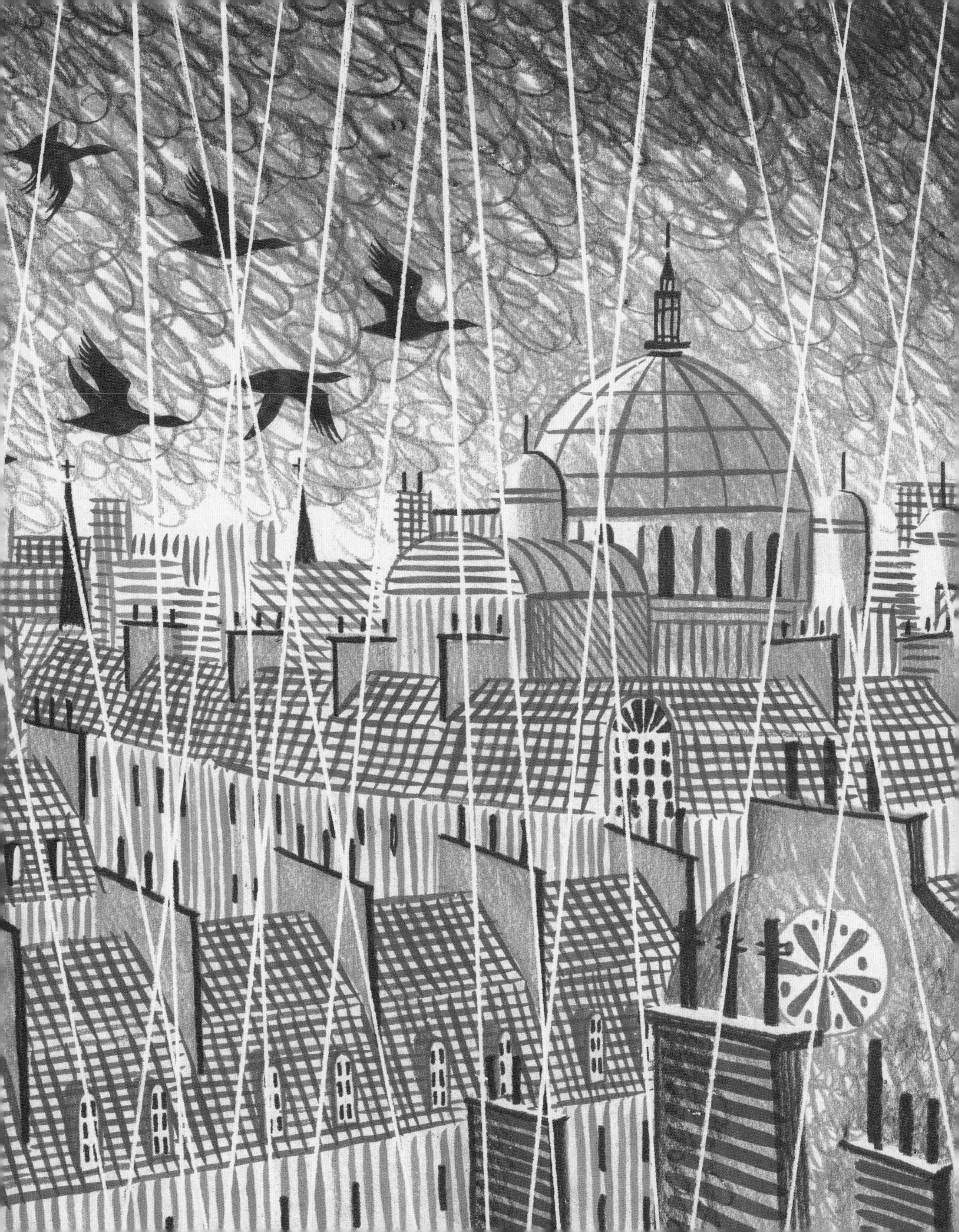

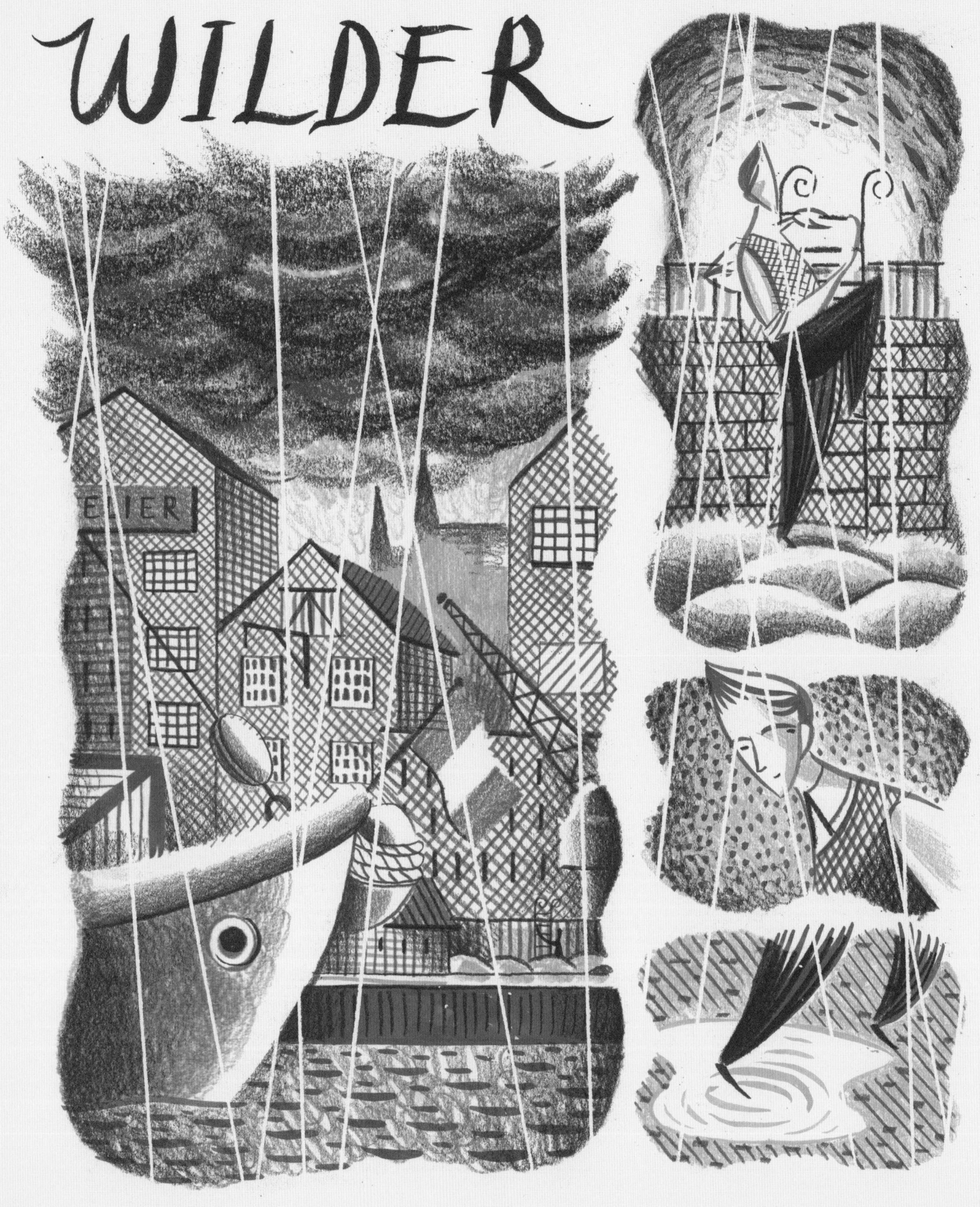
WILDER
ELIER

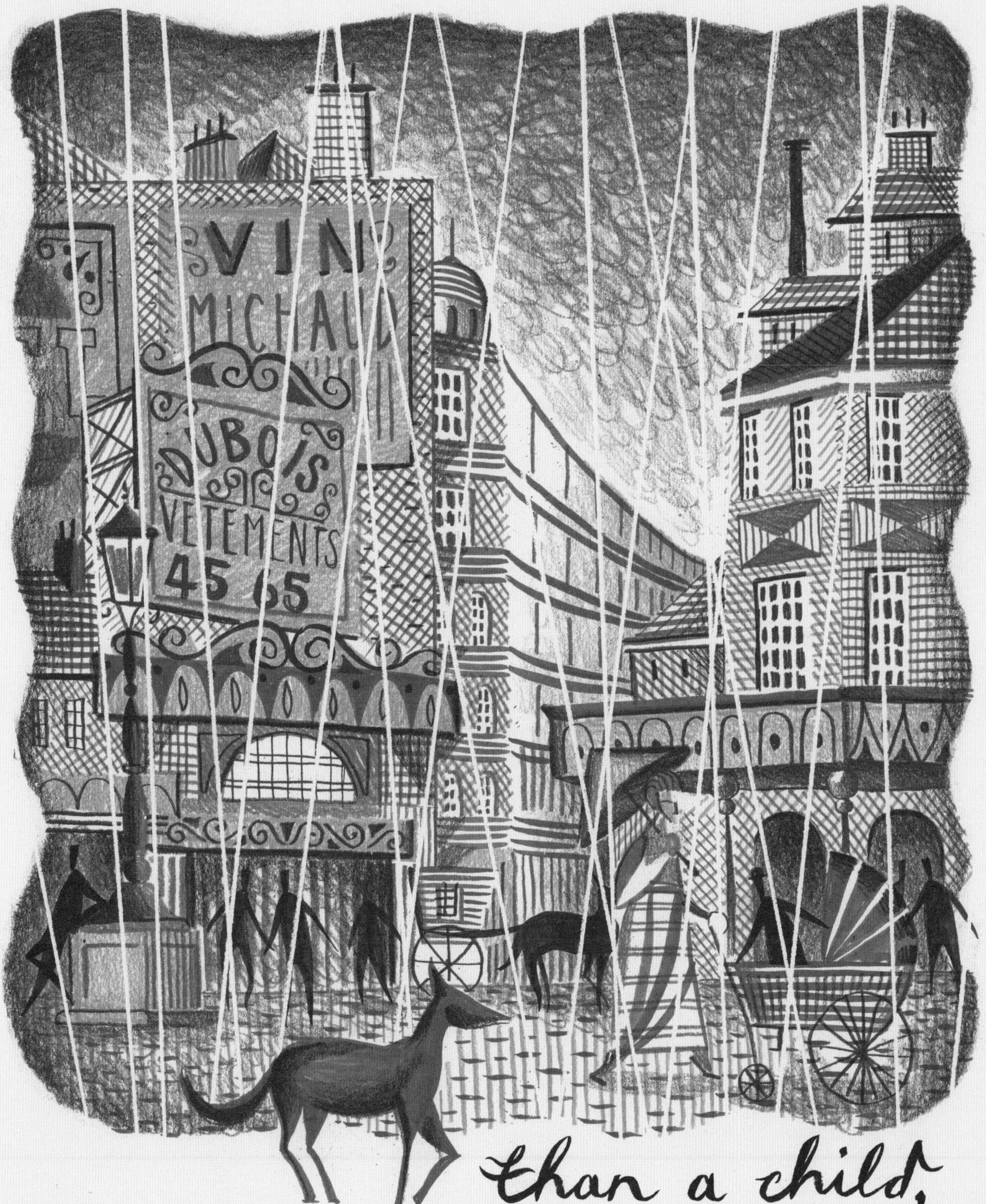
VIN
MICHAUD
DUBOIS
VETEMENTS
45 65

than a child,

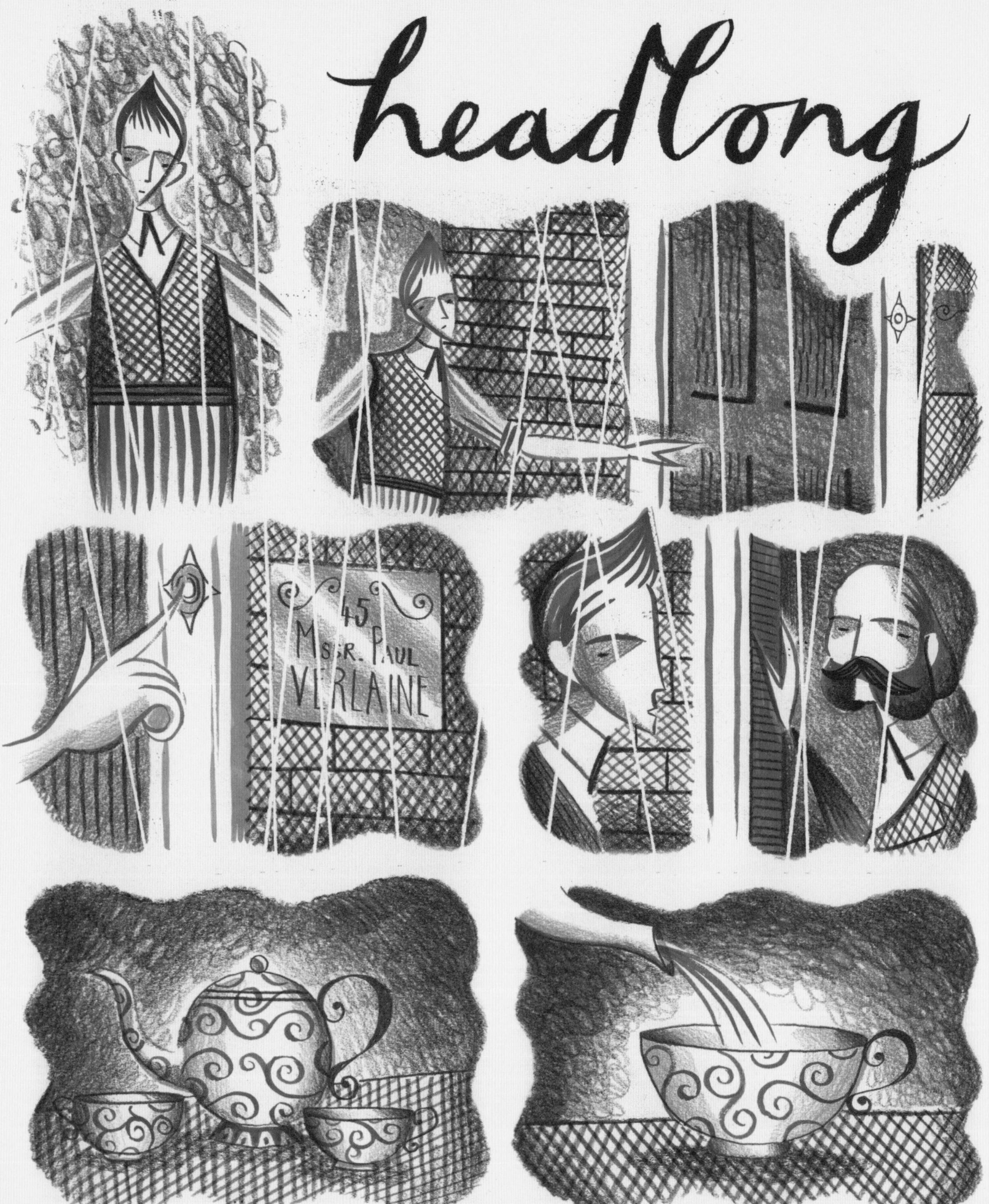
headlong
45
MSSR. PAUL
VERLAINE

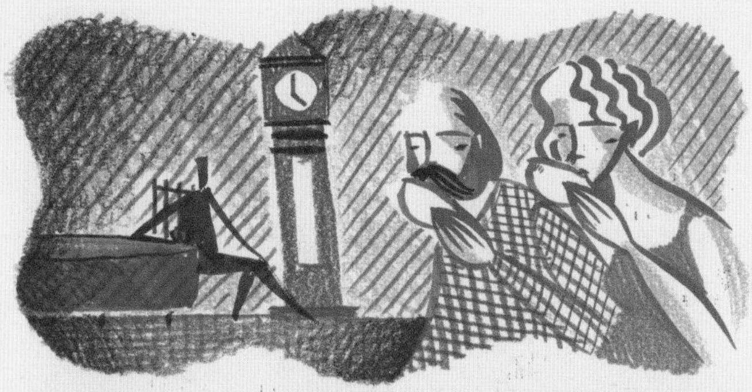

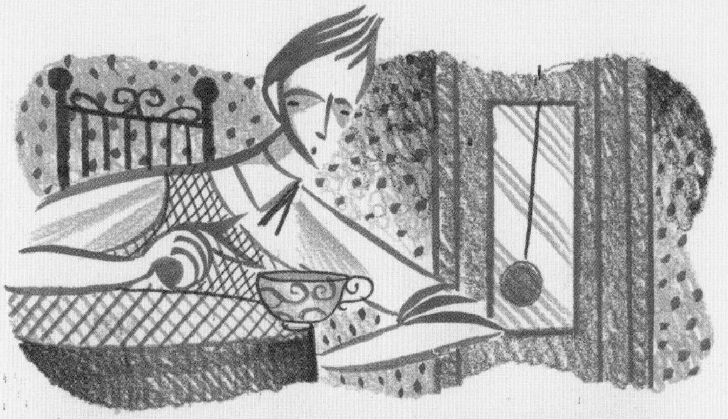

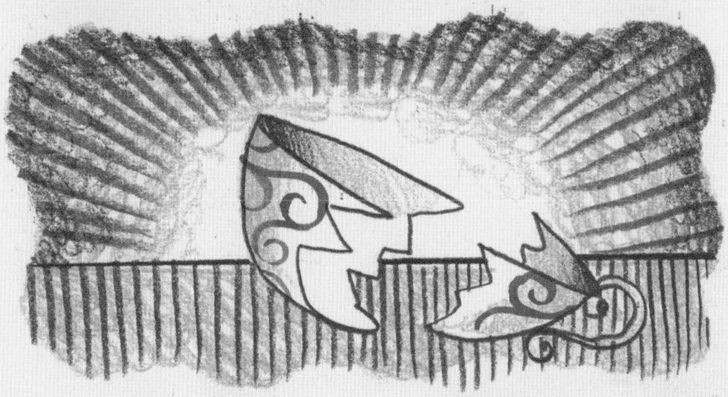

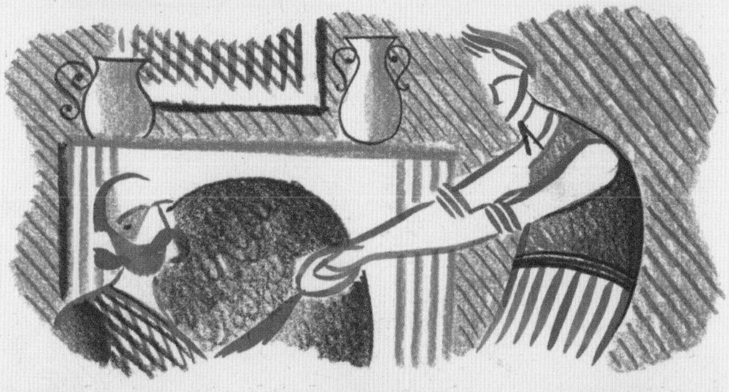

into the raging lash

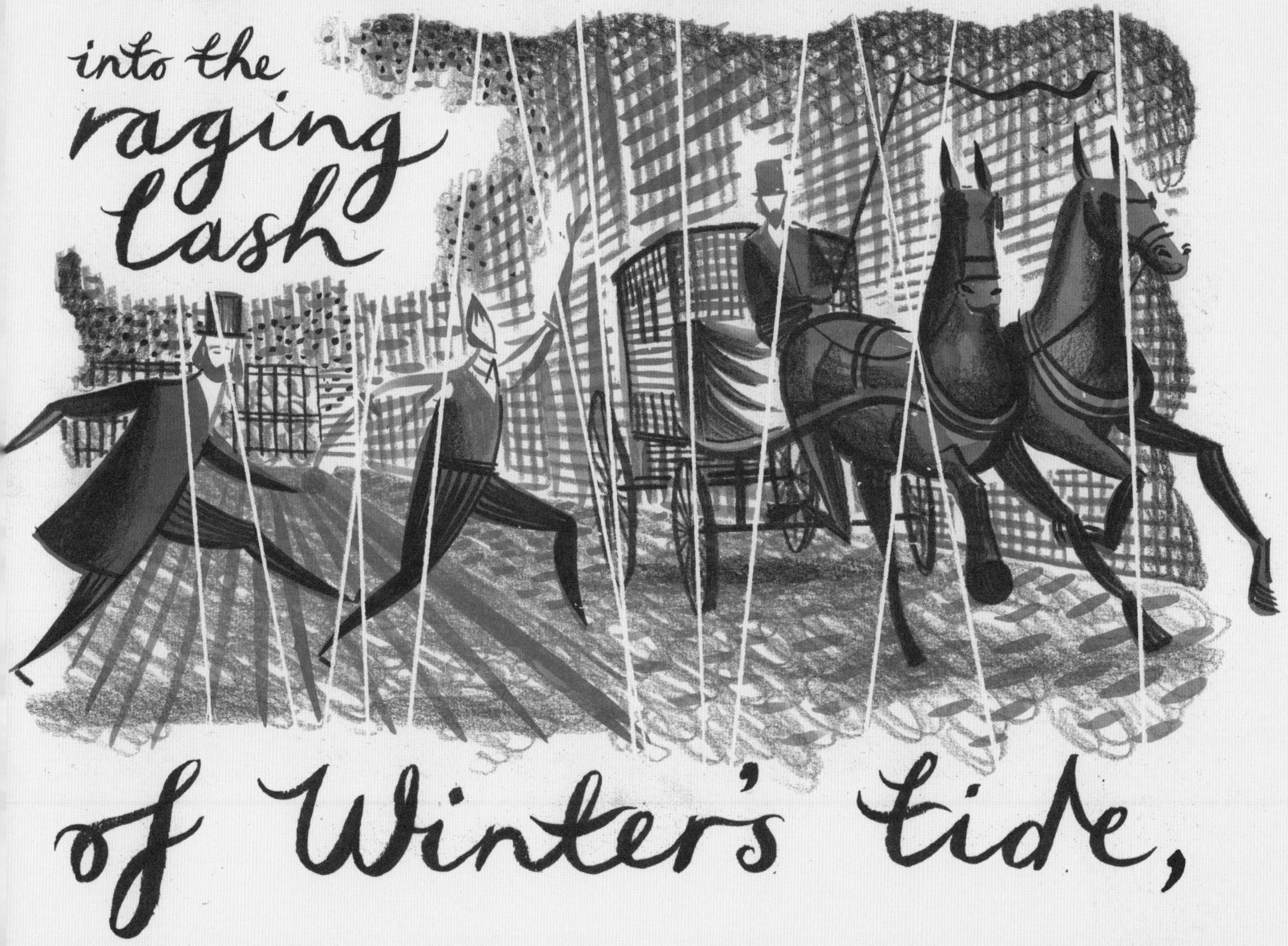

of Winter's tide,

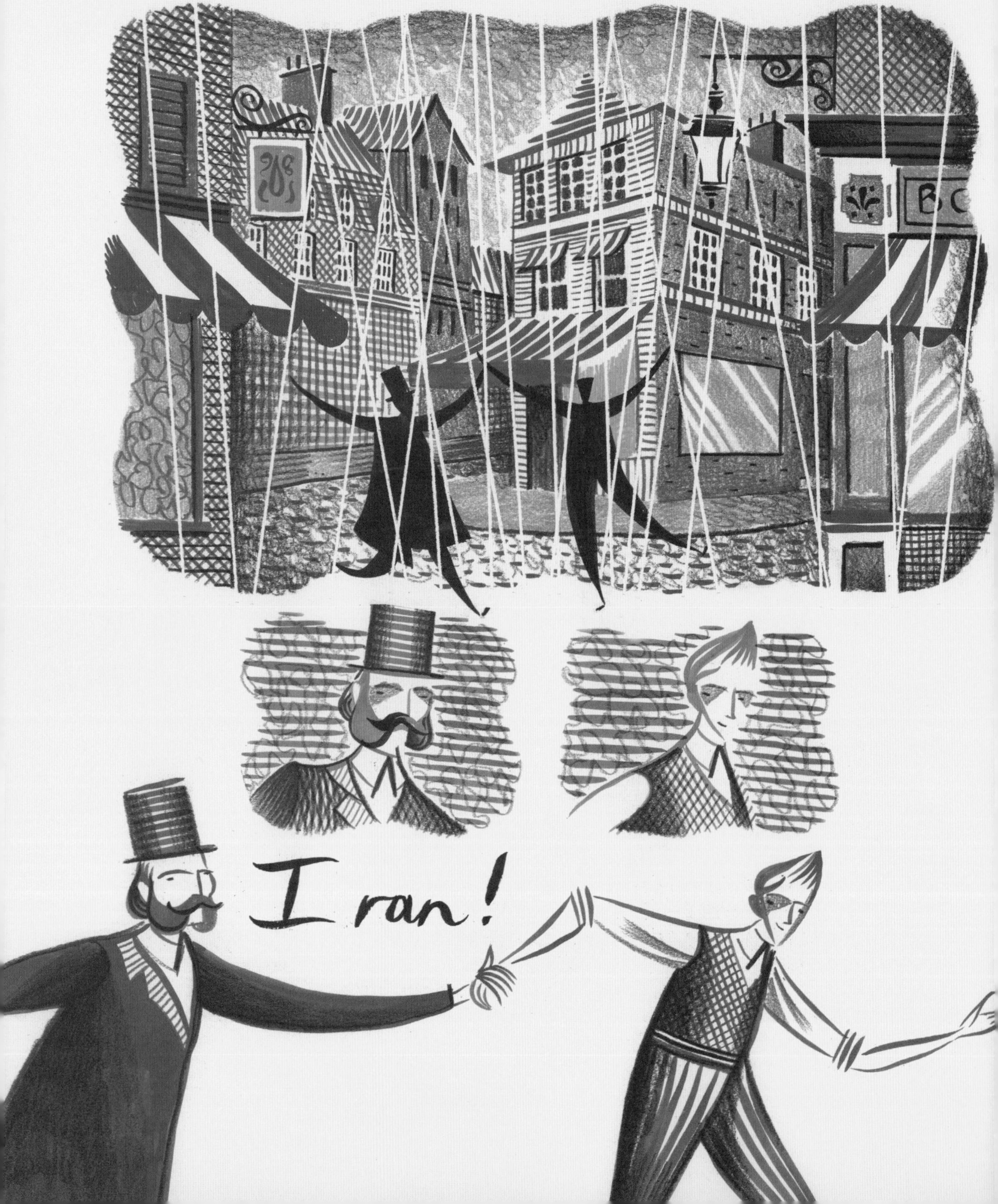
I ran!

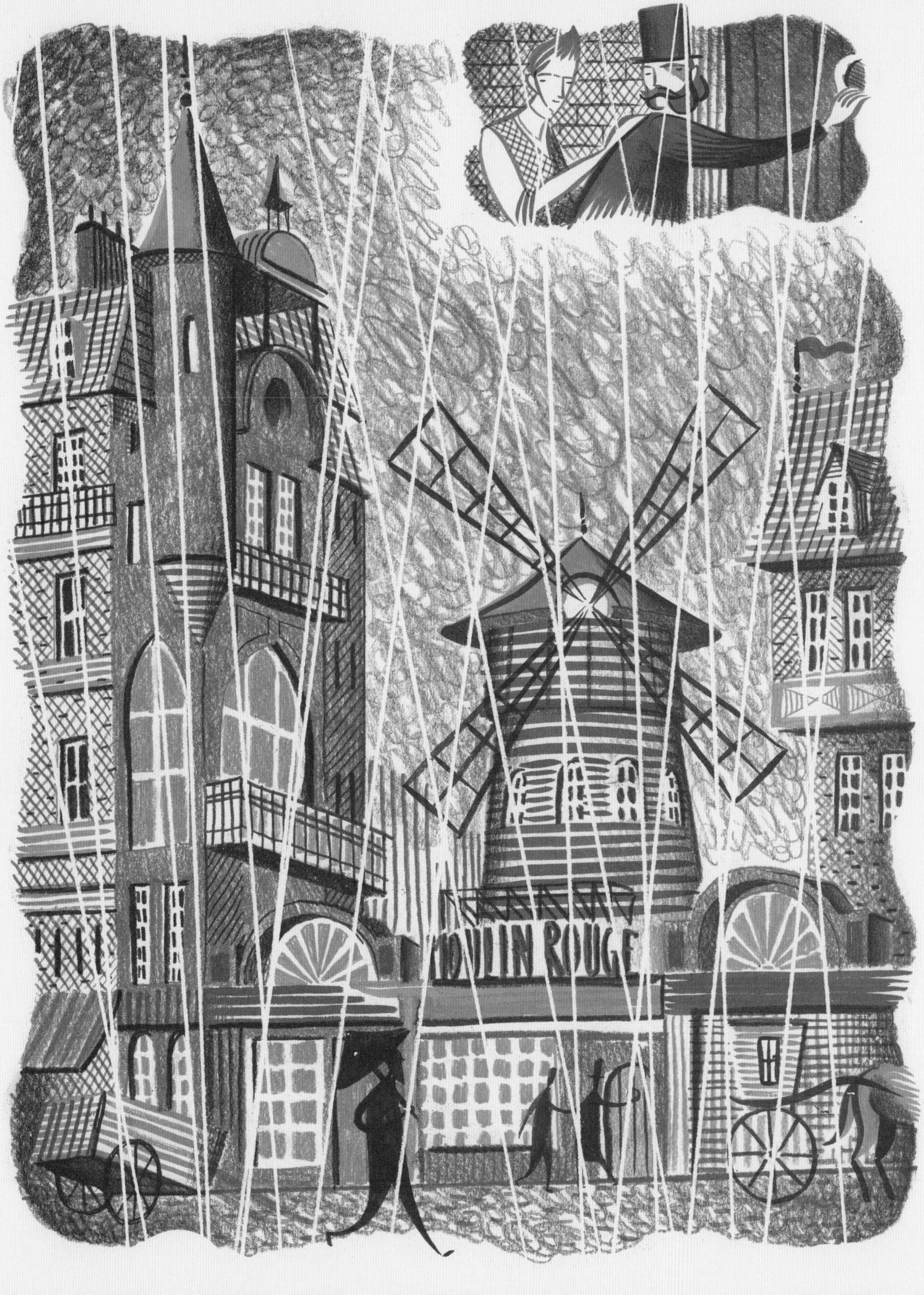
MOULIN ROUGE

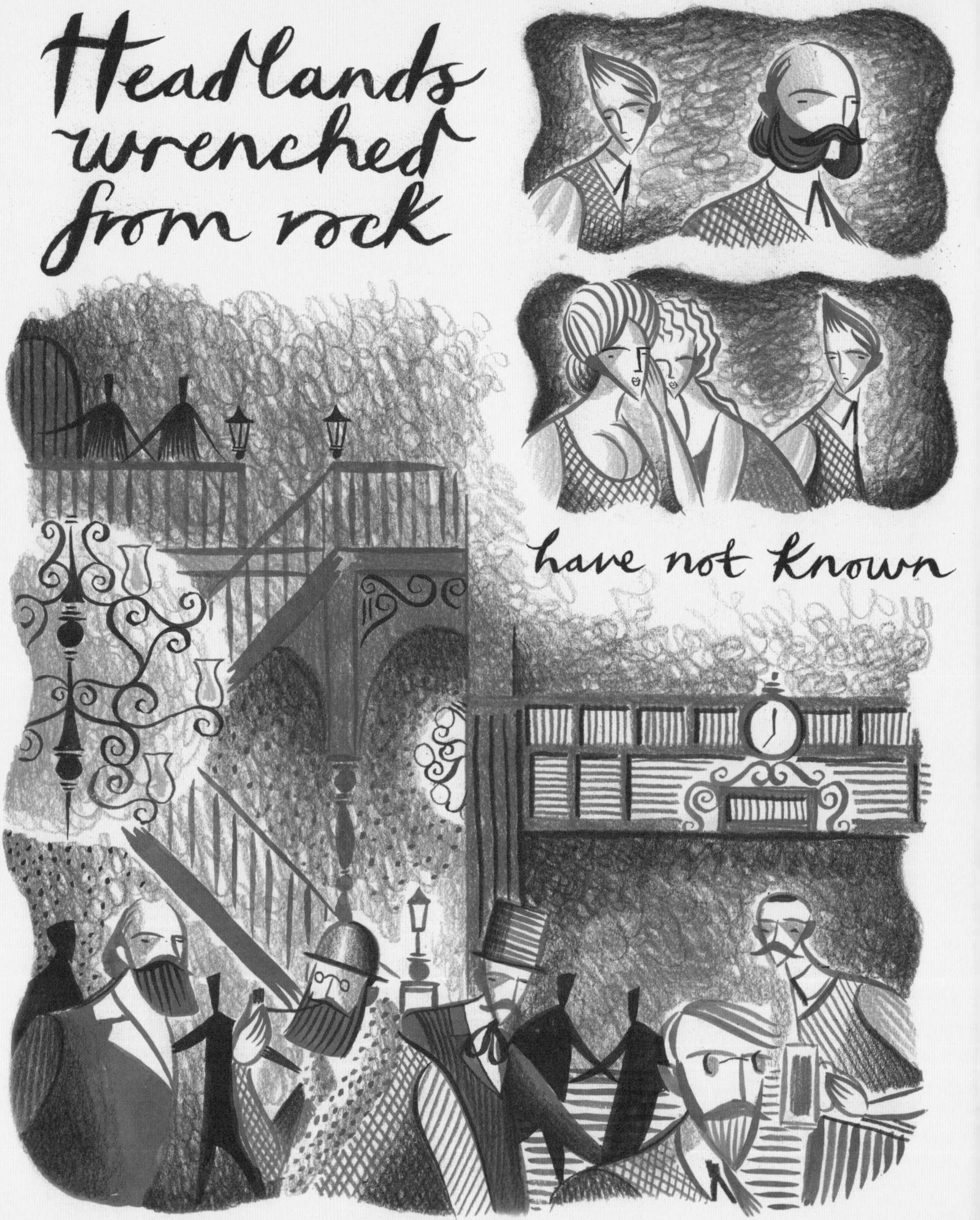
Headlands wrenched from rock
have not known

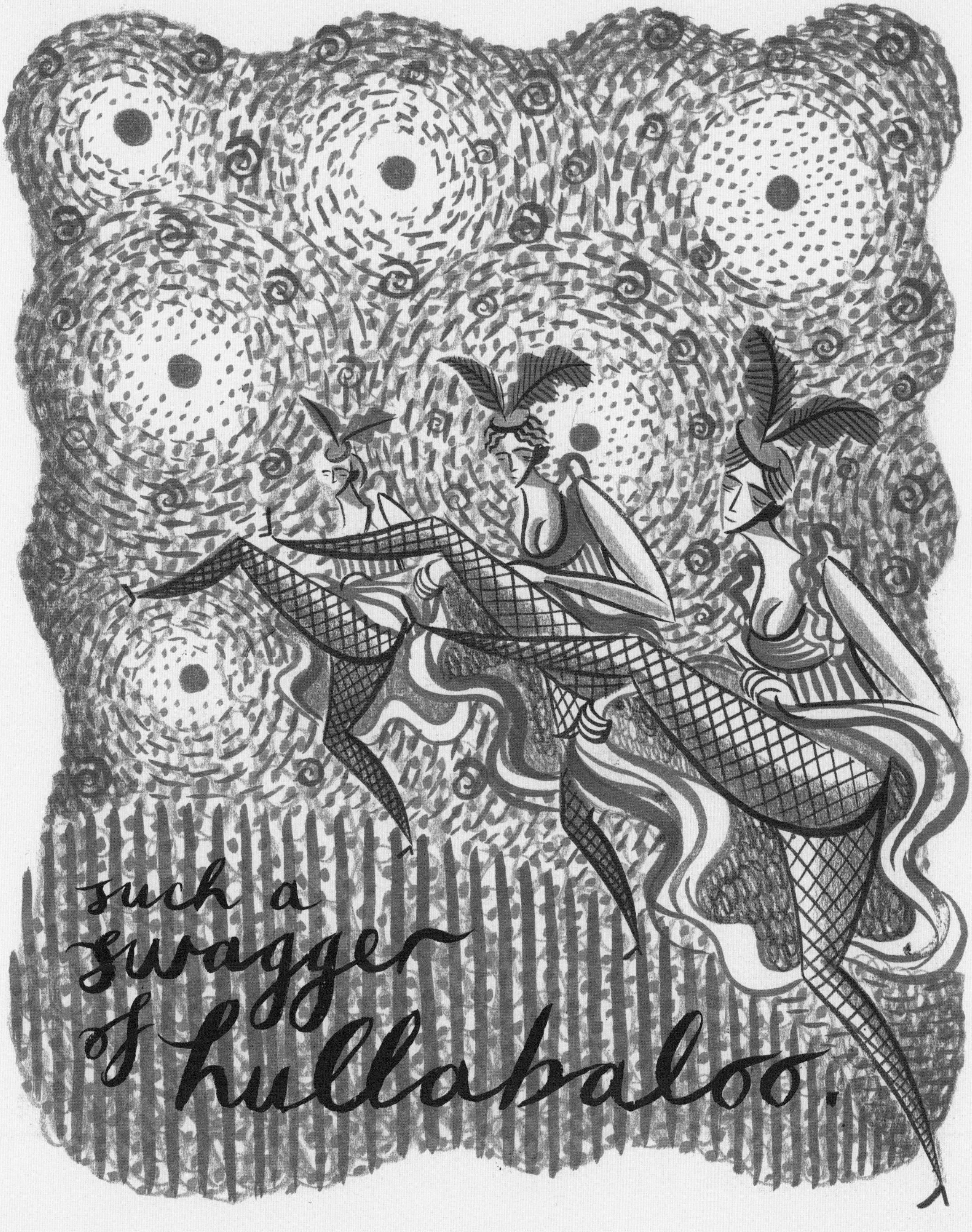
such a
swagger
of hullabaloo.

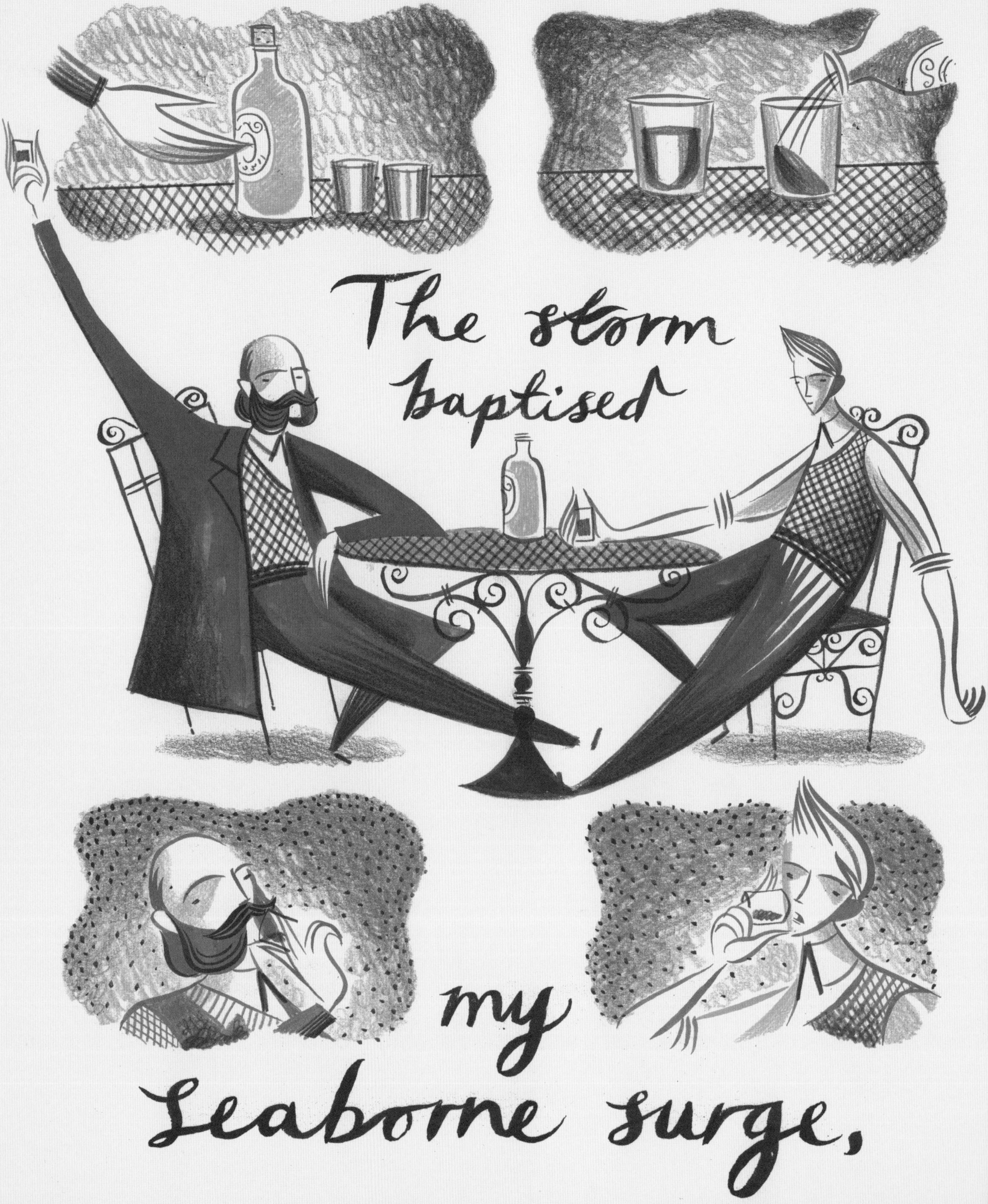
The storm baptised
my
Seaborne surge,

lighter than a cork

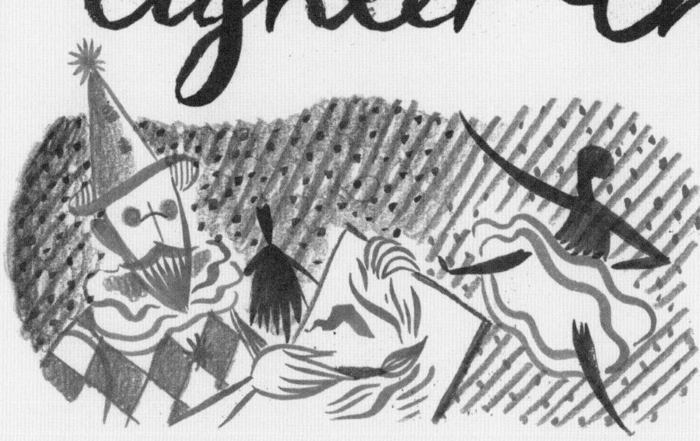

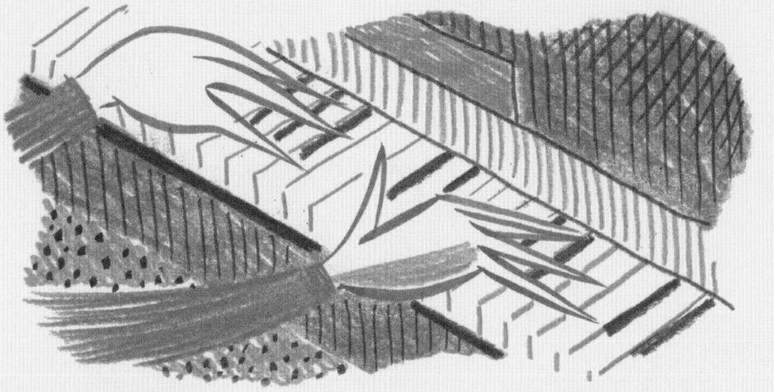

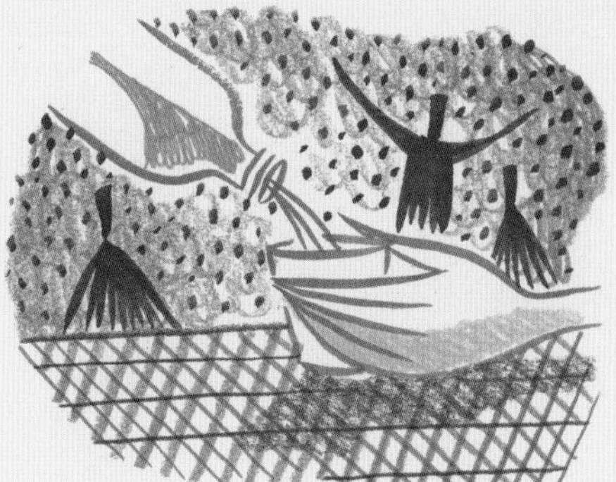

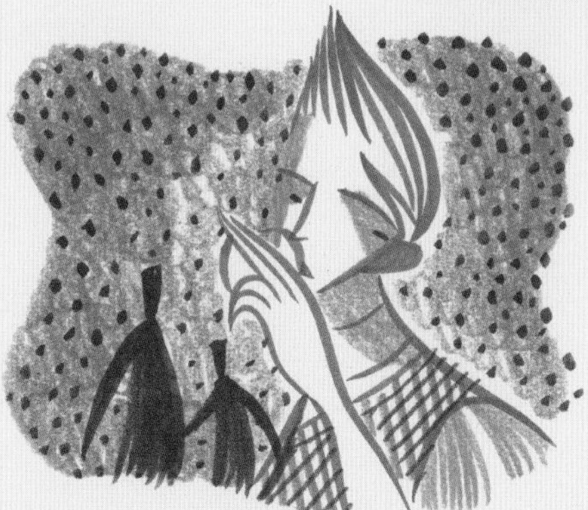

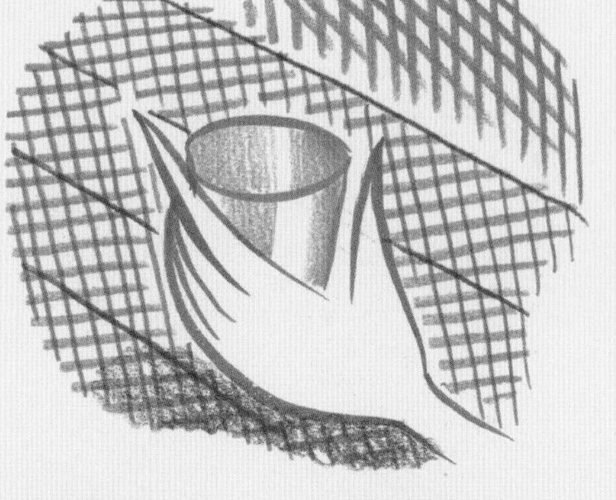

I danced upon the waves

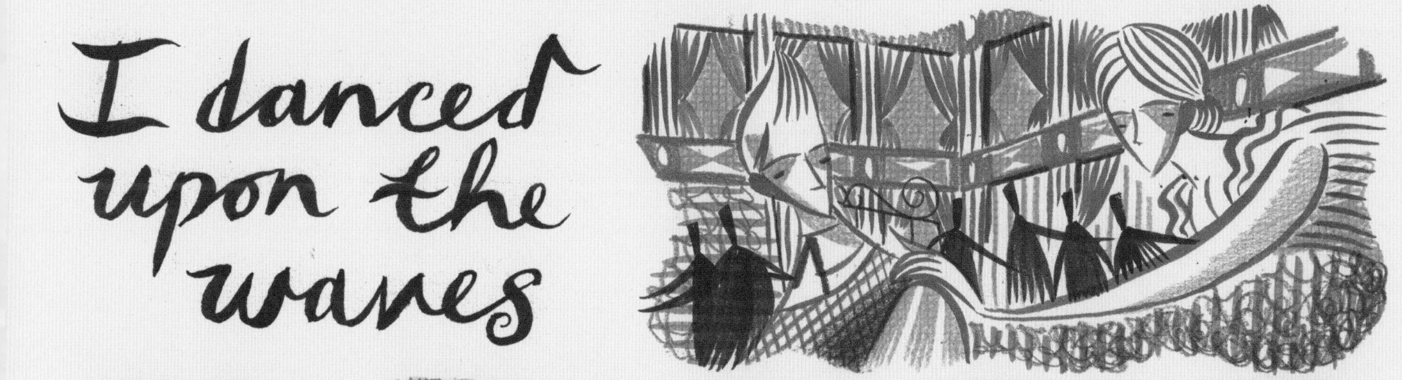

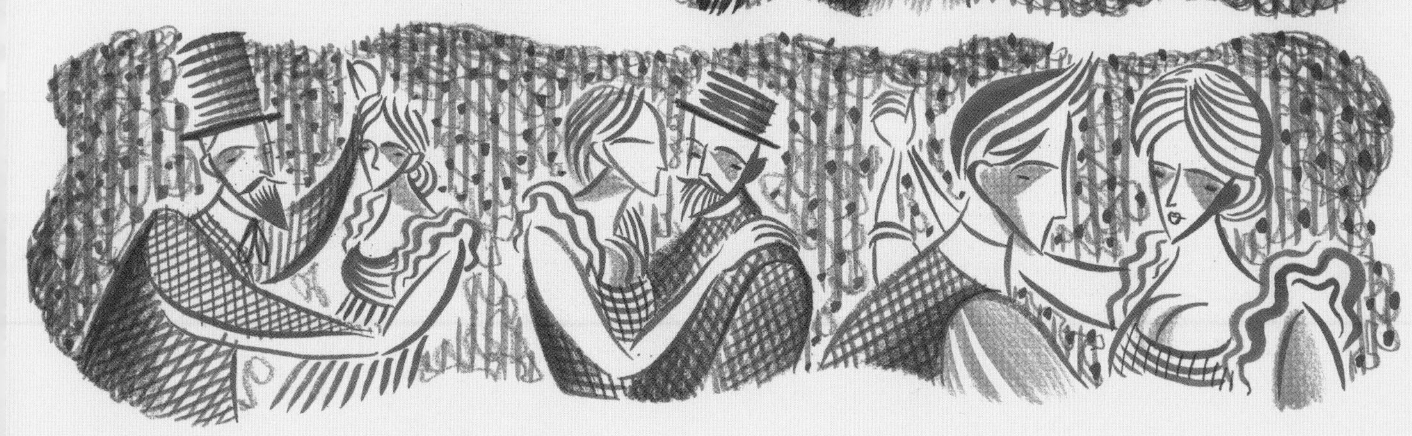

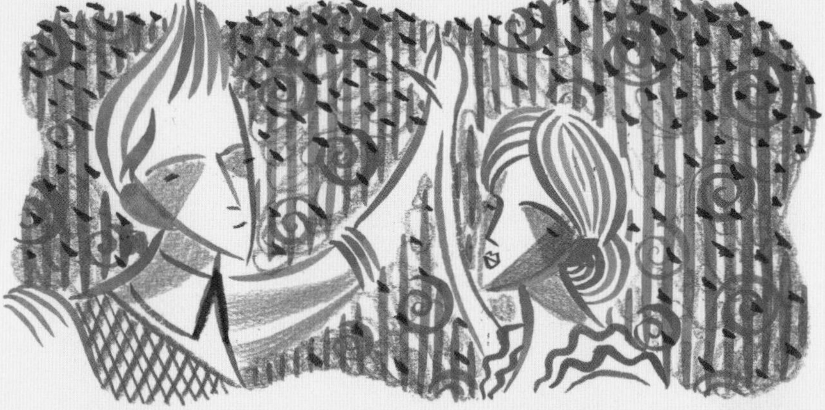

whose martyrs call

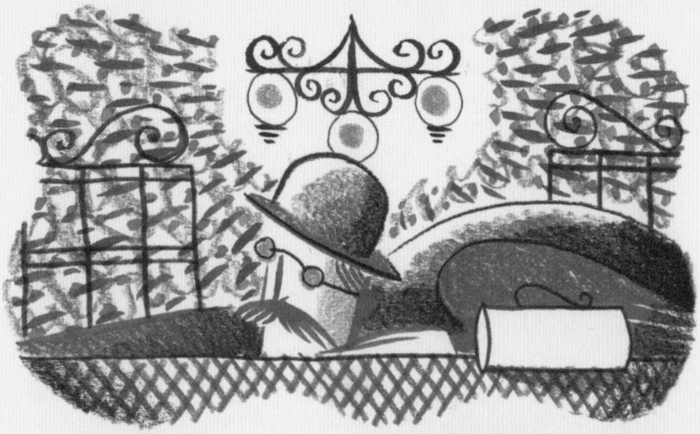

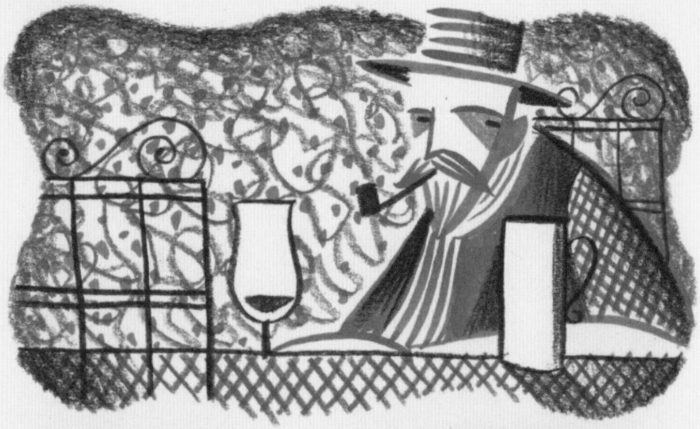

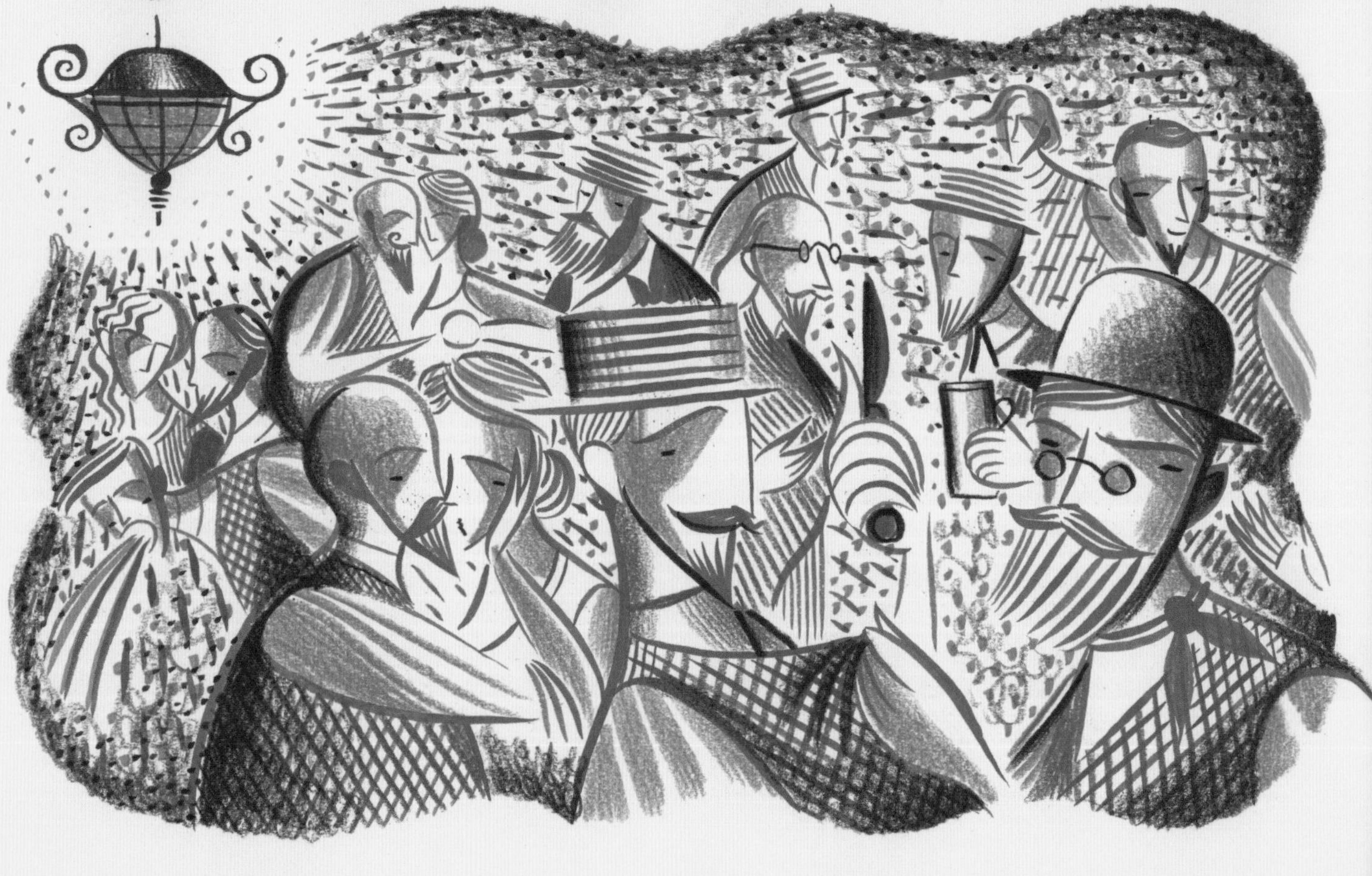

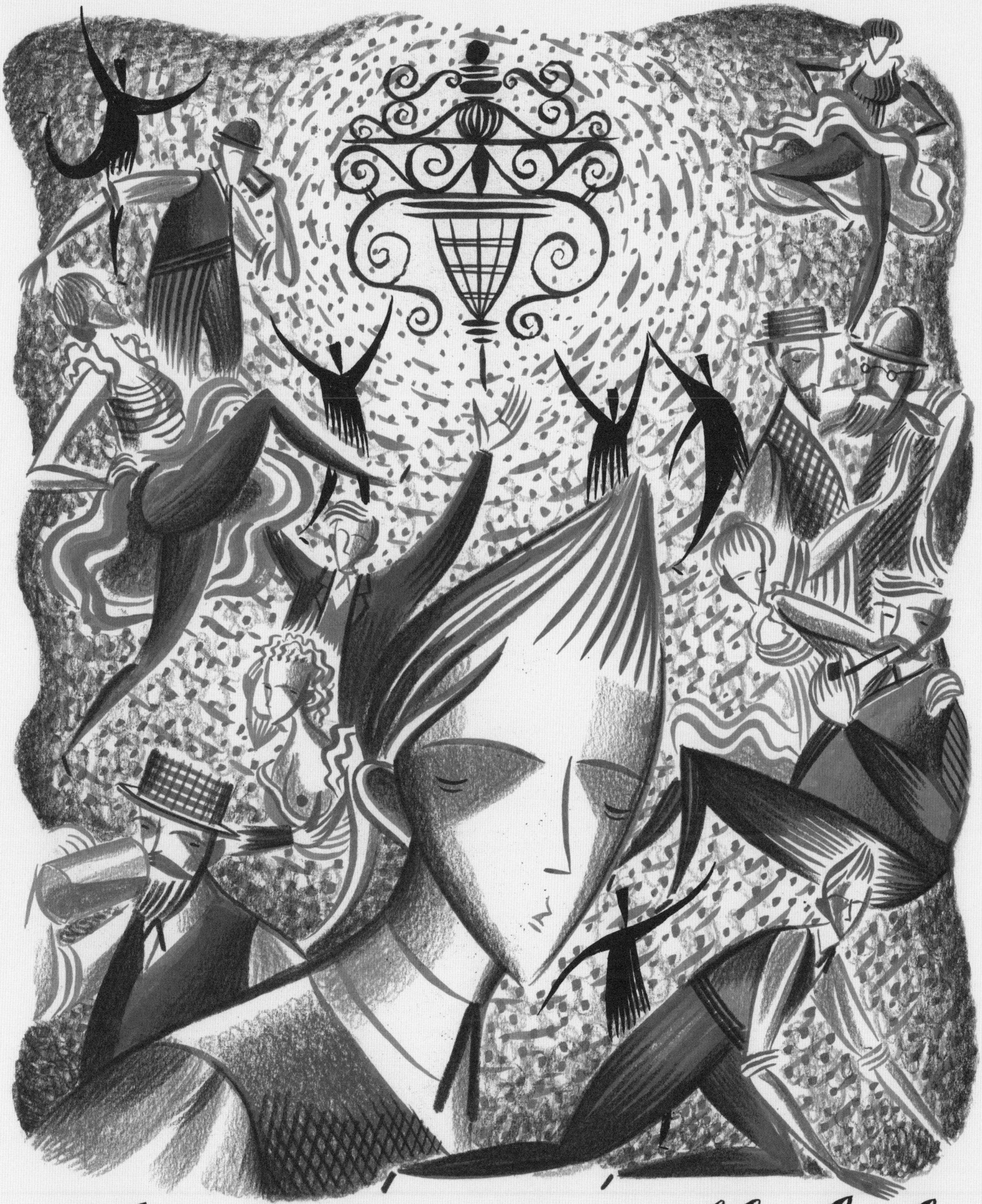

the incessant millwheel,

for ten days,

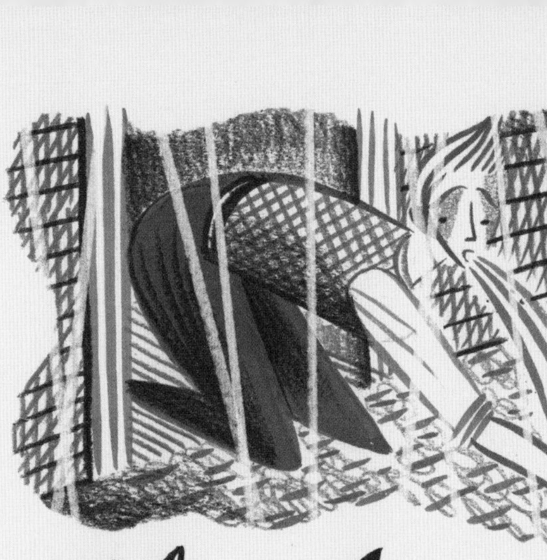

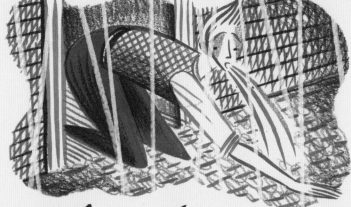

never ruing the beacon's

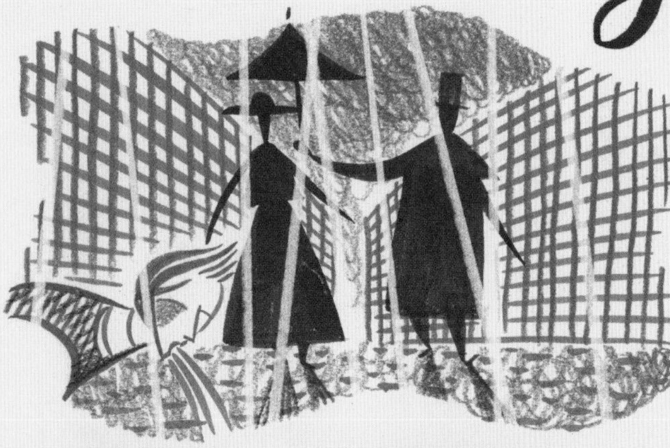

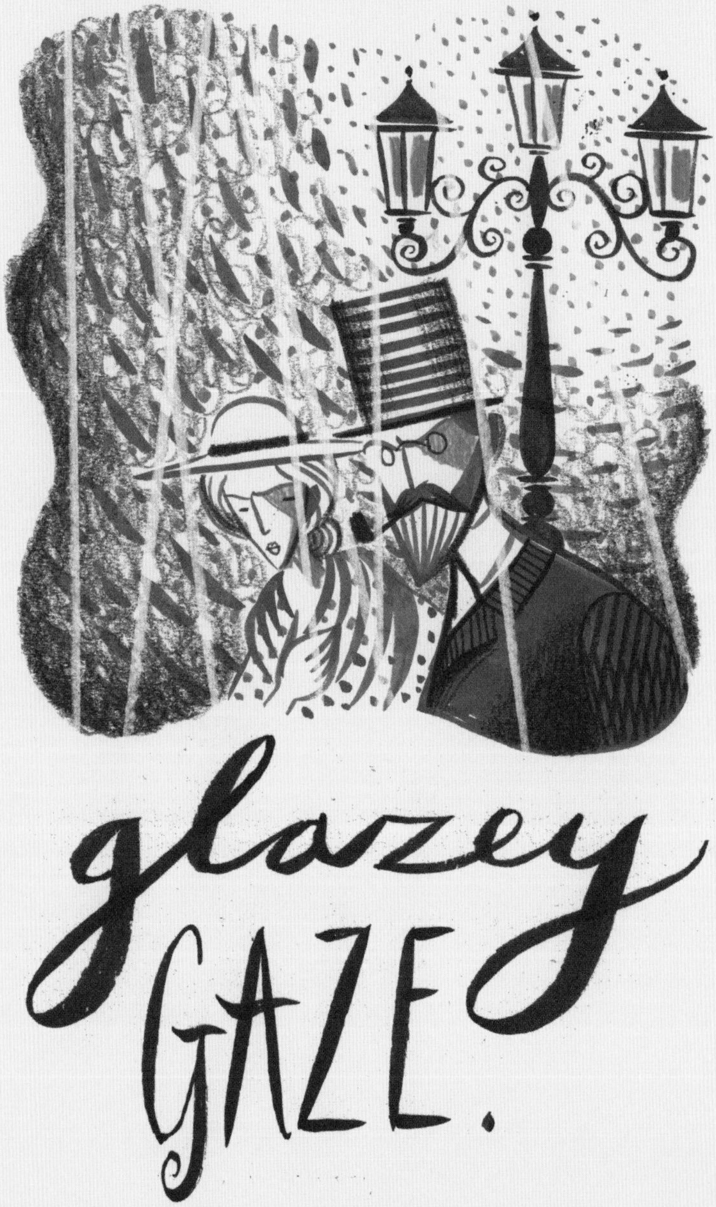

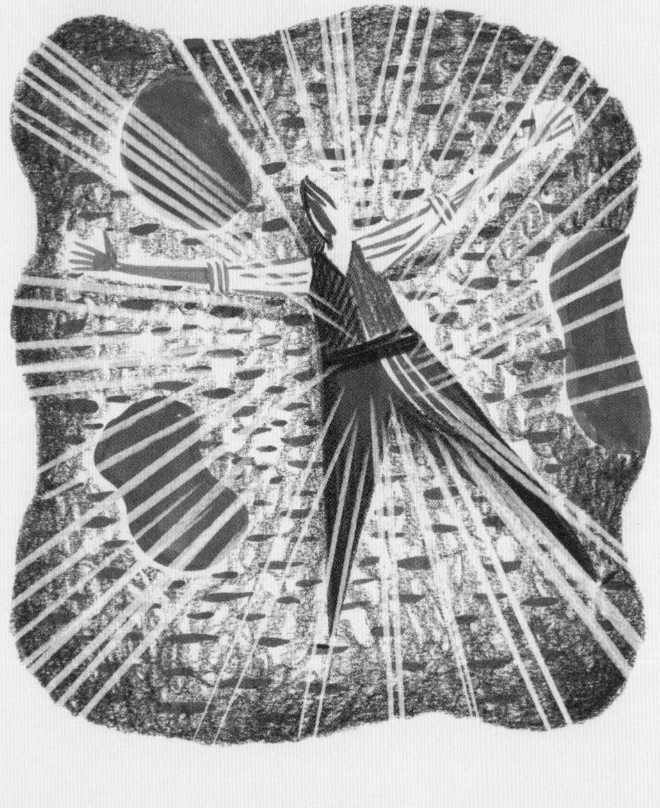

glazey GAZE.

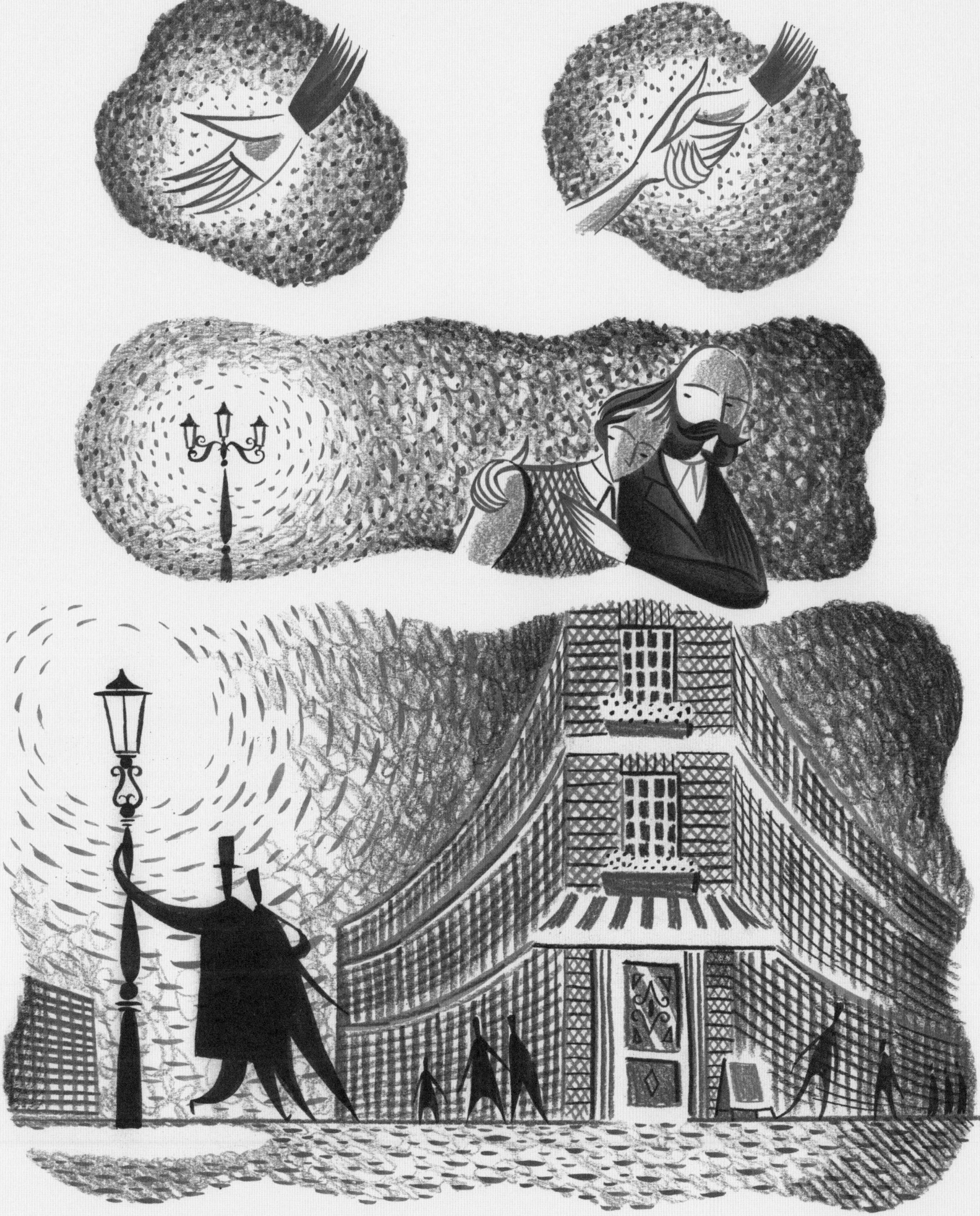

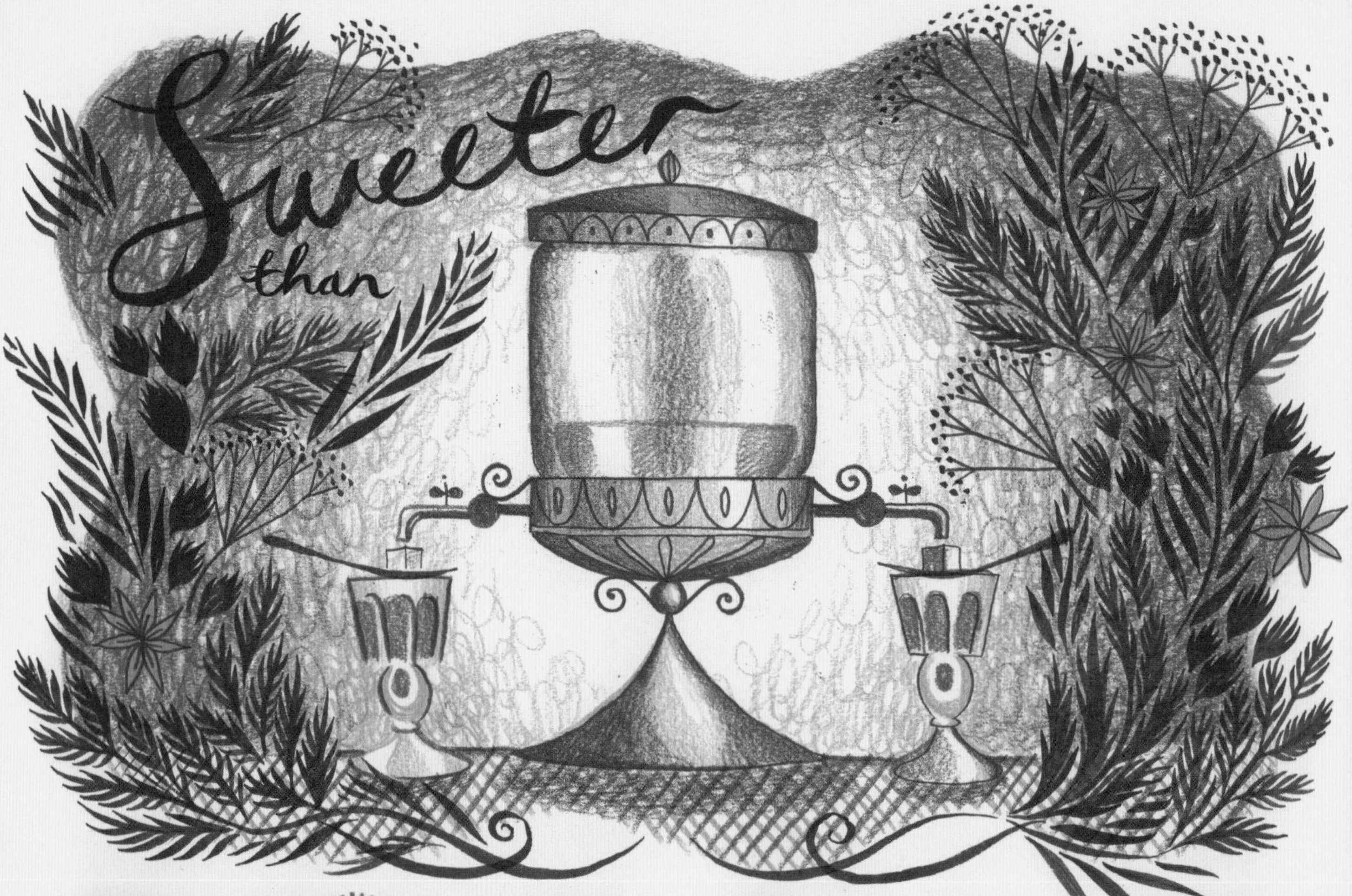
Sweeter
than

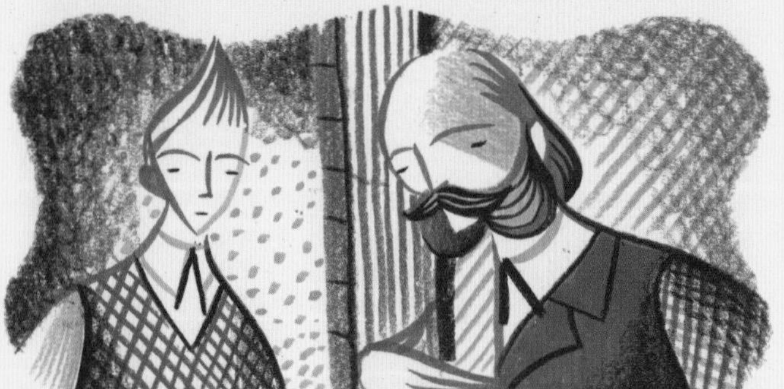

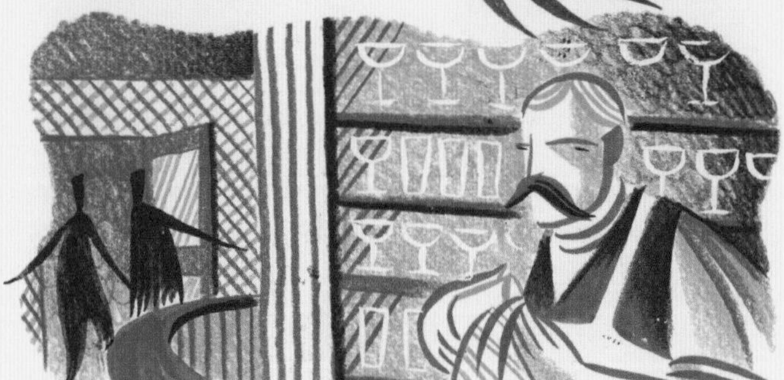

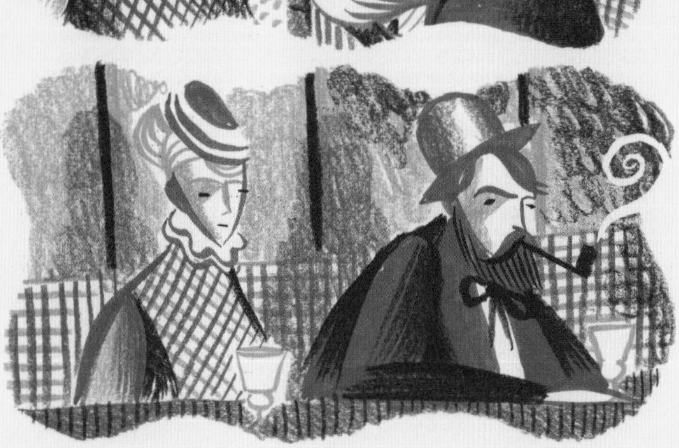

the flesh of
SOUR APPLES
to infants,

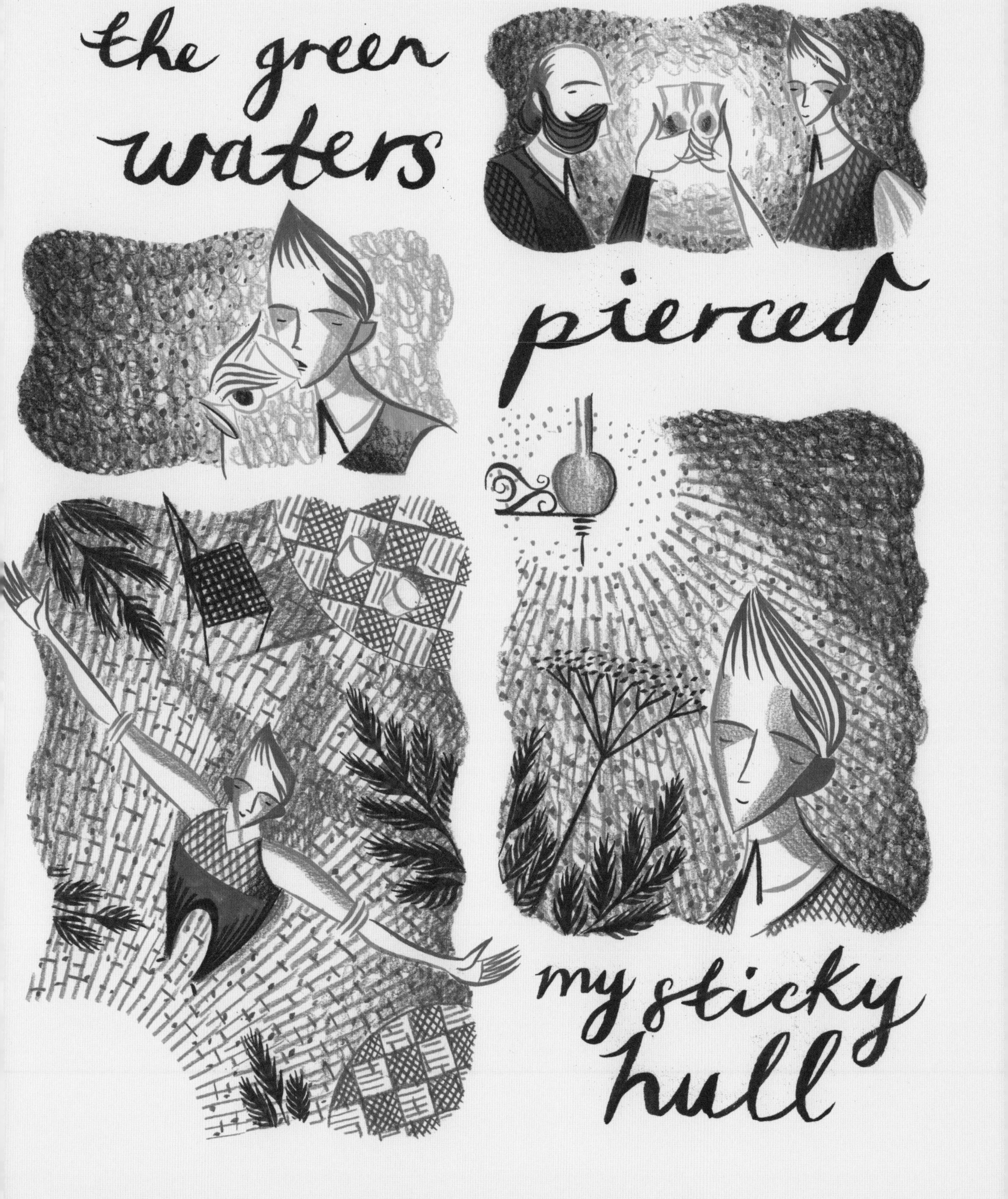
the green waters
pierced
my sticky hull

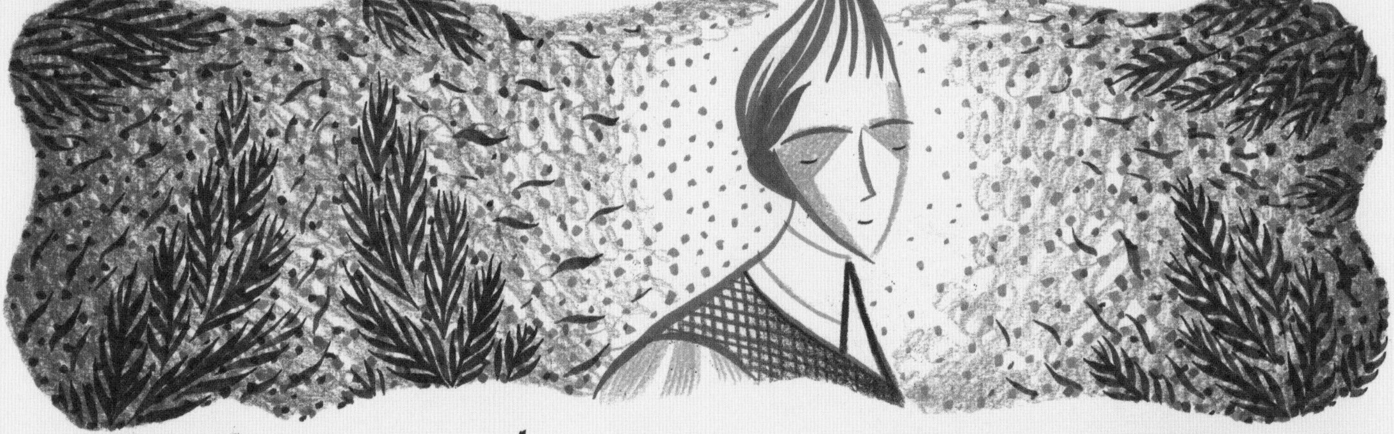

and rinsed
my stains

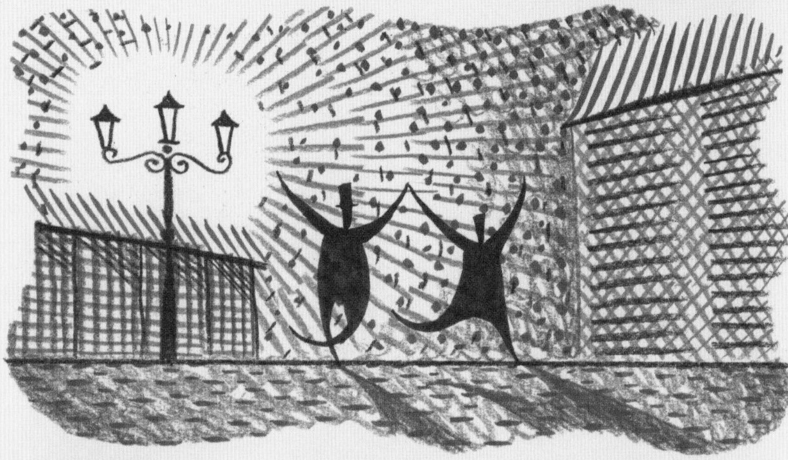

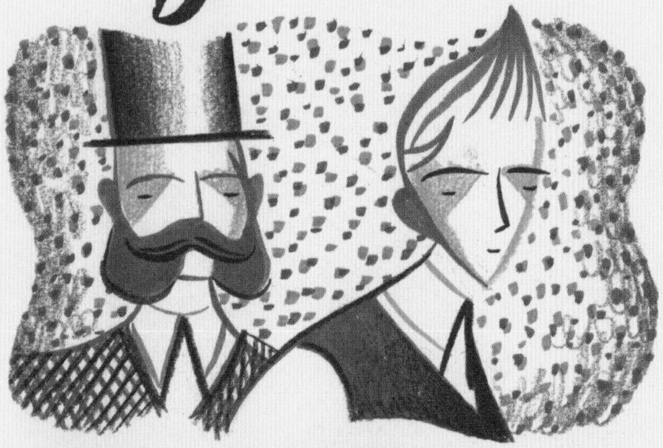

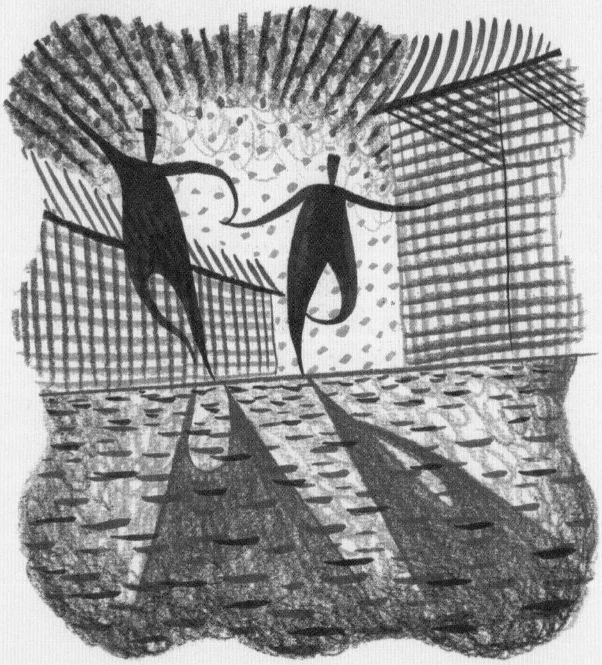

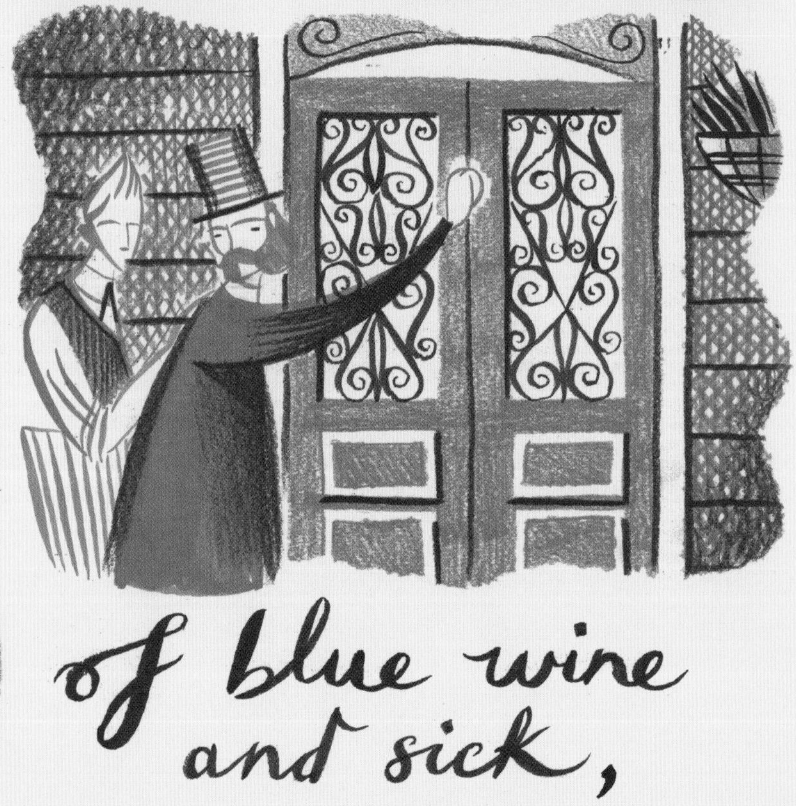

of blue wine
and sick,

sweeping away

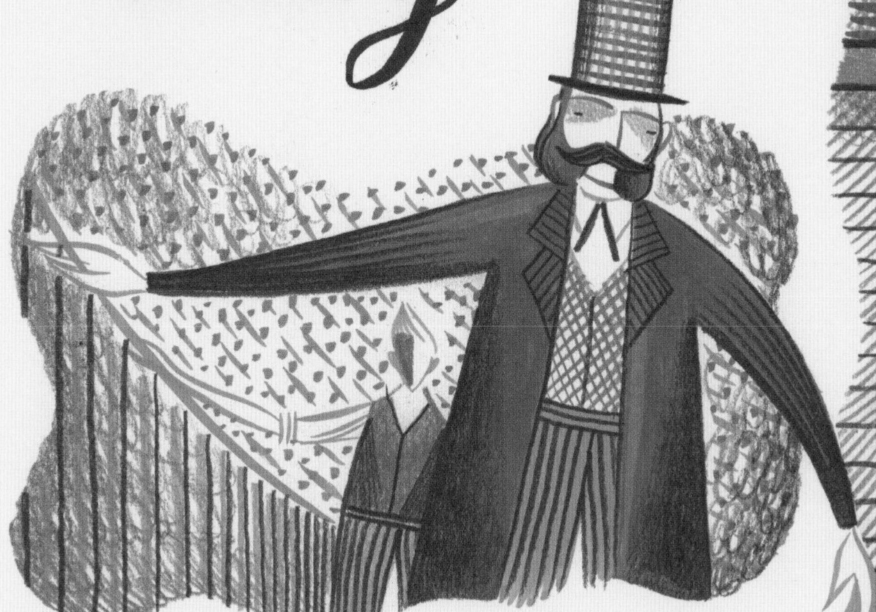

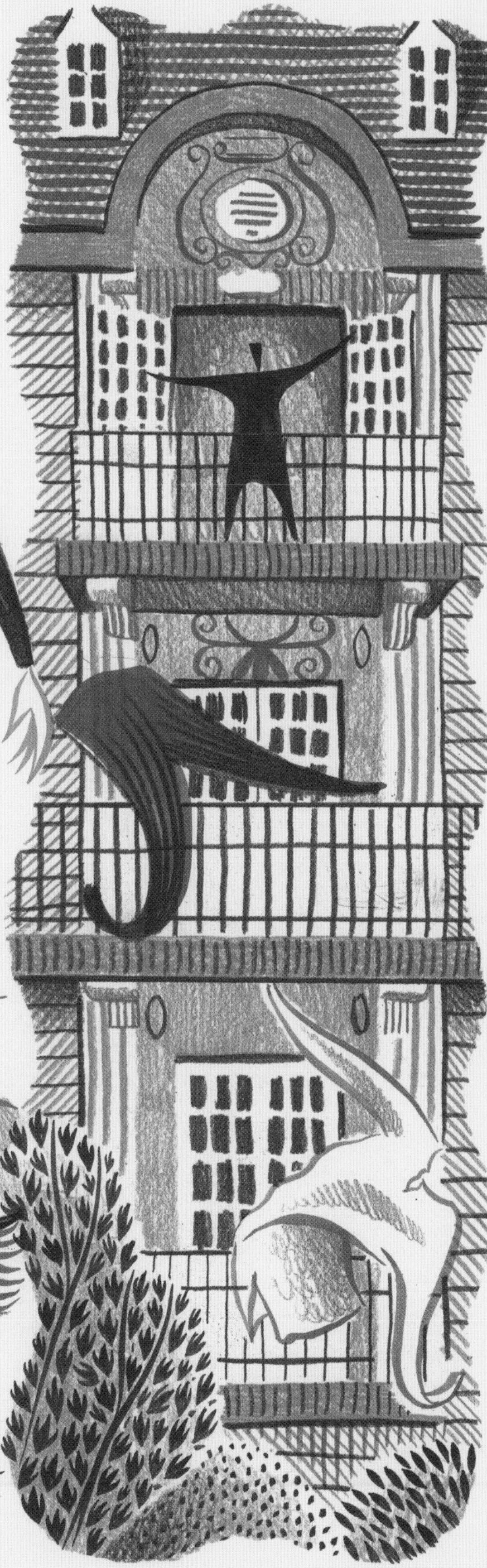

my rudder

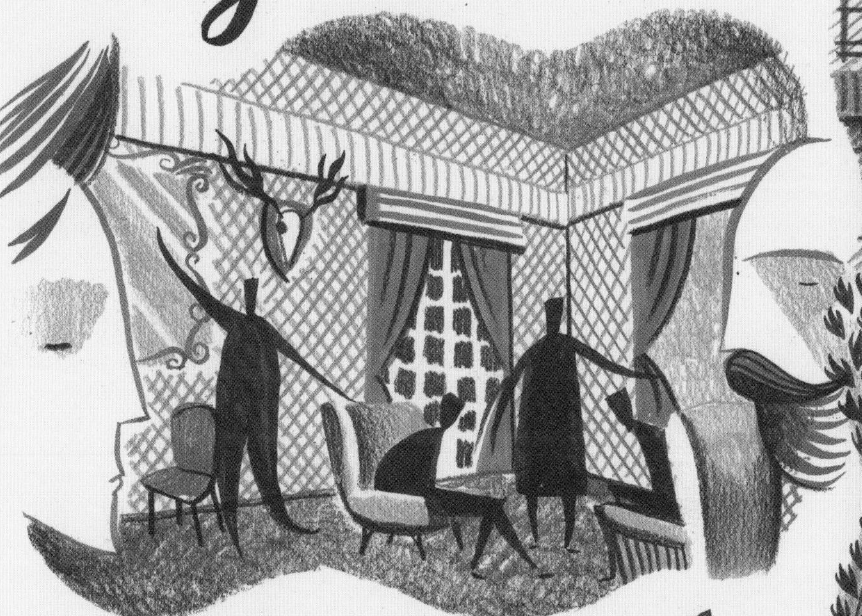

and my anchor.

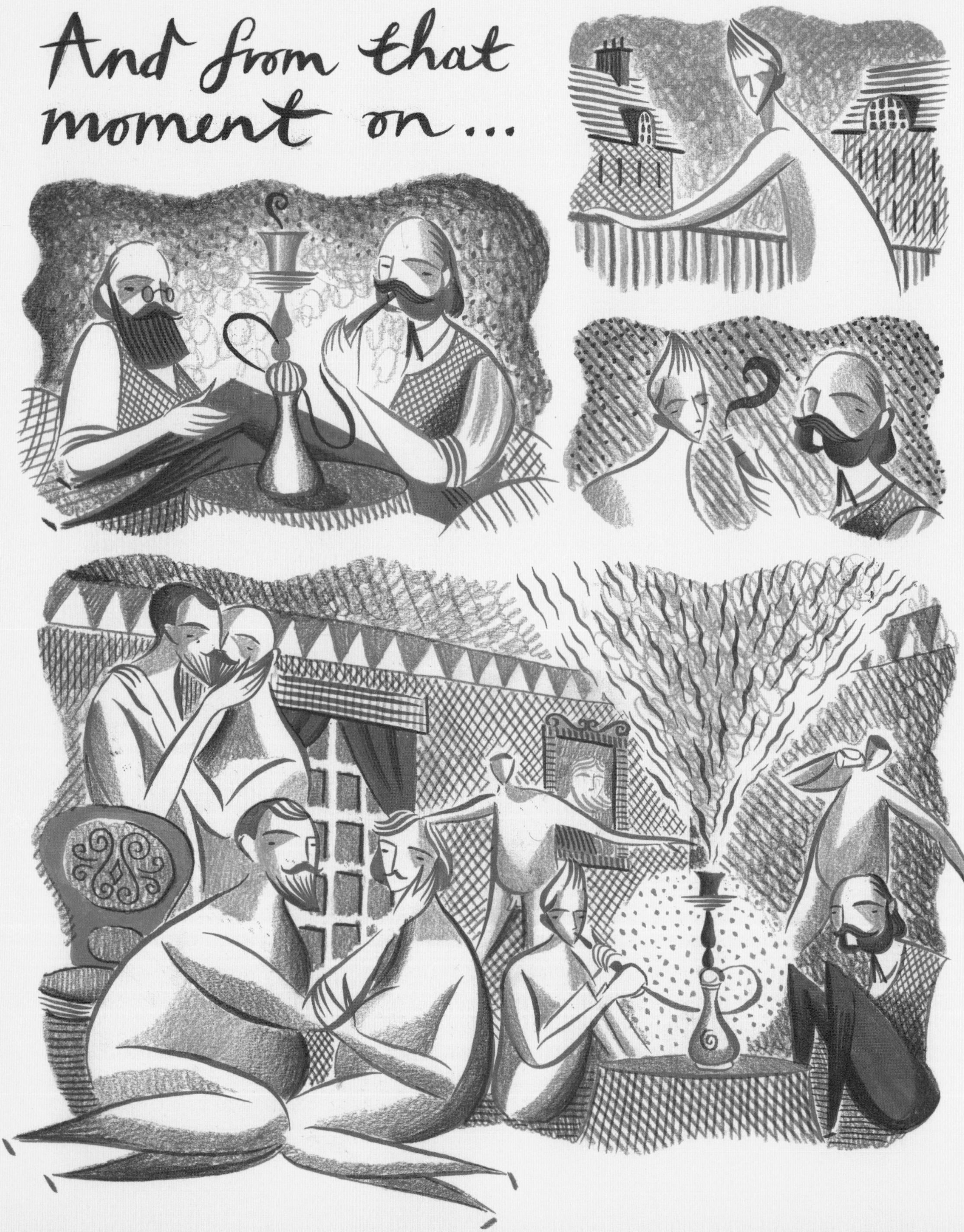
And from that moment on...

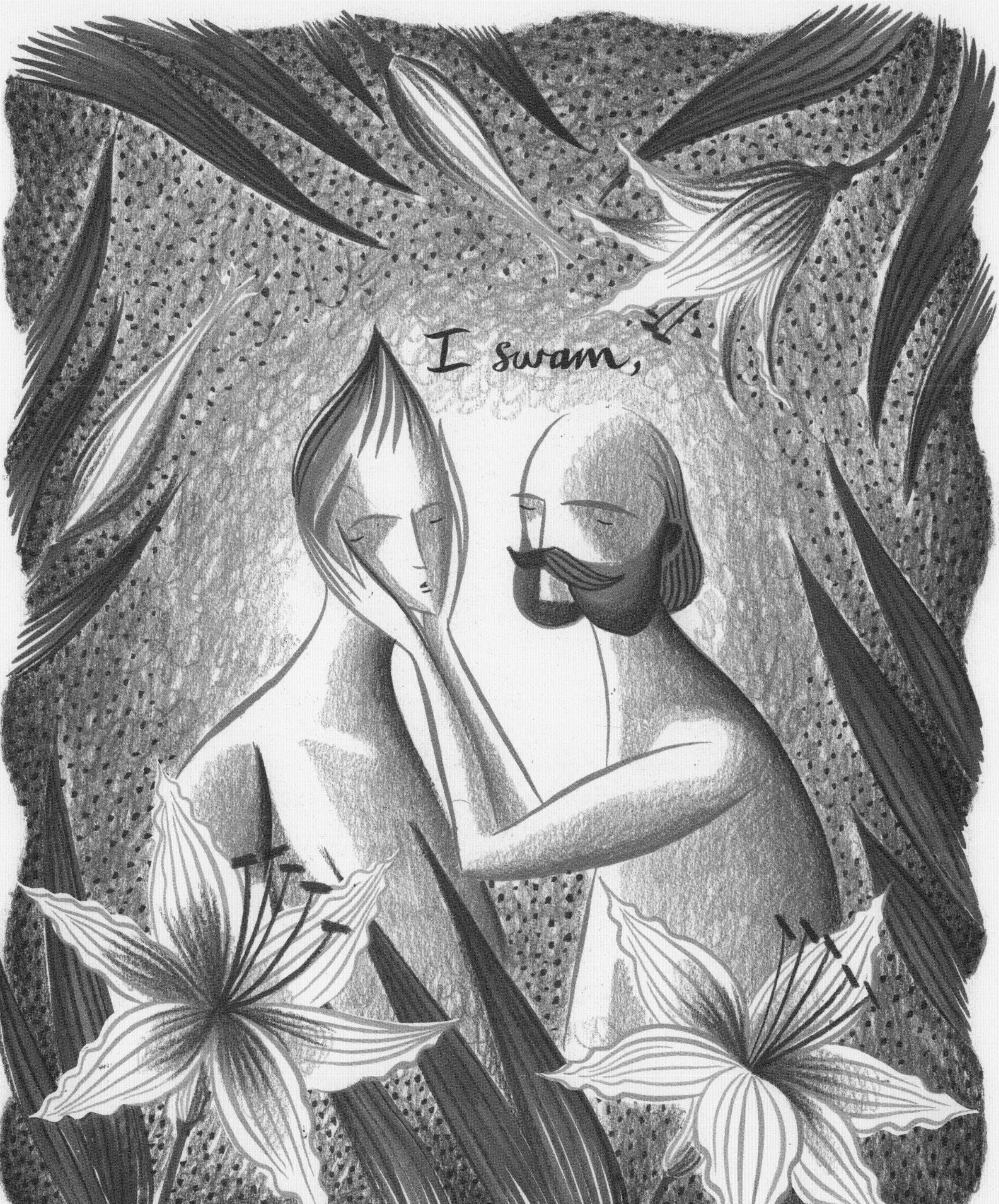
I swam,

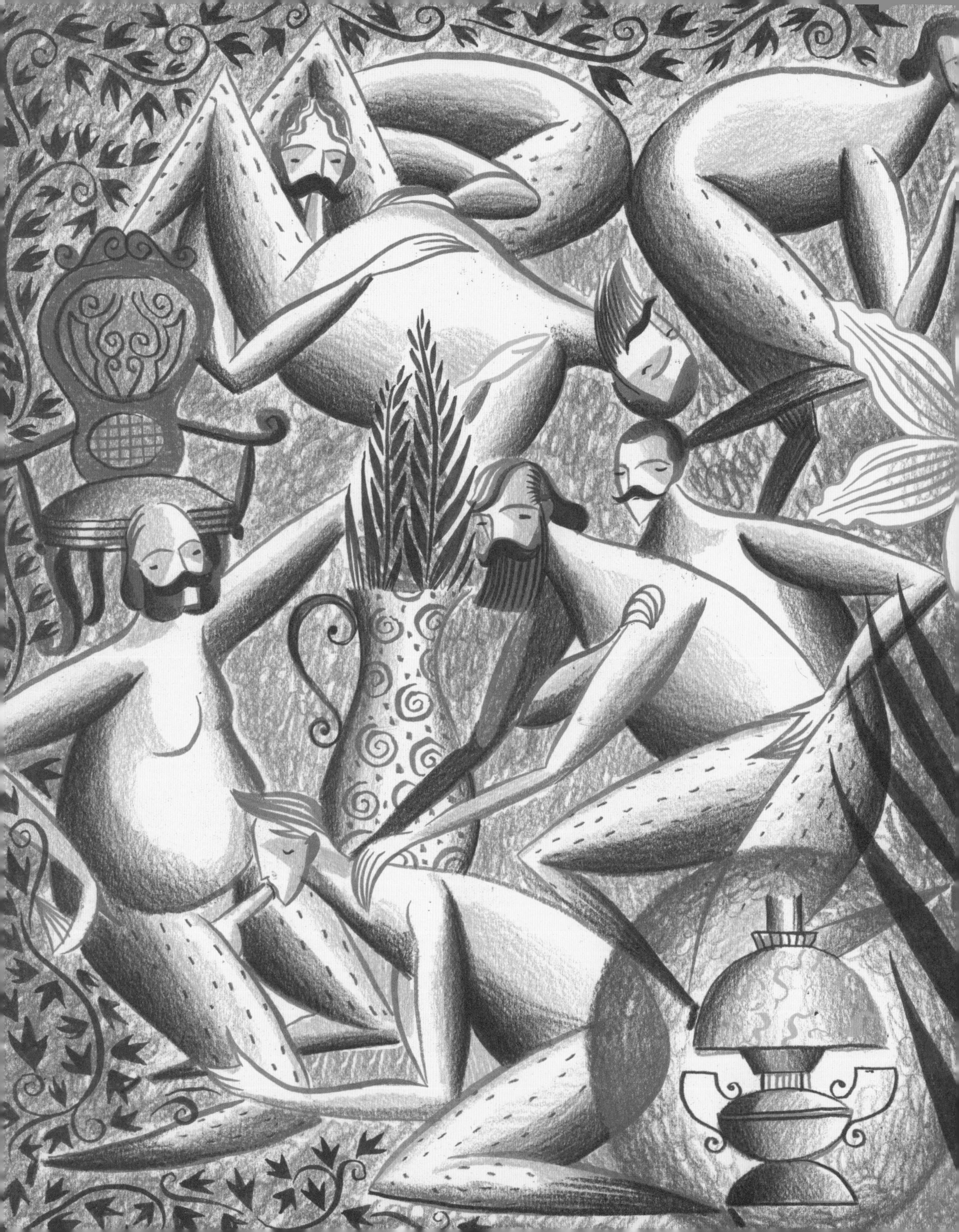

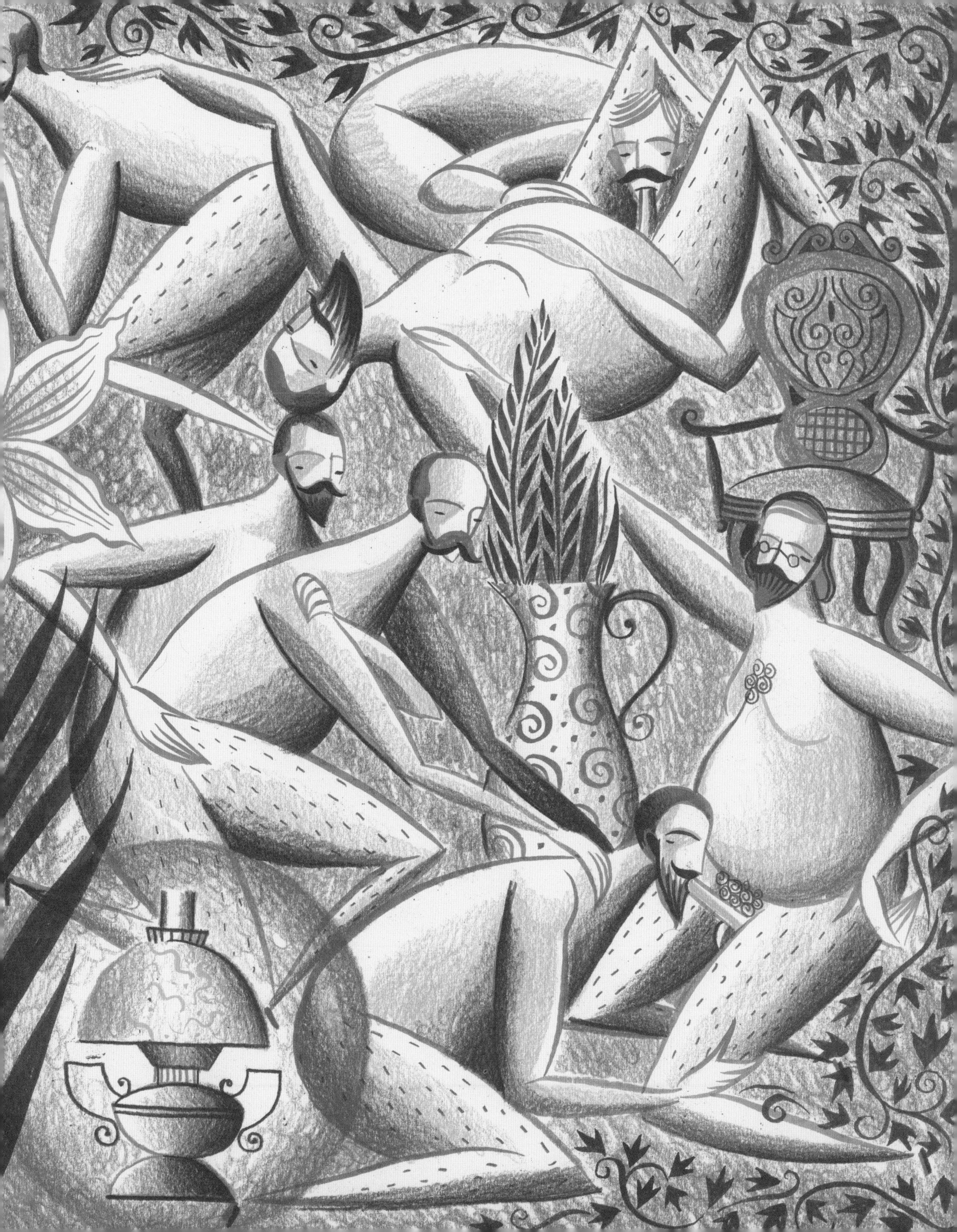

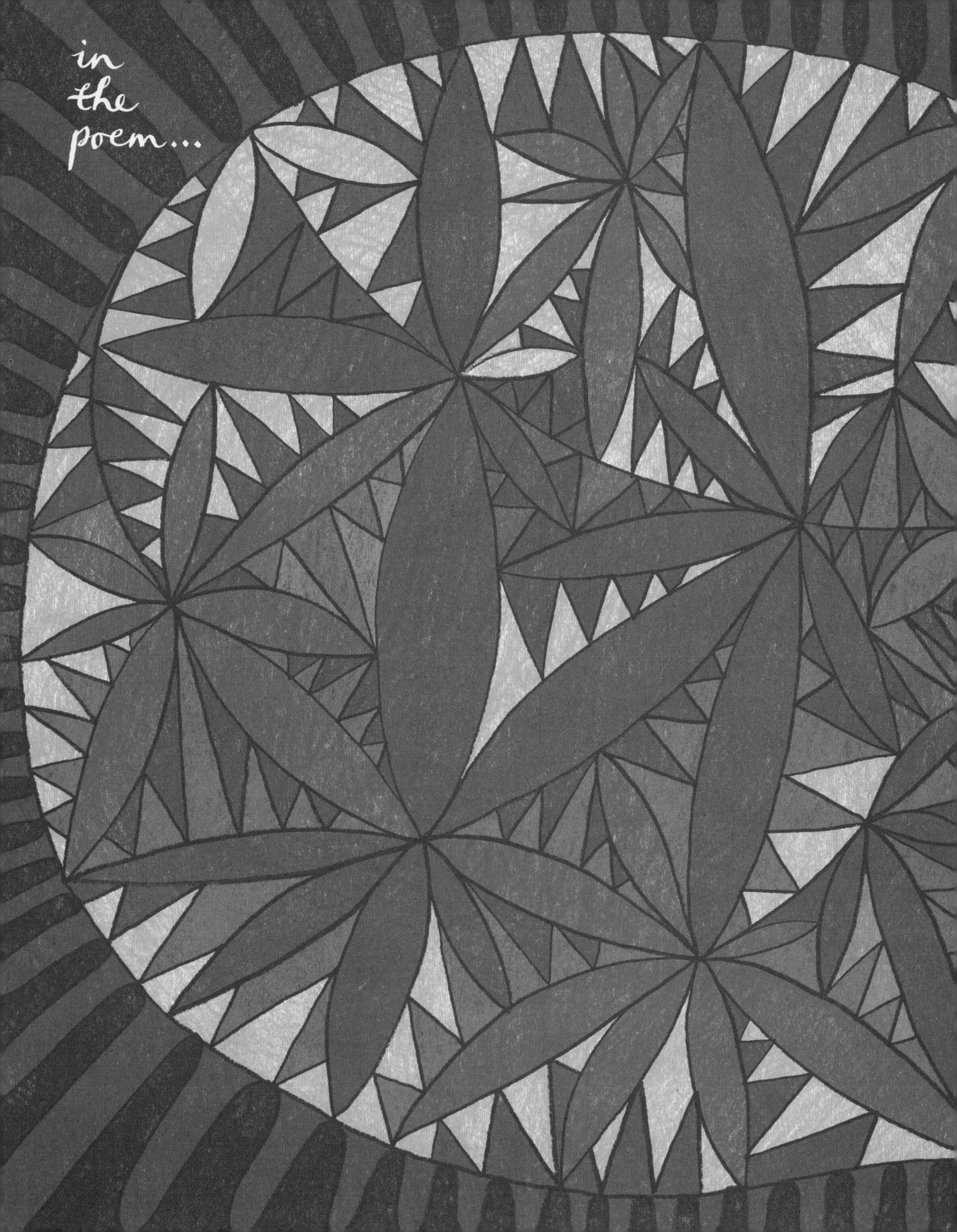
in the poem...

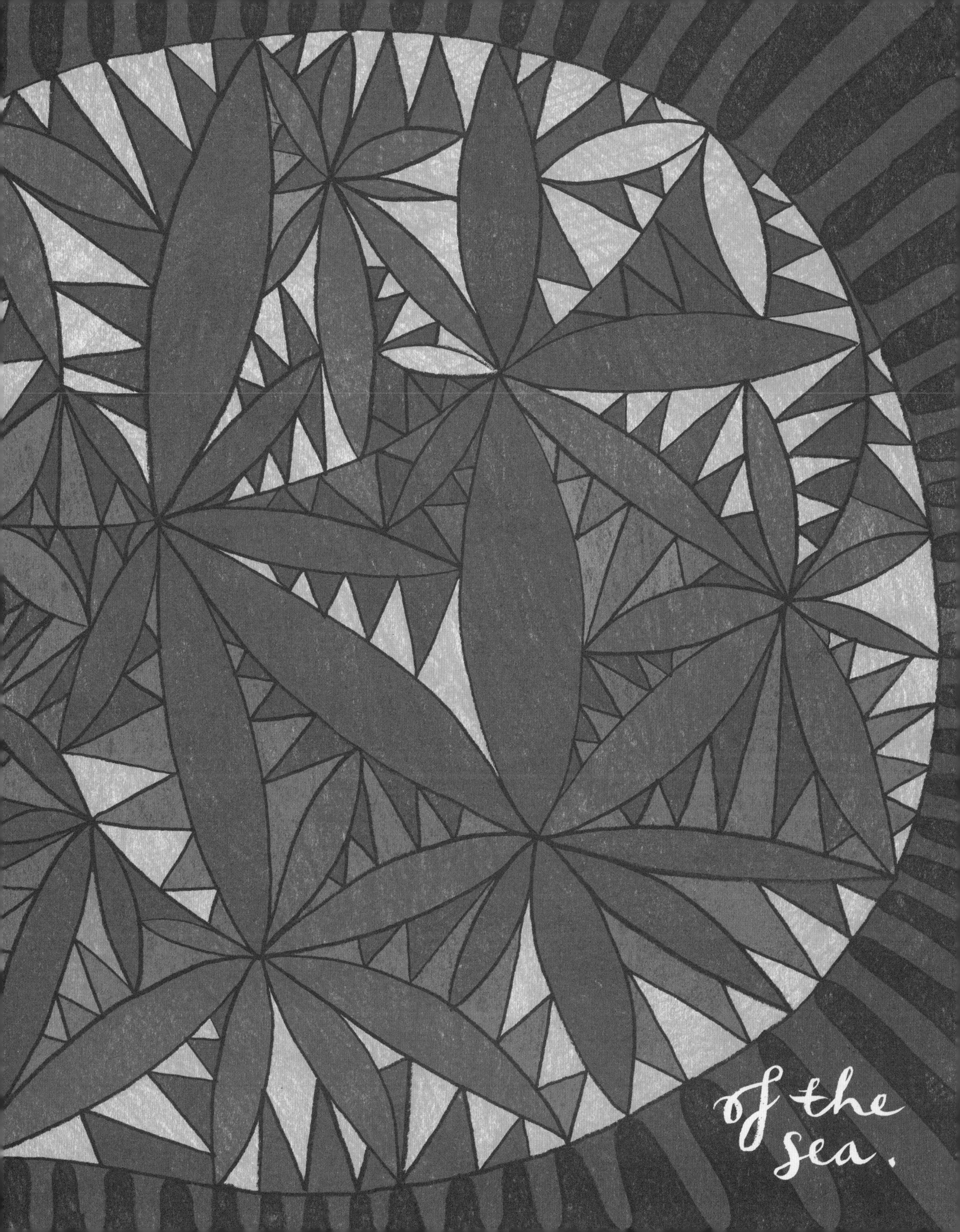
of the
sea.

LACTESCENT,

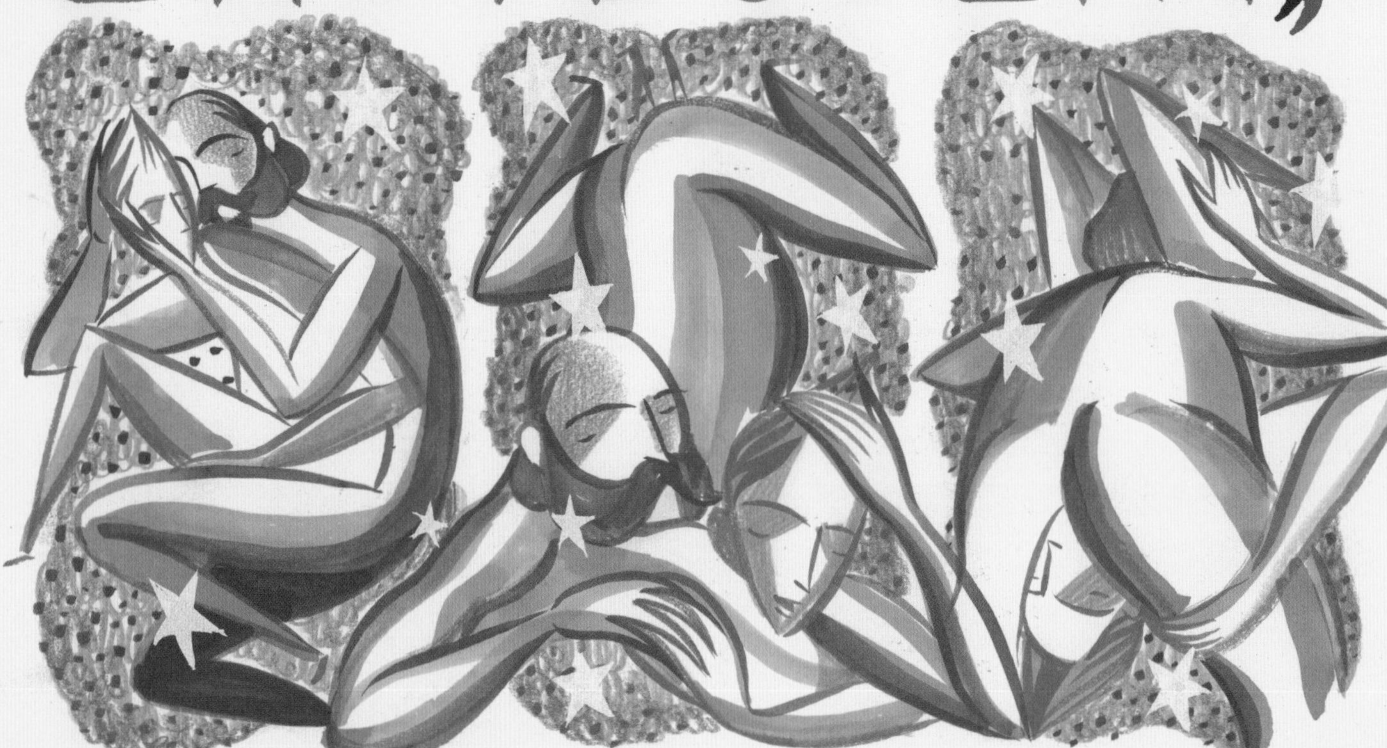

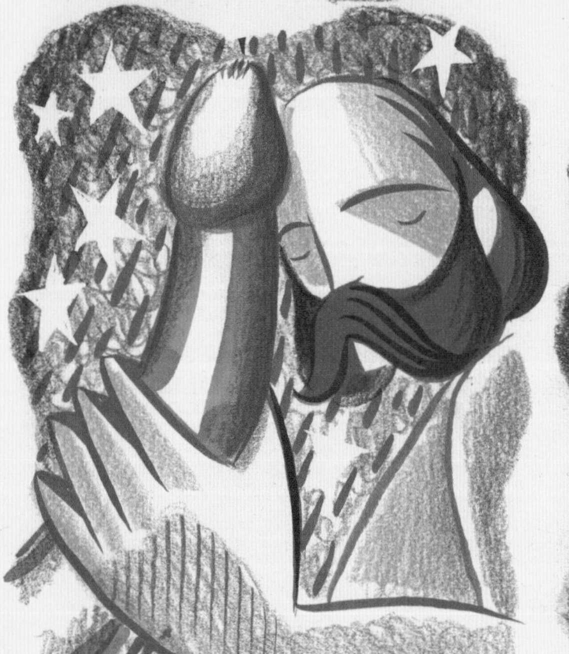

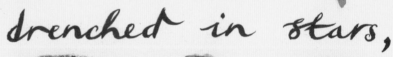

drenched in stars,

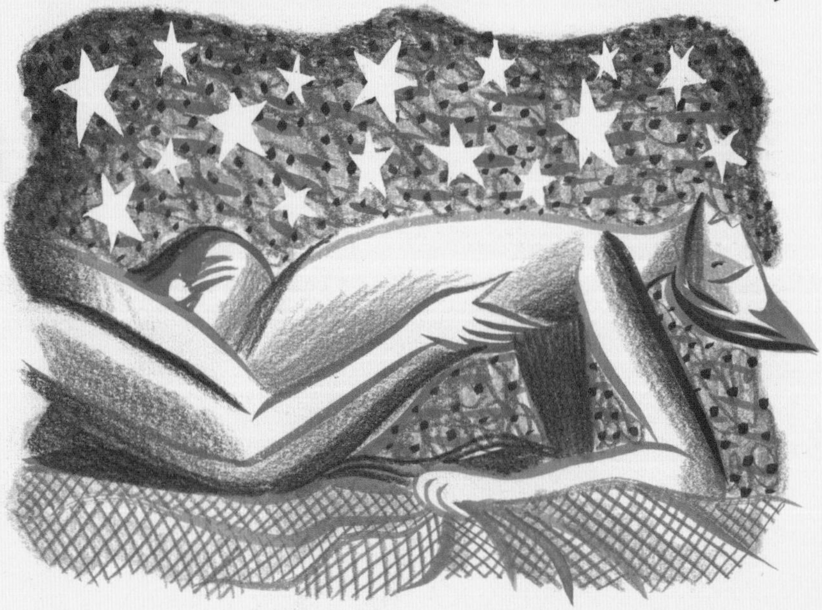

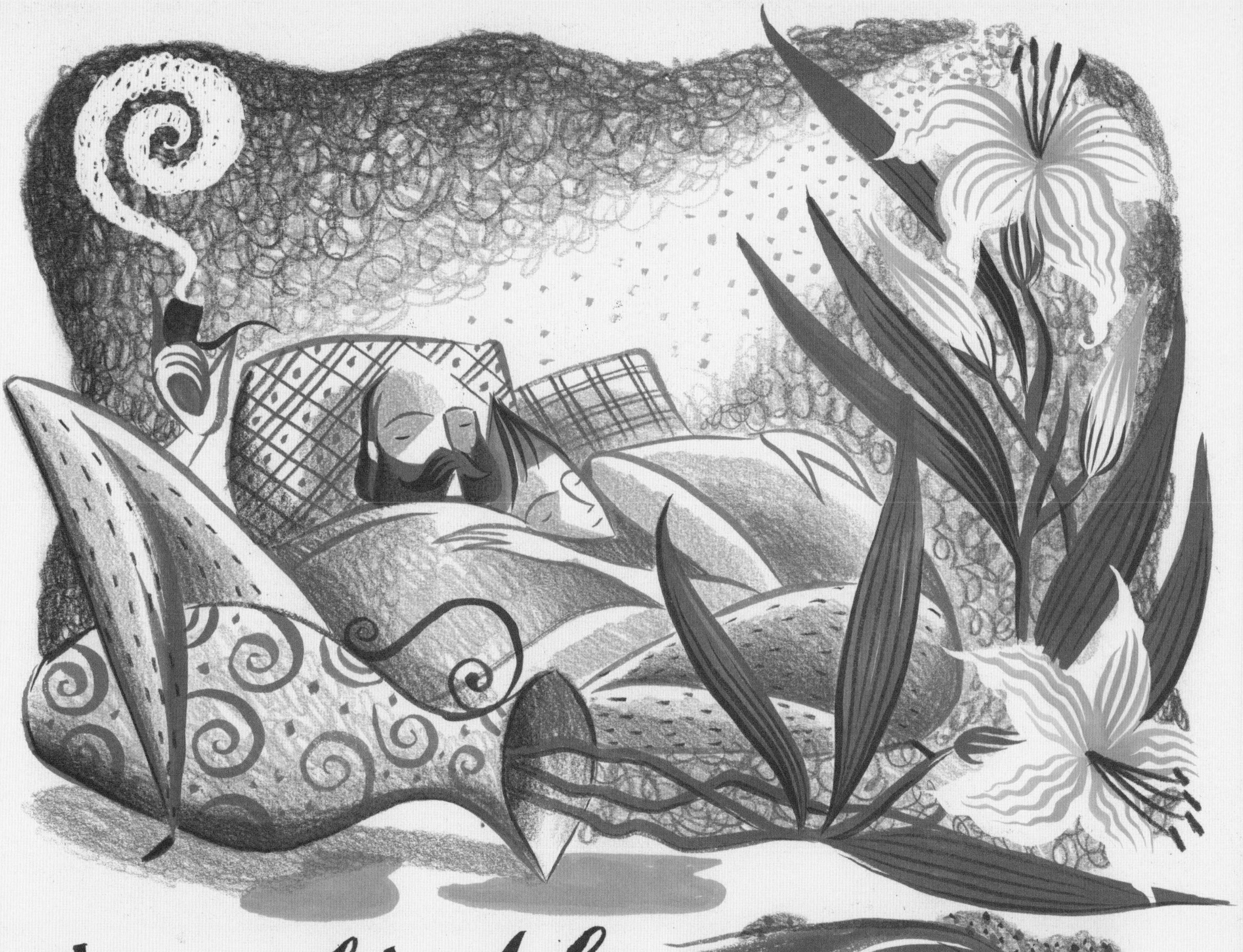

insatiable

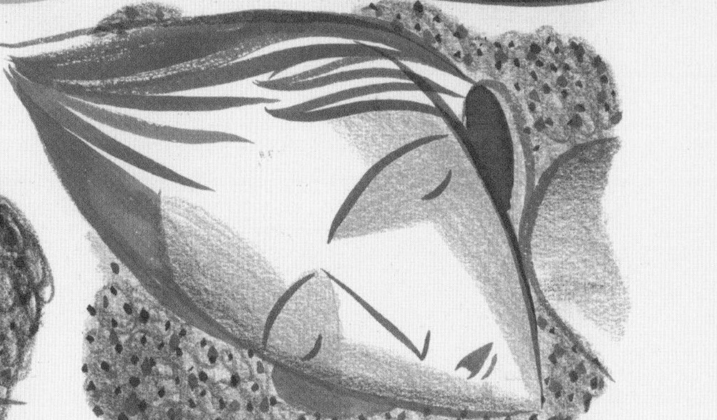

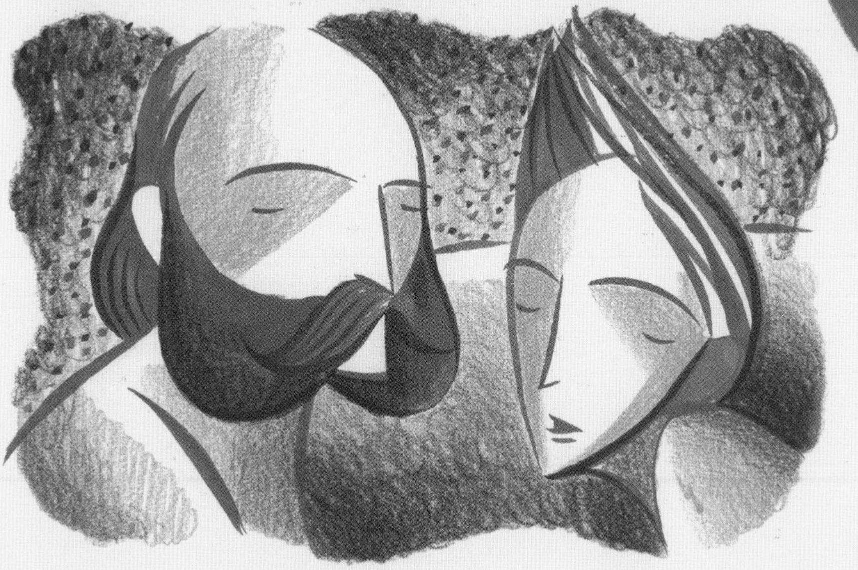

greeny
blue,

Where,

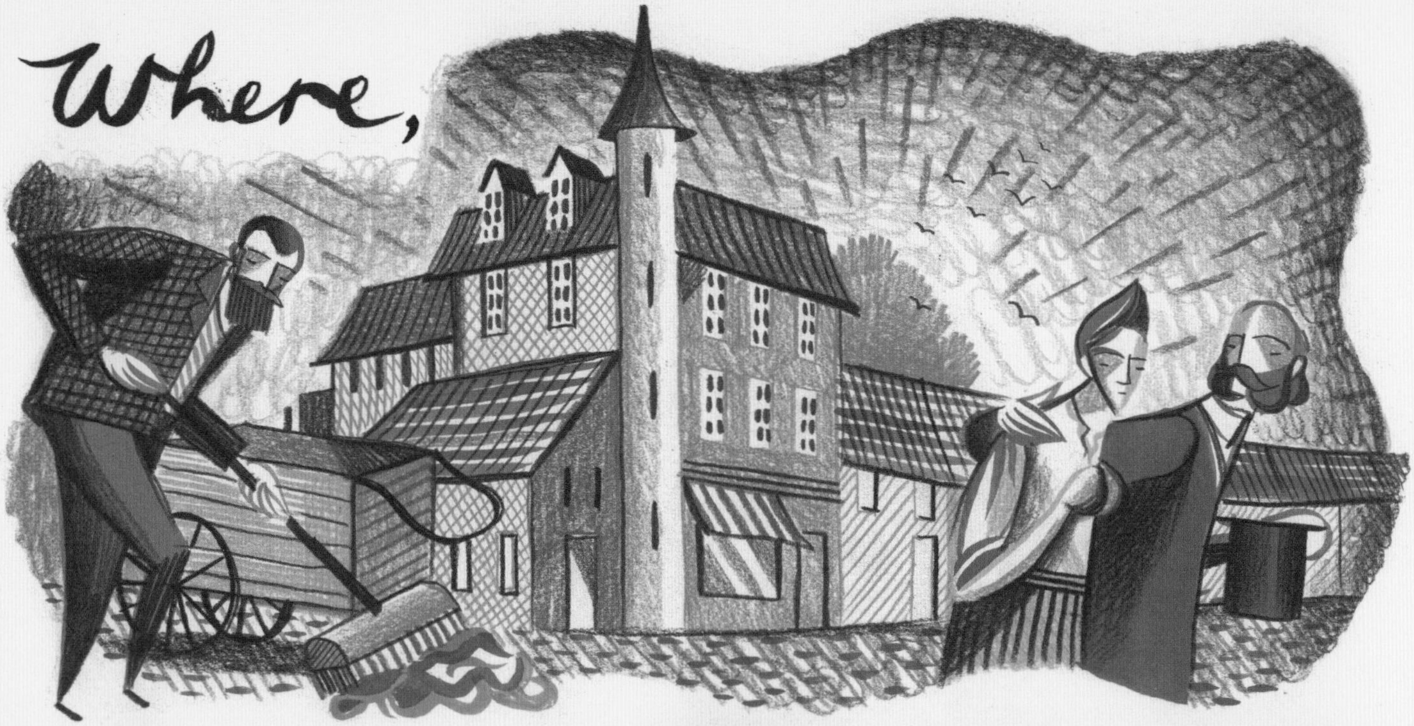

haggard

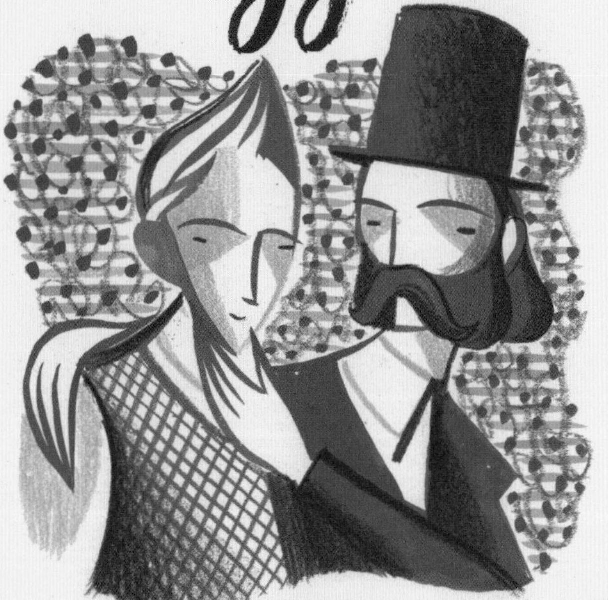

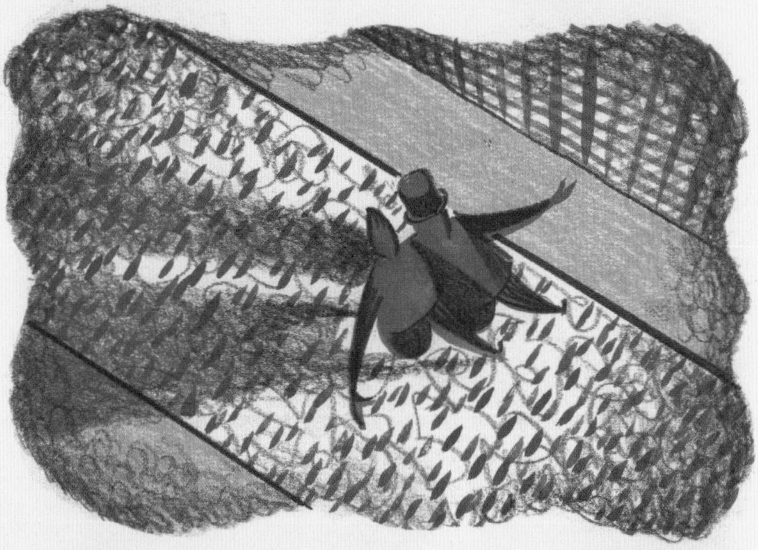

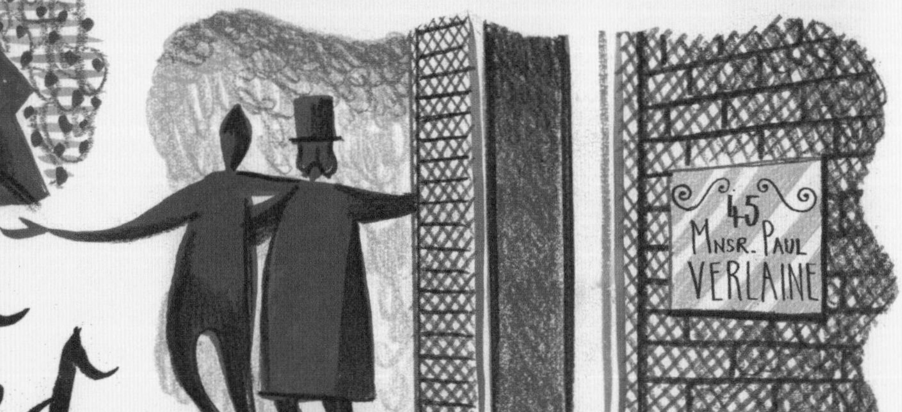
45
MNSR. PAUL
VERLAINE

and goggle-eyed,

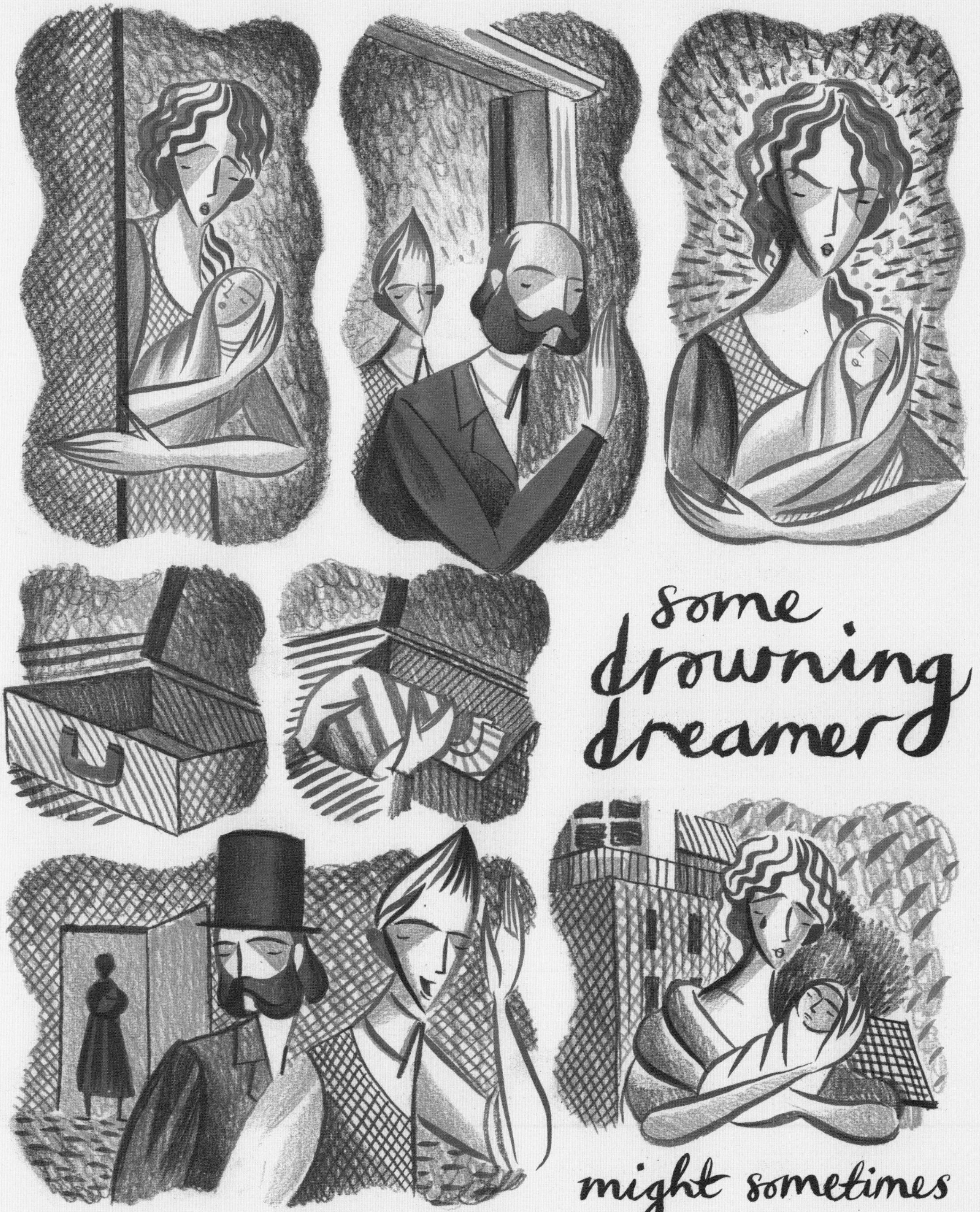some drowning dreamer
might sometimes

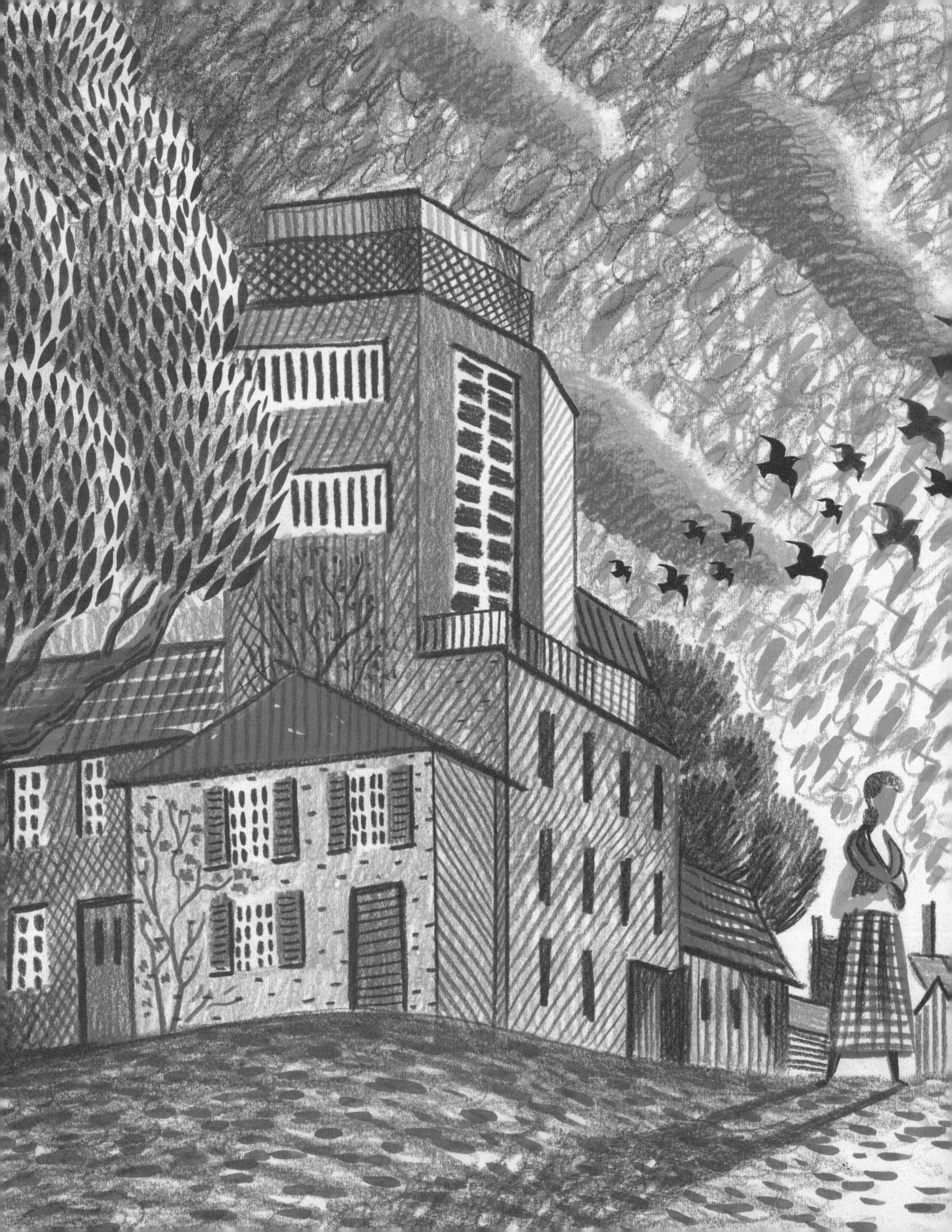

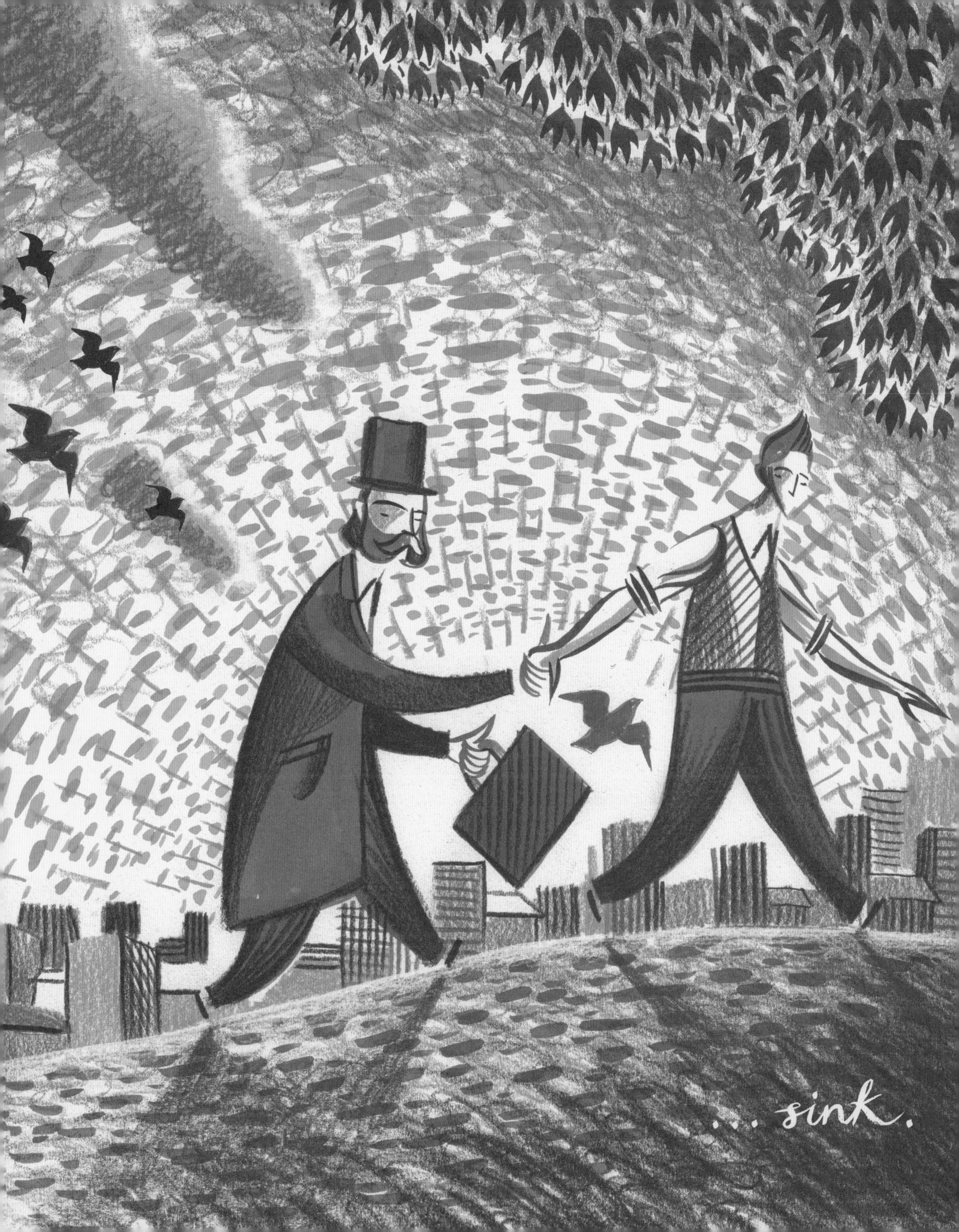
. . . sink.

Where,

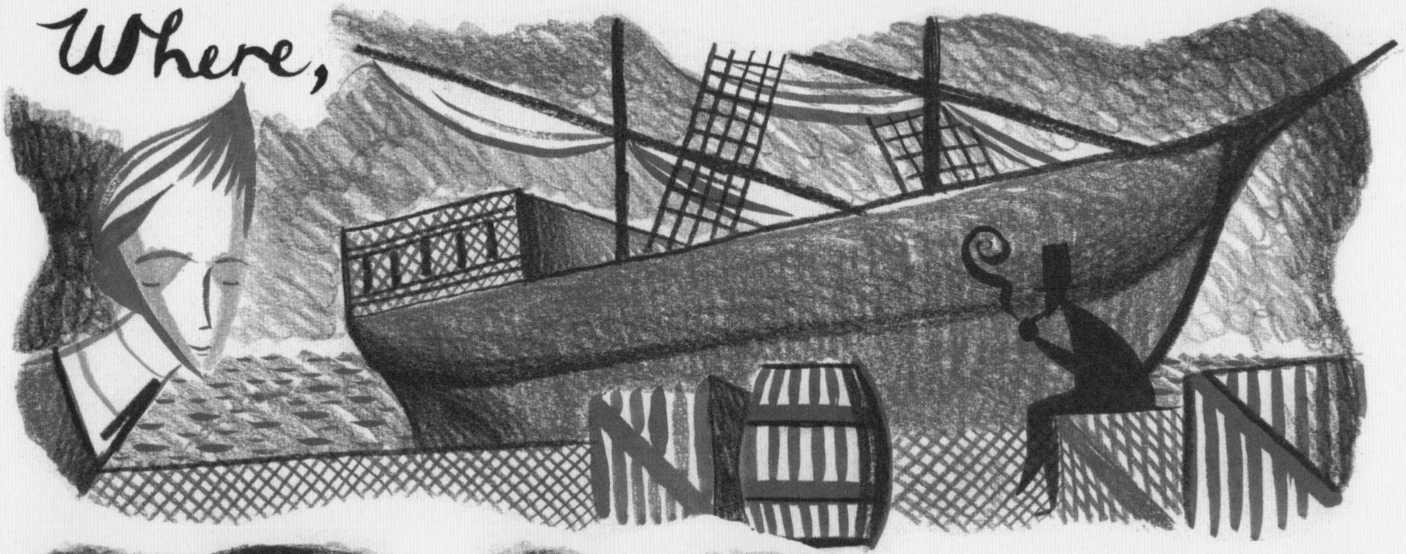

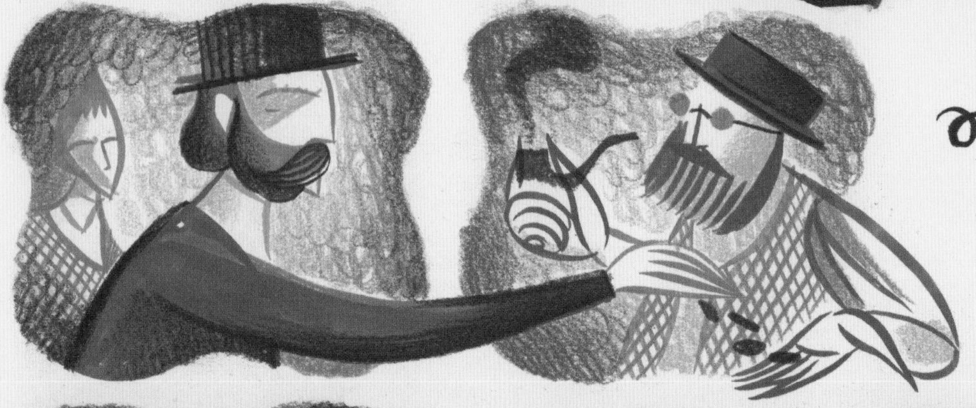

out of the blue,

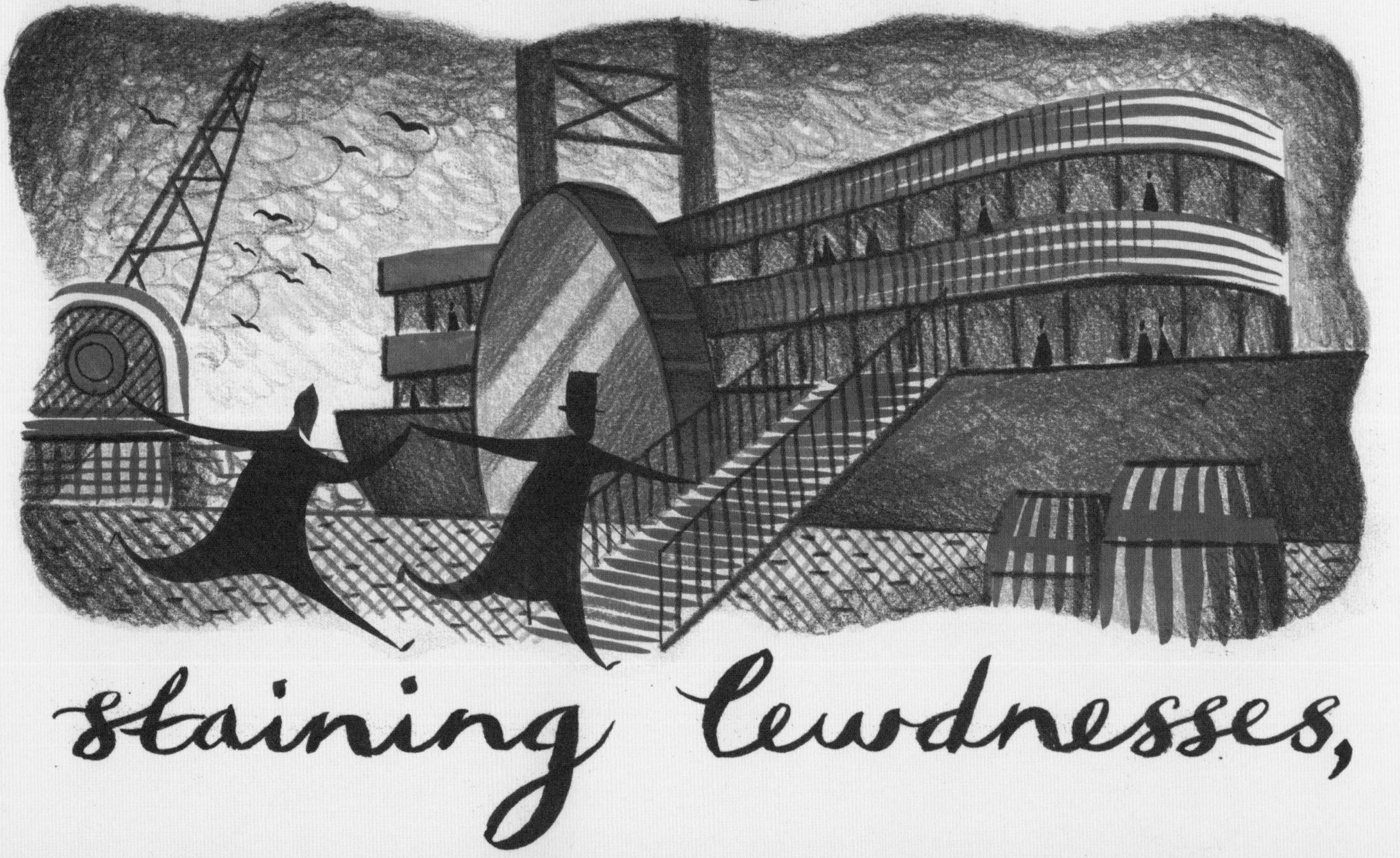

staining lewdnesses,

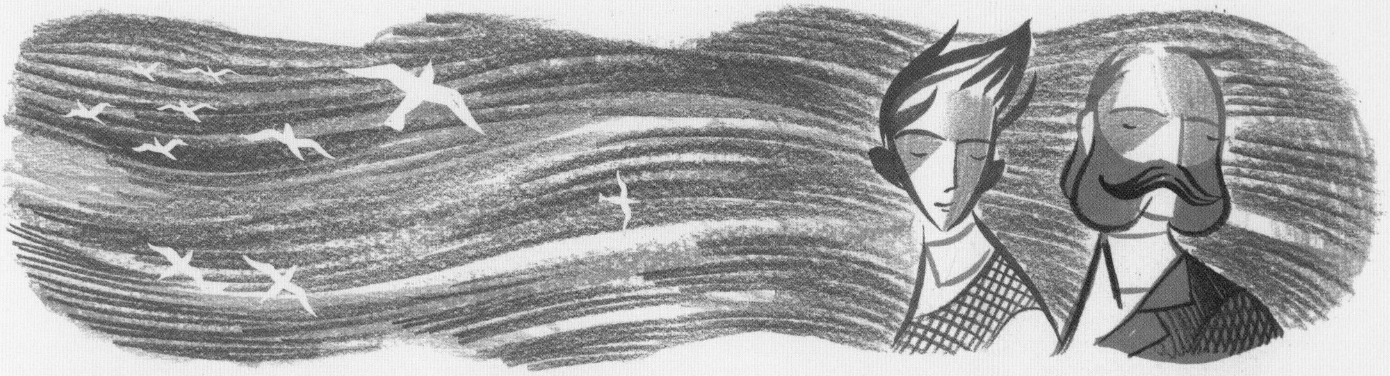

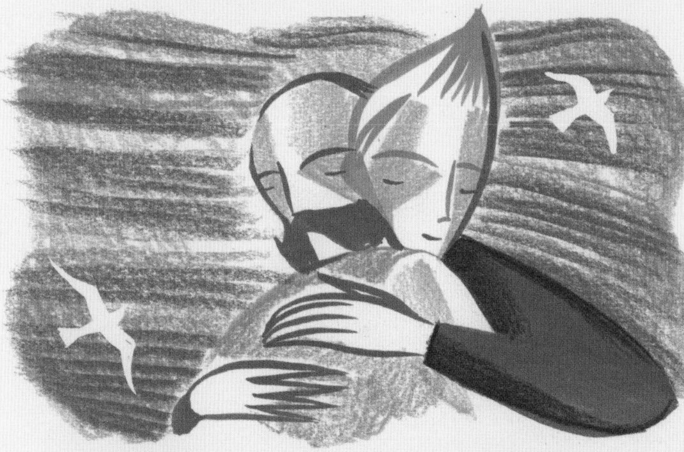

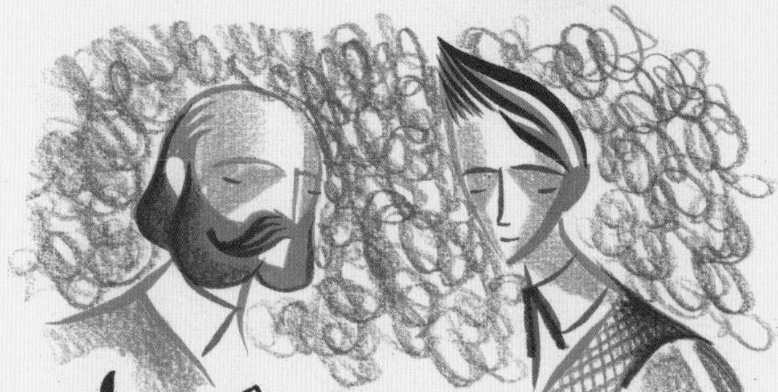

deliriums,

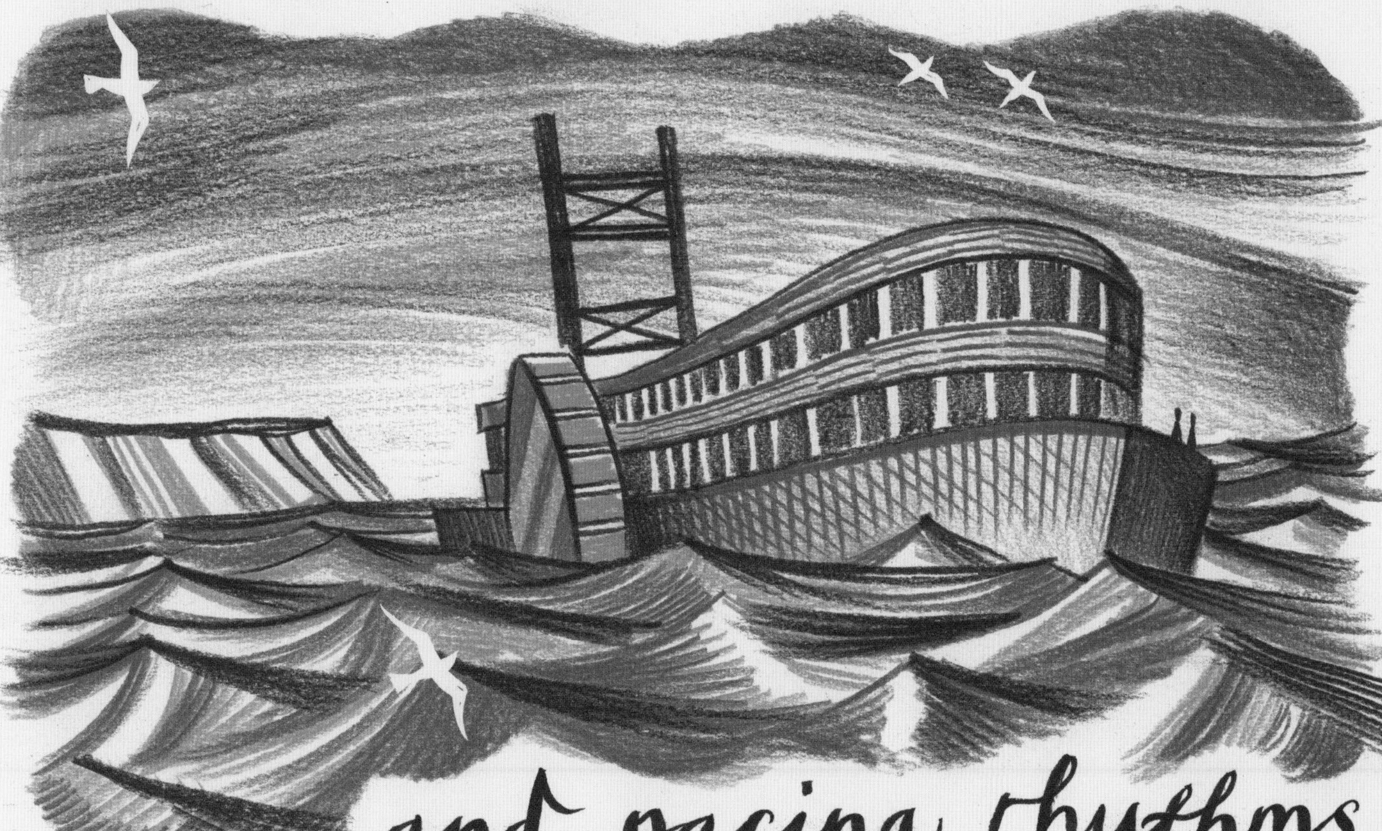

and pacing rhythms,

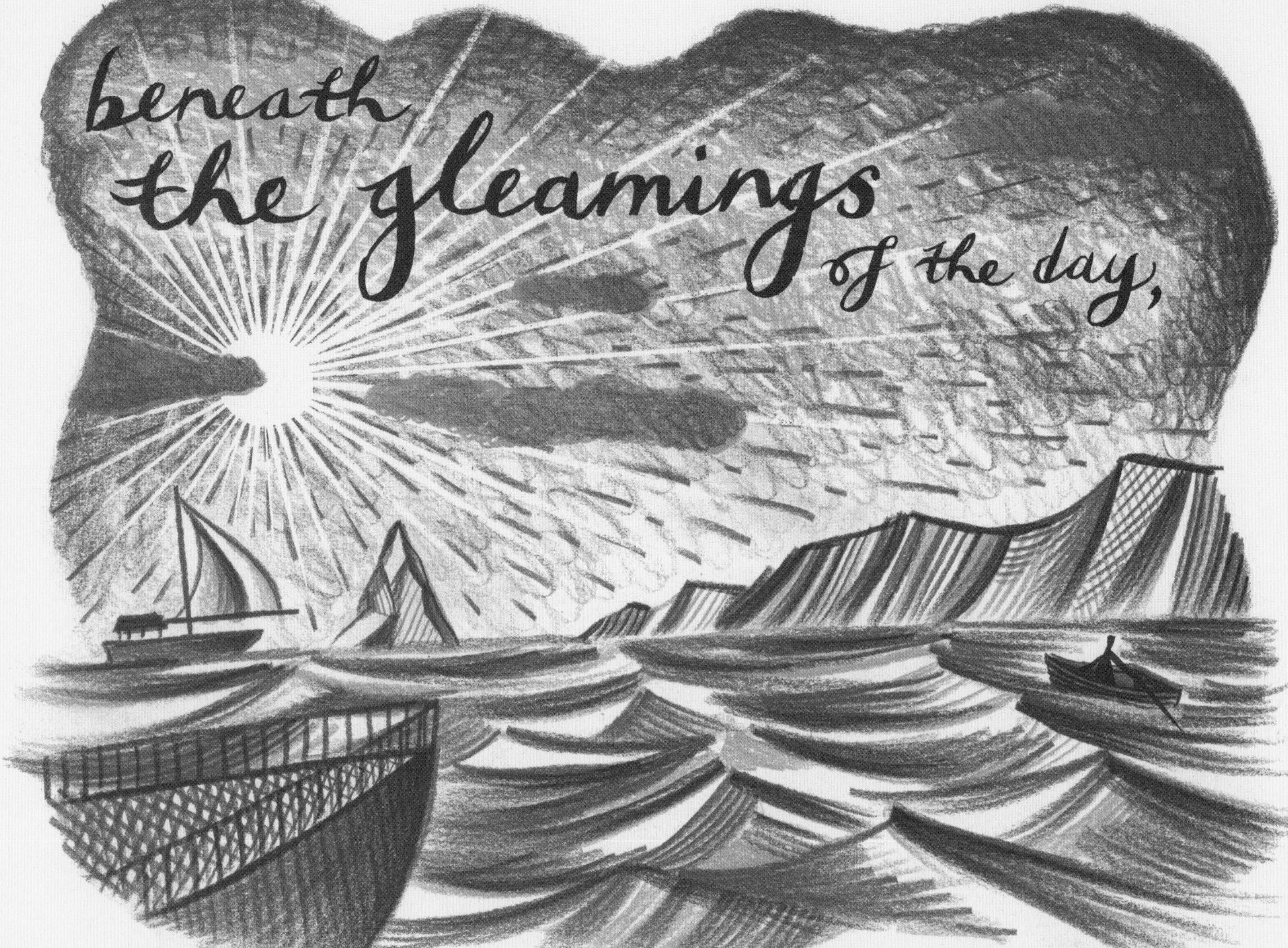
beneath the gleamings of the day,

stronger than alcohol,

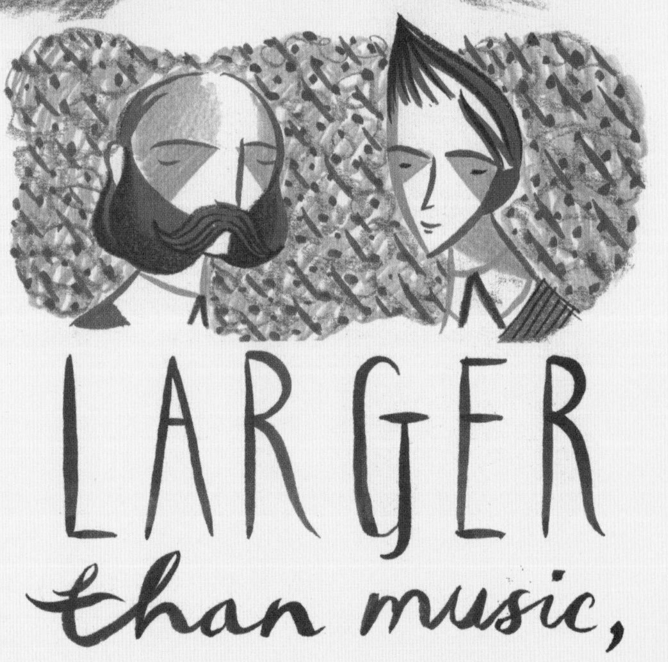

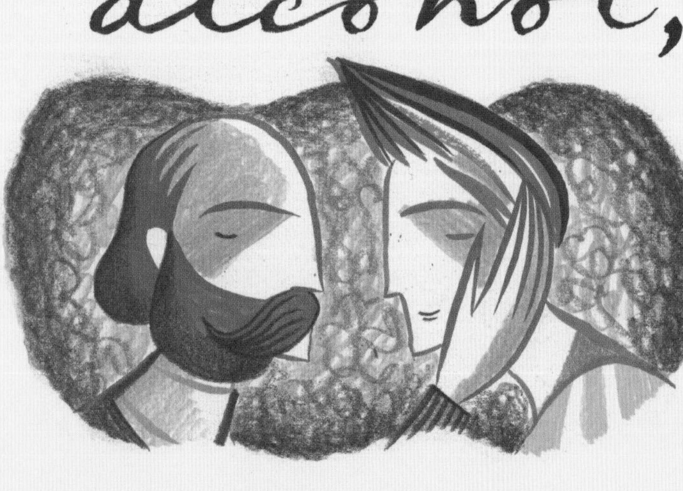

LARGER than music,

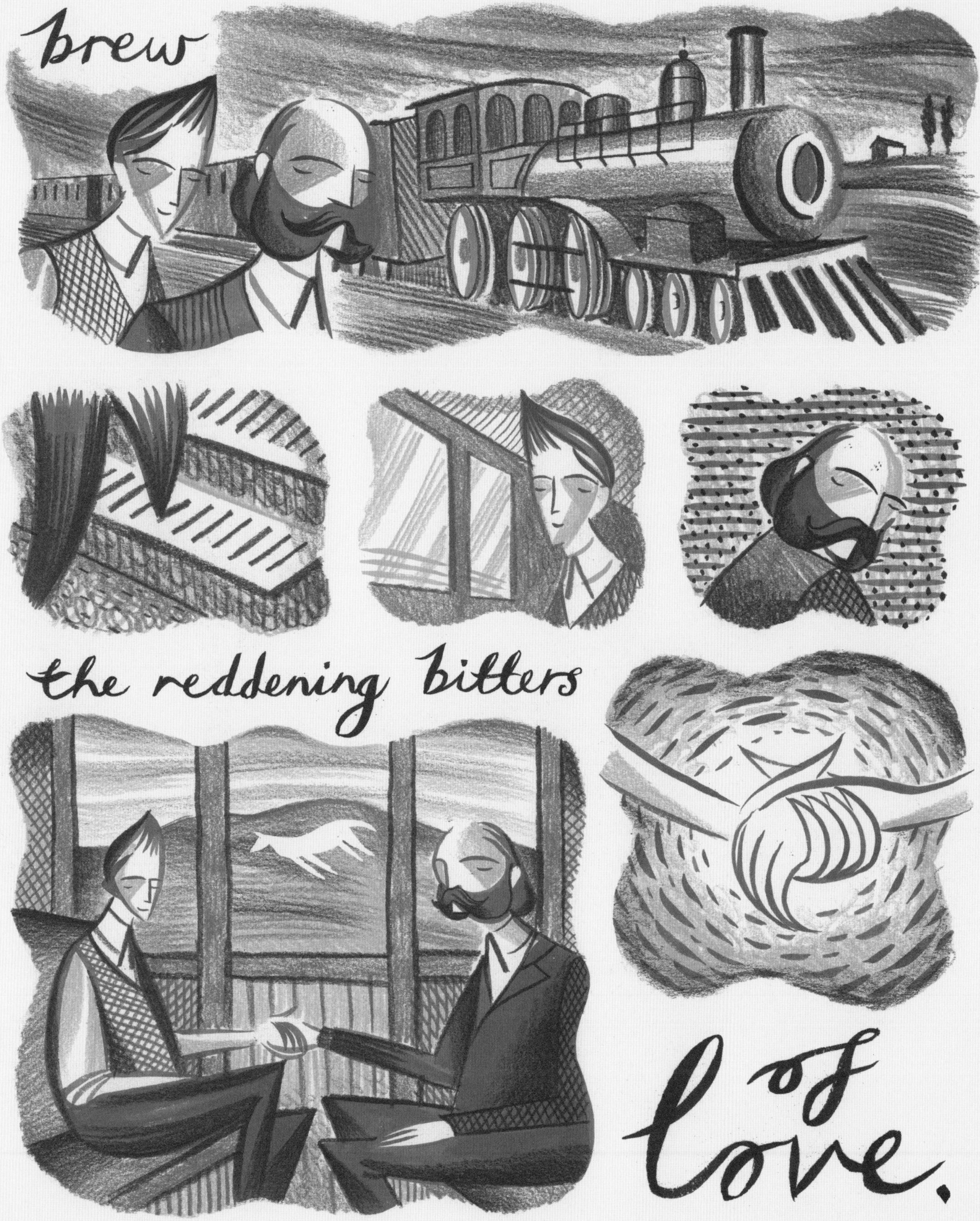
brew
the reddening bitters
of love.

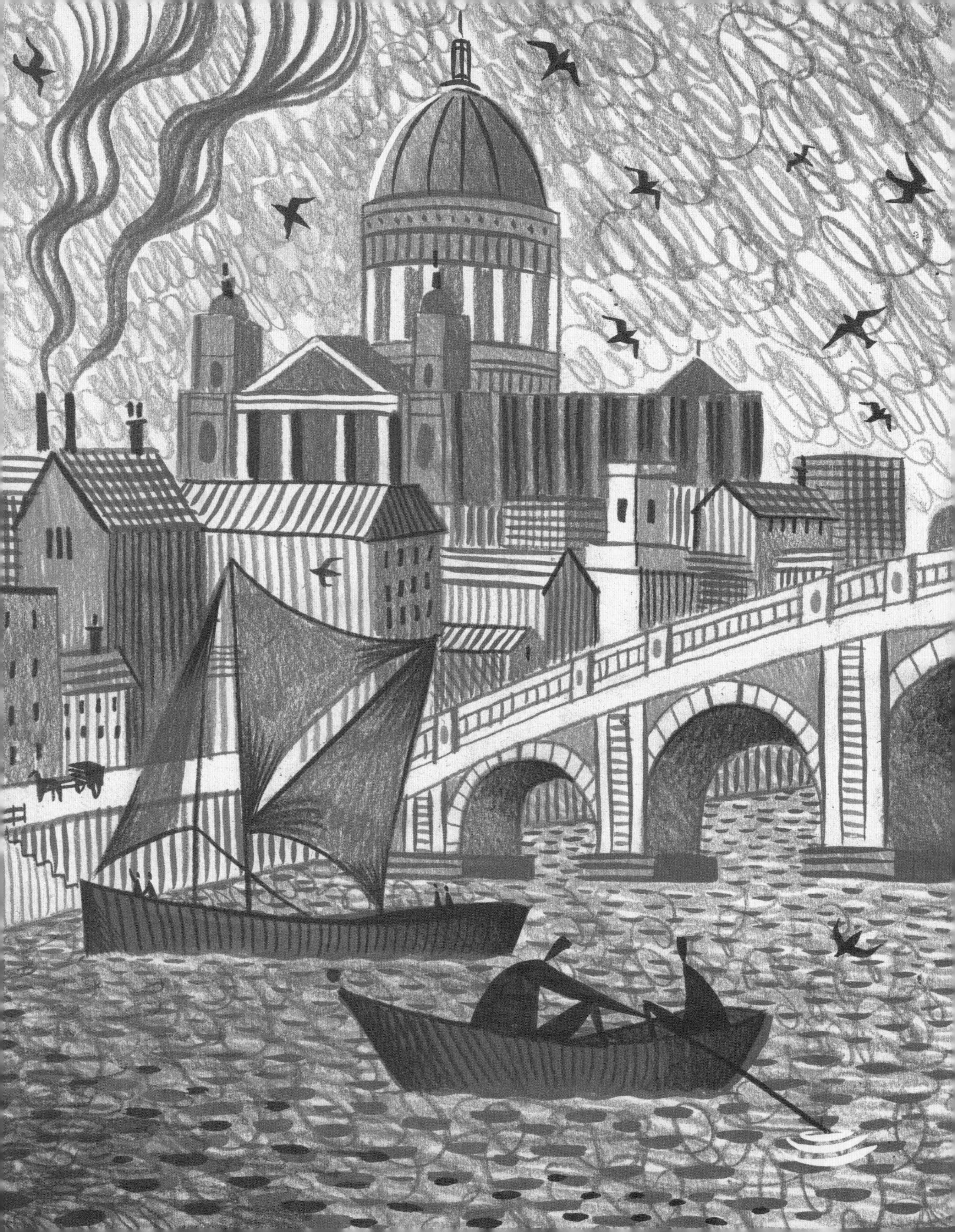

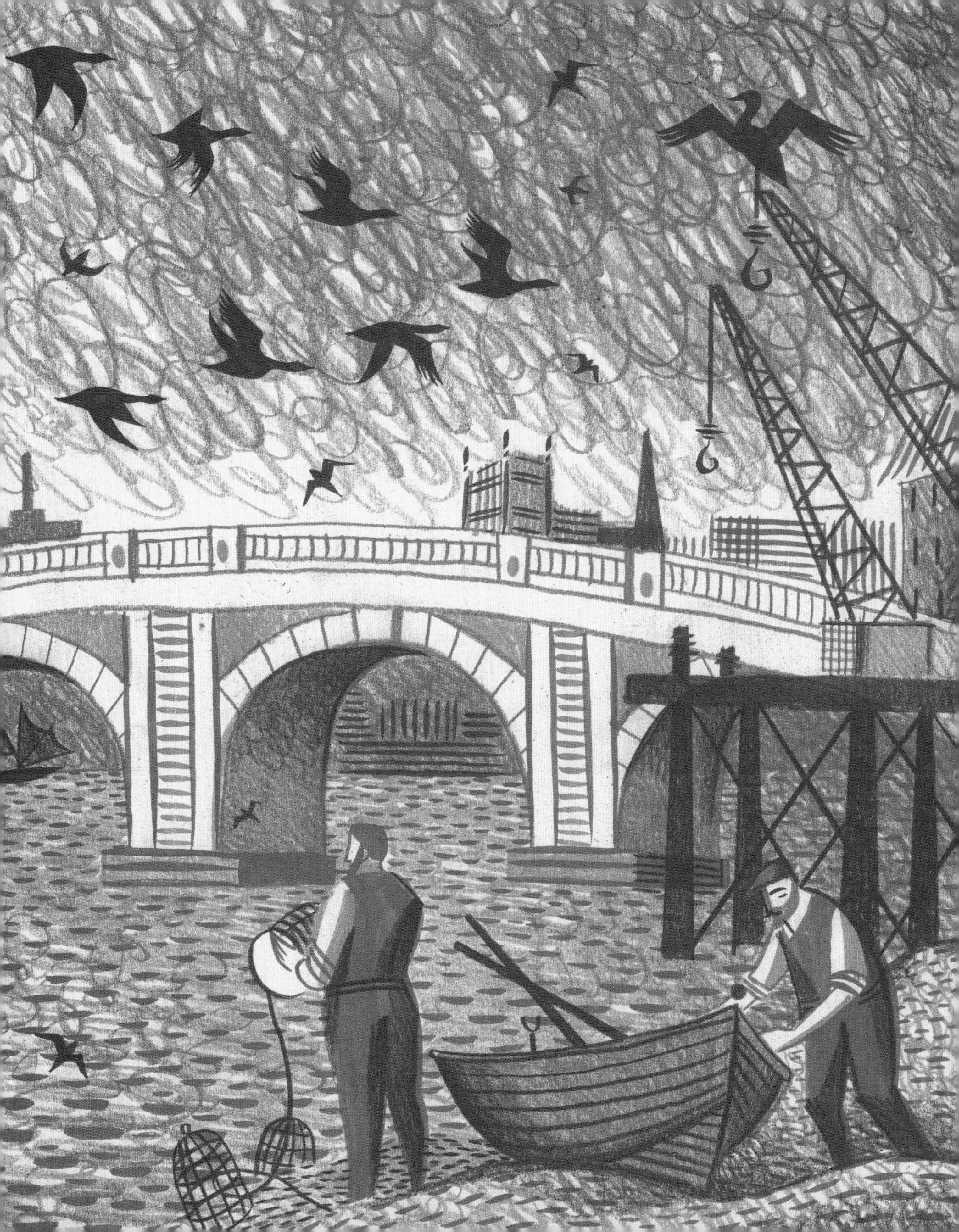

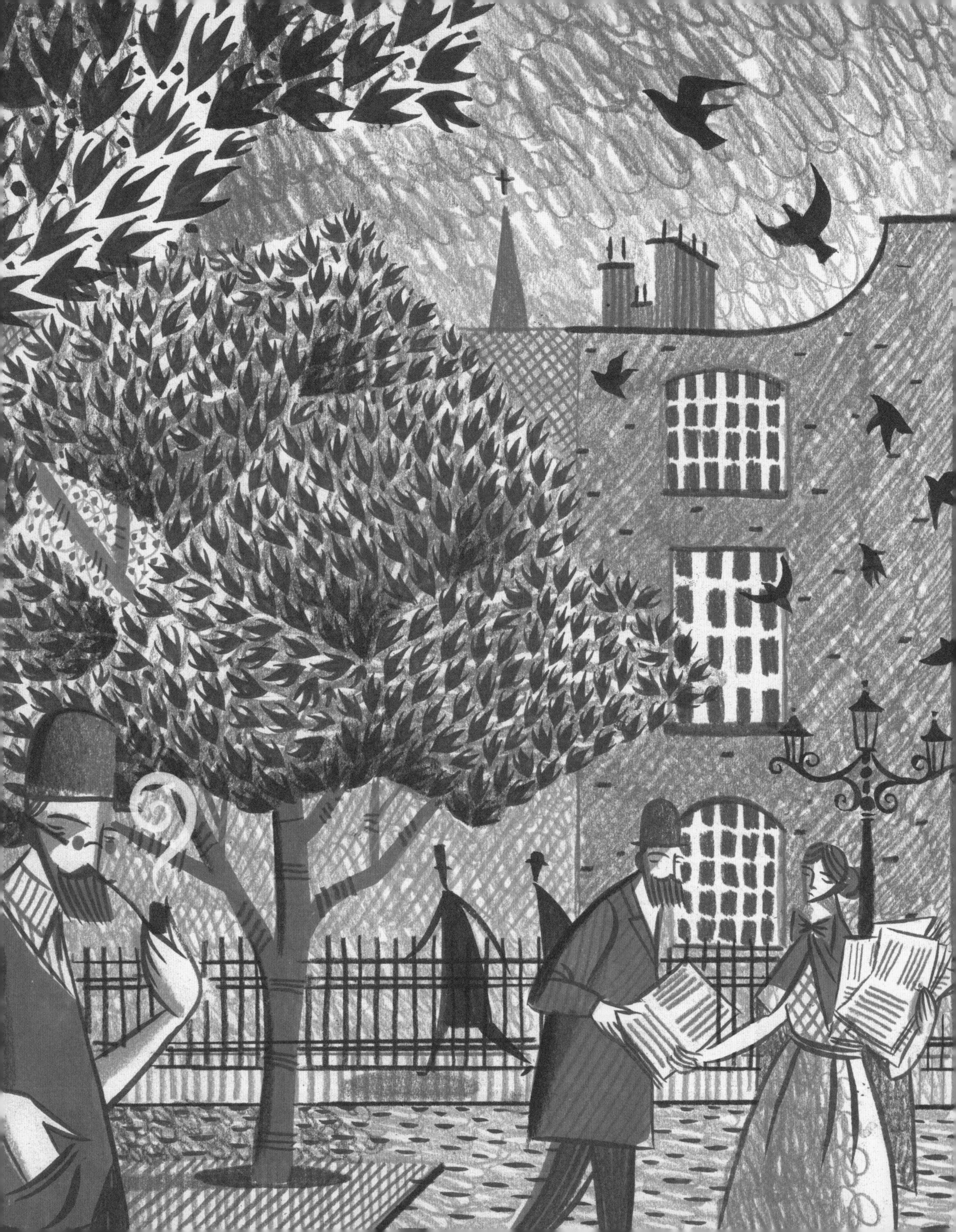

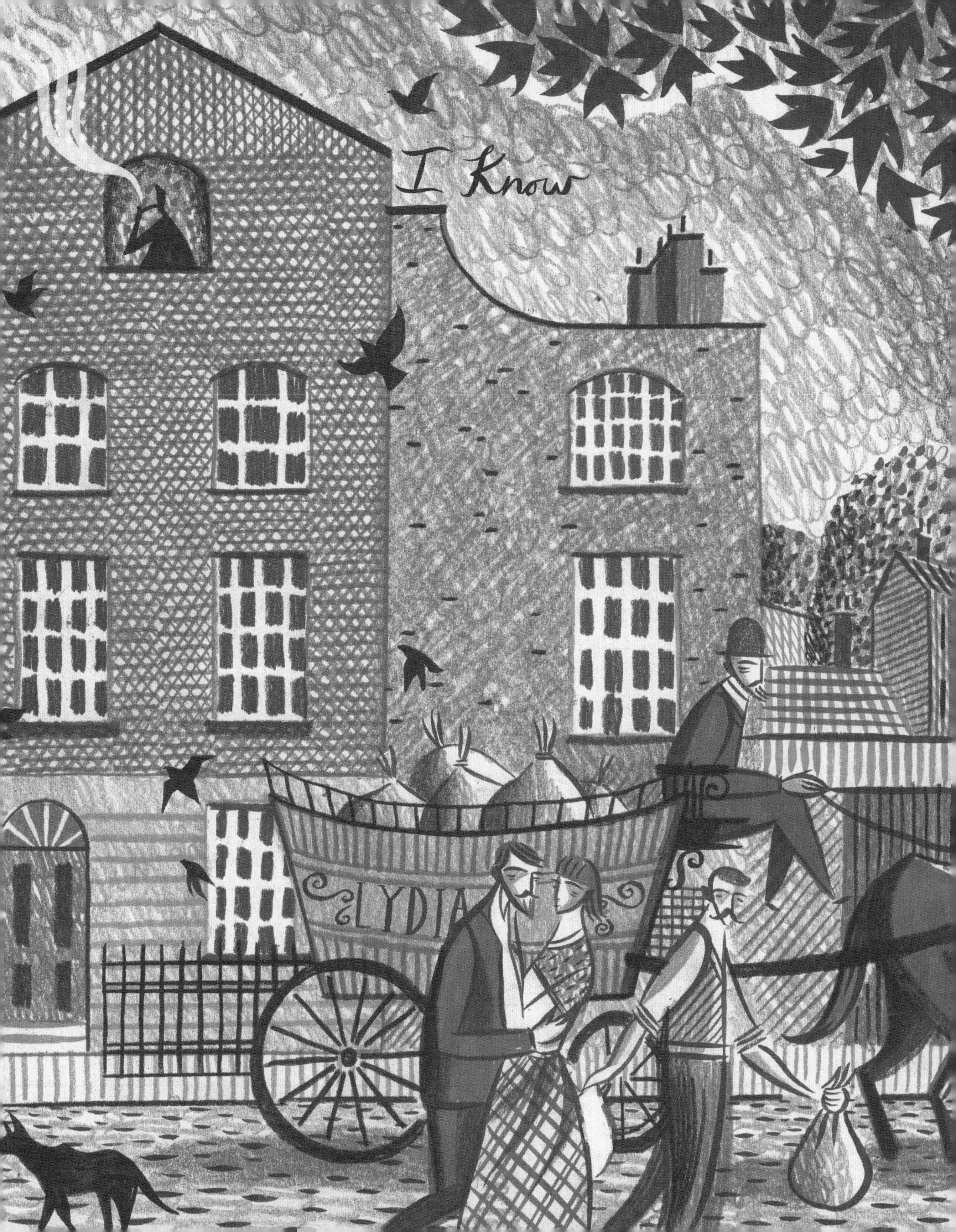
I Know
LYDIA

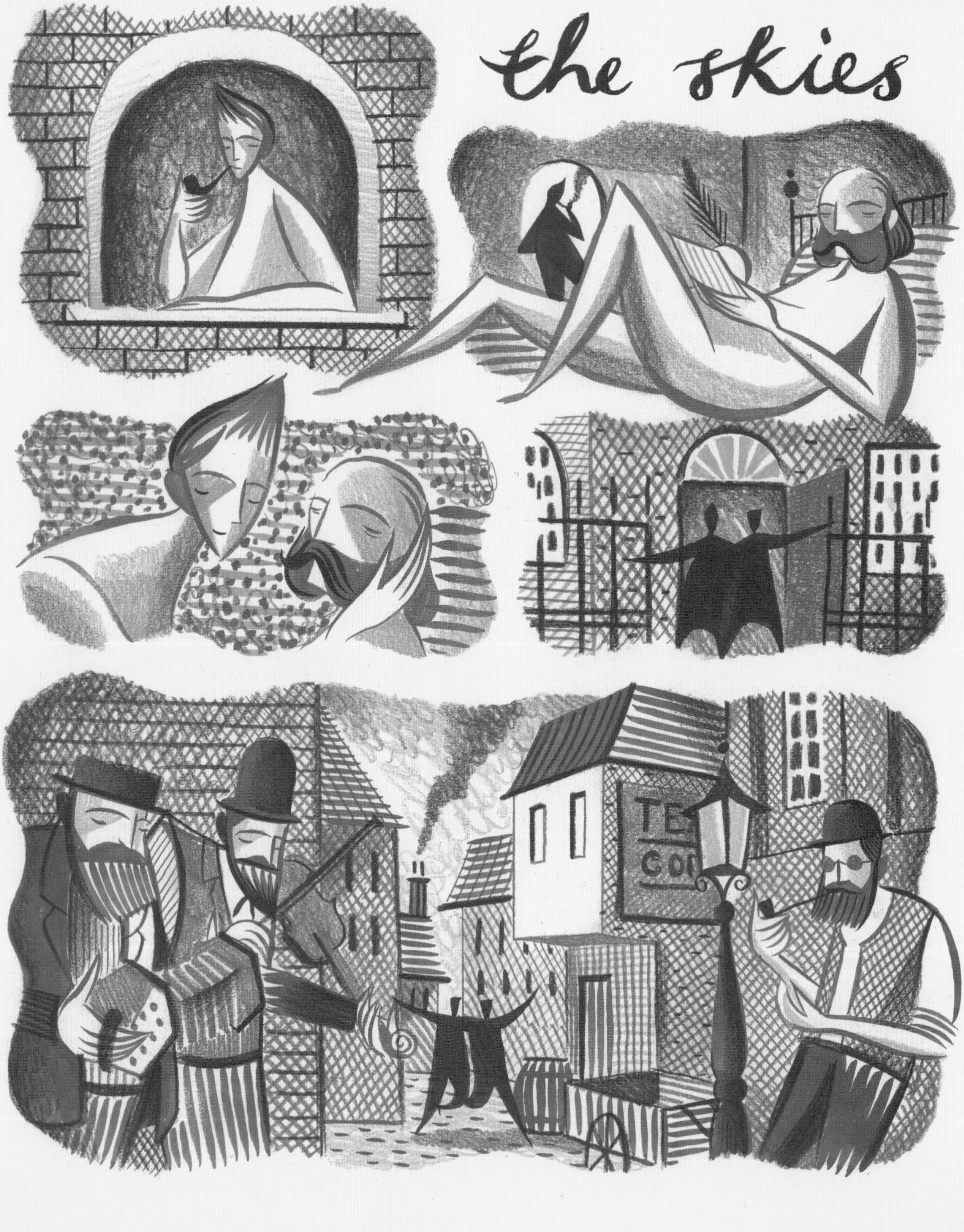
the skies

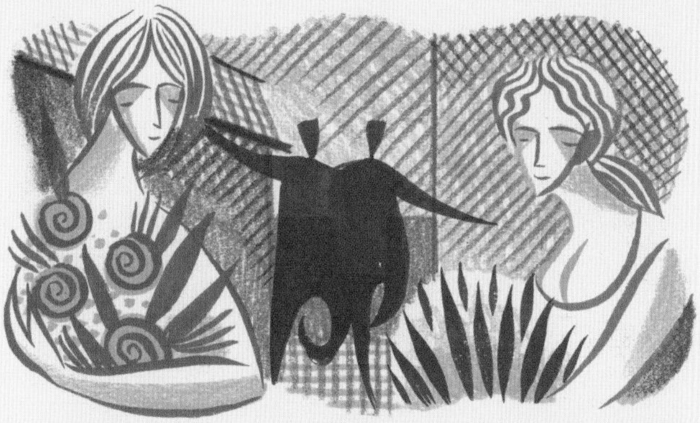

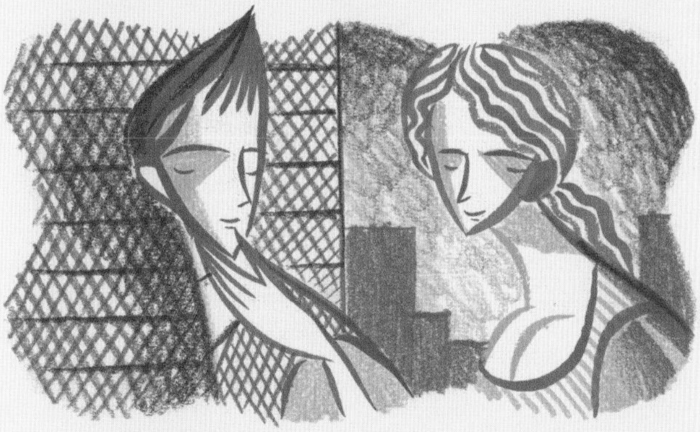

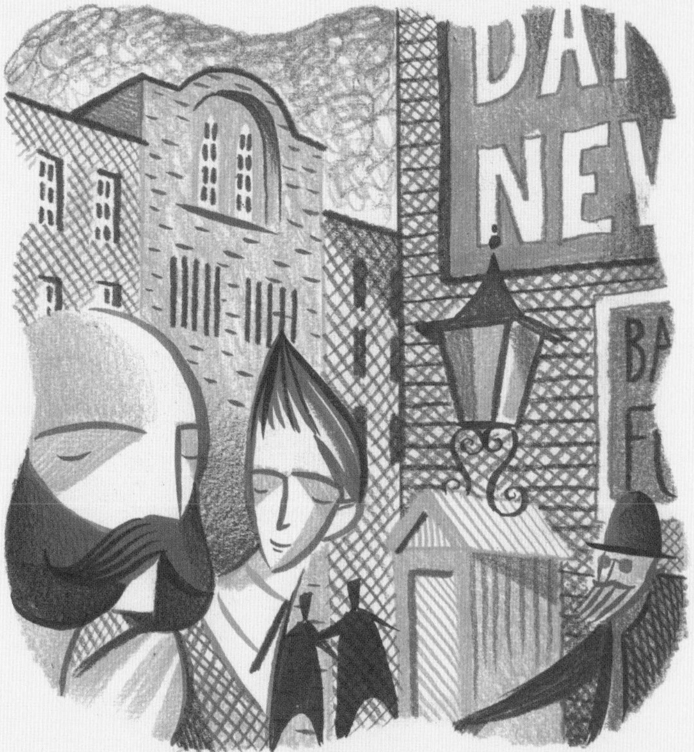

split with lightning,

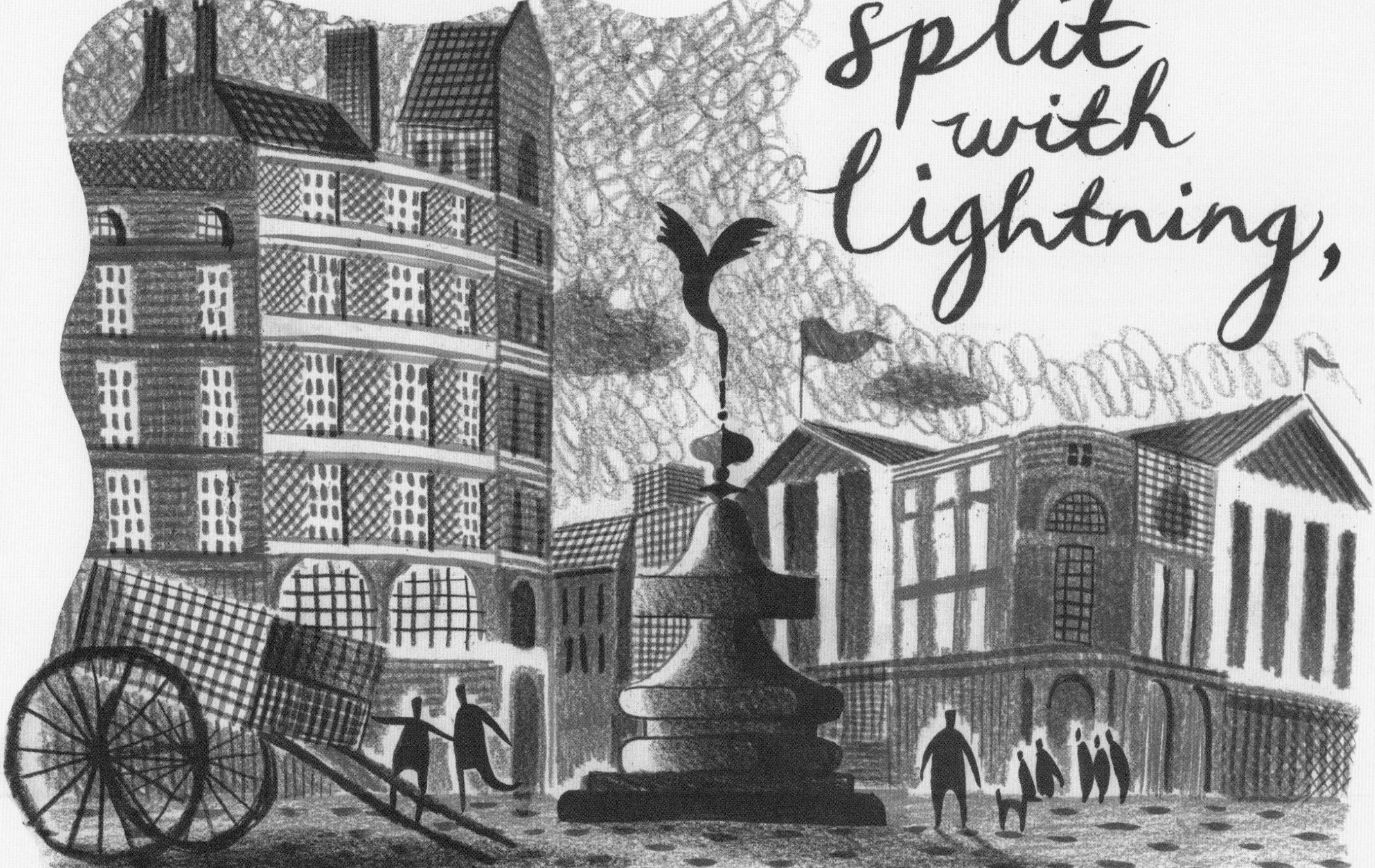

and the whirlpools

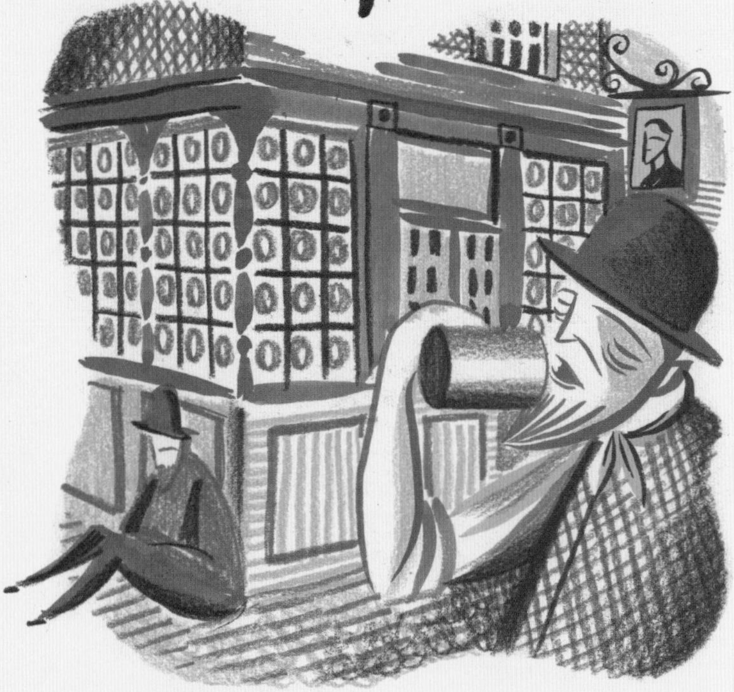

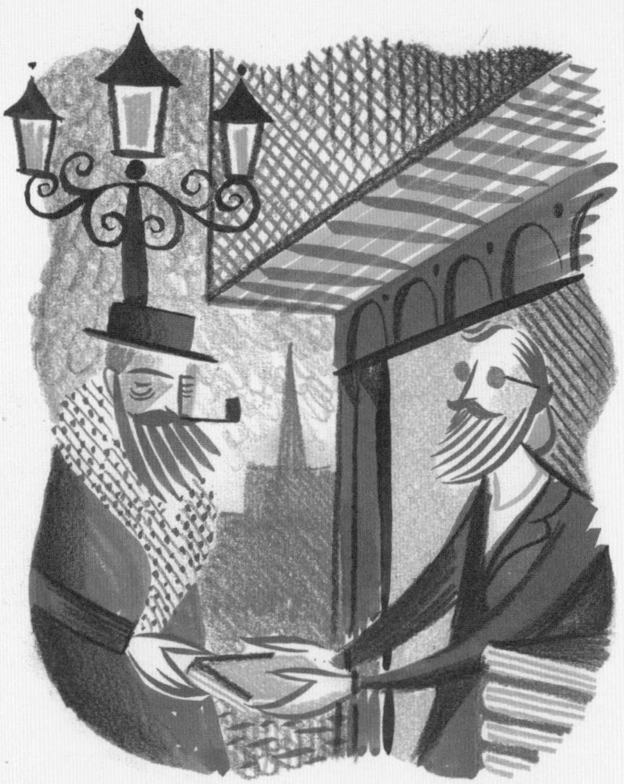

and currents

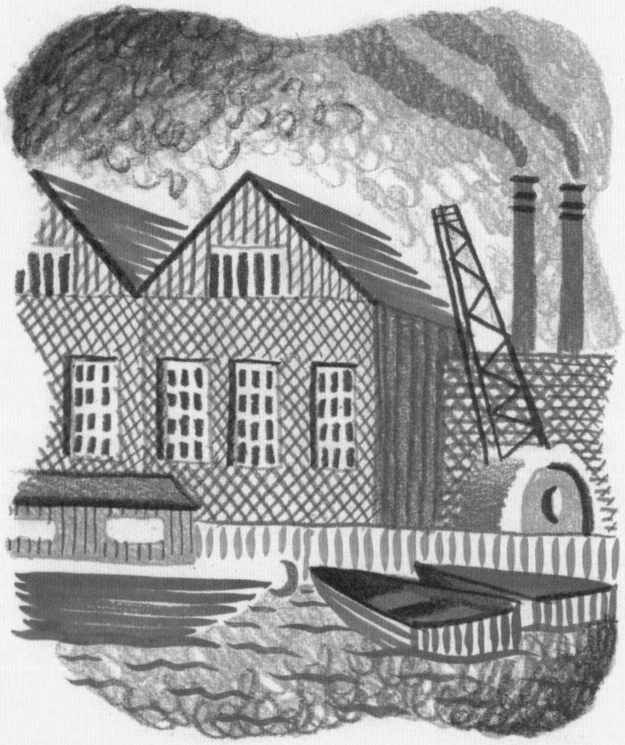

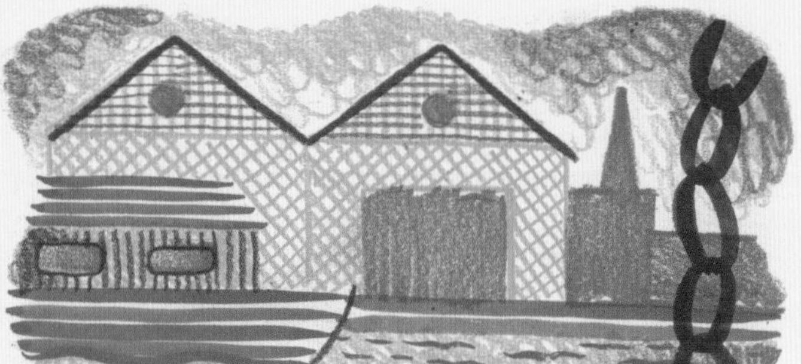

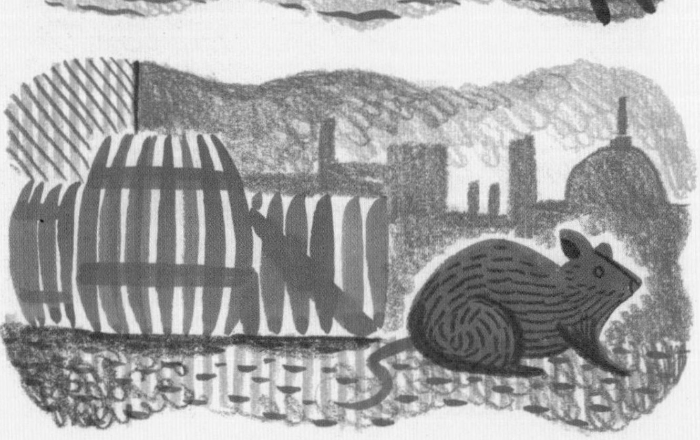

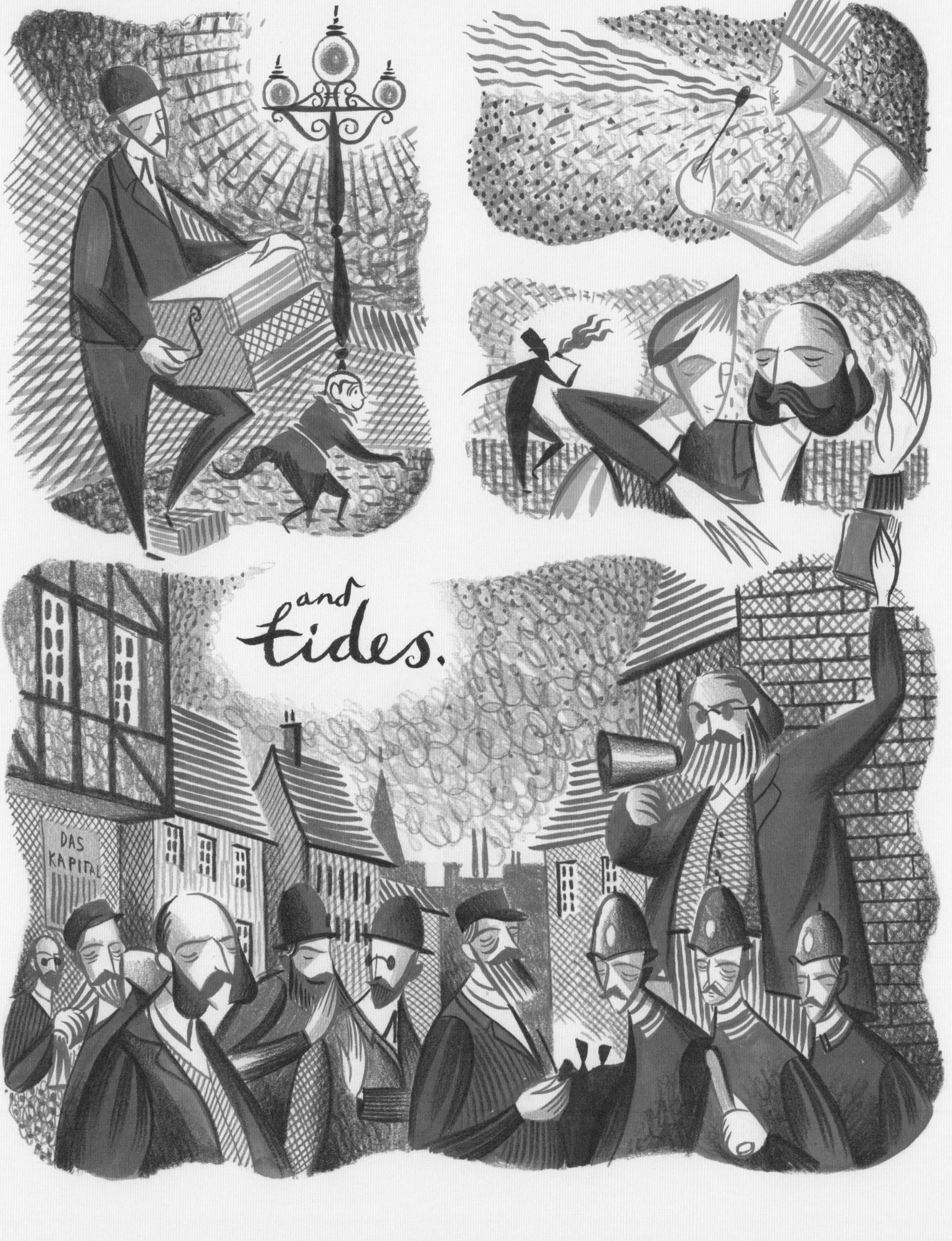
and tides.
DAS KAPITAL

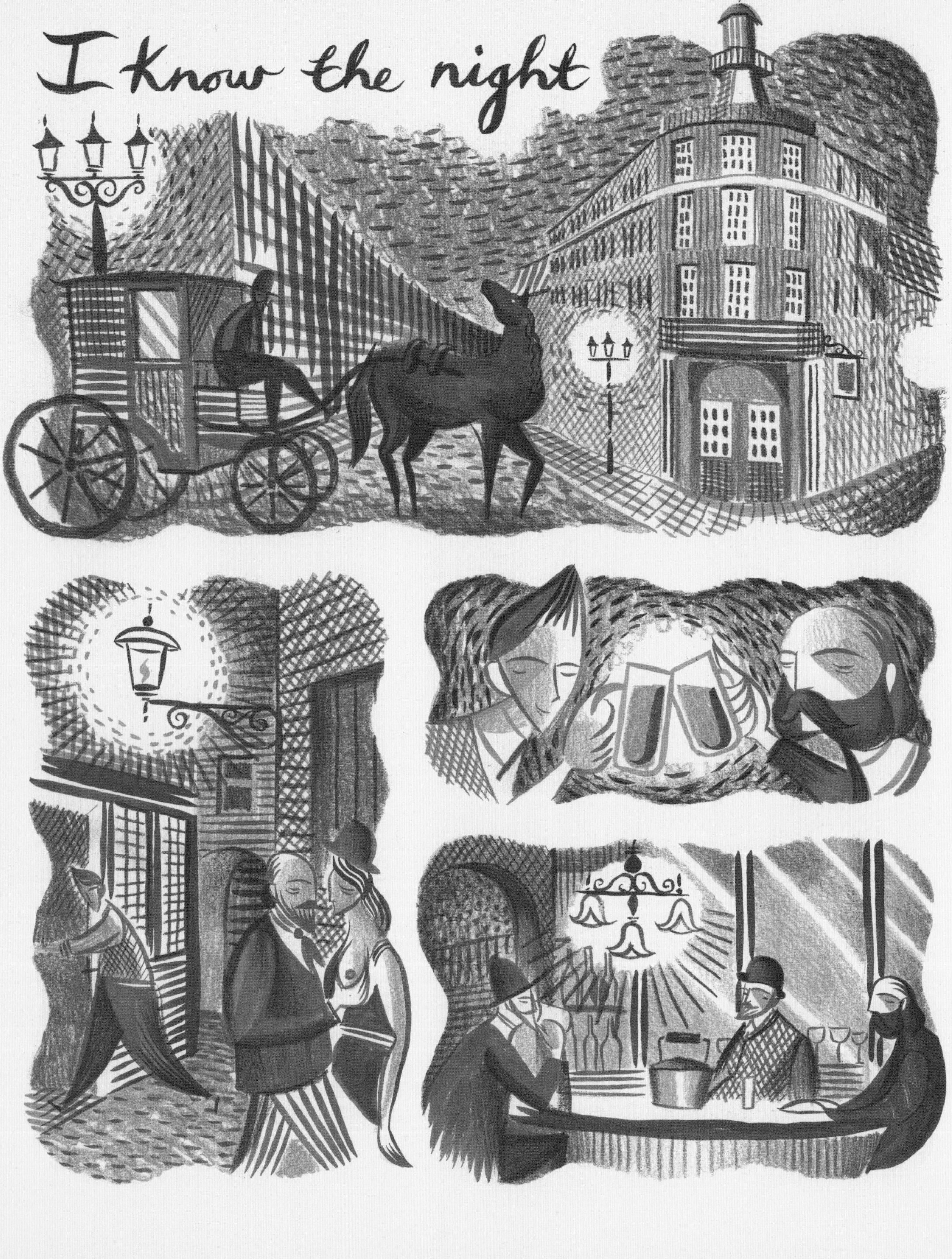
I know the night

and dawn,

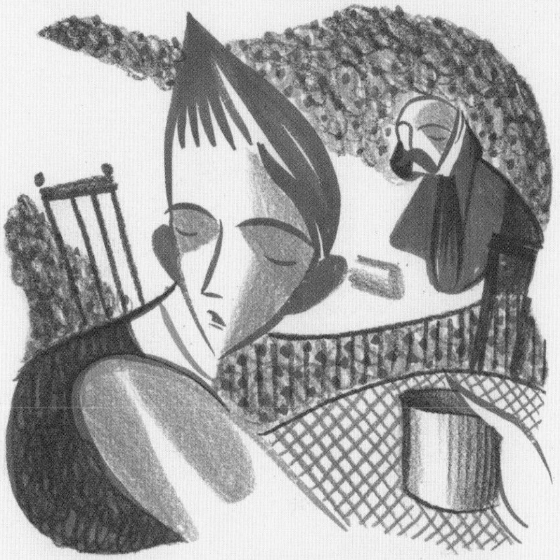

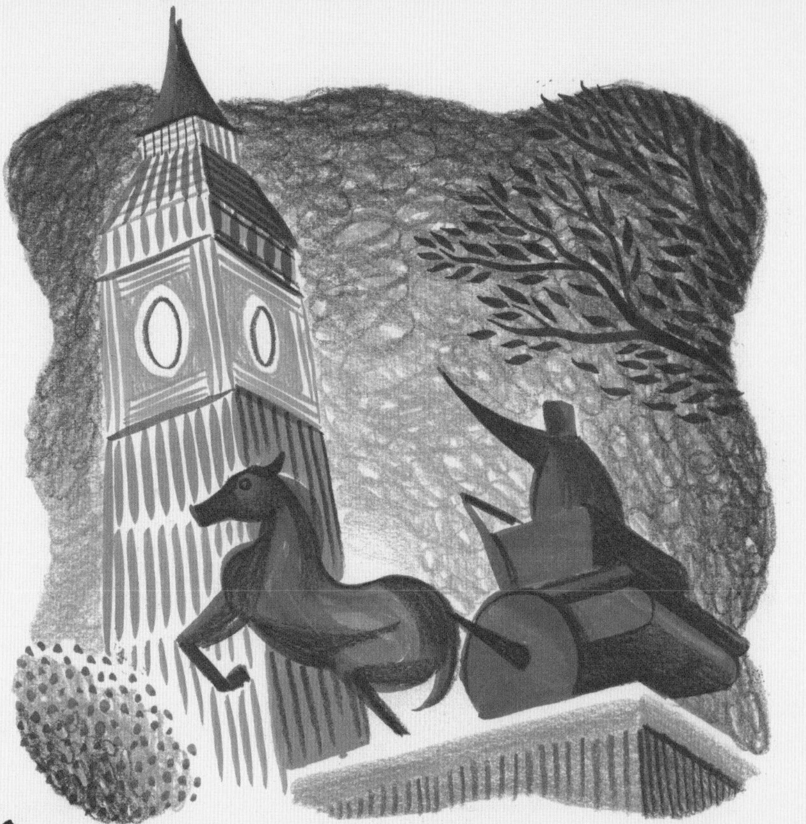

soaring…

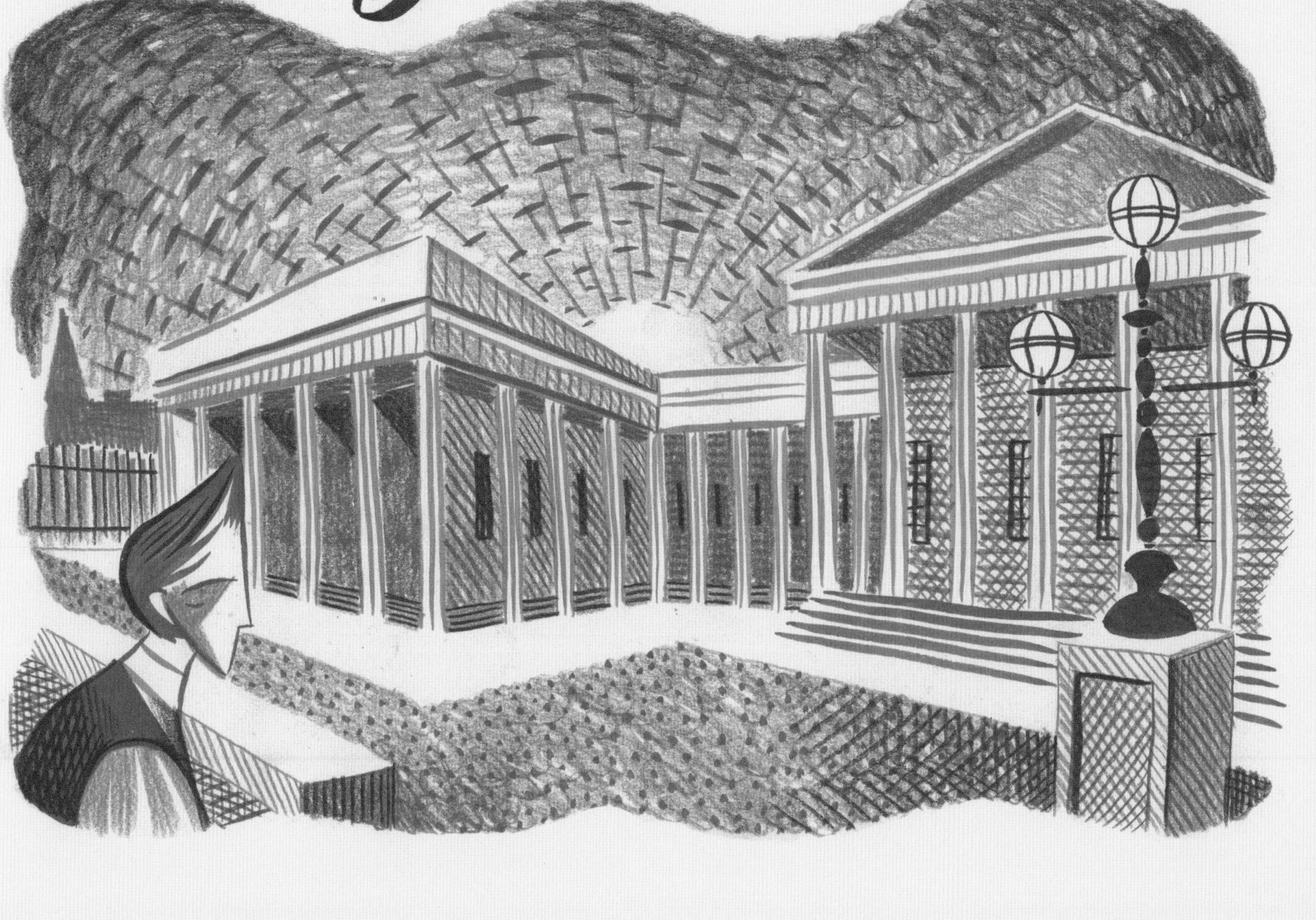

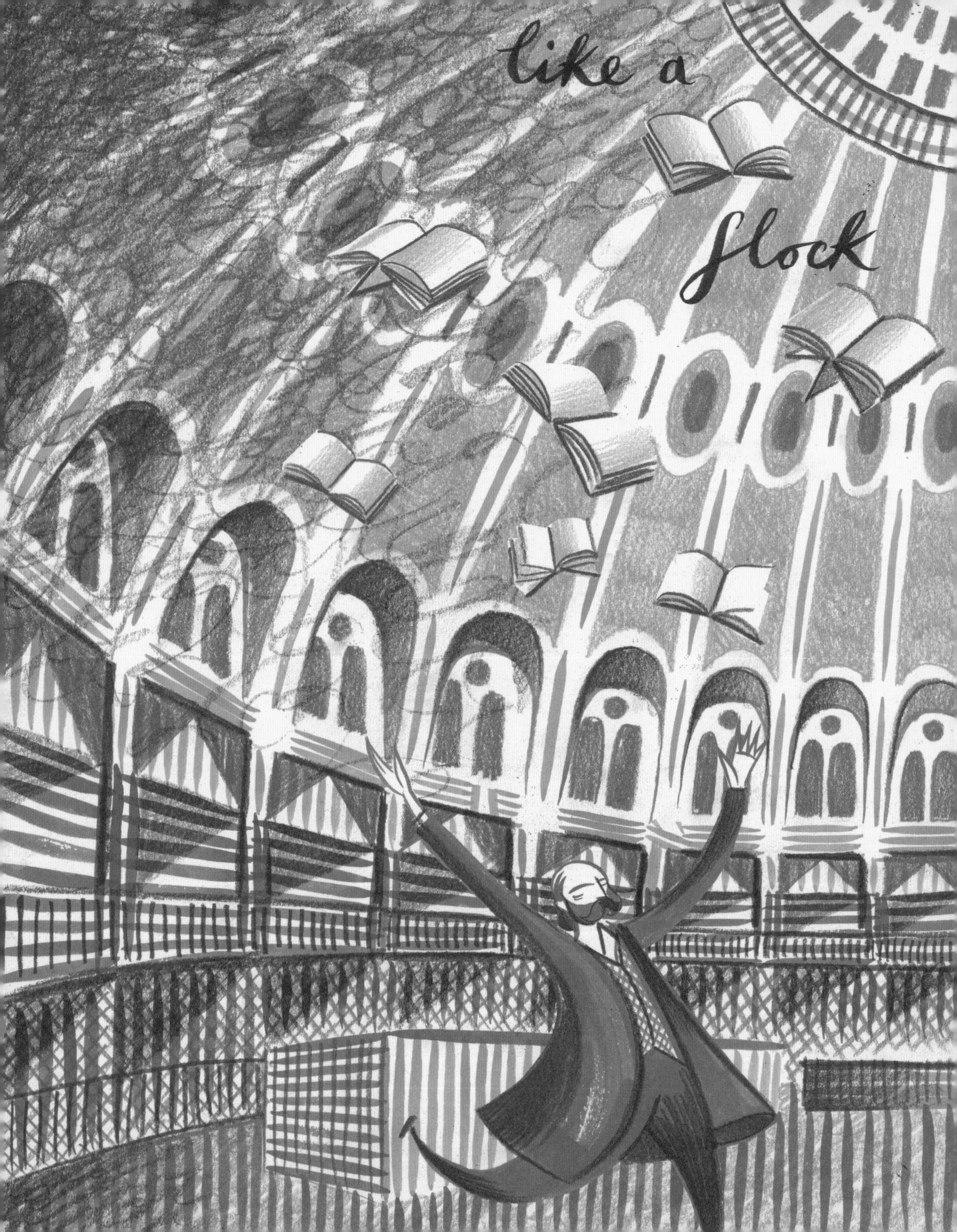
like a
flock

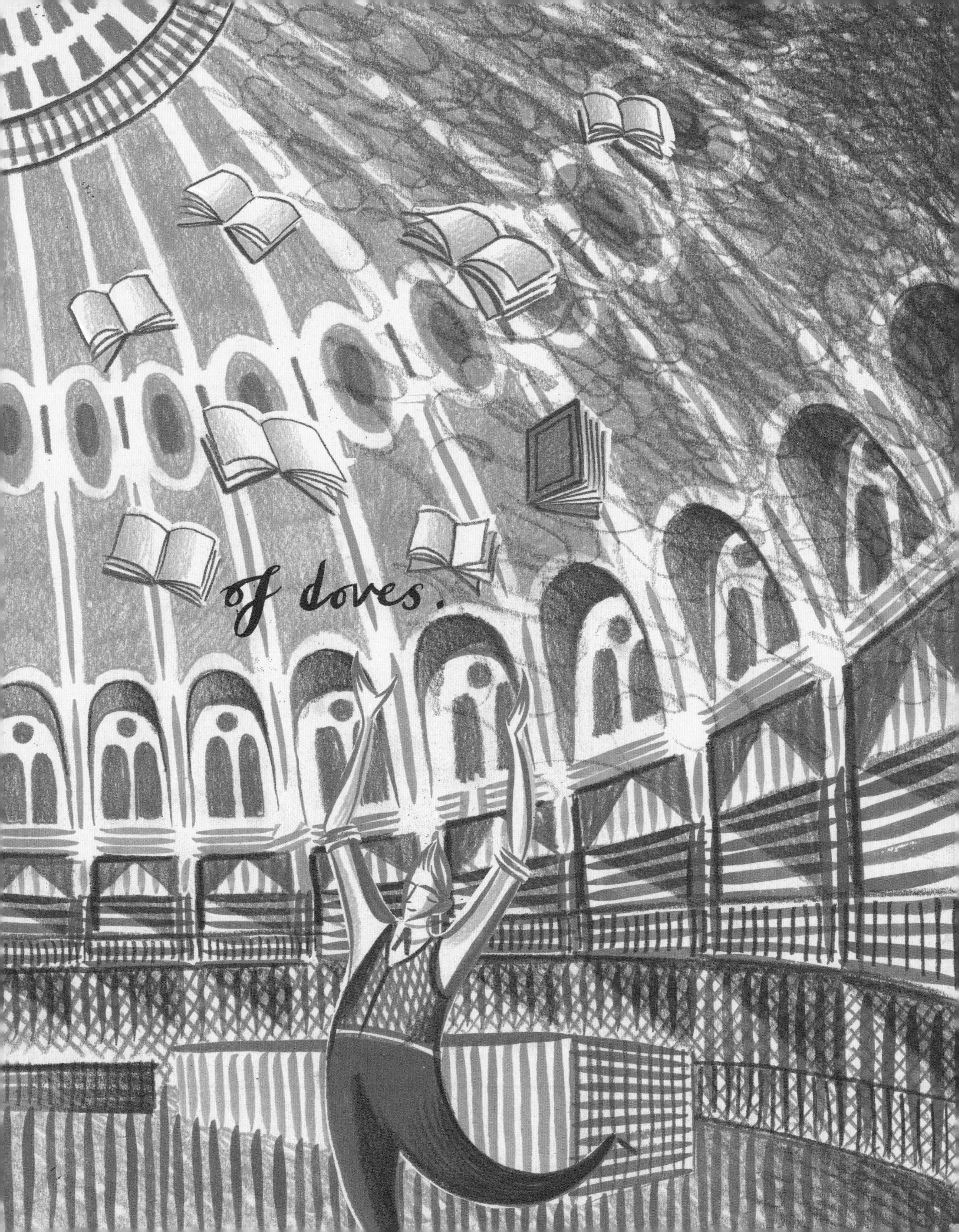
of doves.

I have seen

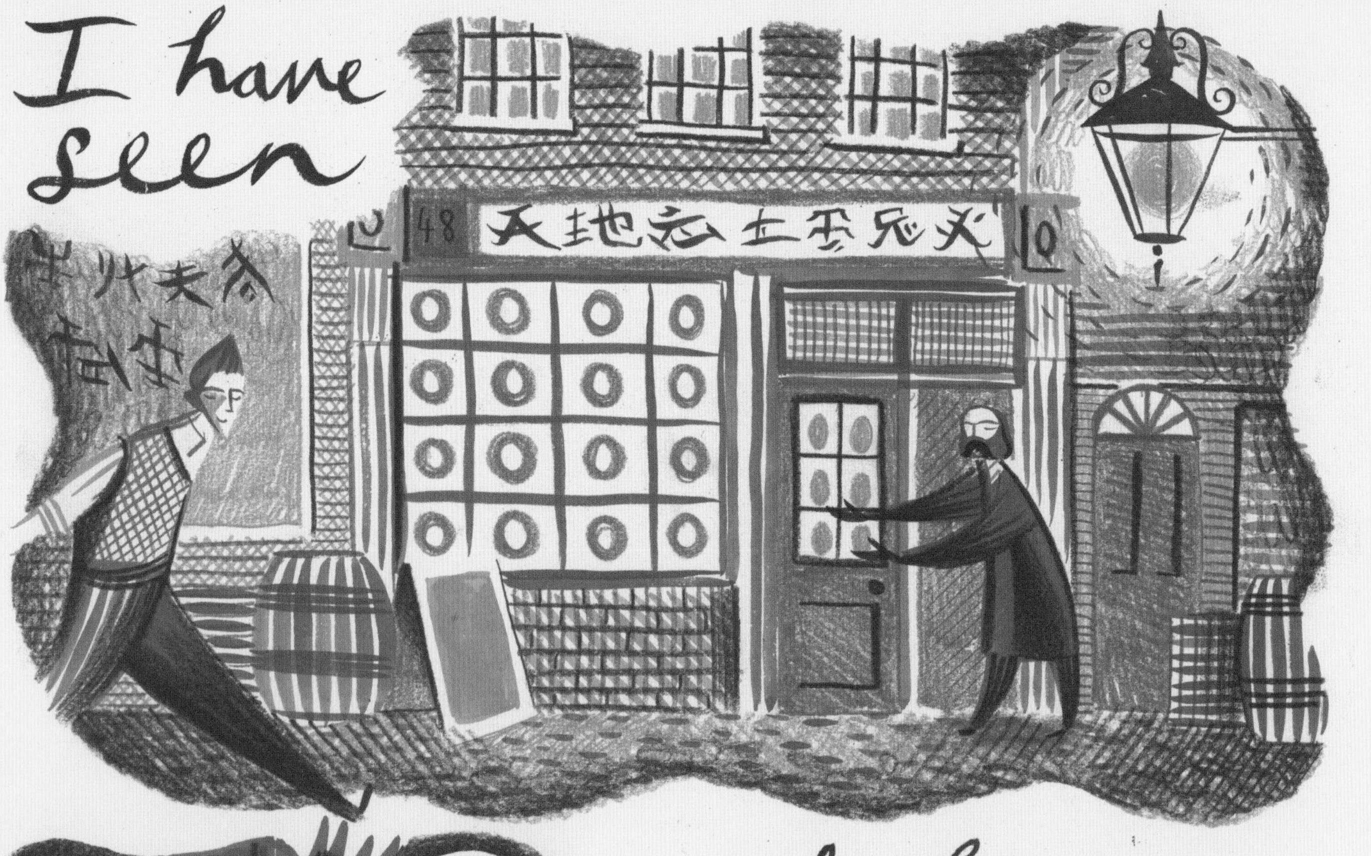

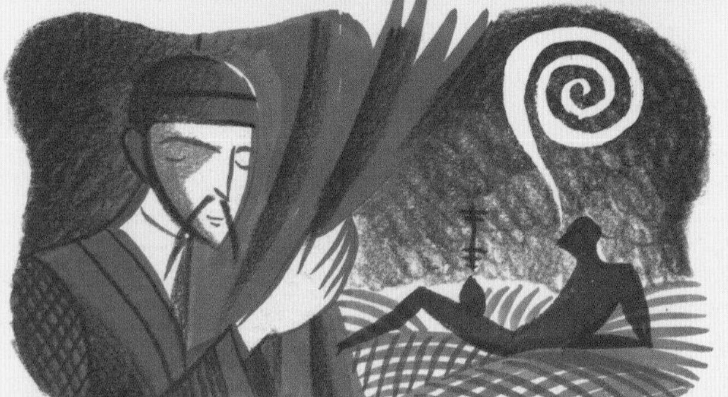

at times

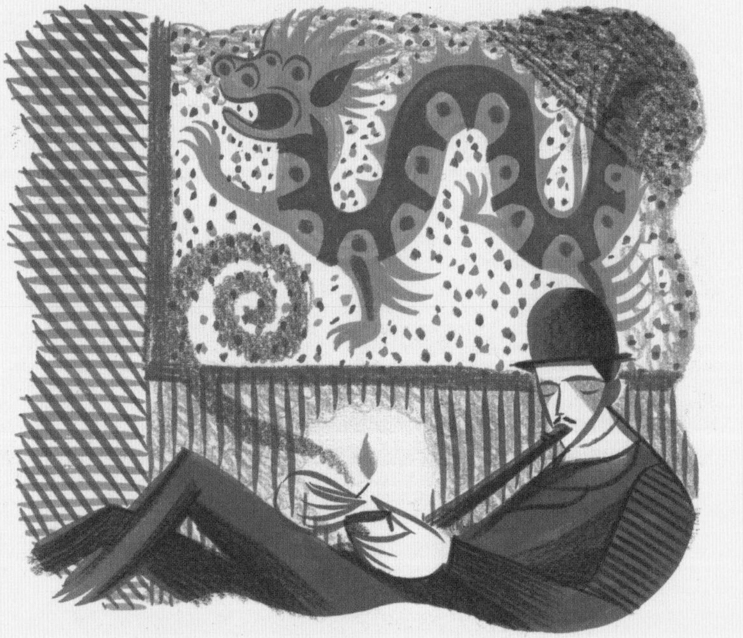

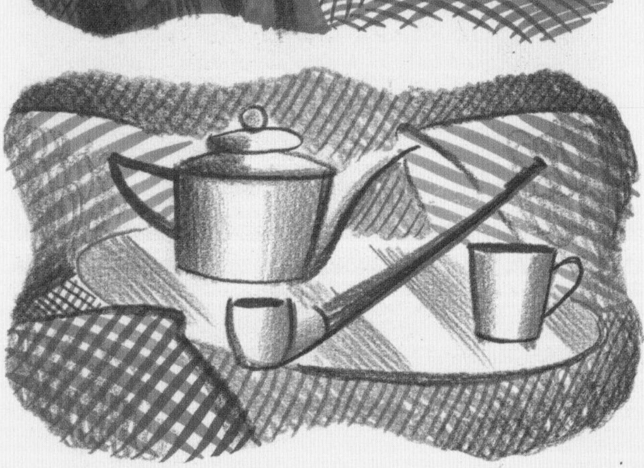

what men thought they saw.

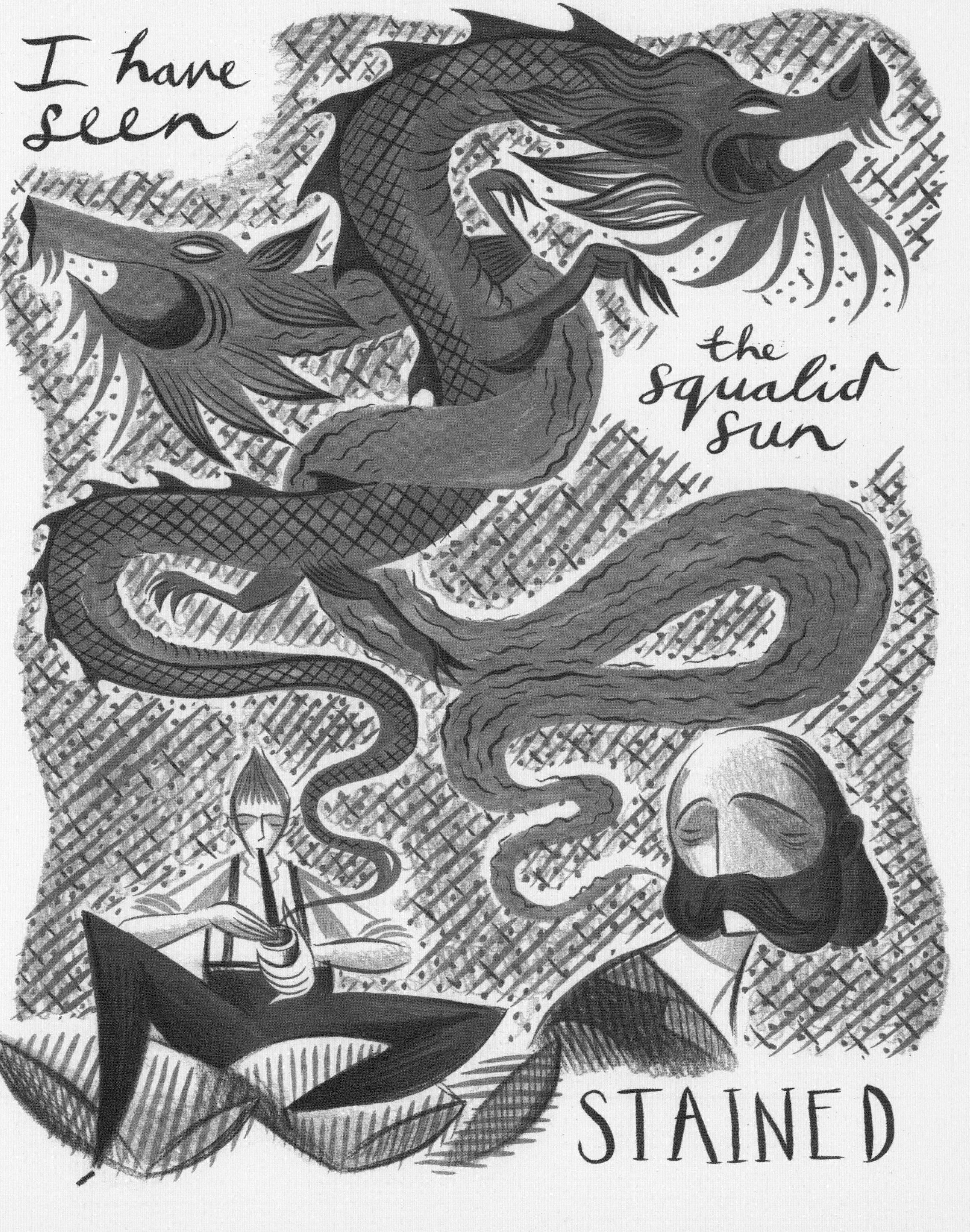
I have seen
the squalid sun
STAINED

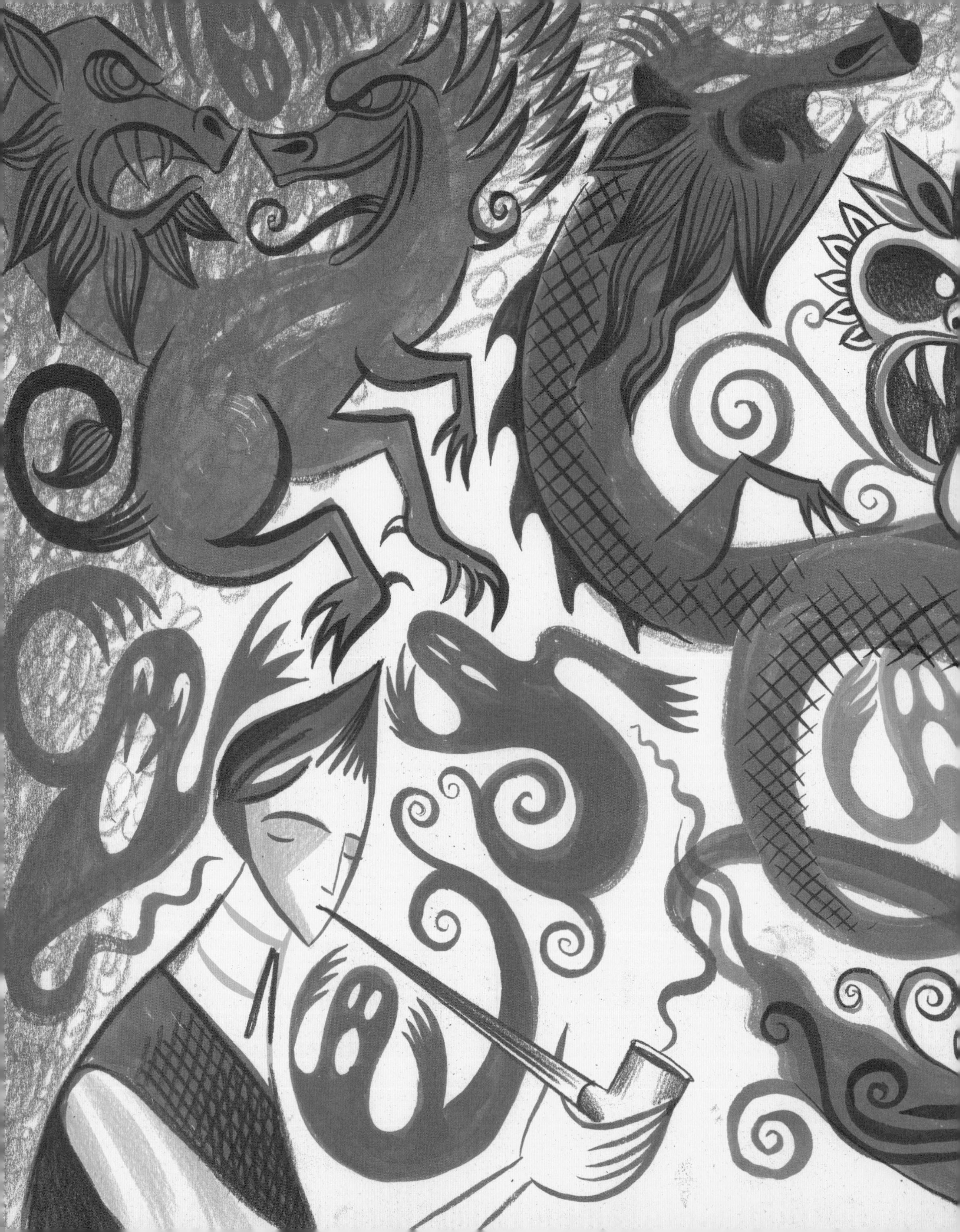

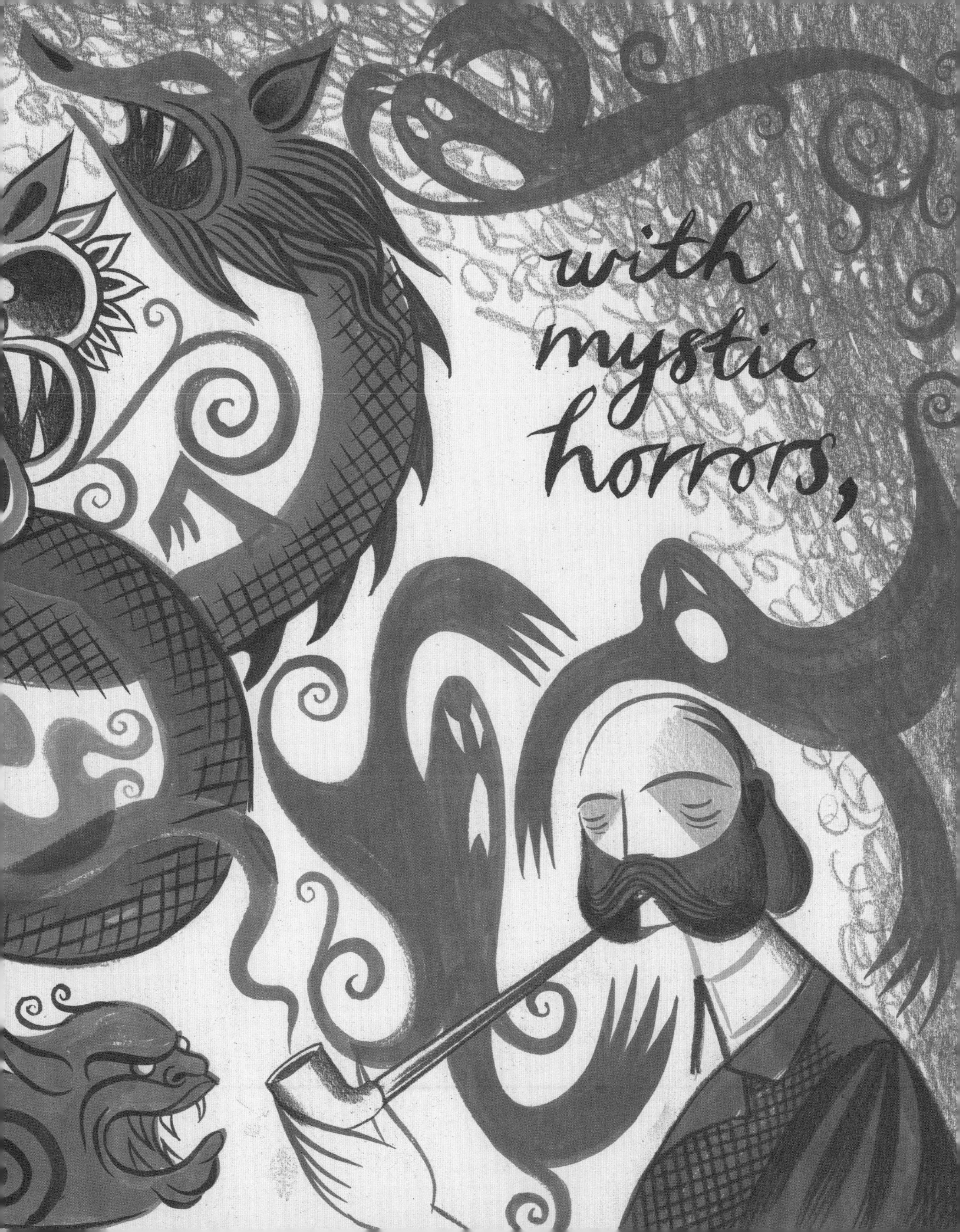
with
mystic
horrors,

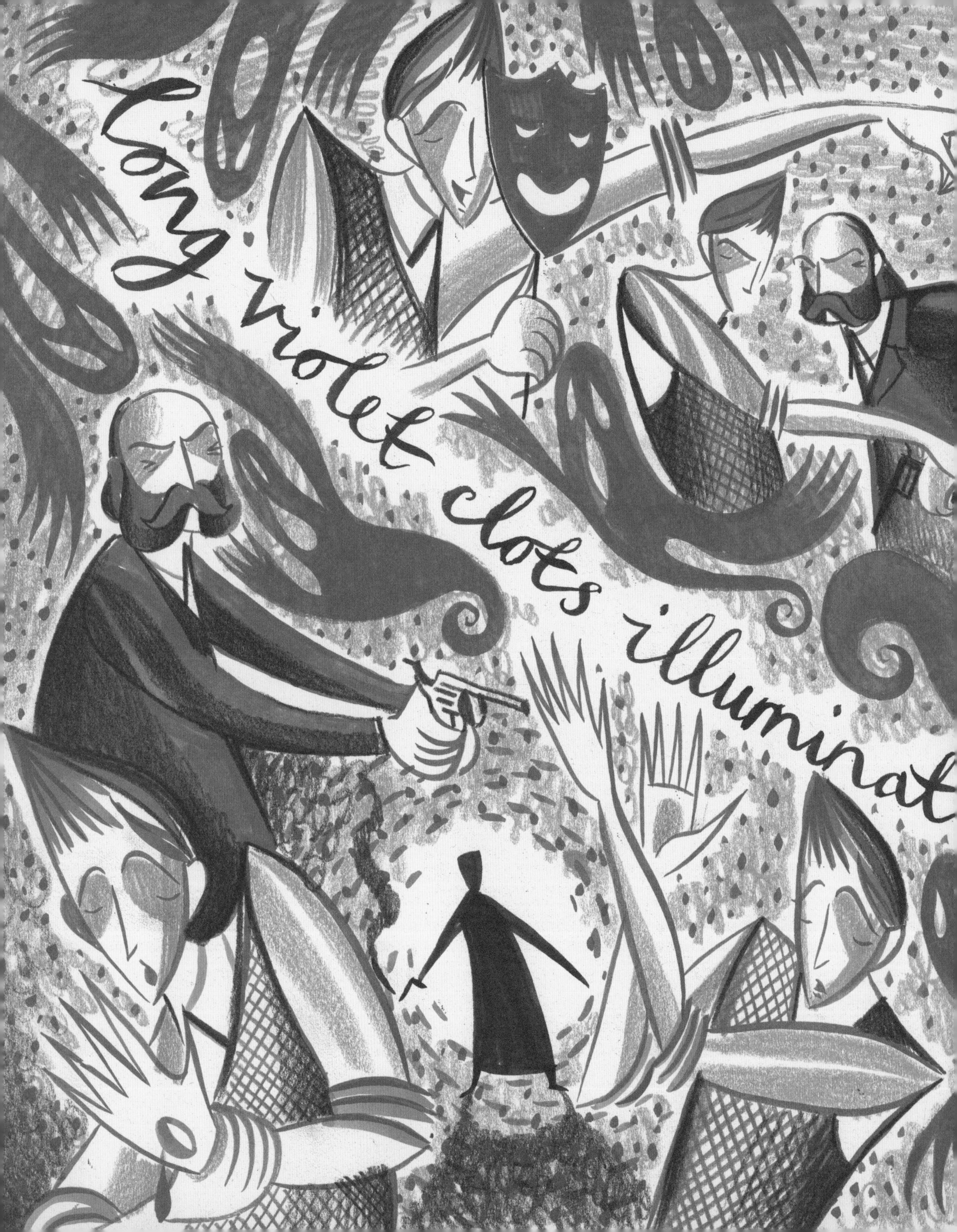
Long violet clots illuminat

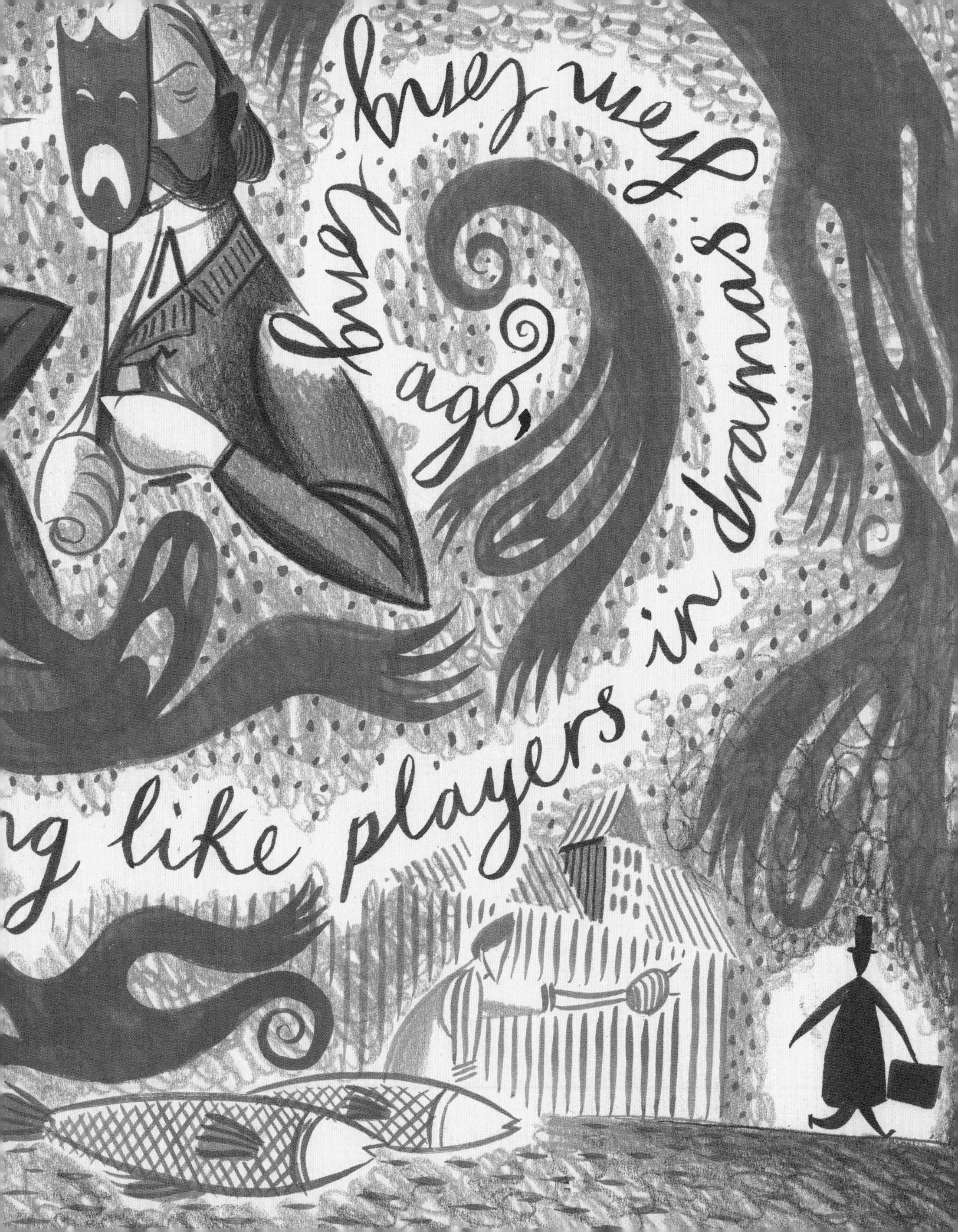
ng like players in dramas from long ago,

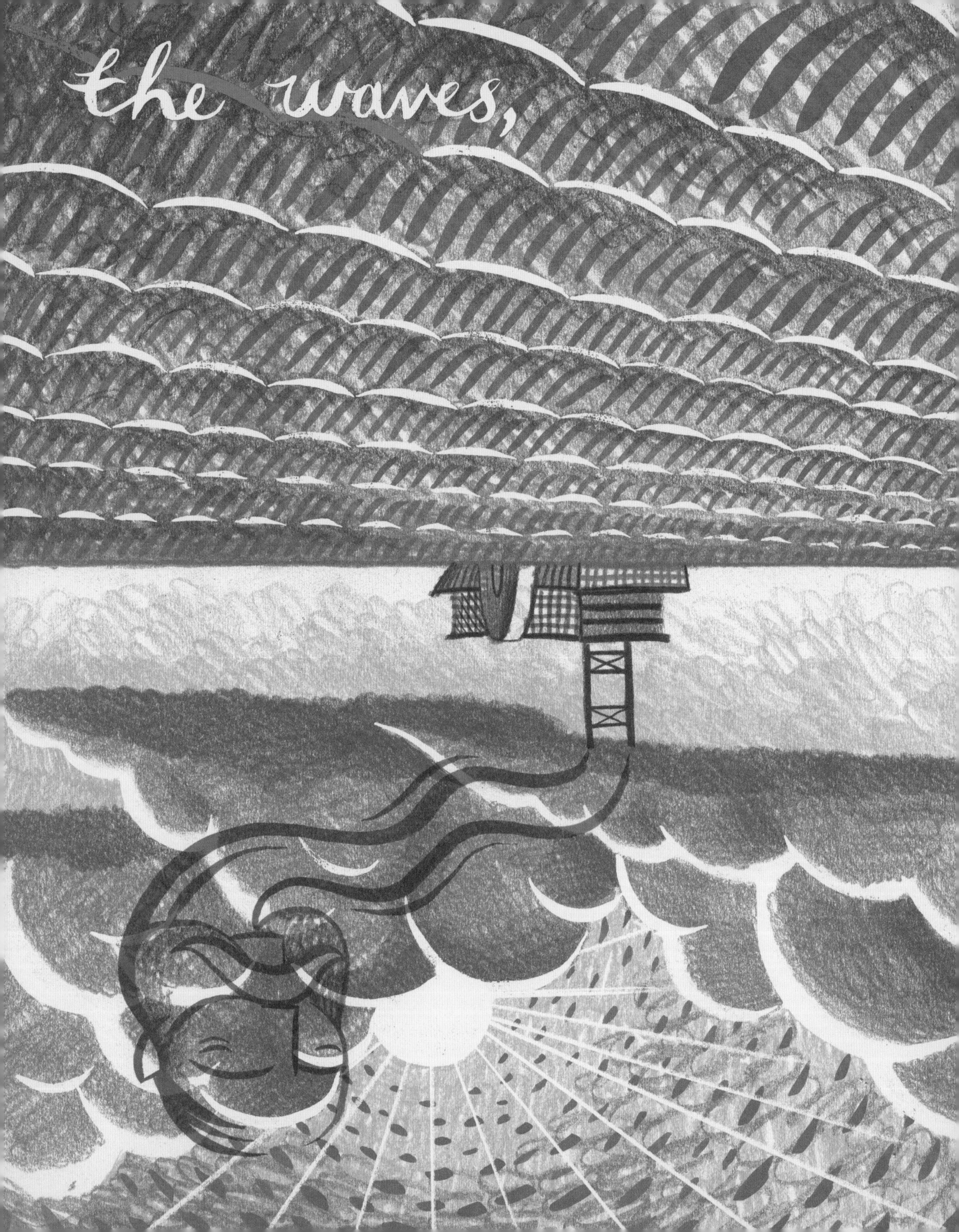
the waves,

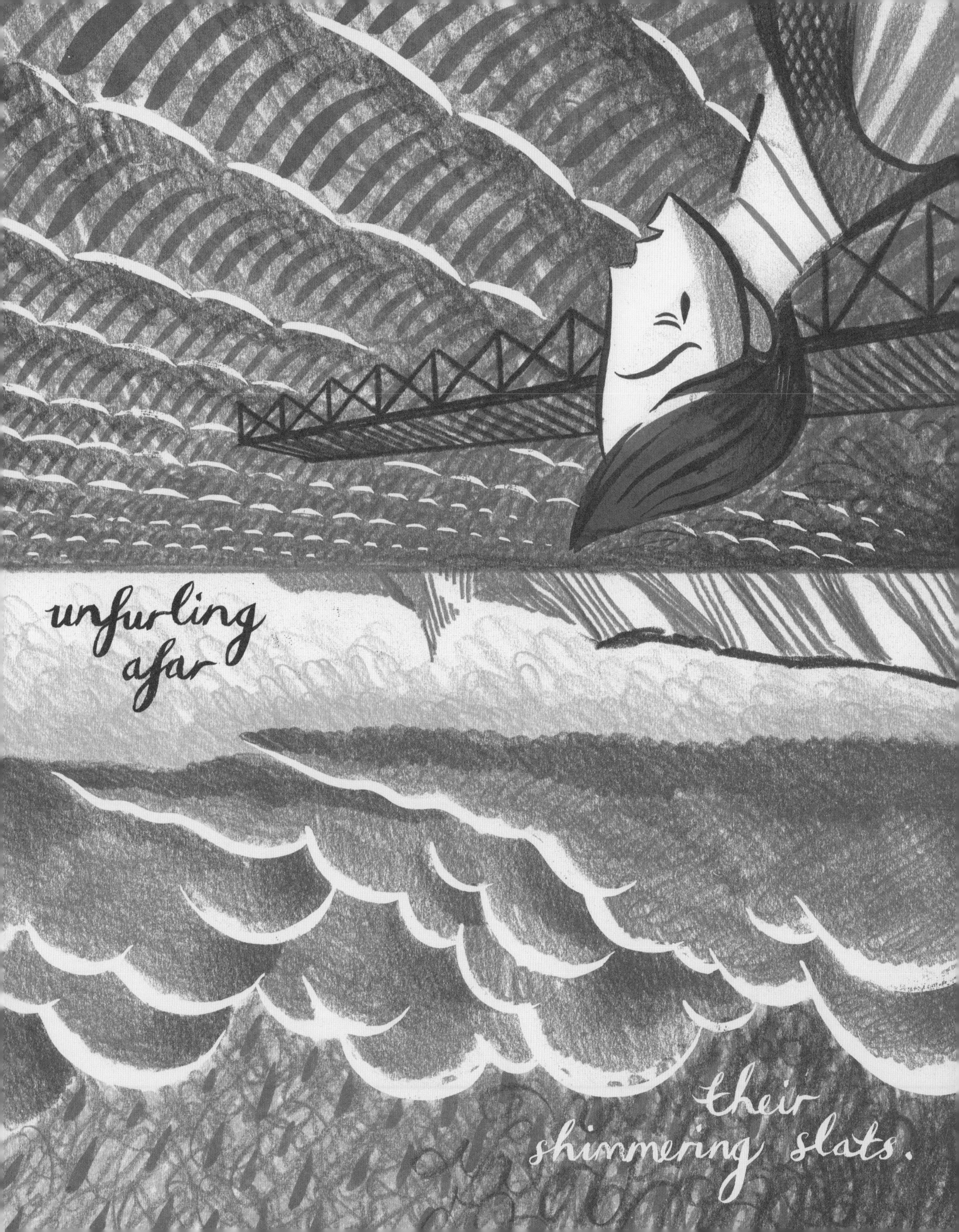
unfurling
afar
their
shimmering slats.

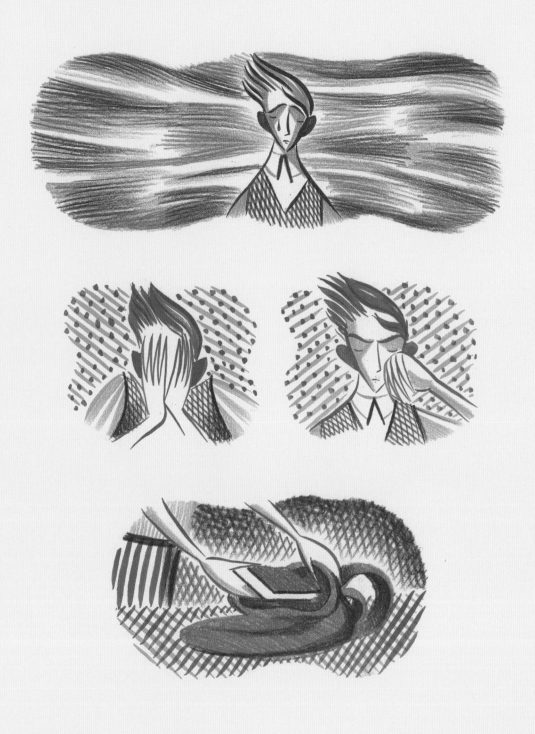

I have dreamed

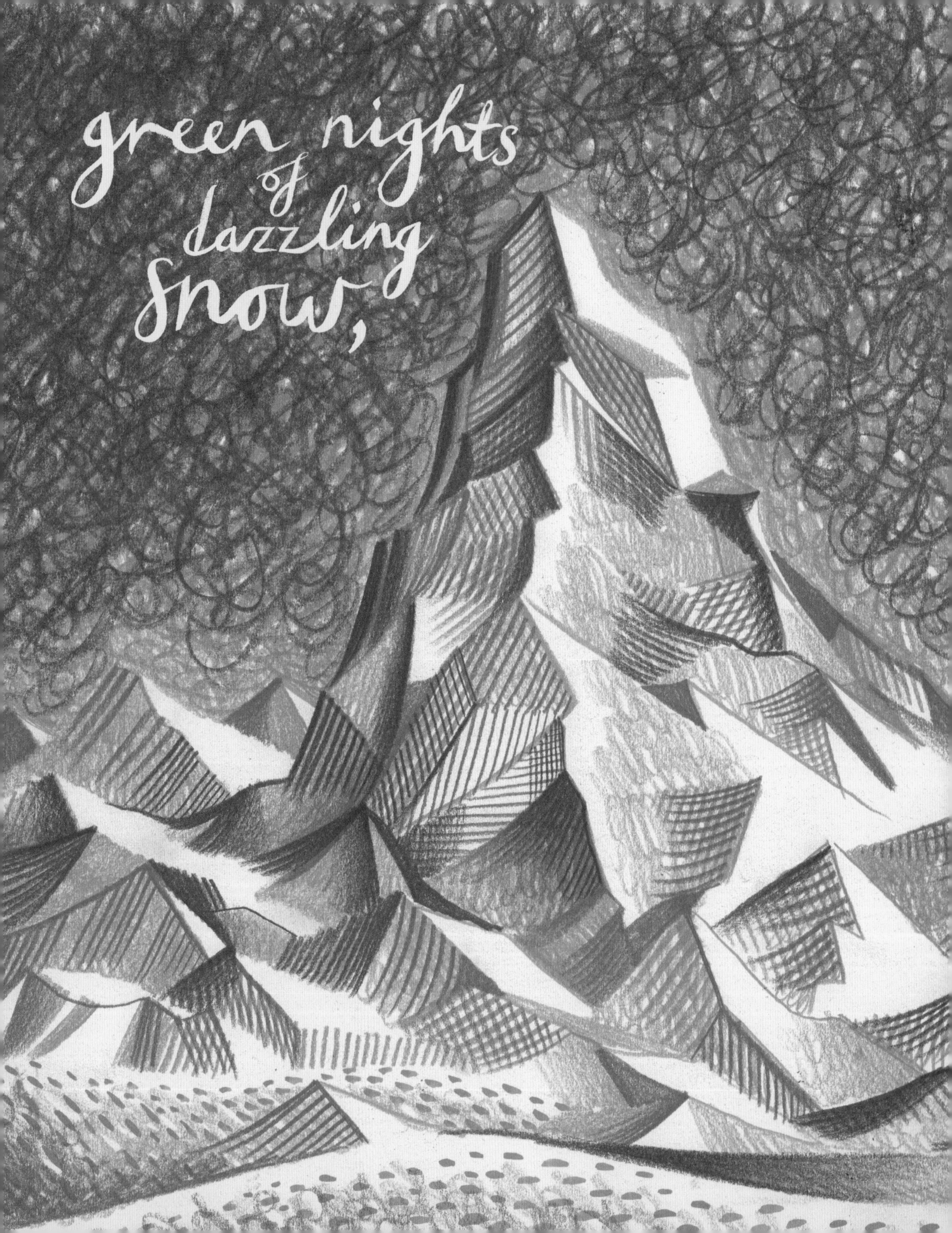
green nights
of
dazzling
snow,

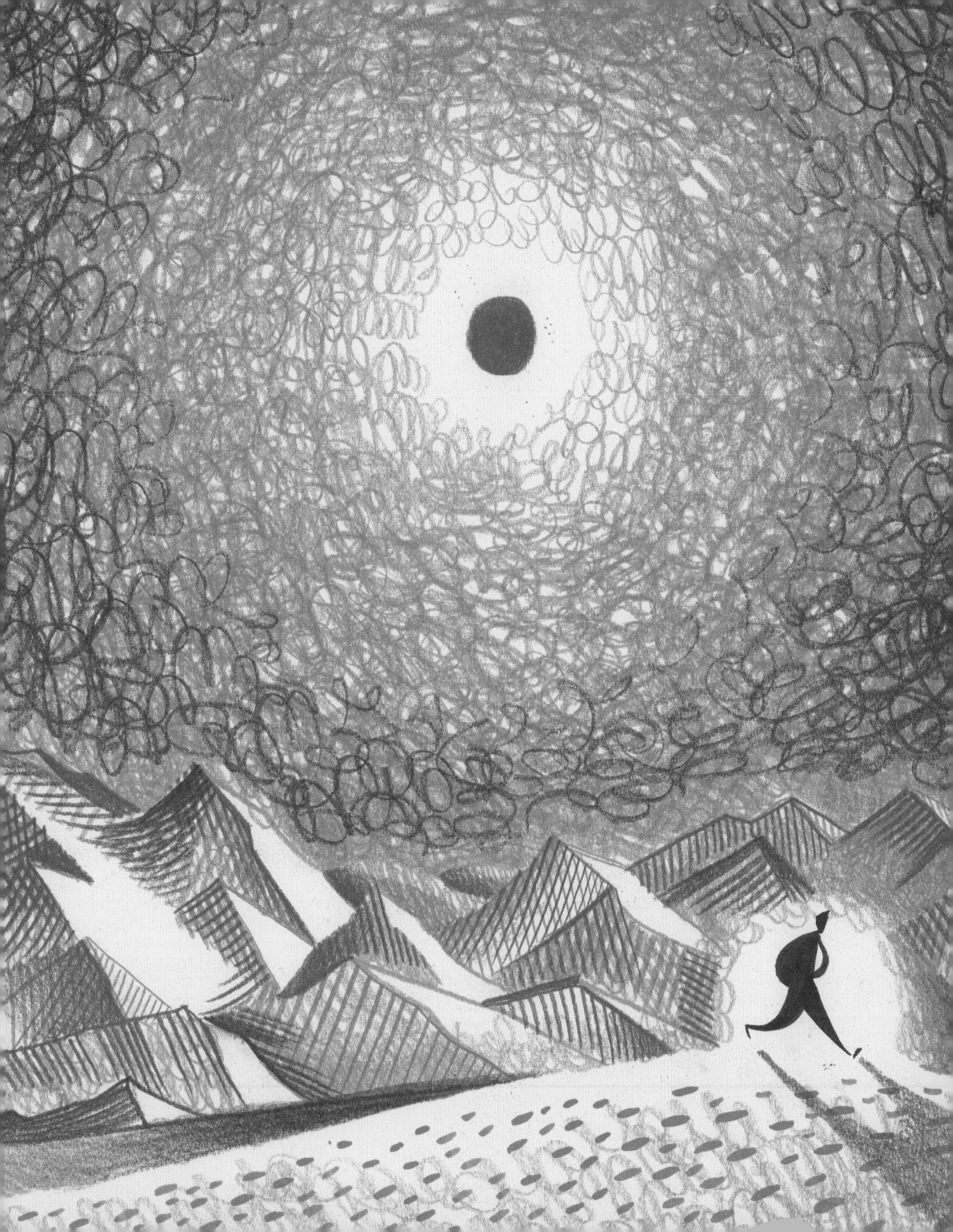

the Kiss

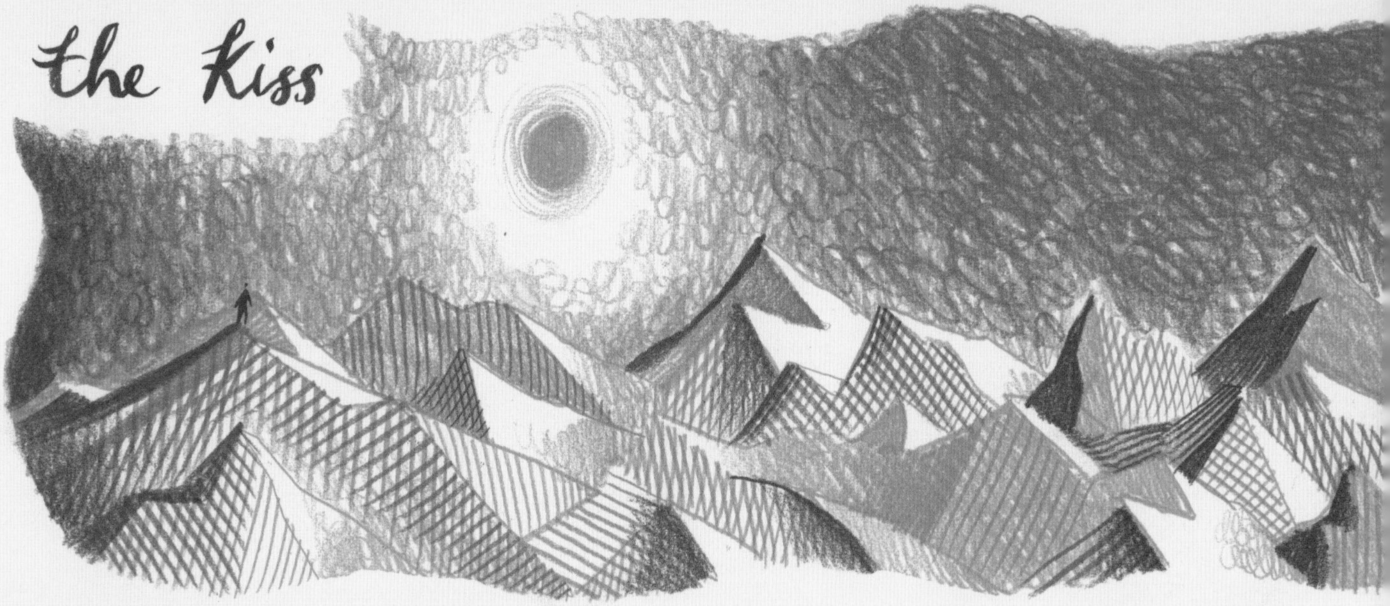

rising

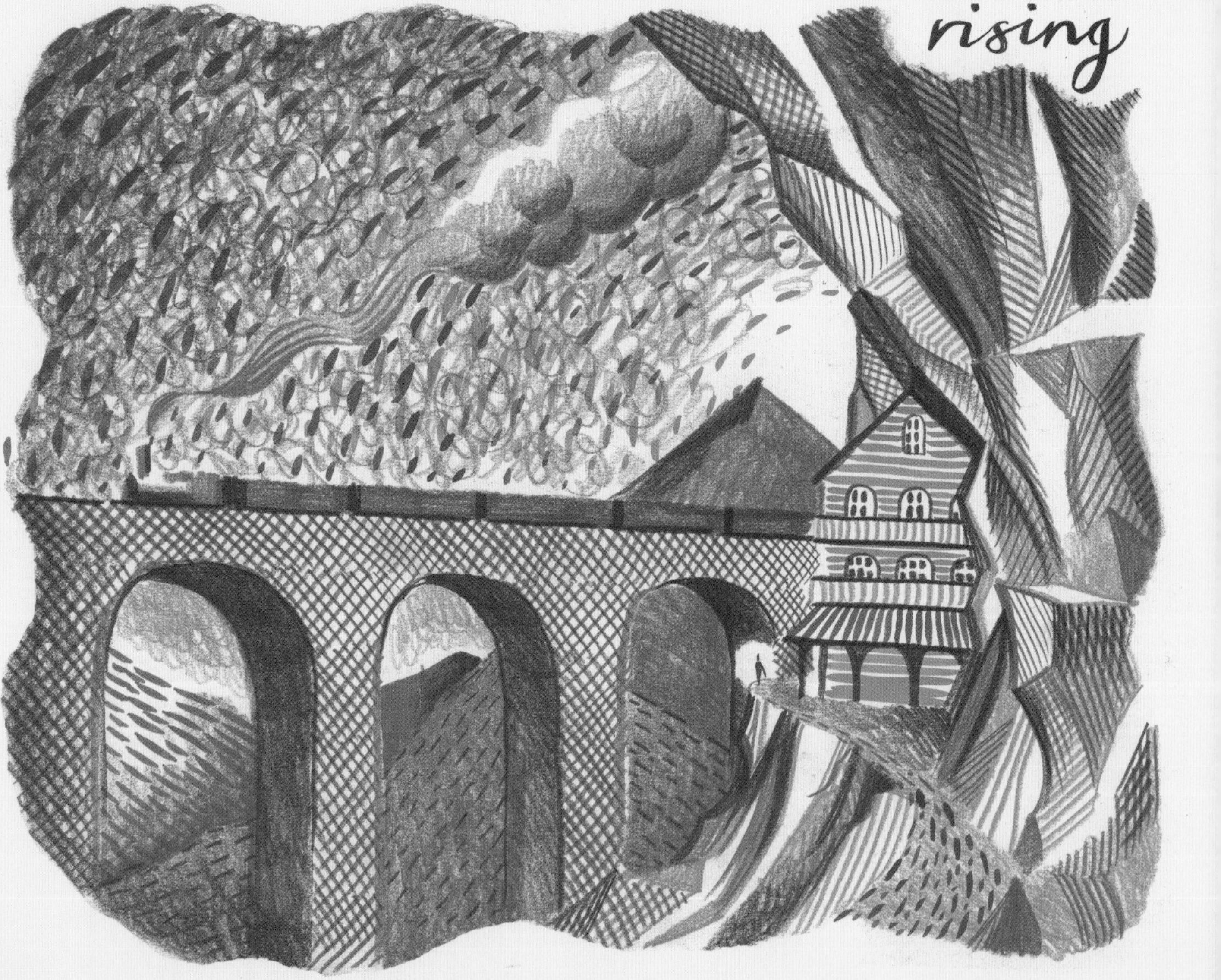

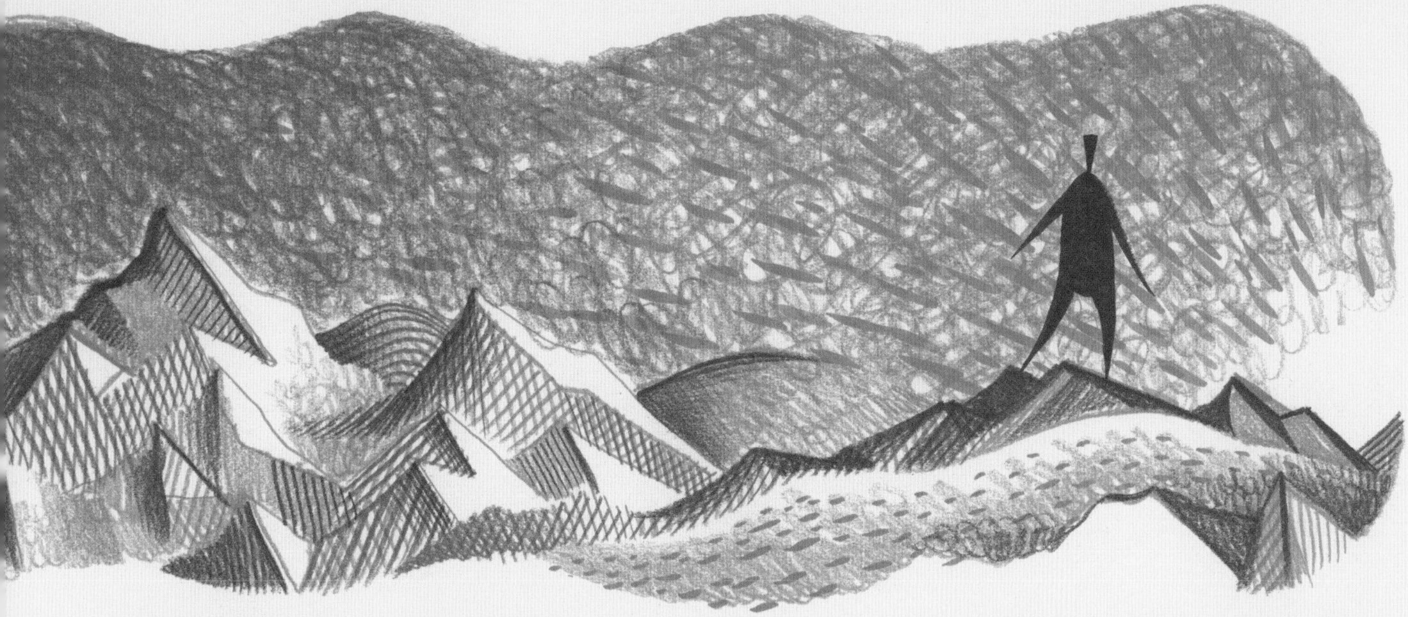

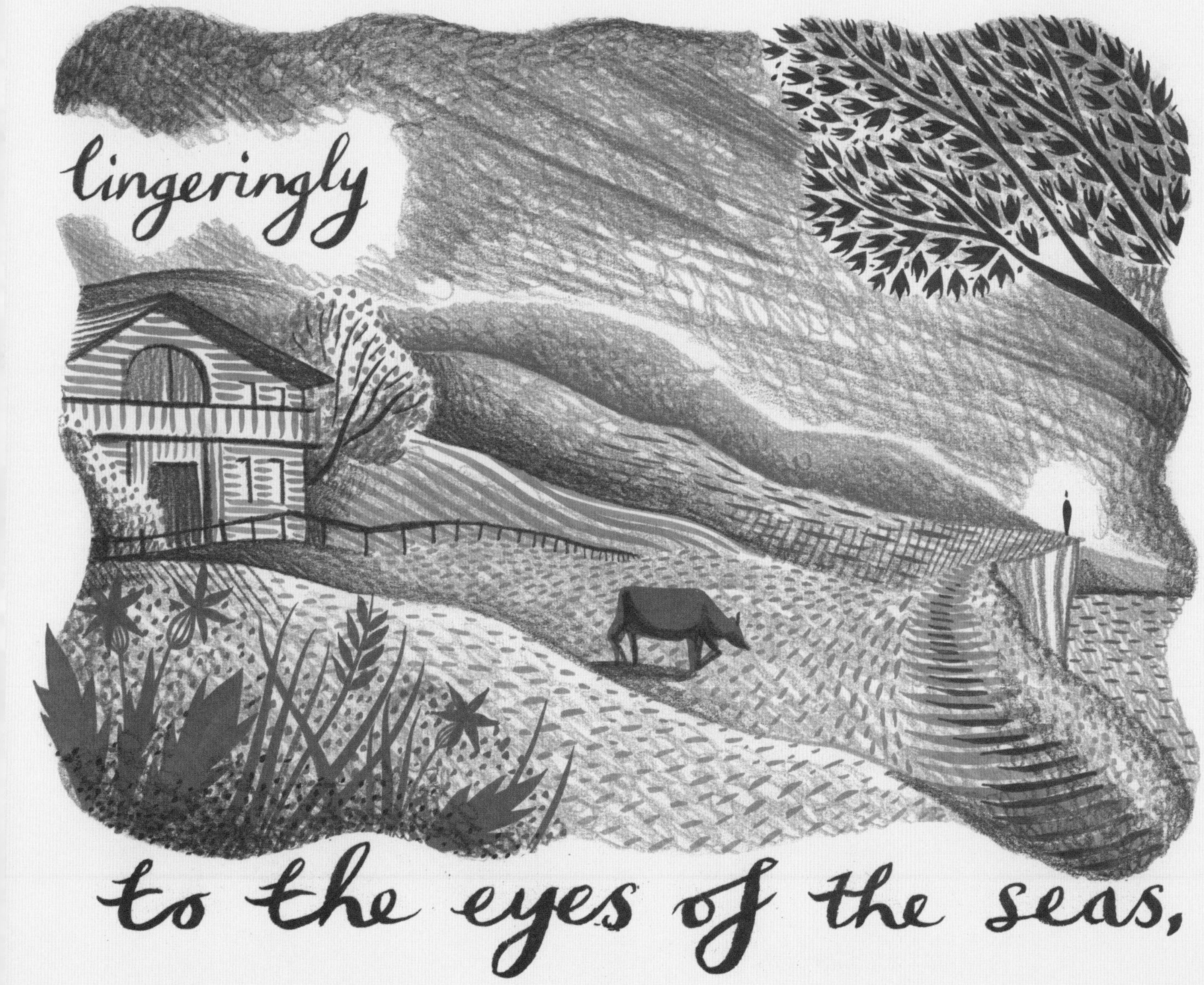
lingeringly

to the eyes of the seas,

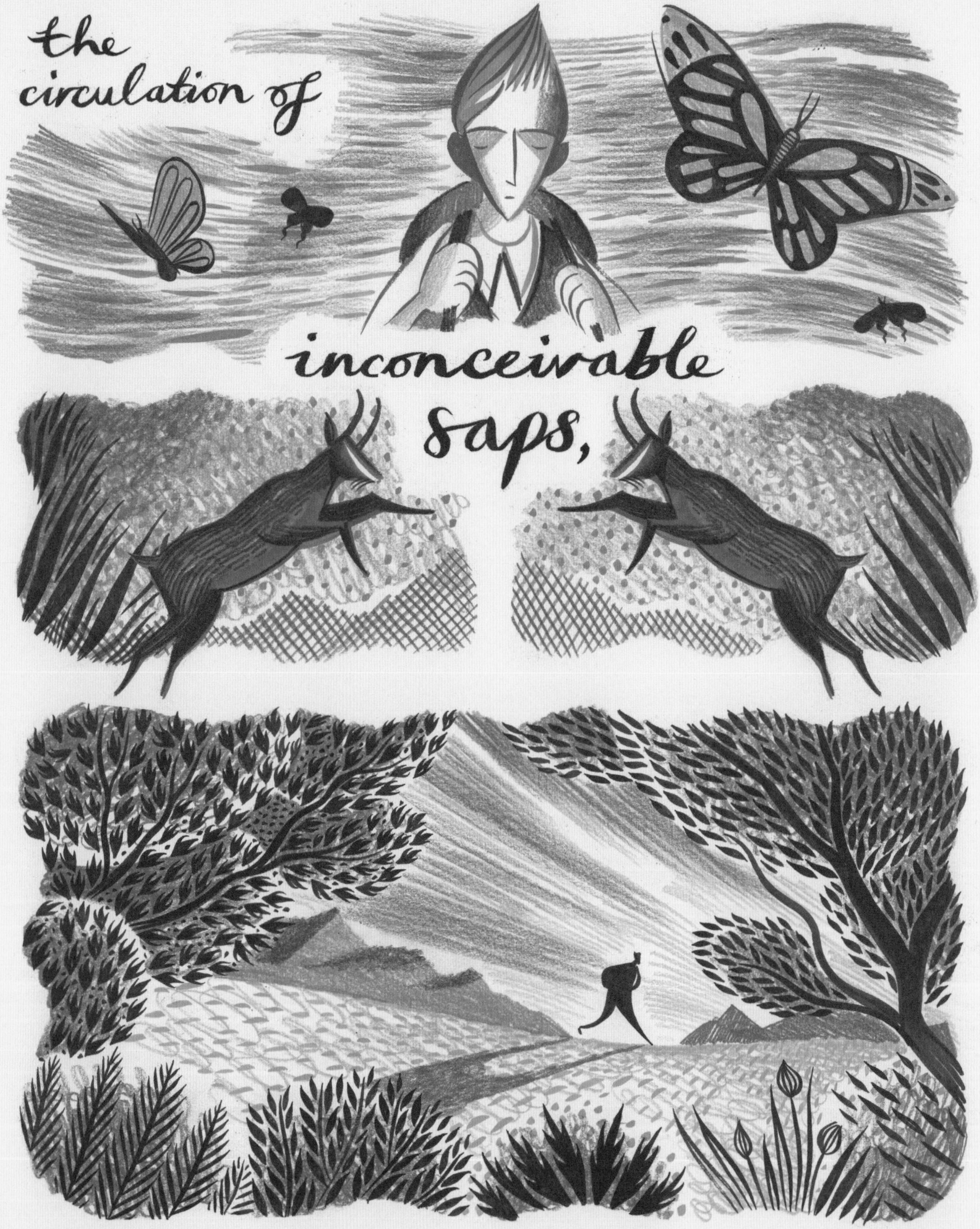
the circulation of
inconceivable
saps,

the citroen

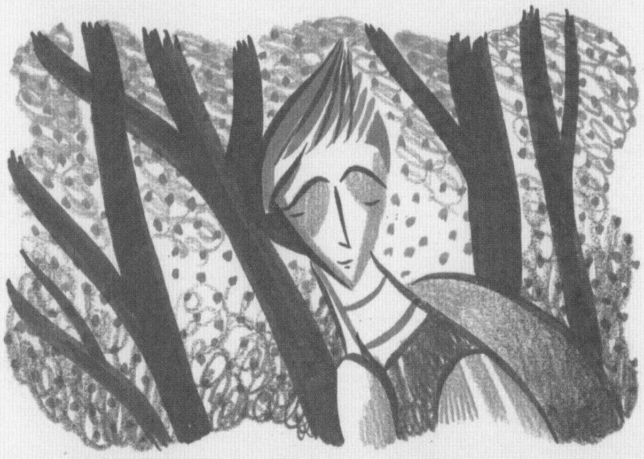

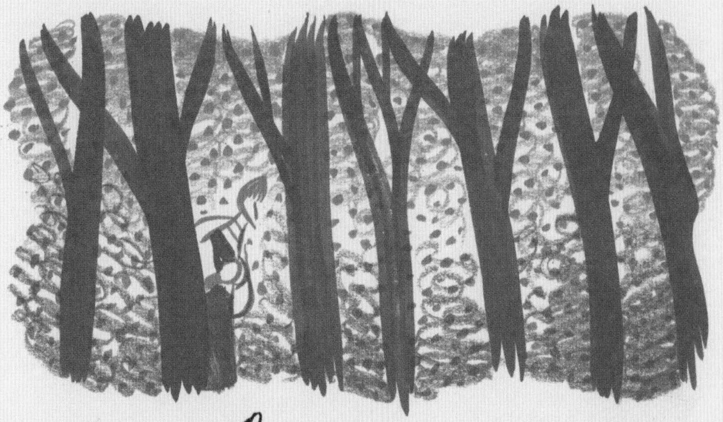

cerulean surge

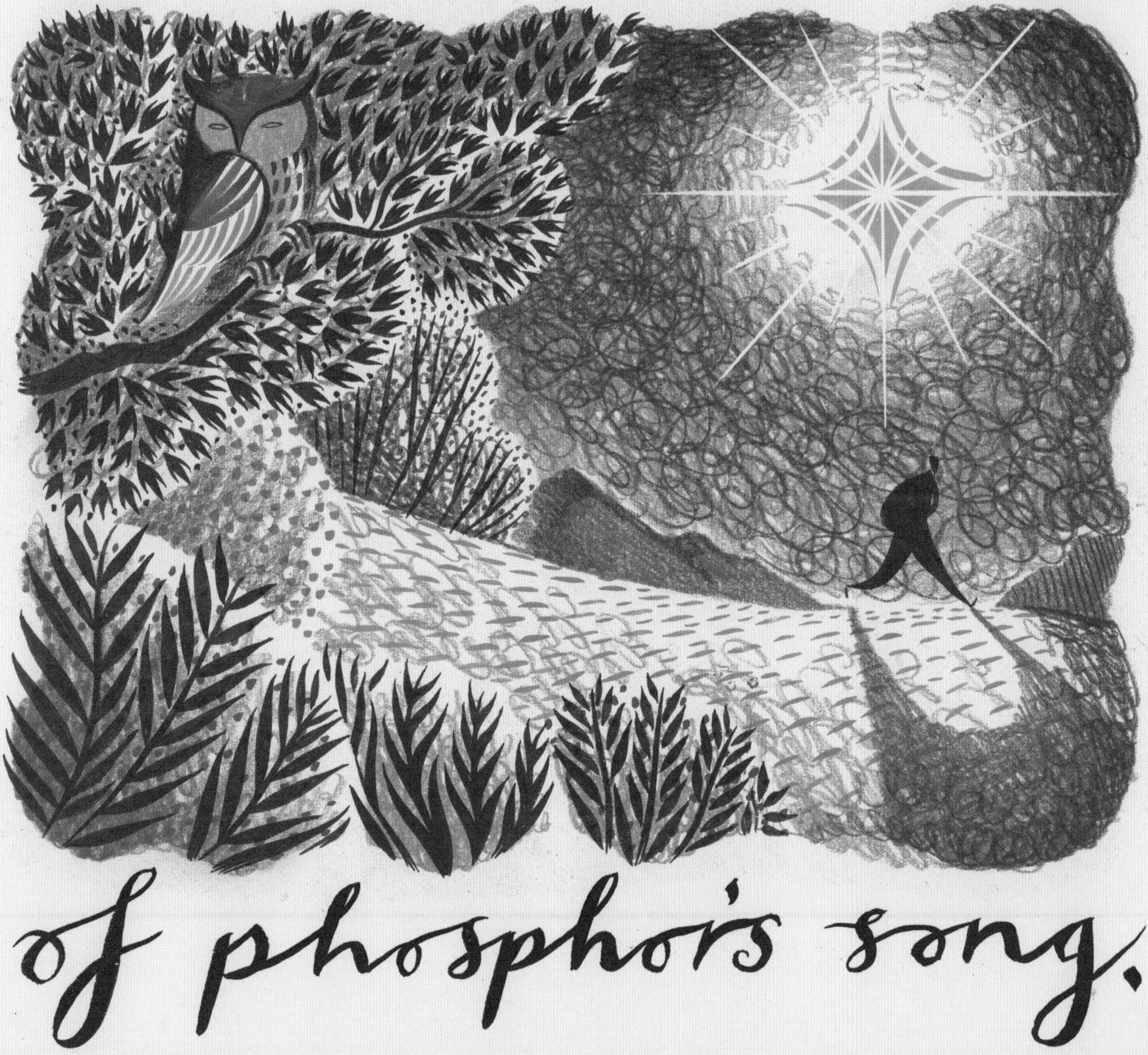

of phosphor's song.

I have followed,

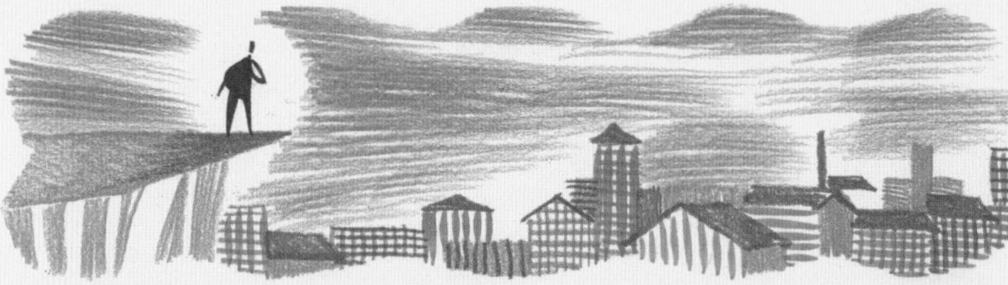

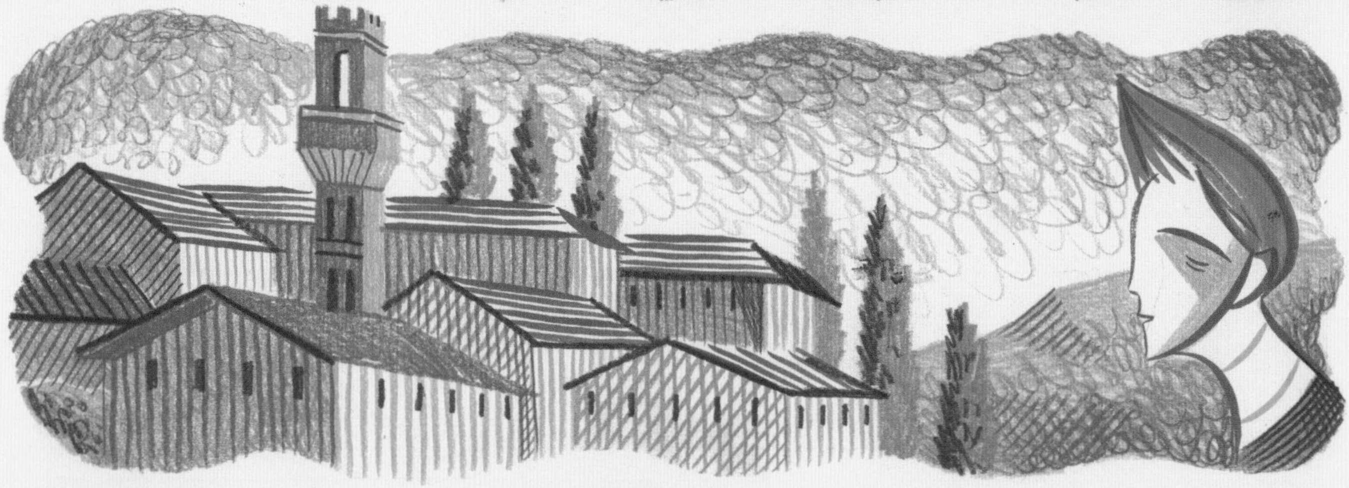

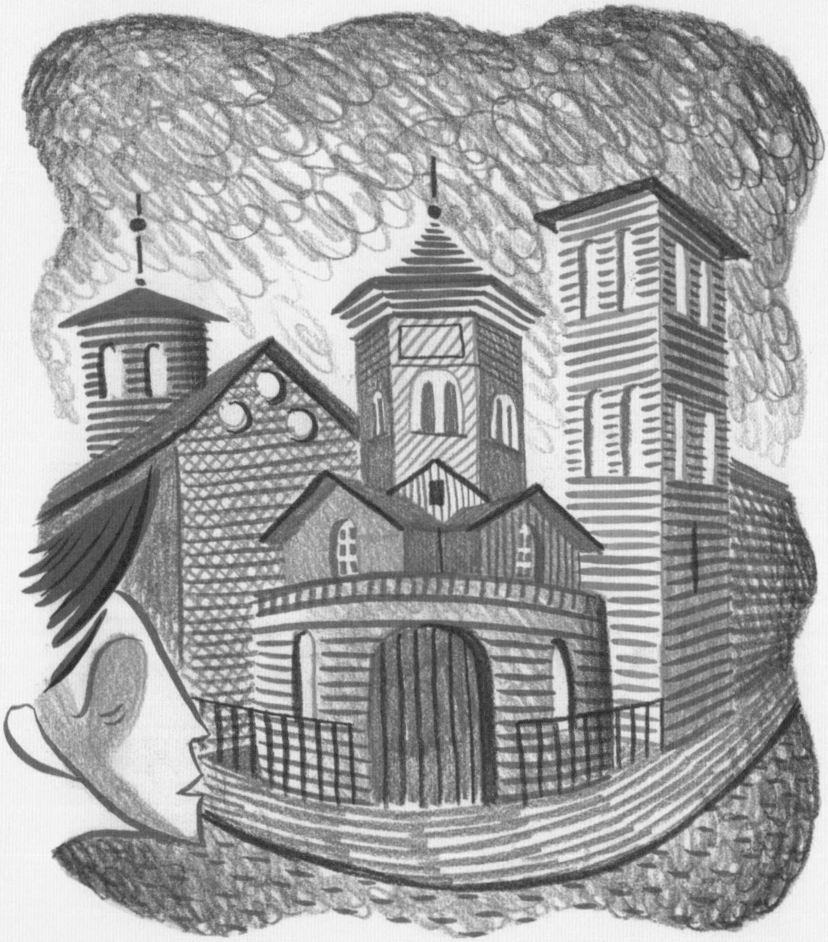

for months on end,

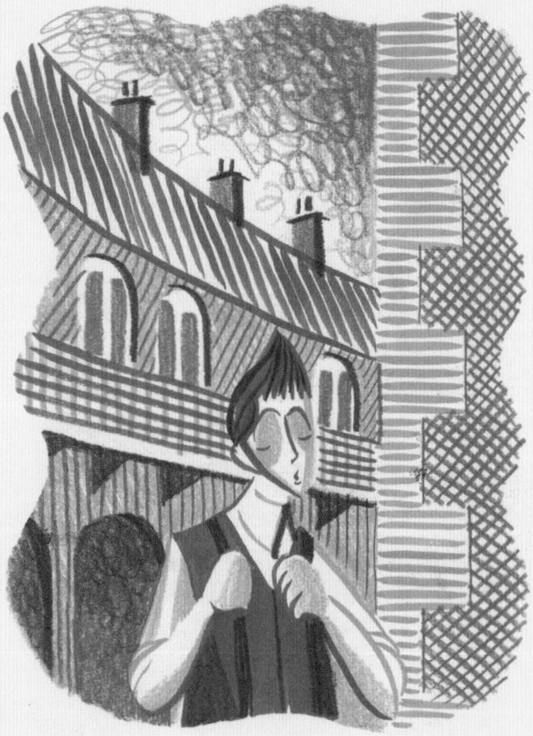

the frenzied stampede

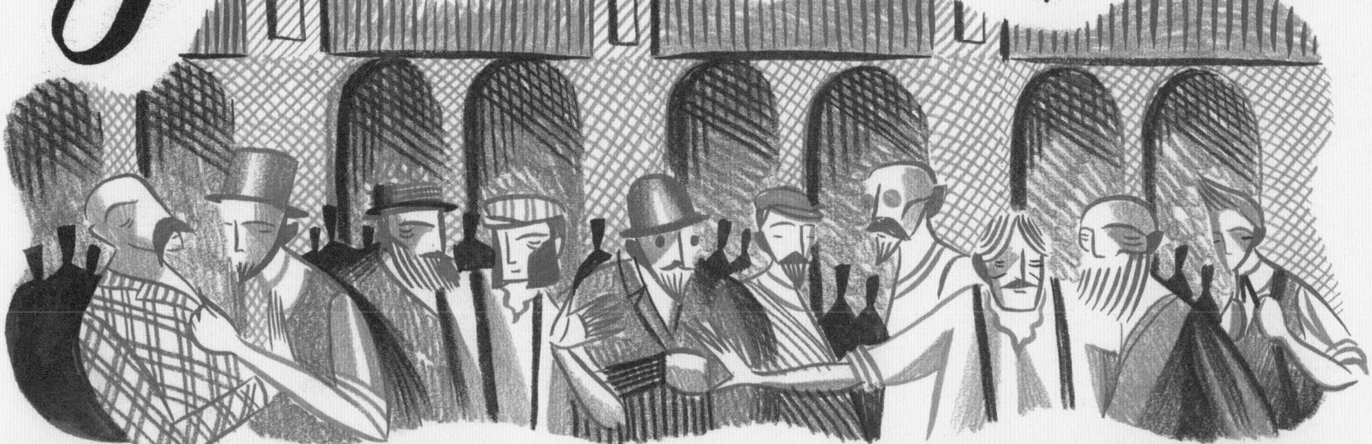

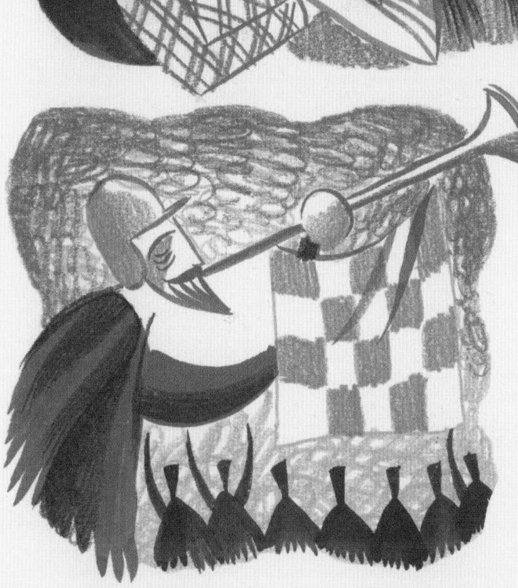

of the swell of the reefs,

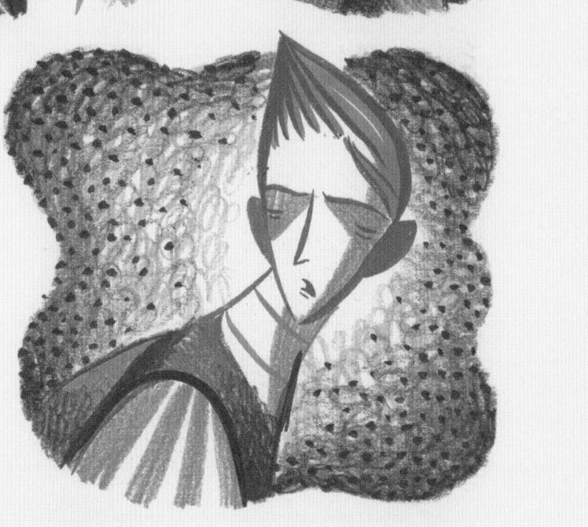

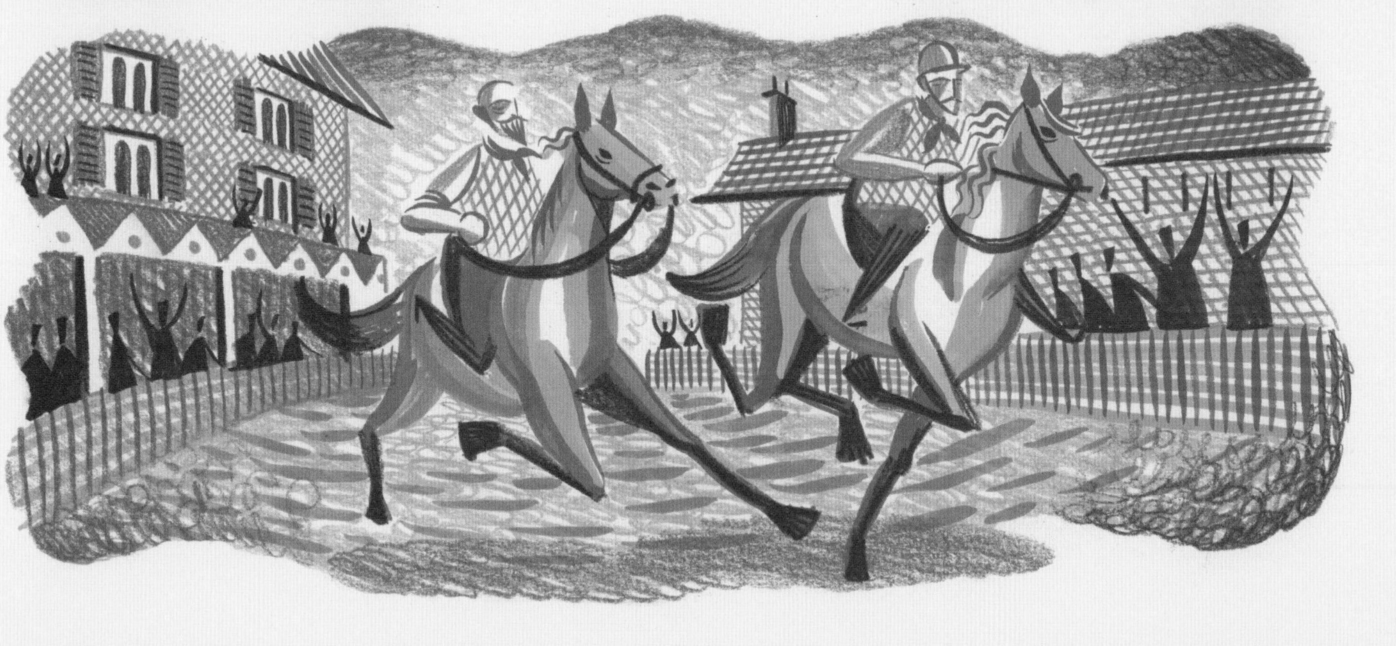

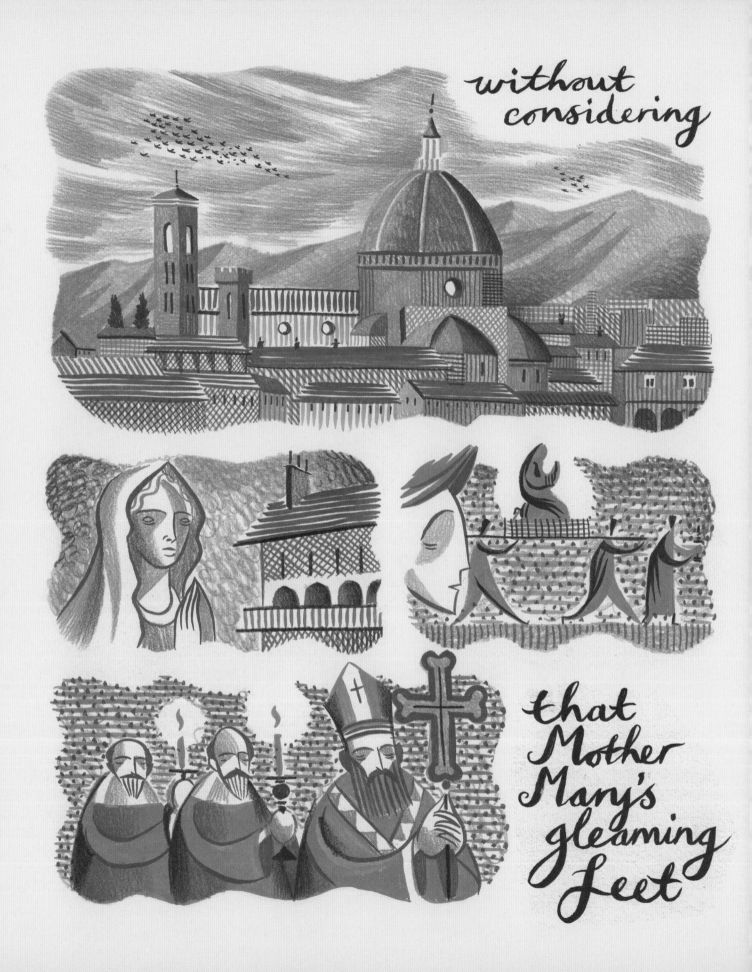

without considering

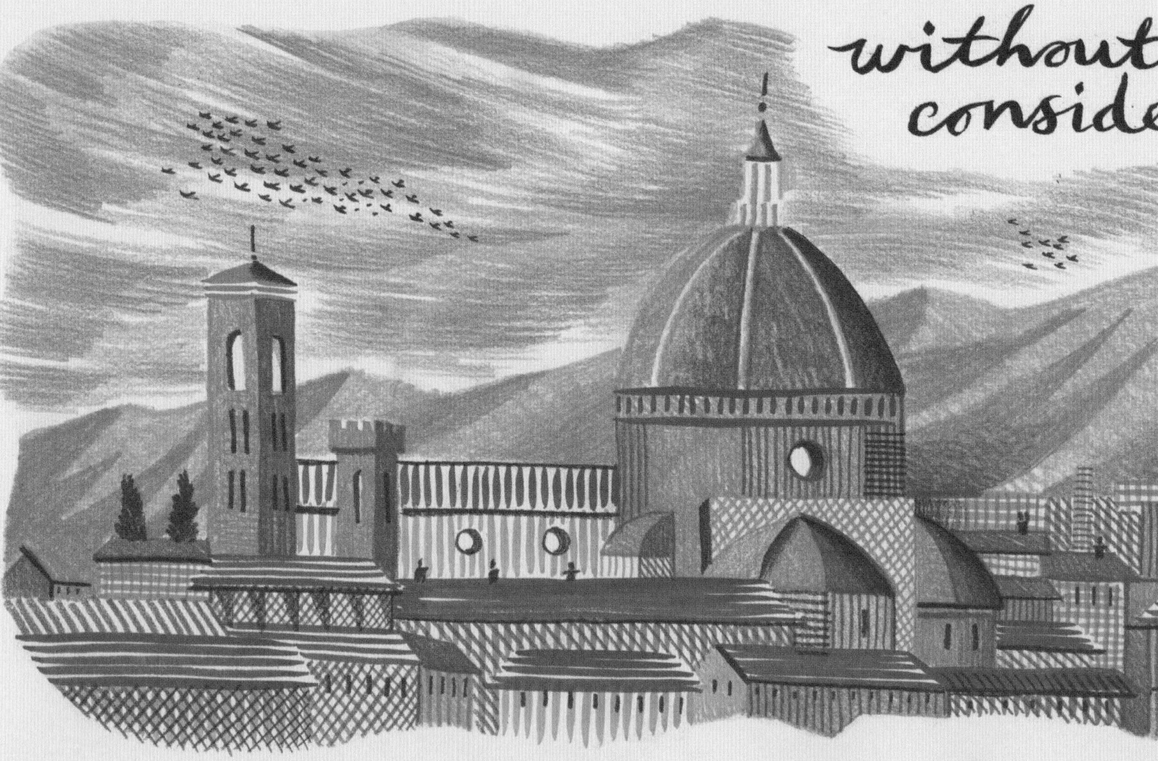

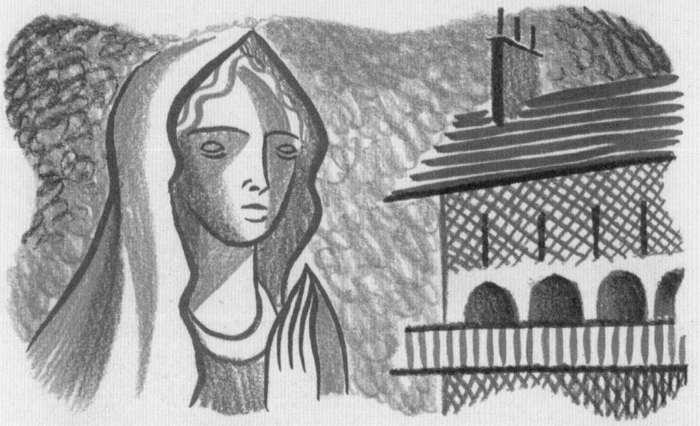

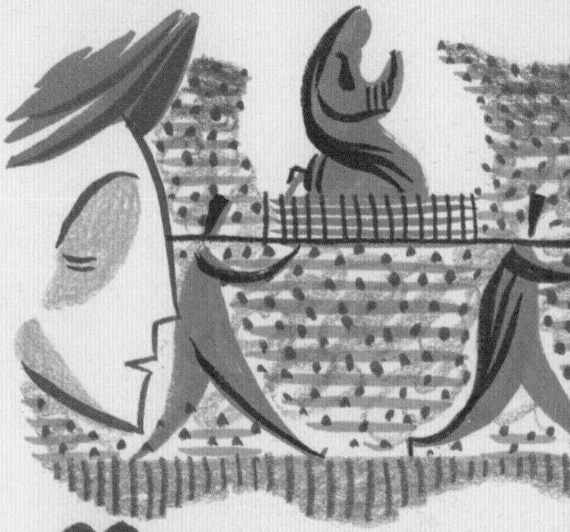

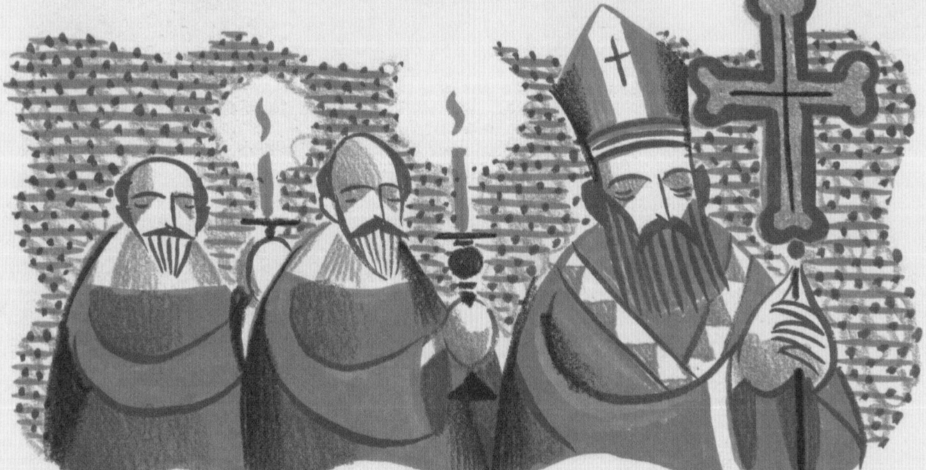

that Mother Mary's gleaming feet

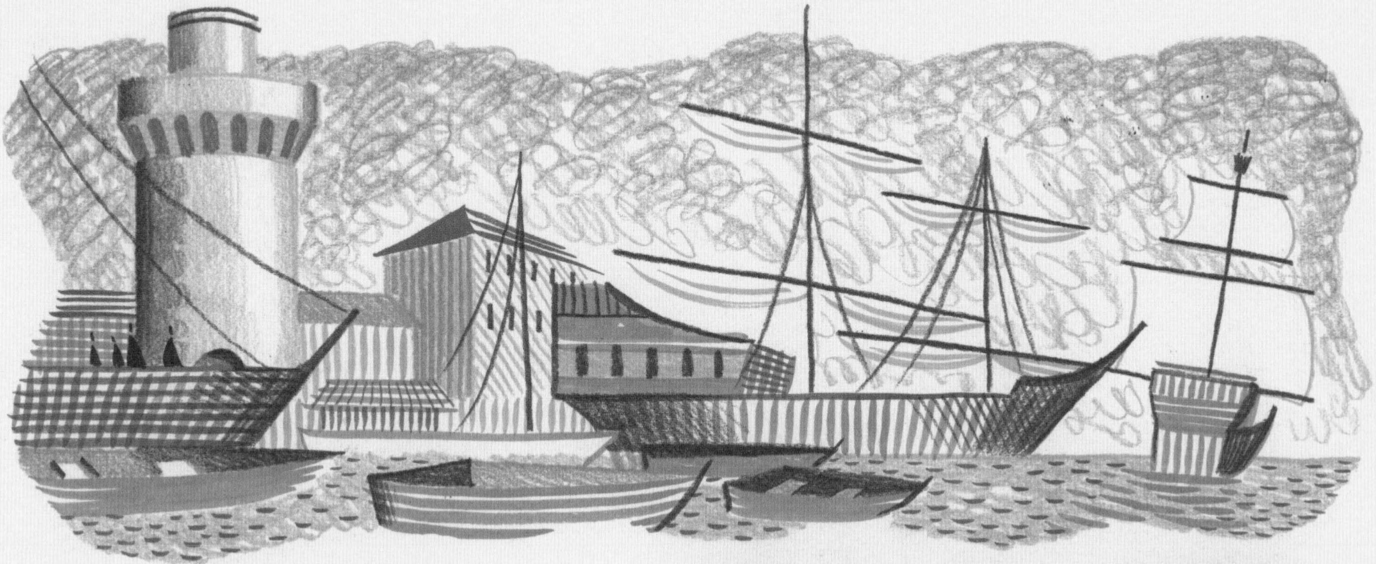

could MUZZLE these gasping seas.

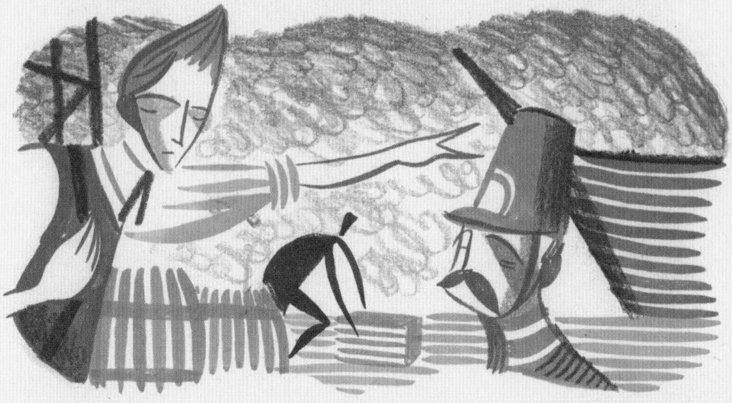

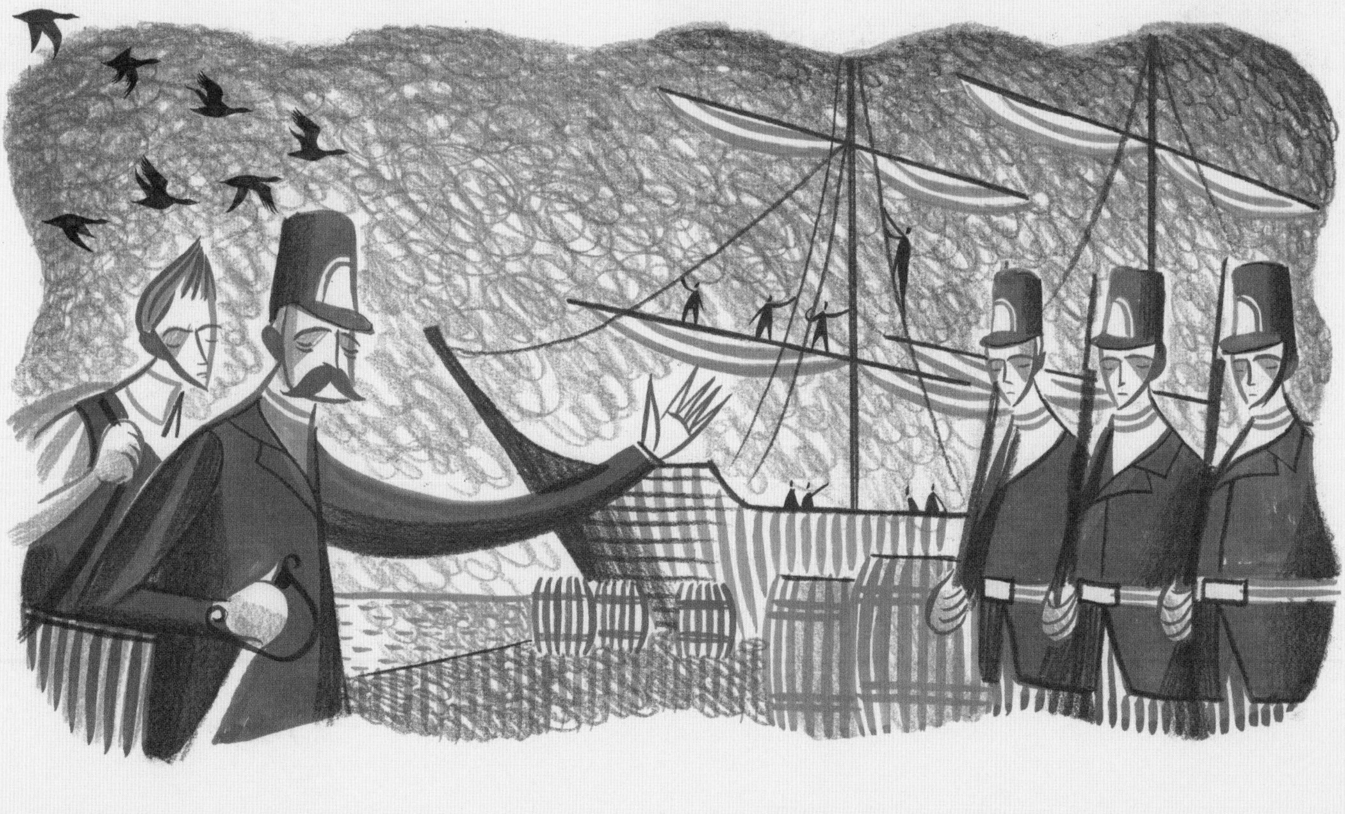

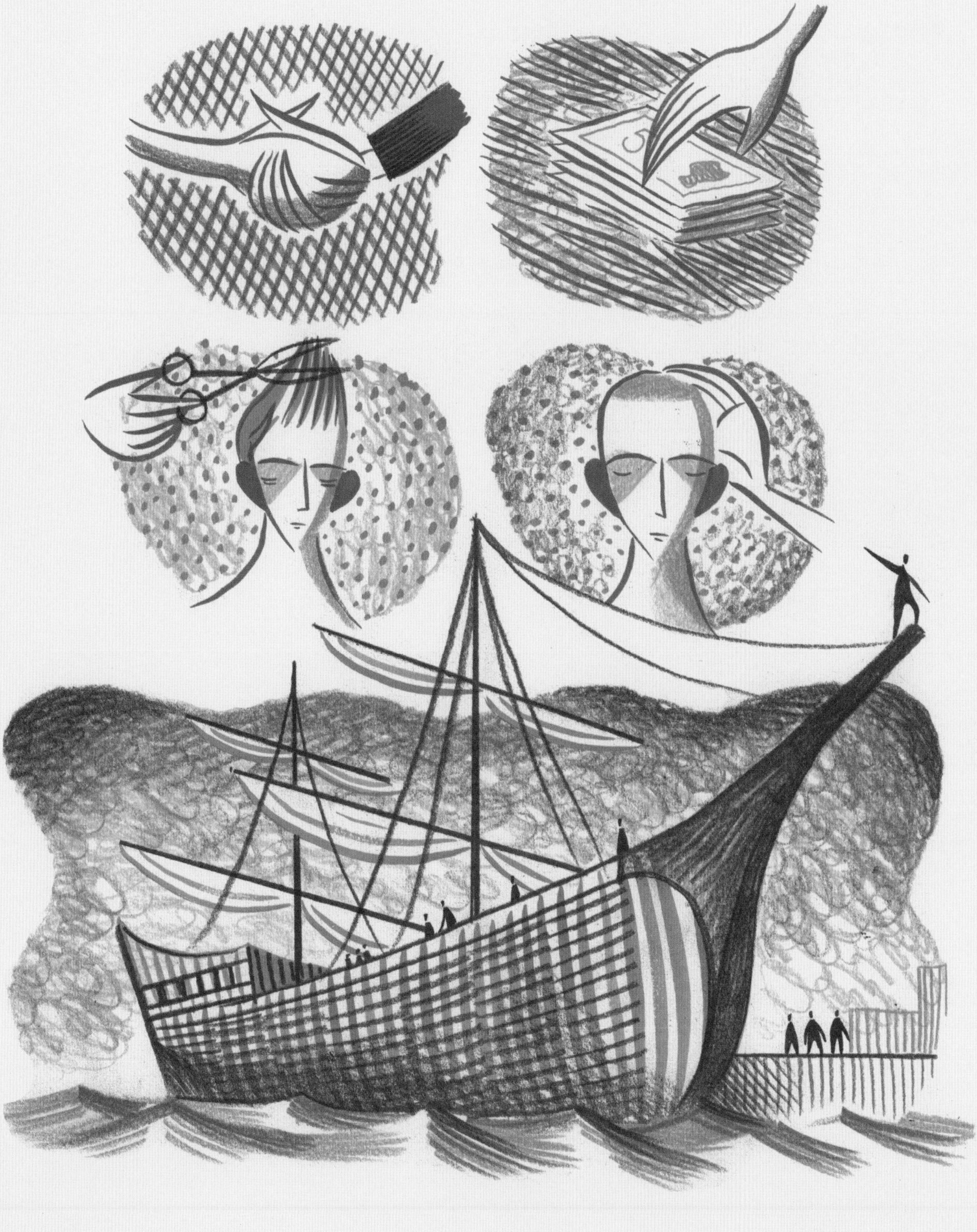

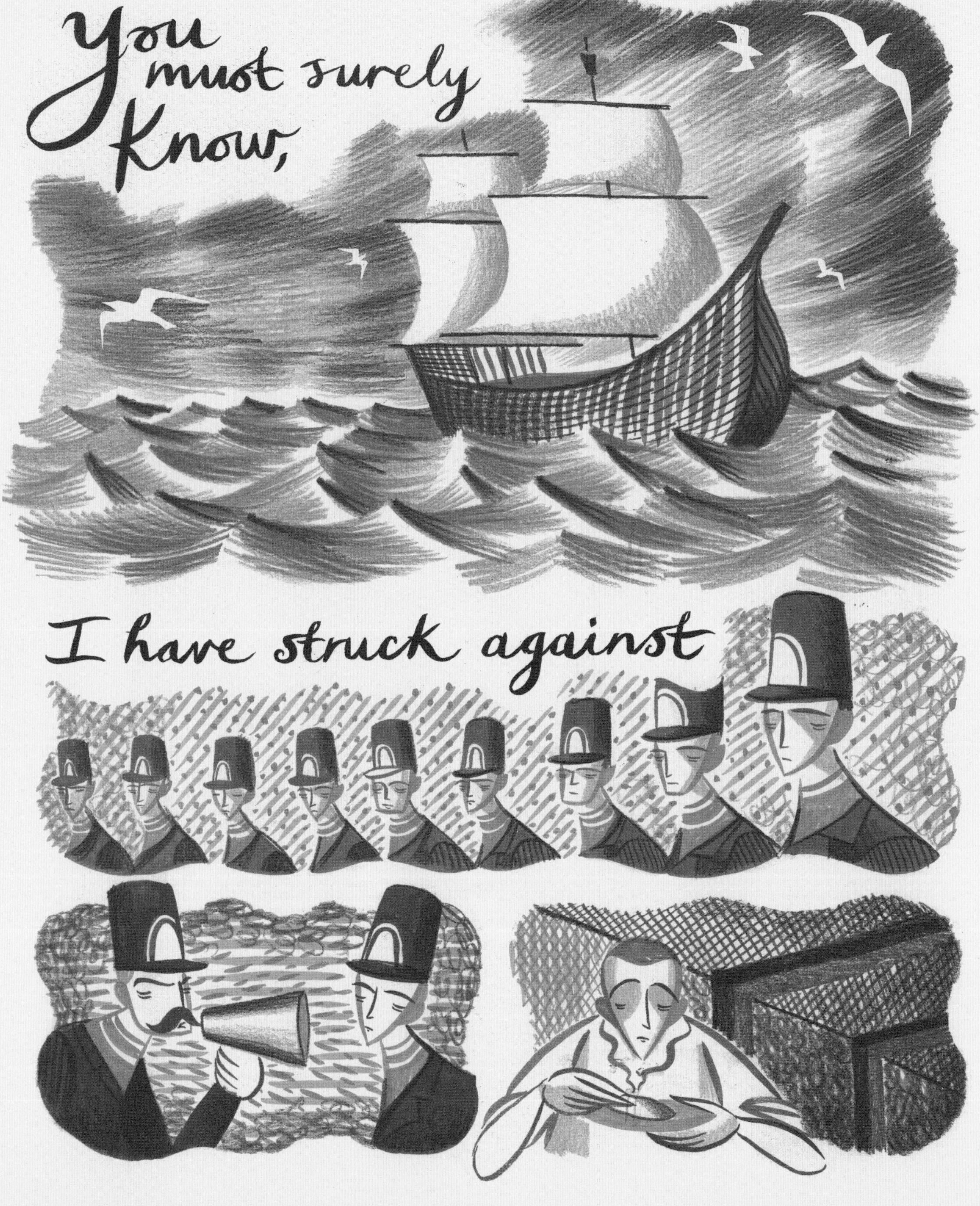
You must surely know,
I have struck against

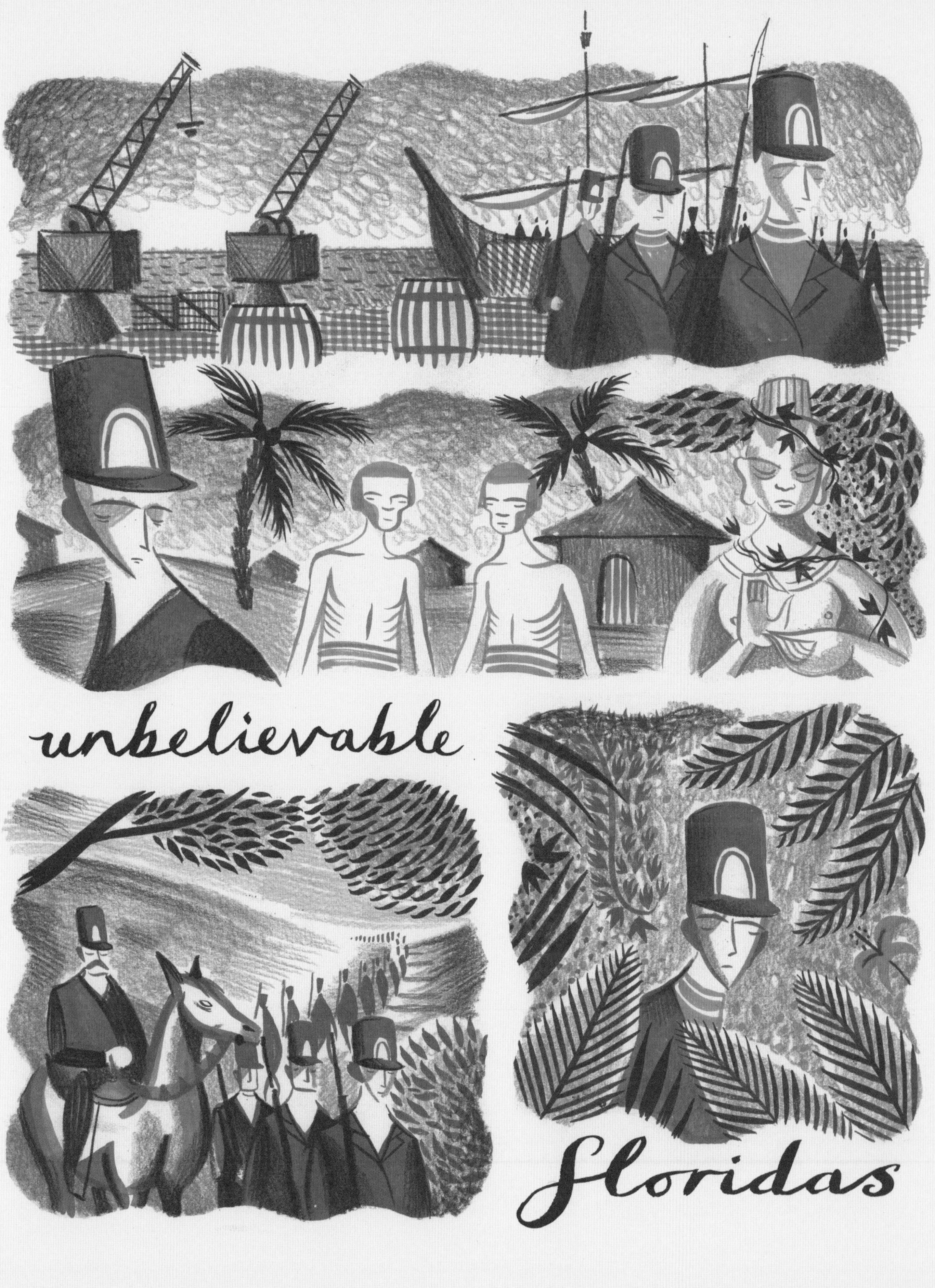
unbelievable
floridas

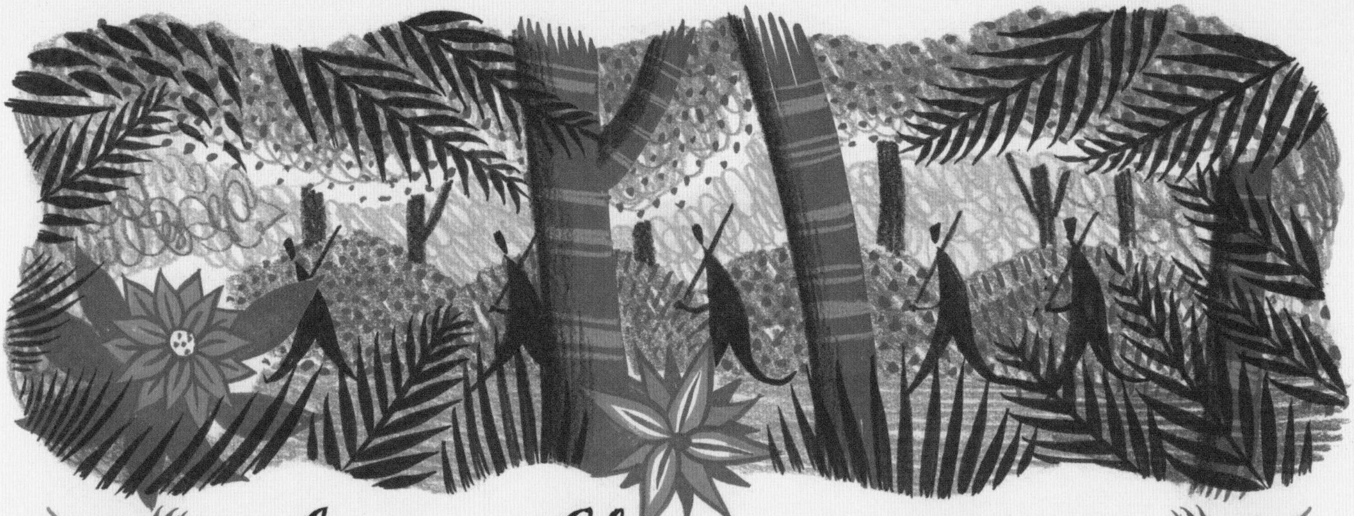

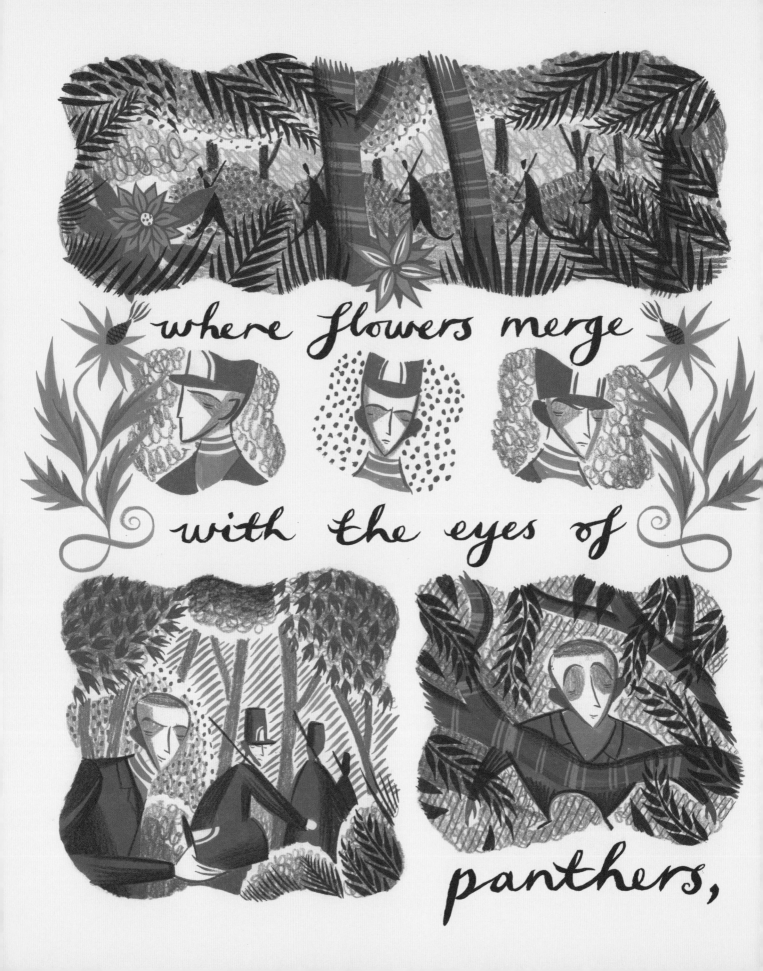

where flowers merge

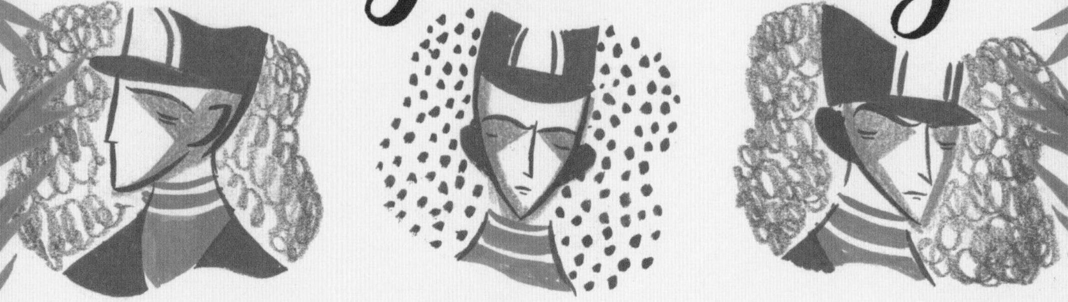

with the eyes of

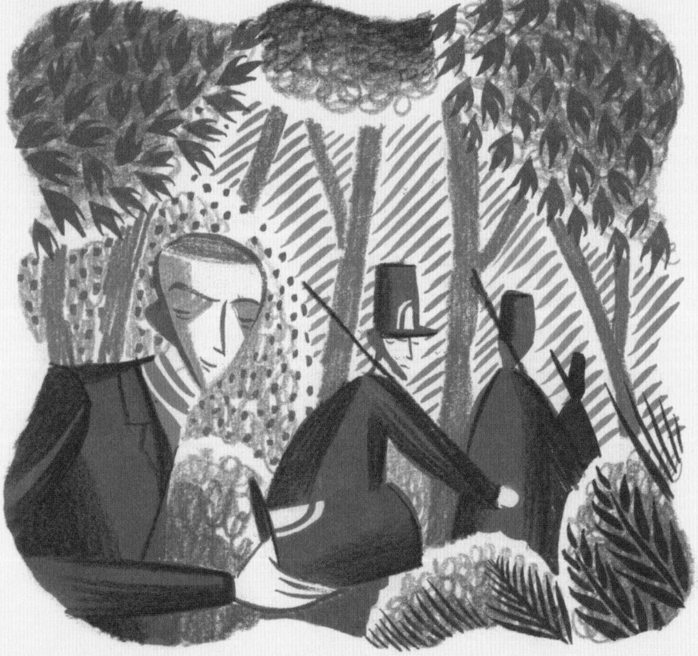

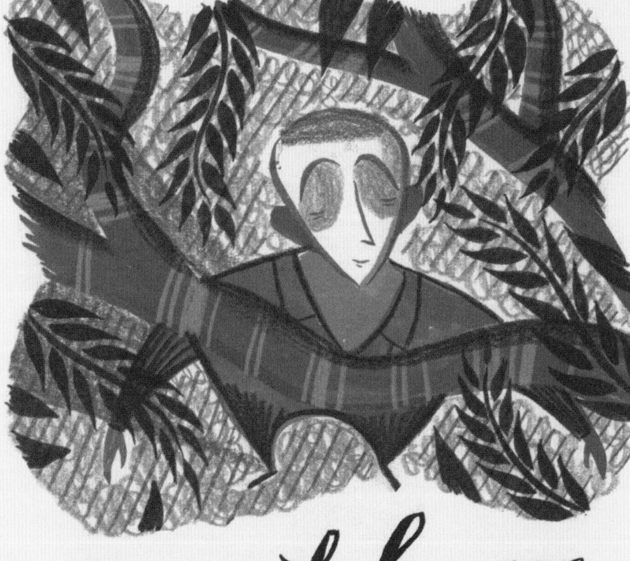

panthers,

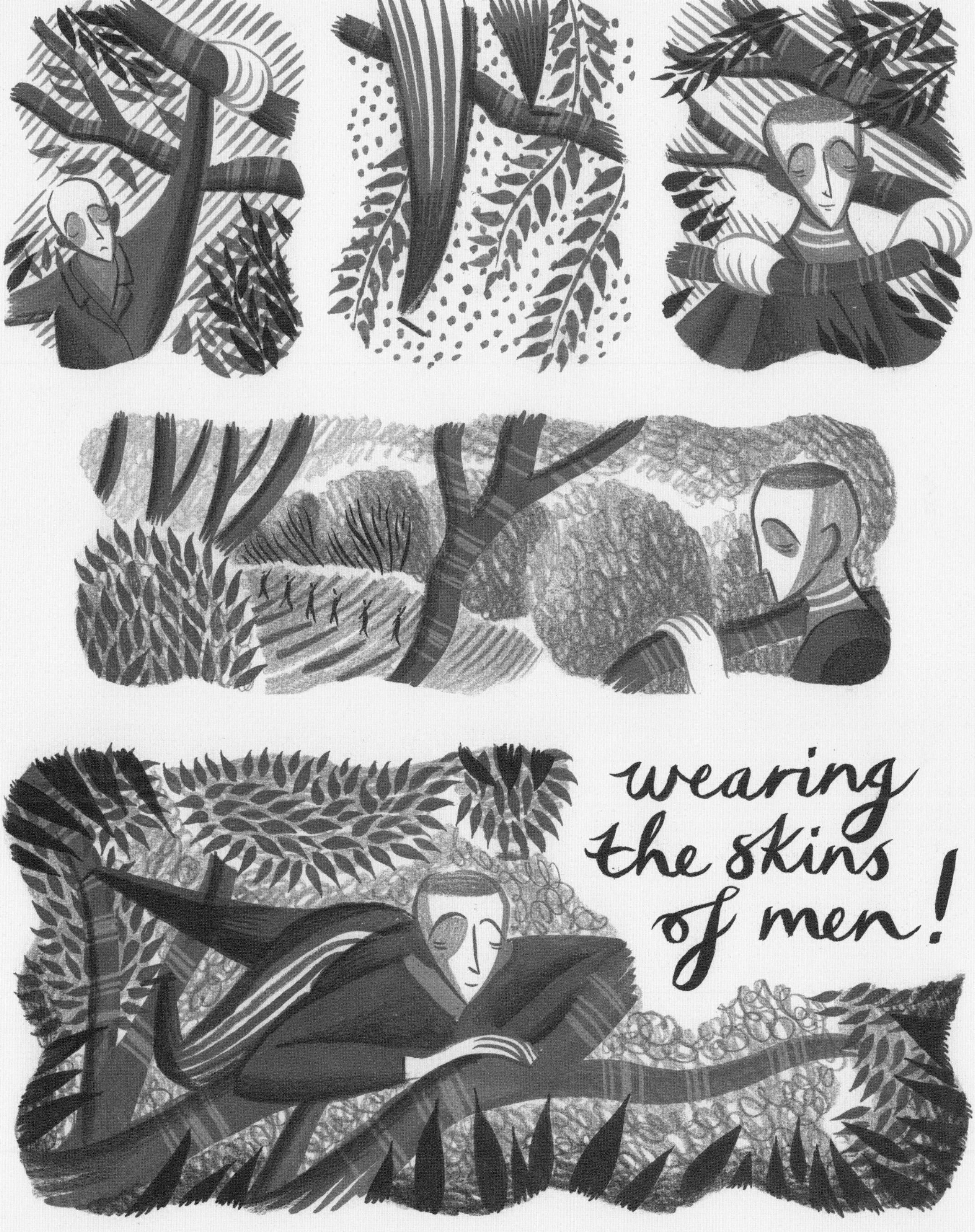
wearing
the skins
of men!

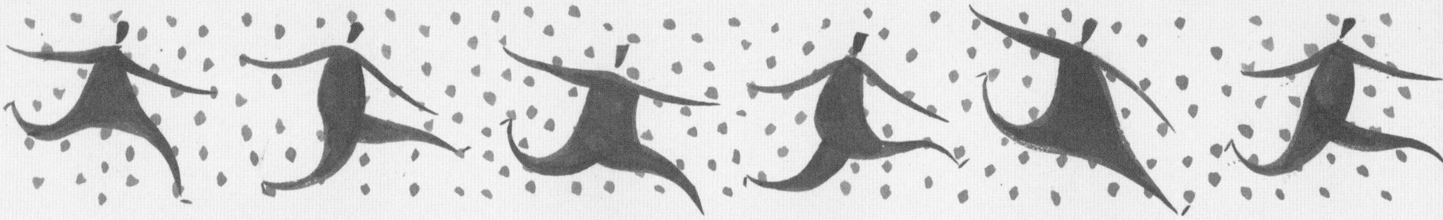

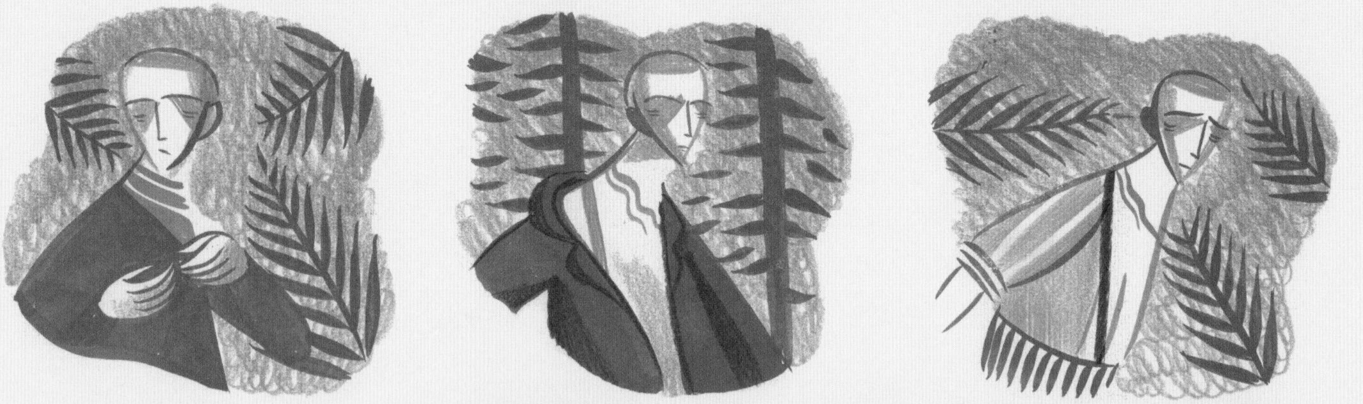

Where rainbows stretched

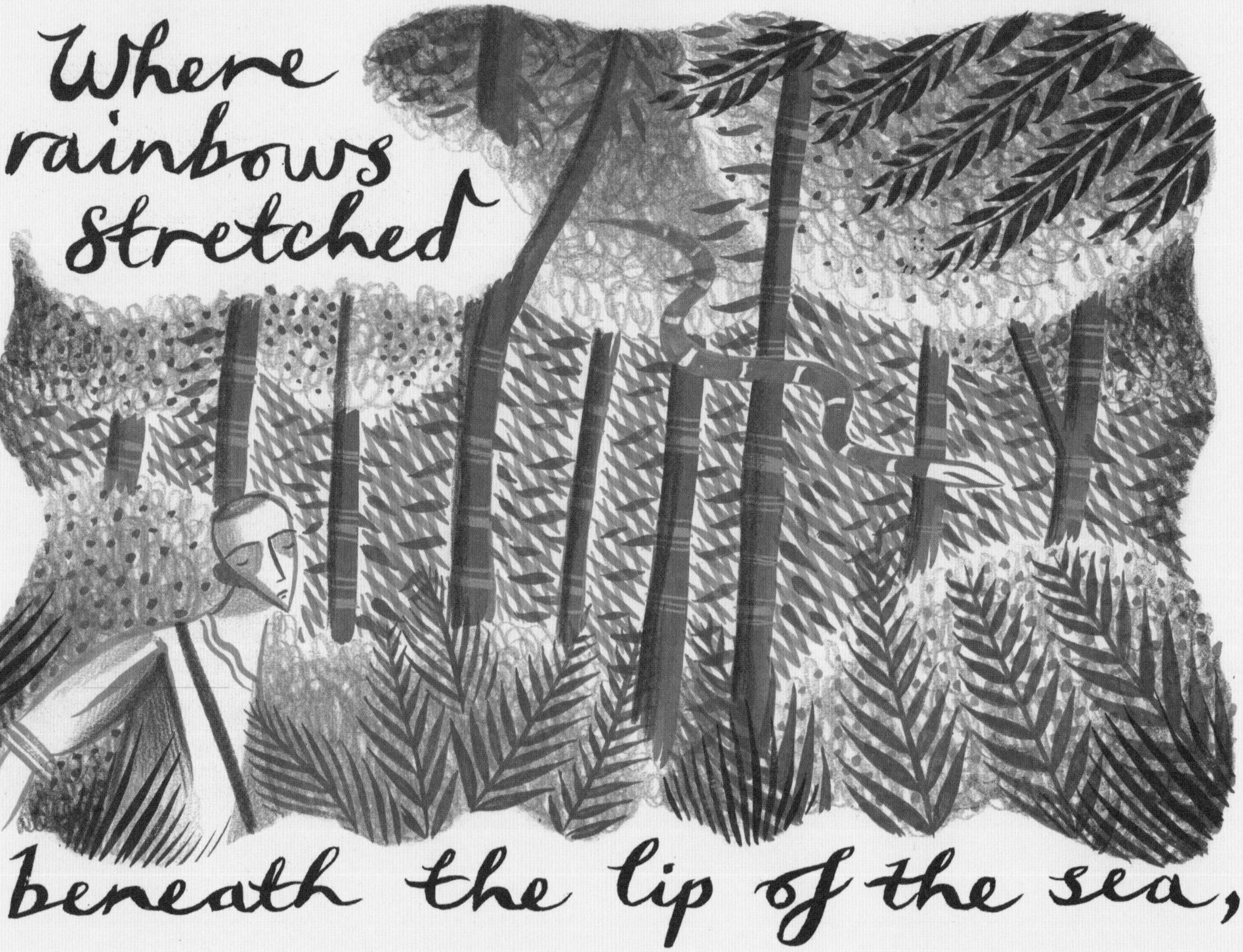

beneath the lip of the sea,

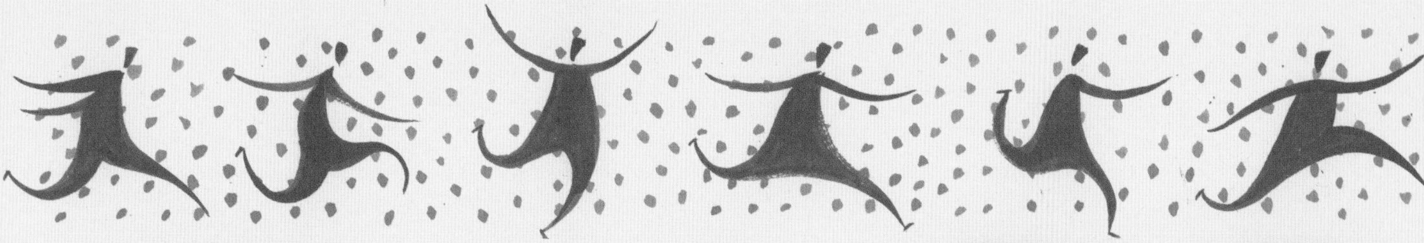

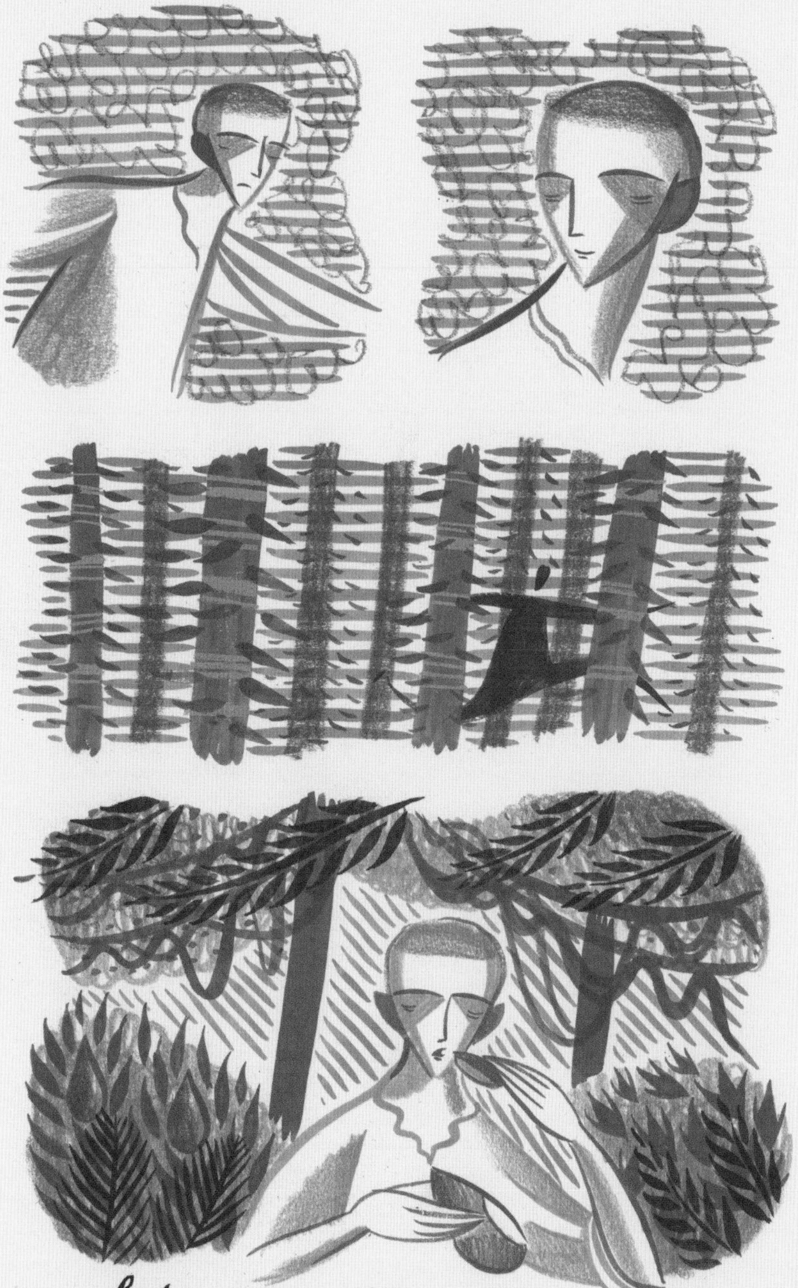

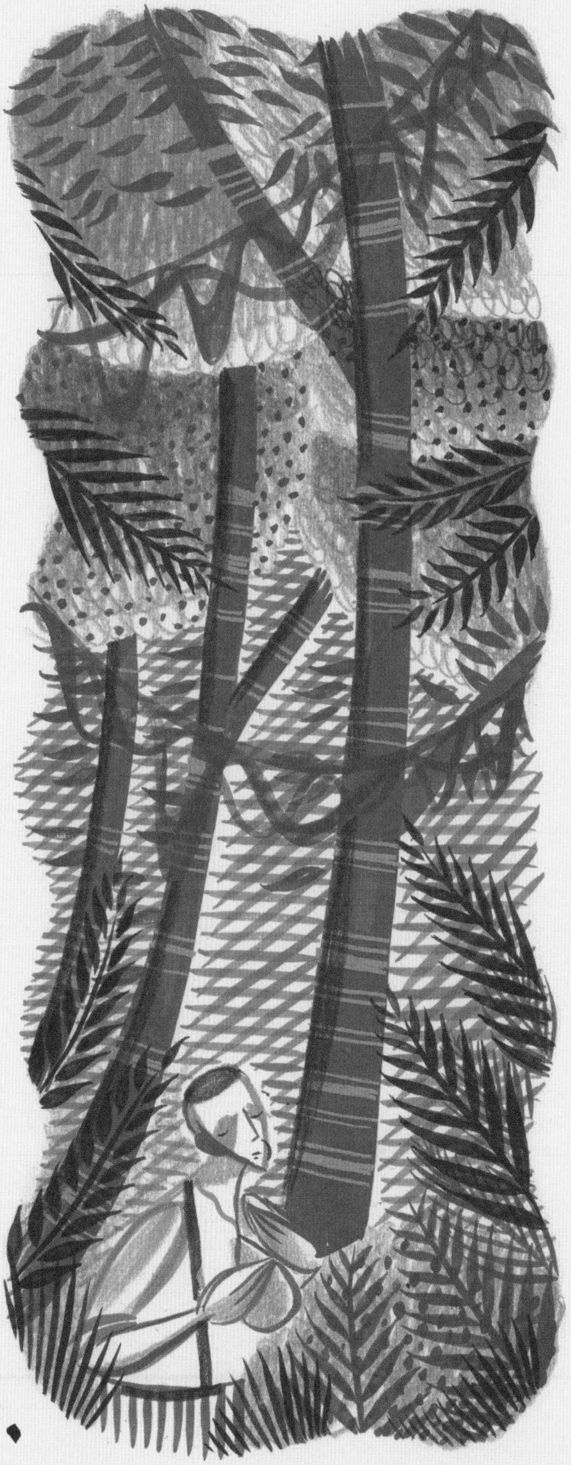

like the stirrups of
glaucous herds.

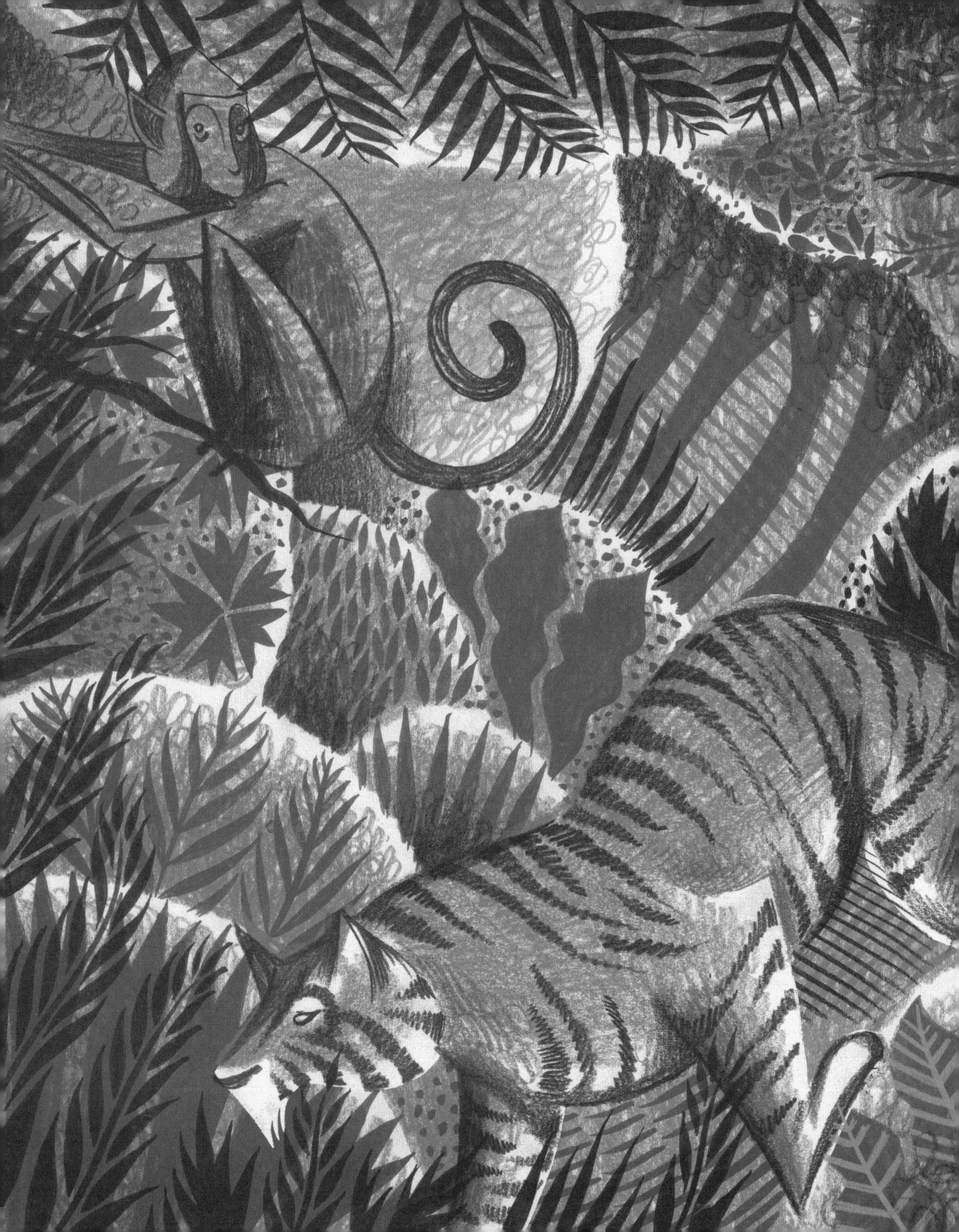

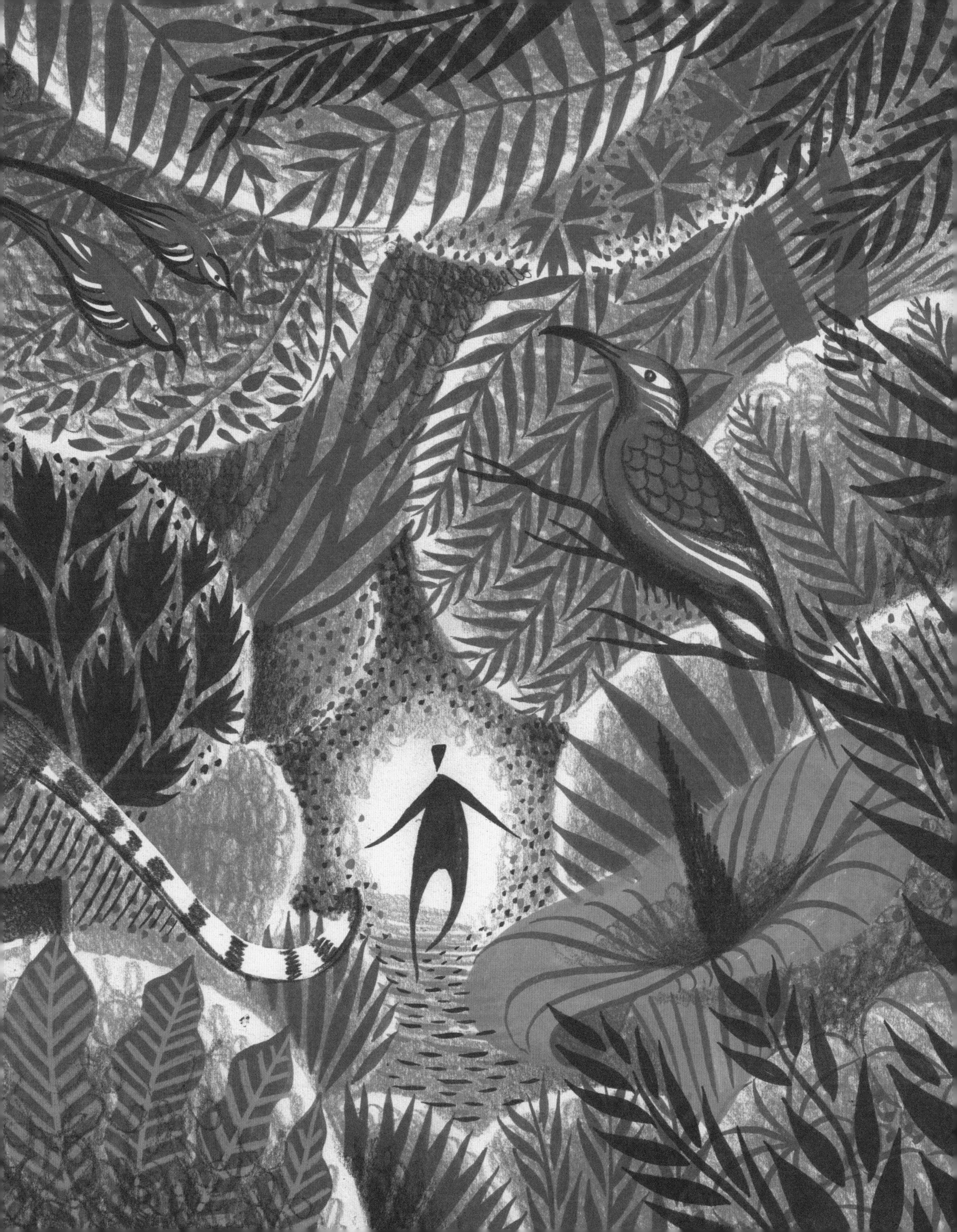

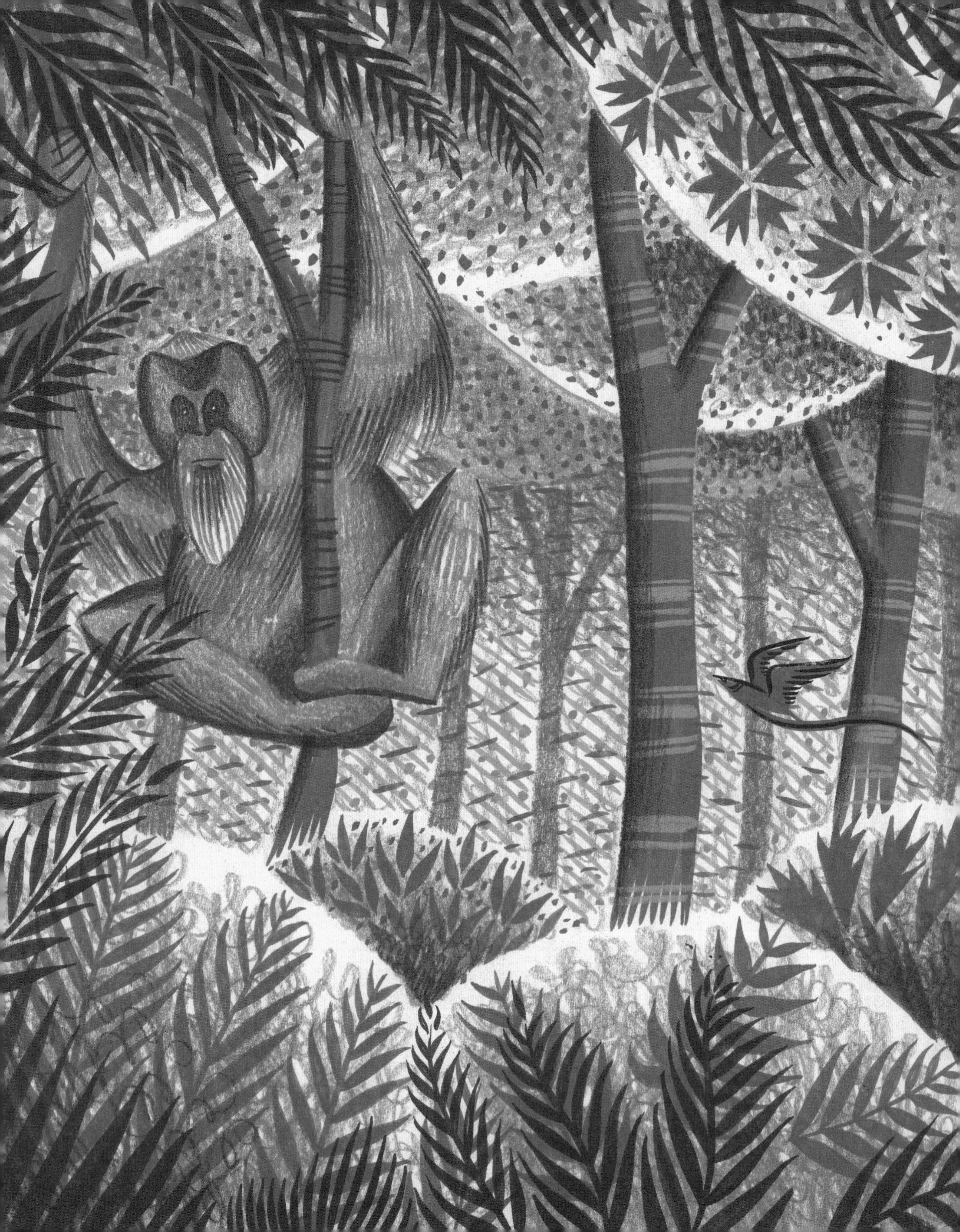

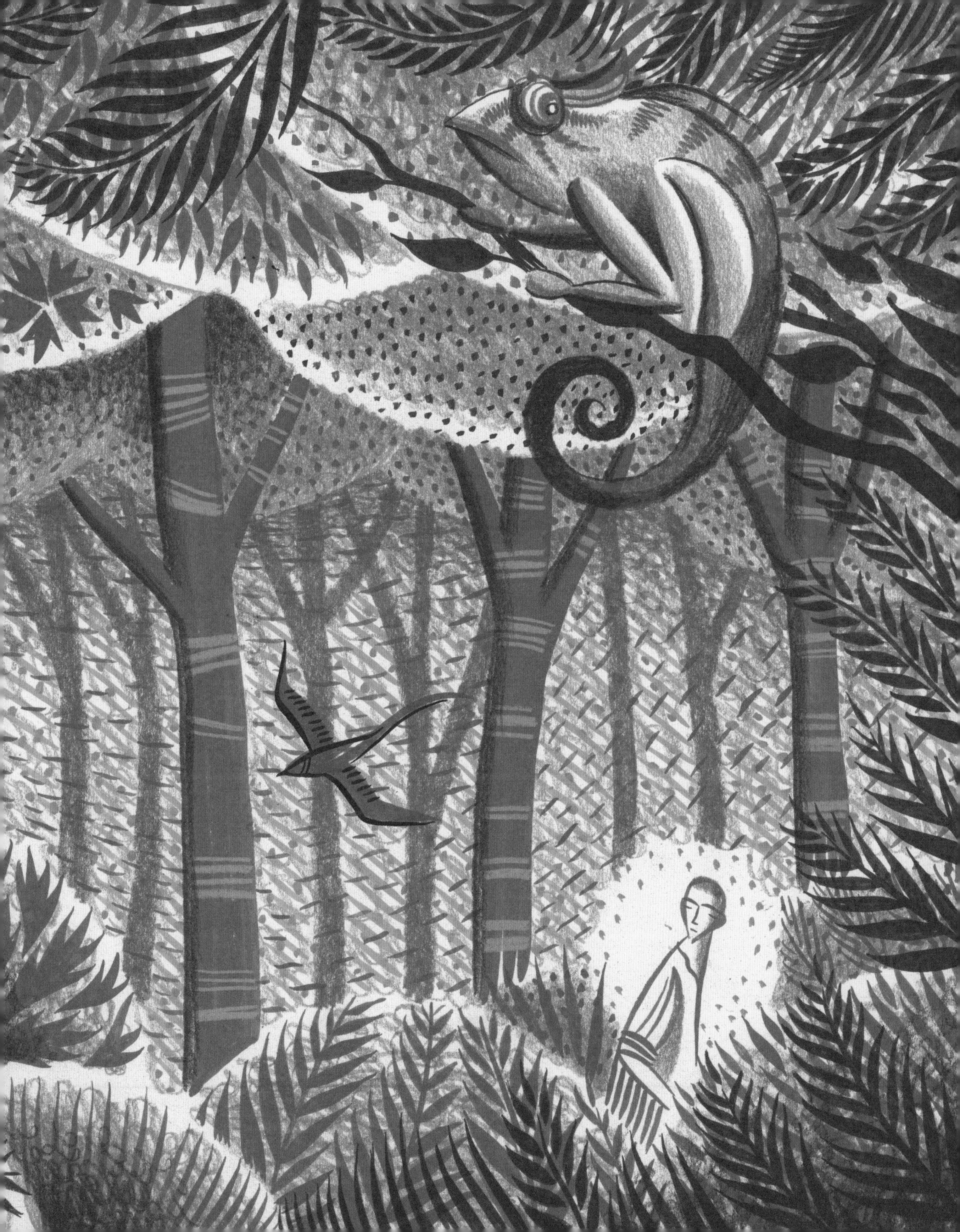

I have seen

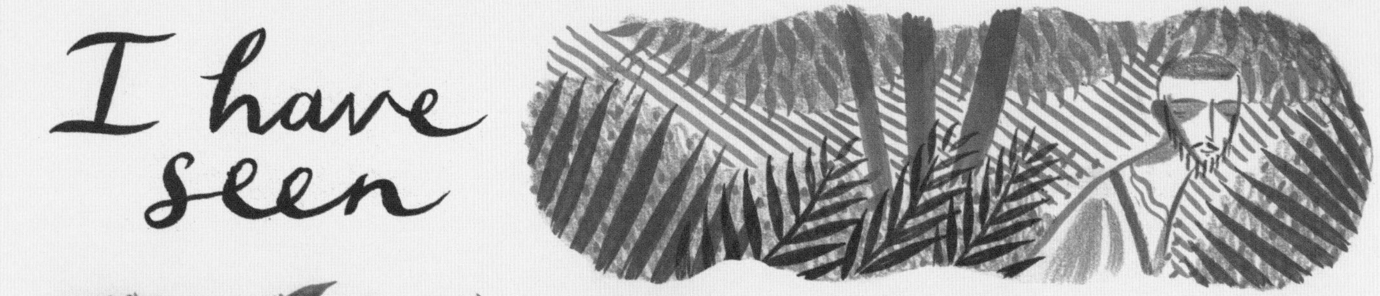

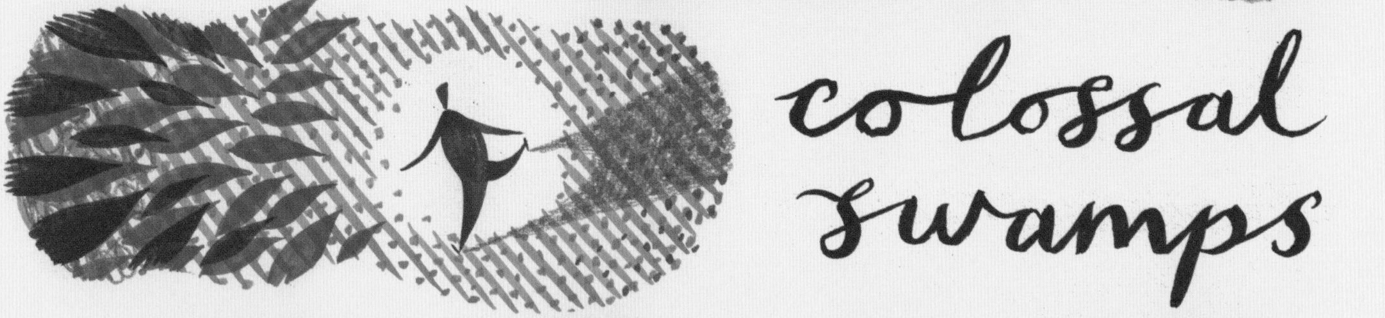

colossal swamps

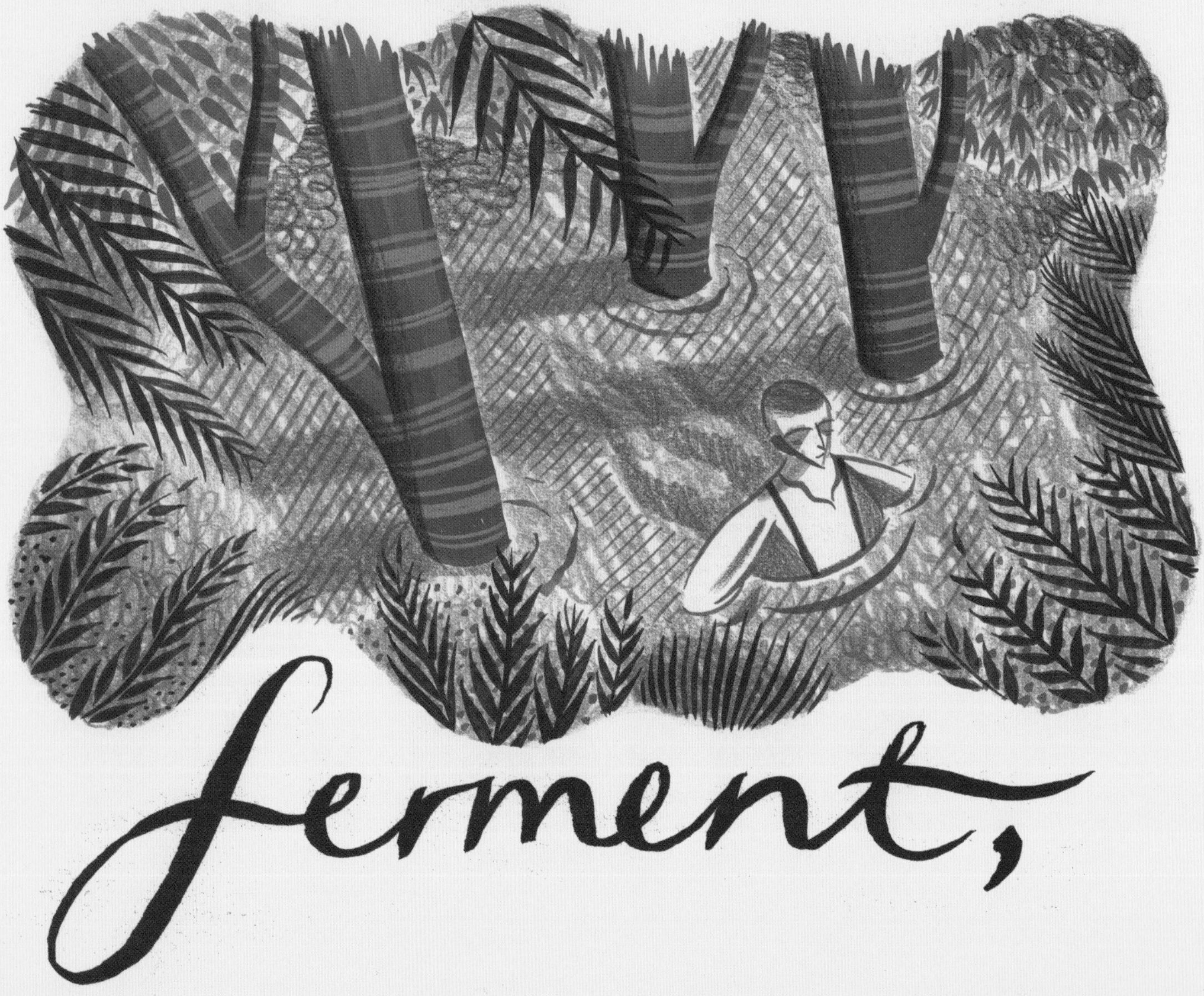

ferment,

traps

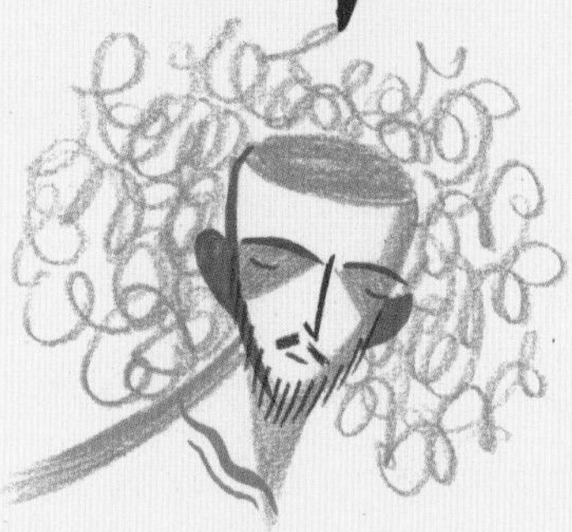

where,

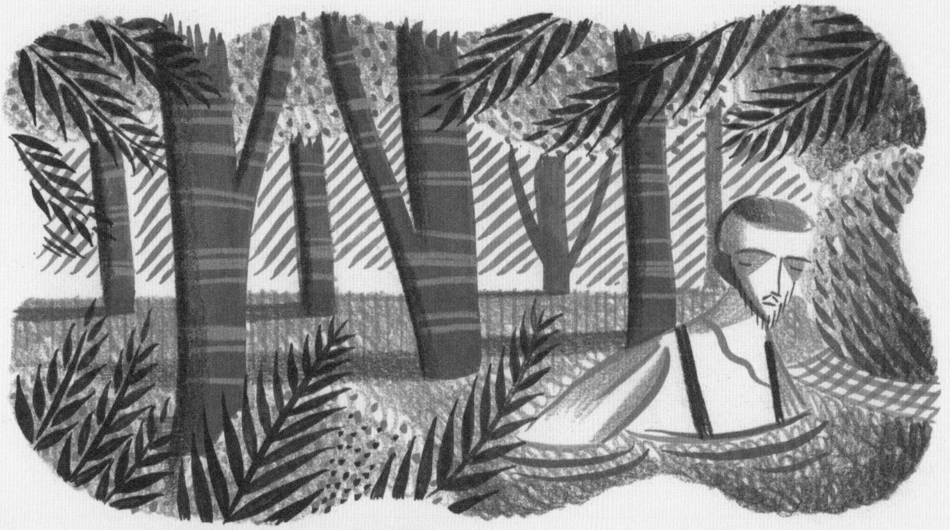

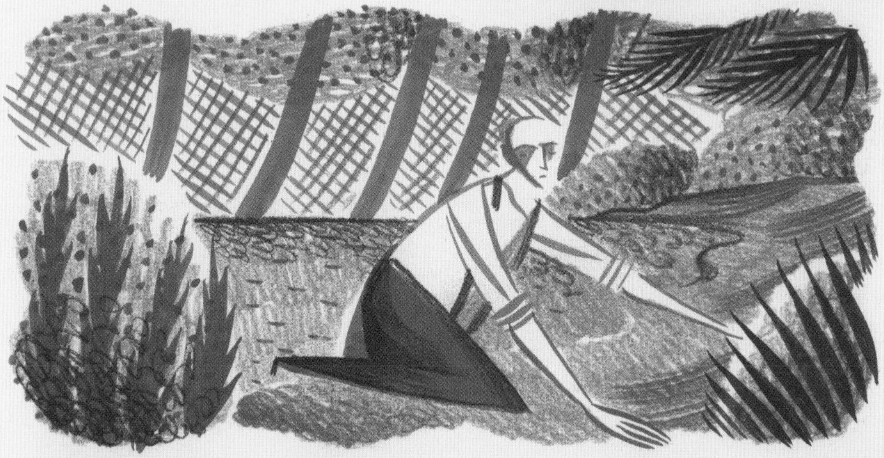

in the rushes,

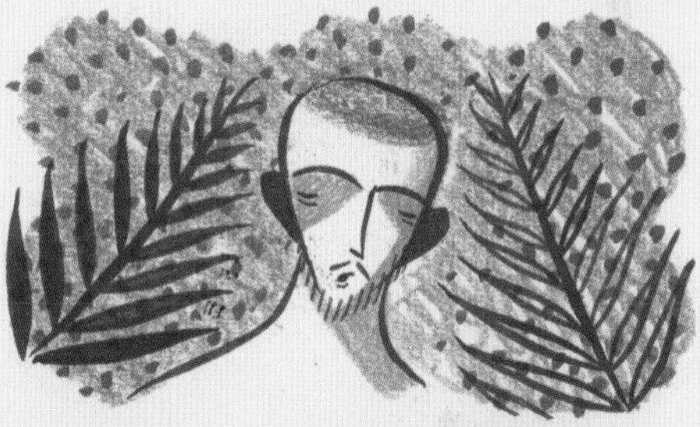

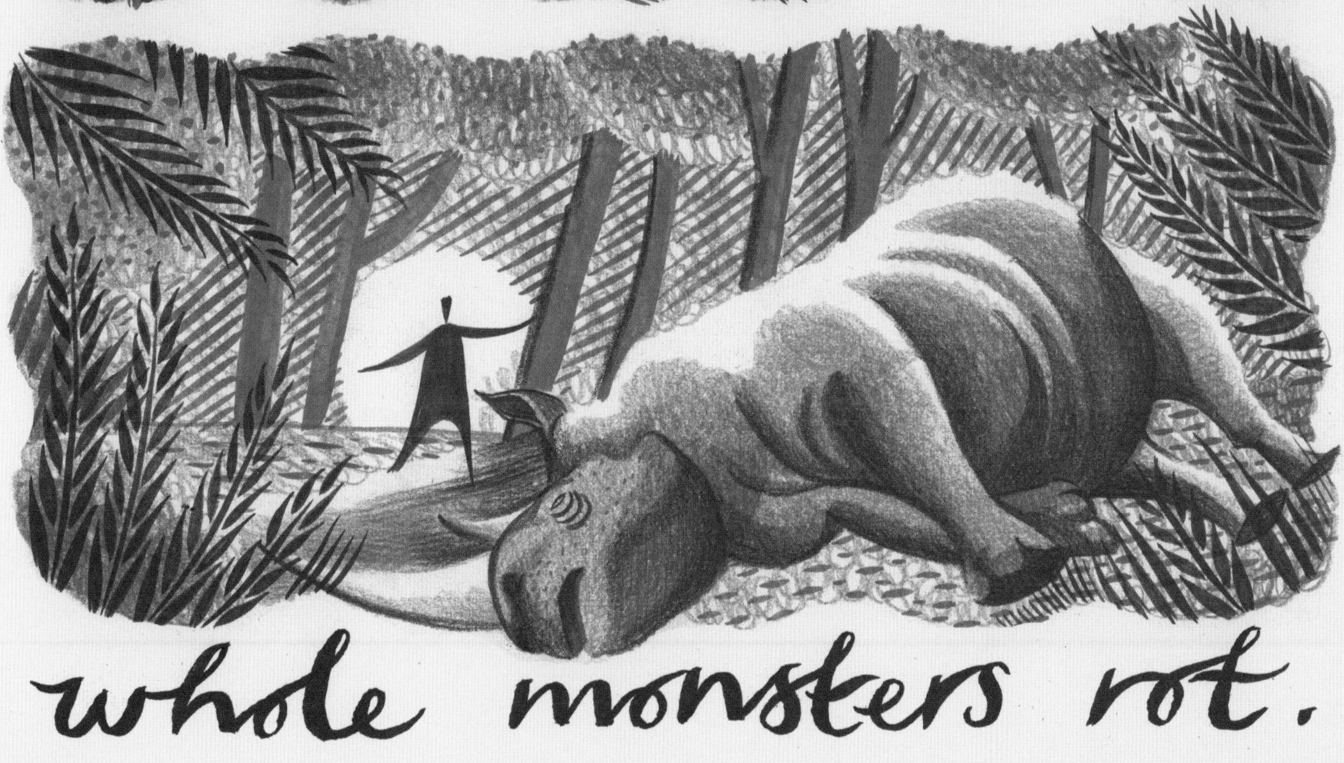

whole monsters rot.

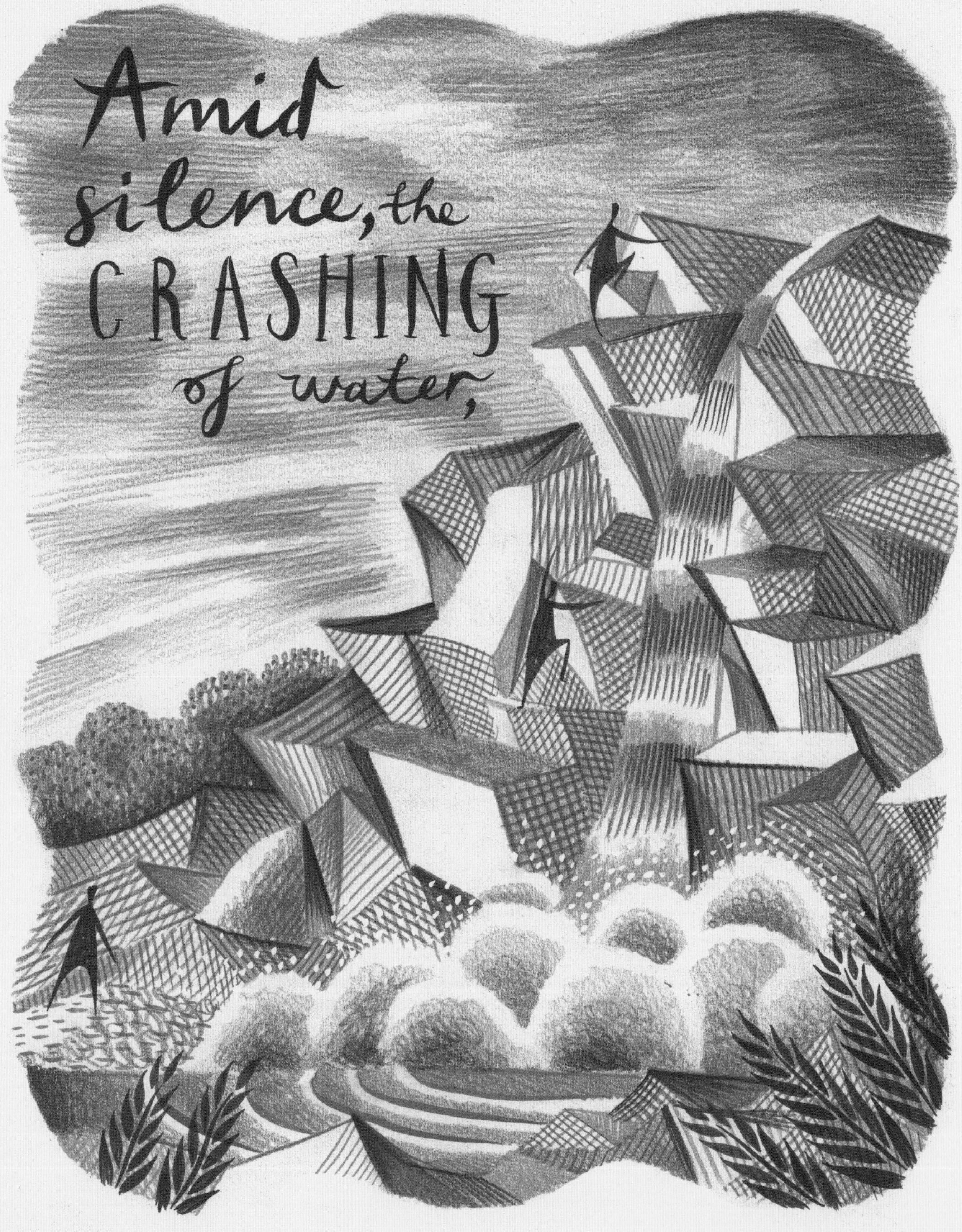
Amid
silence, the
CRASHING
of water,

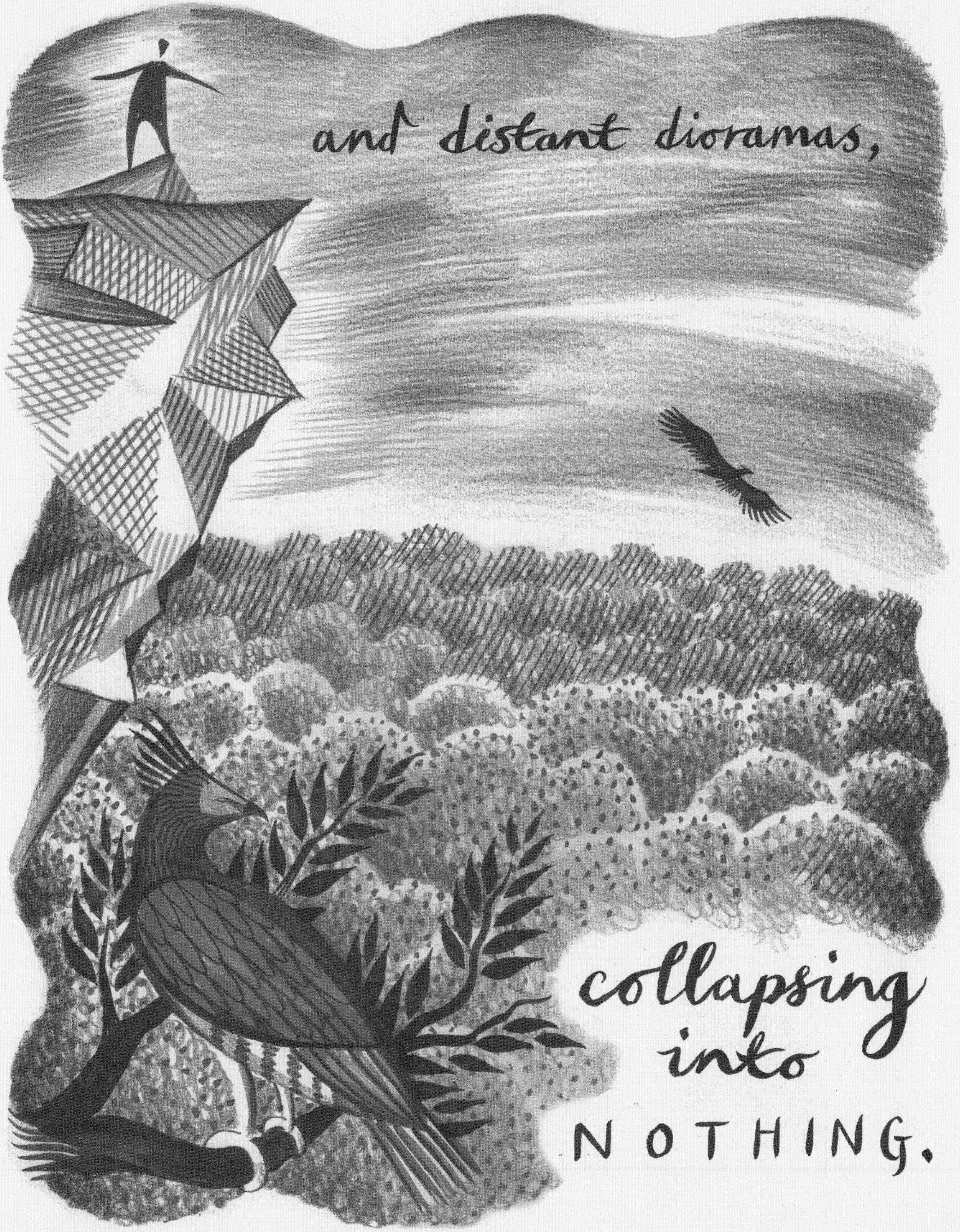
and distant dioramas,
collapsing
into
NOTHING.

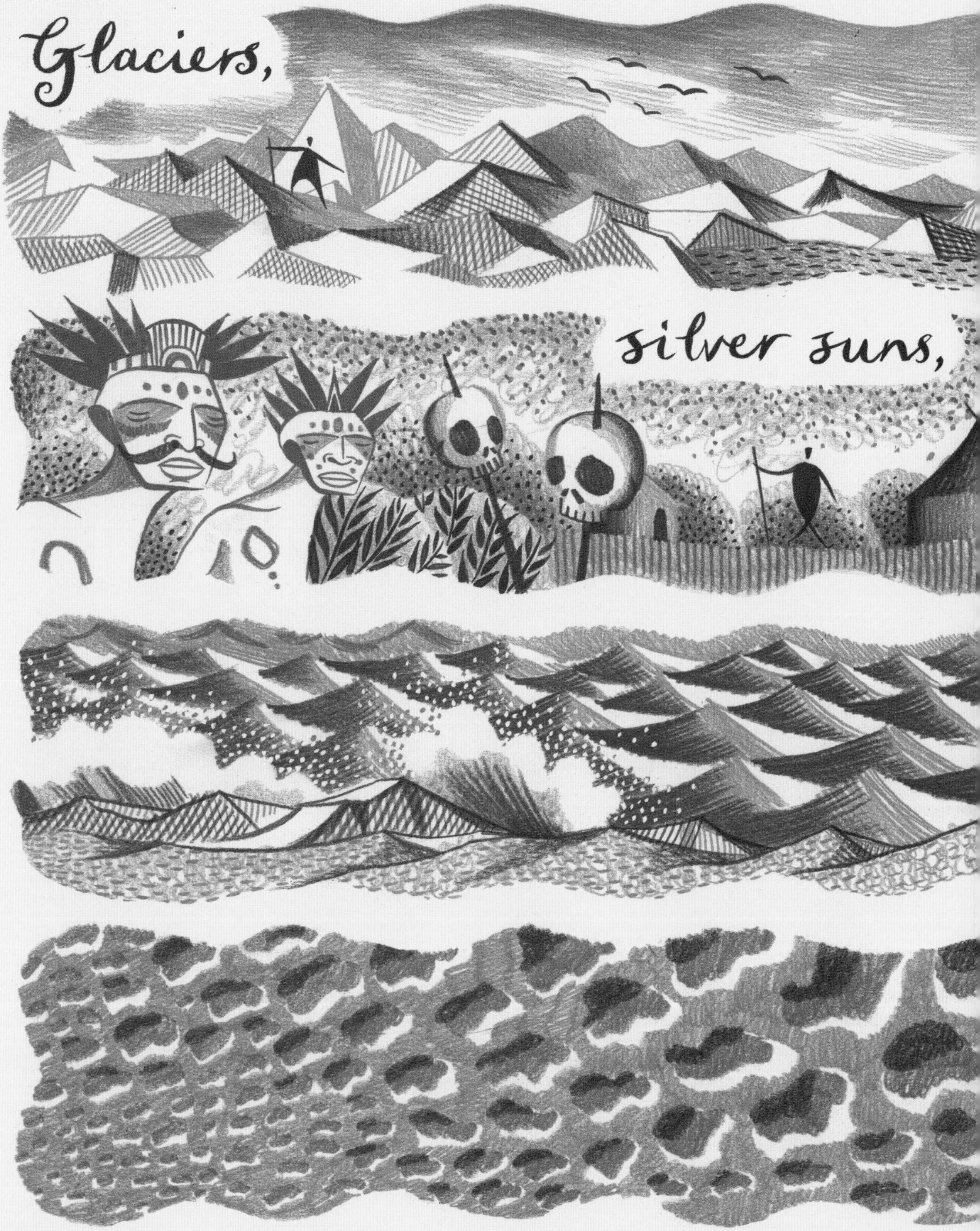
Glaciers,
silver suns,

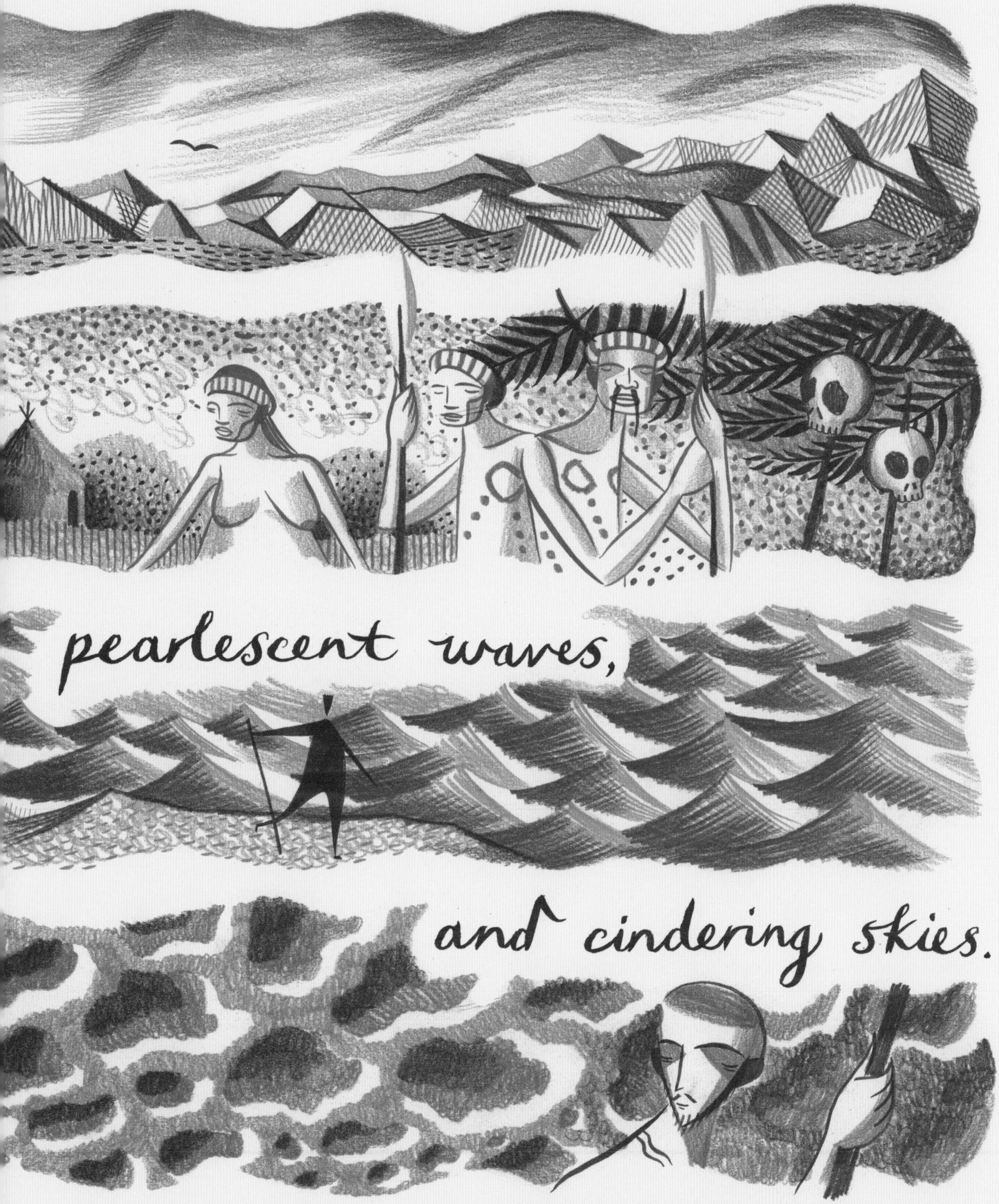
pearlescent waves,
and cindering skies.

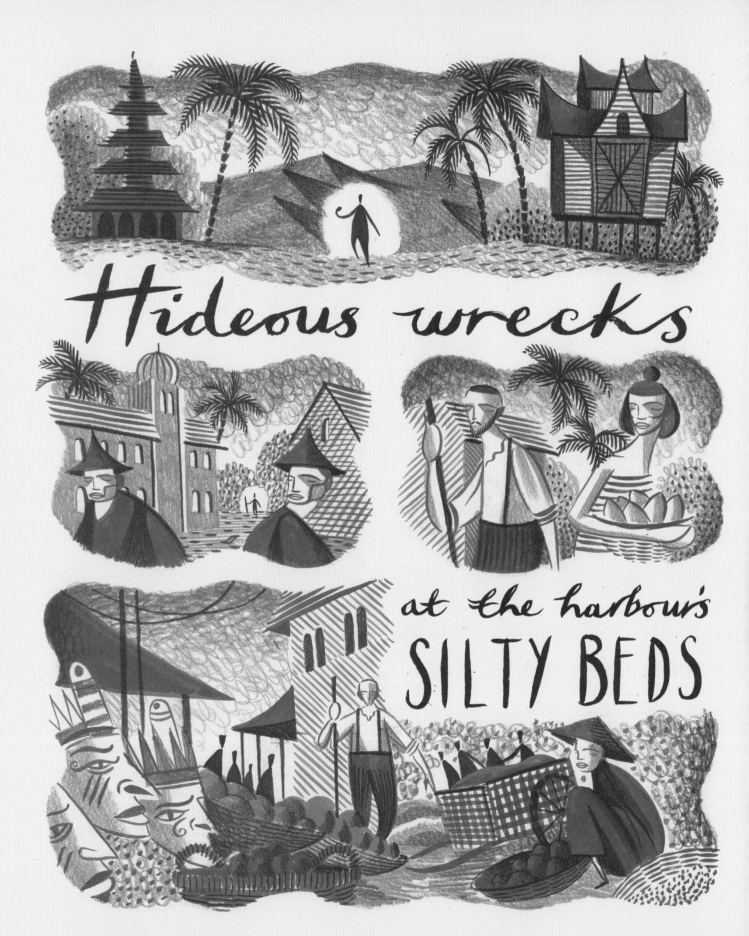

Hideous wrecks at the harbour's SILTY BEDS

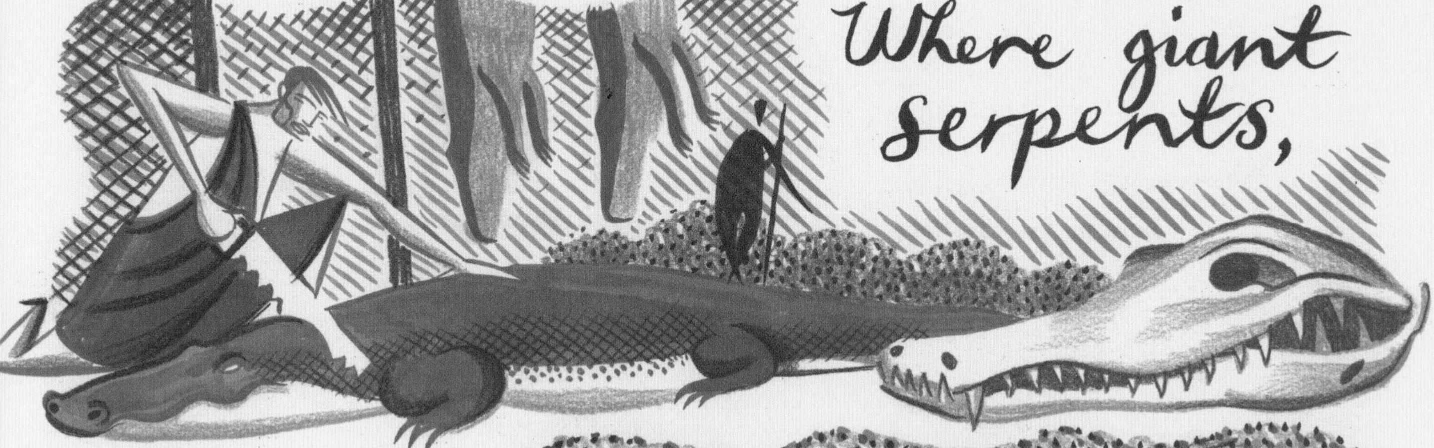

Where giant serpents,

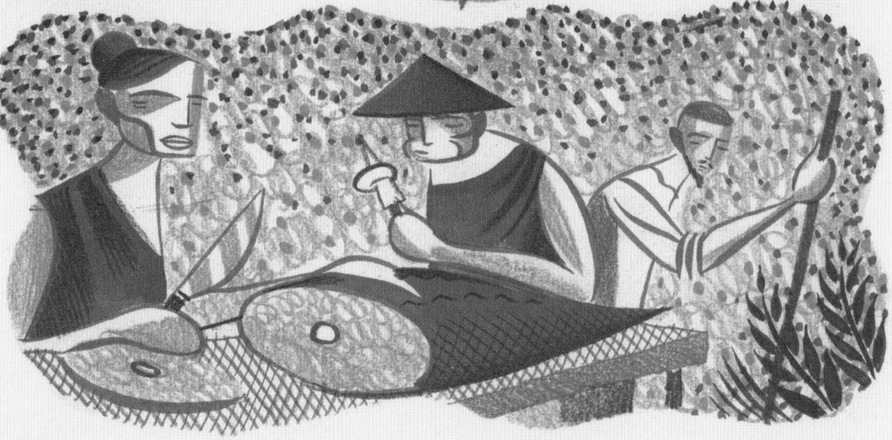

gorged by pampered parasites,

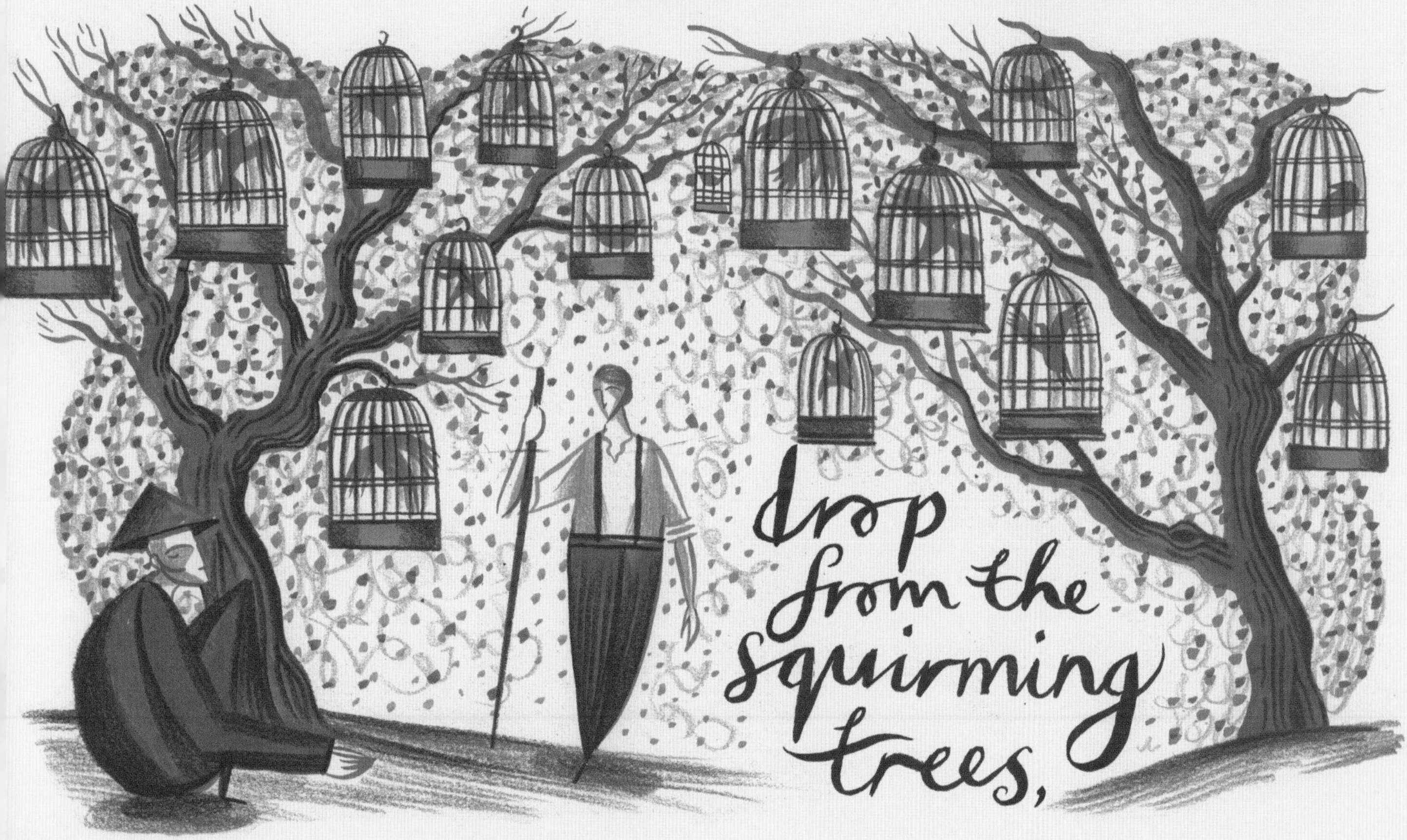

drop from the squirming trees,

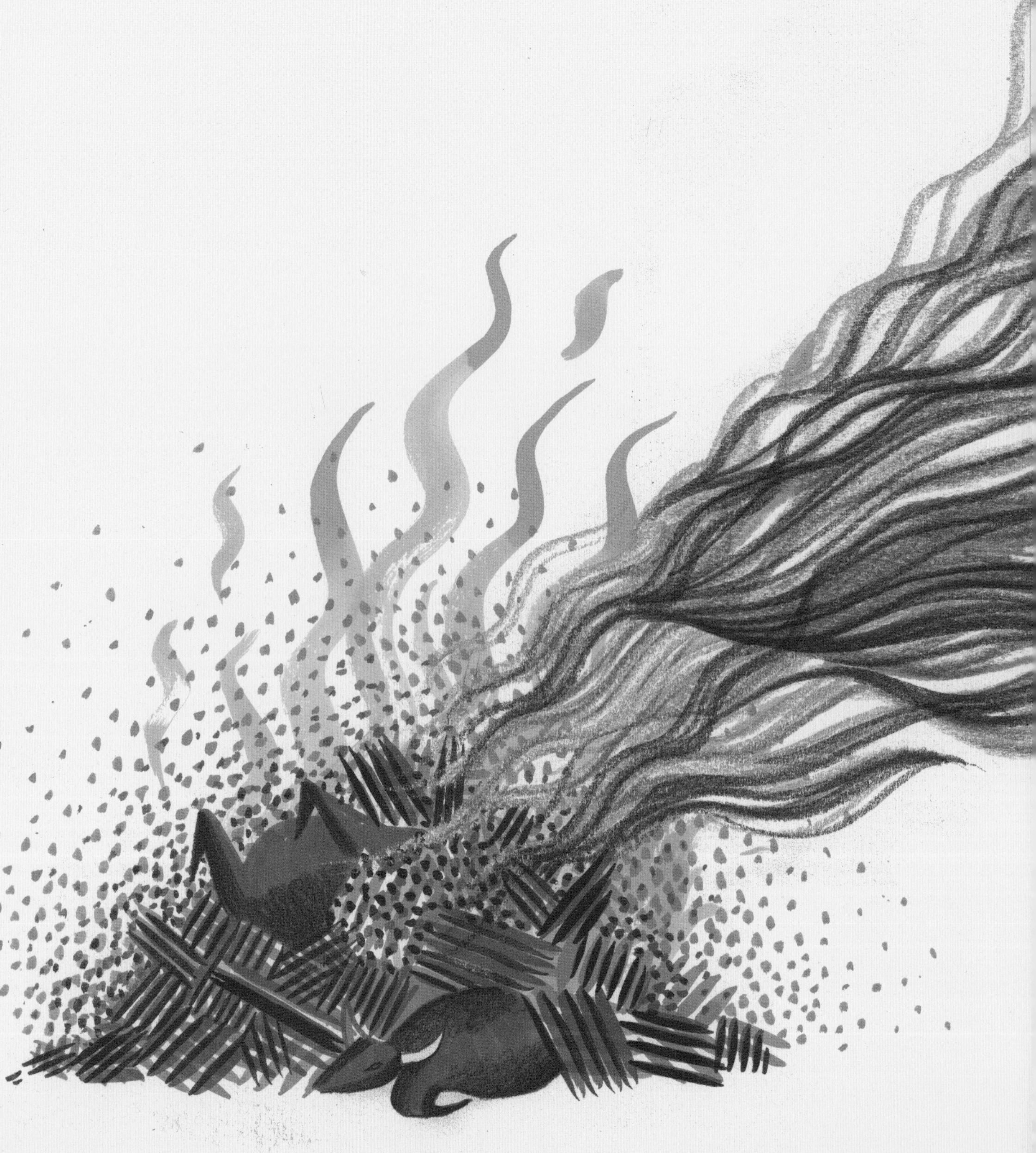

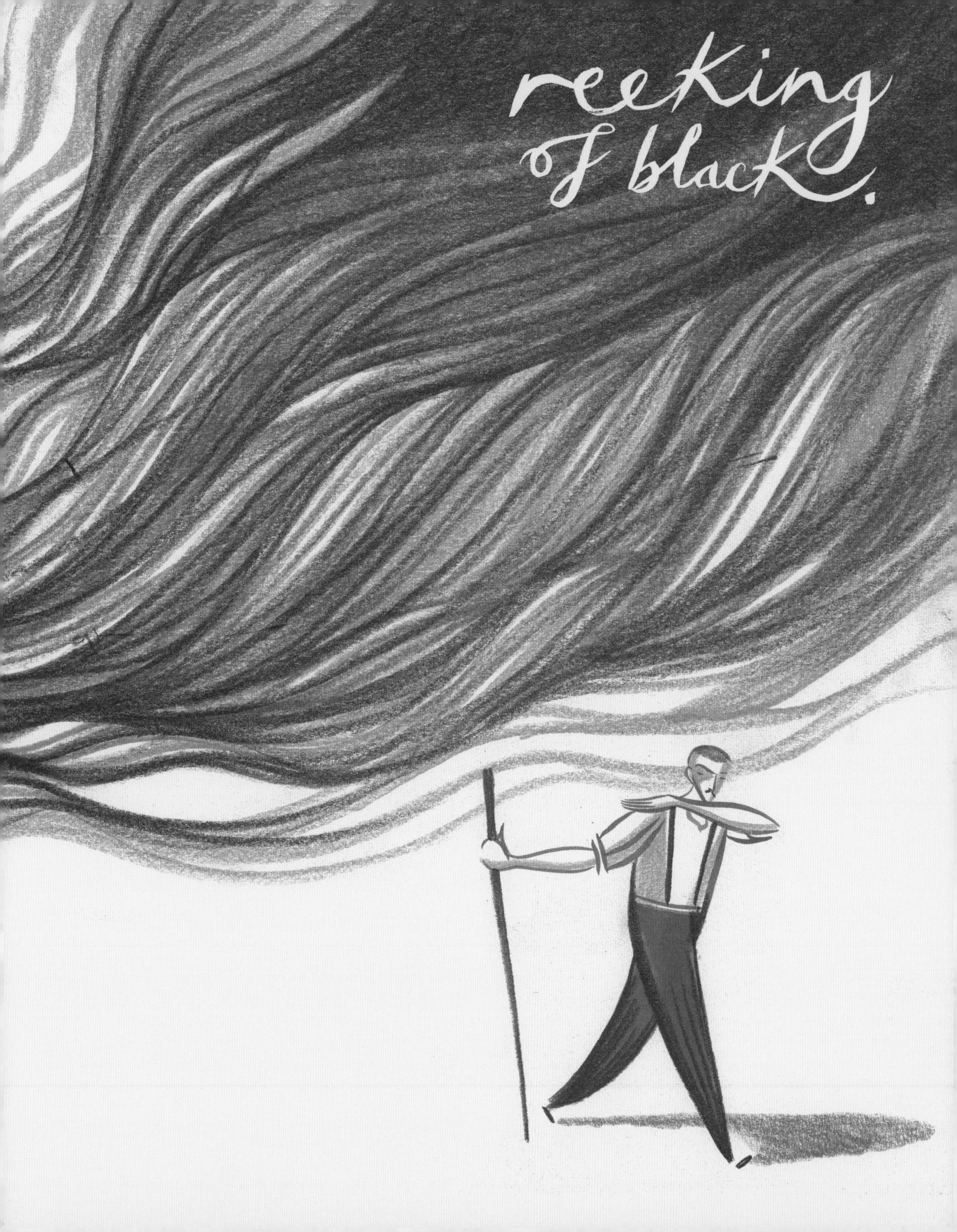
reeking
of black.

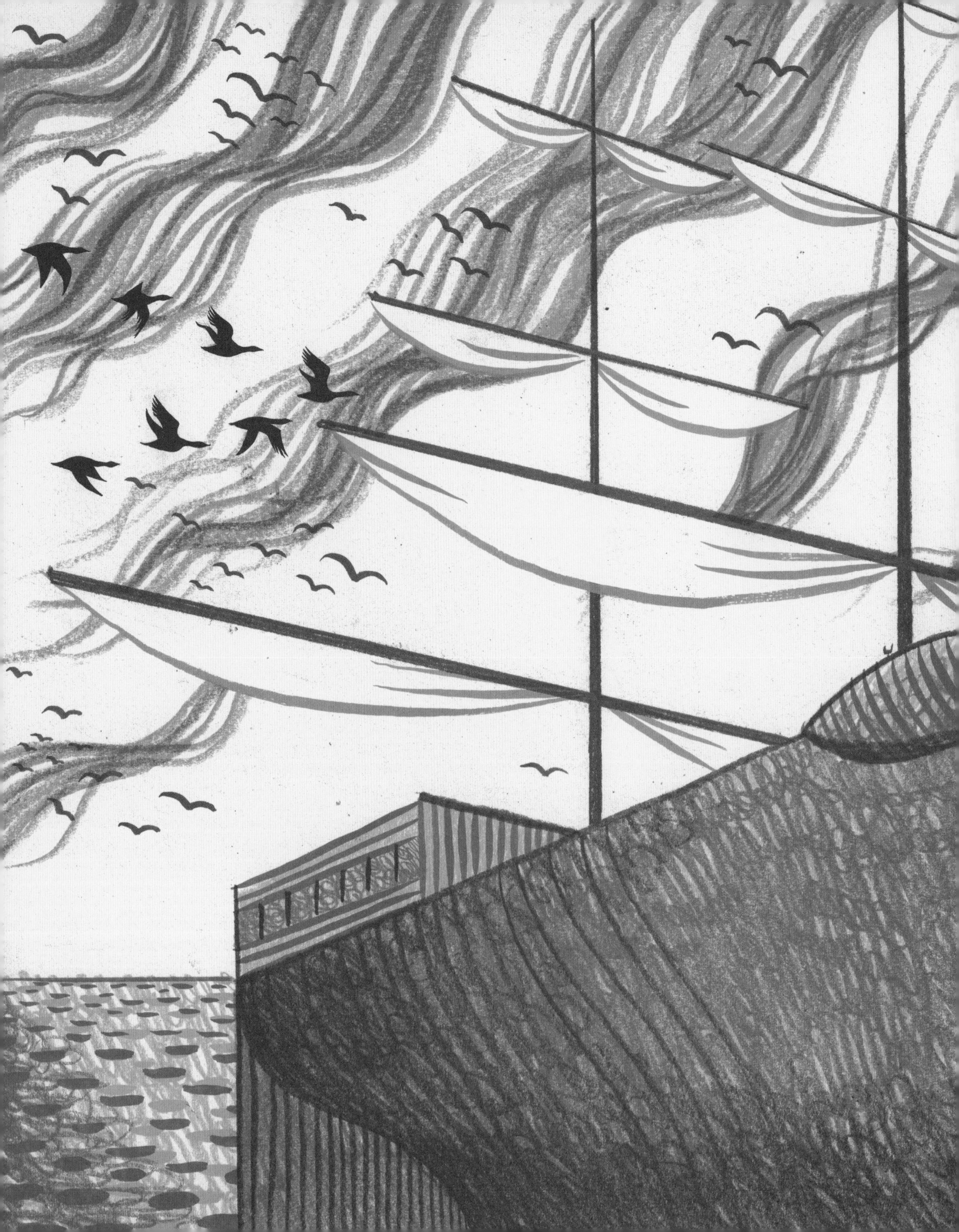

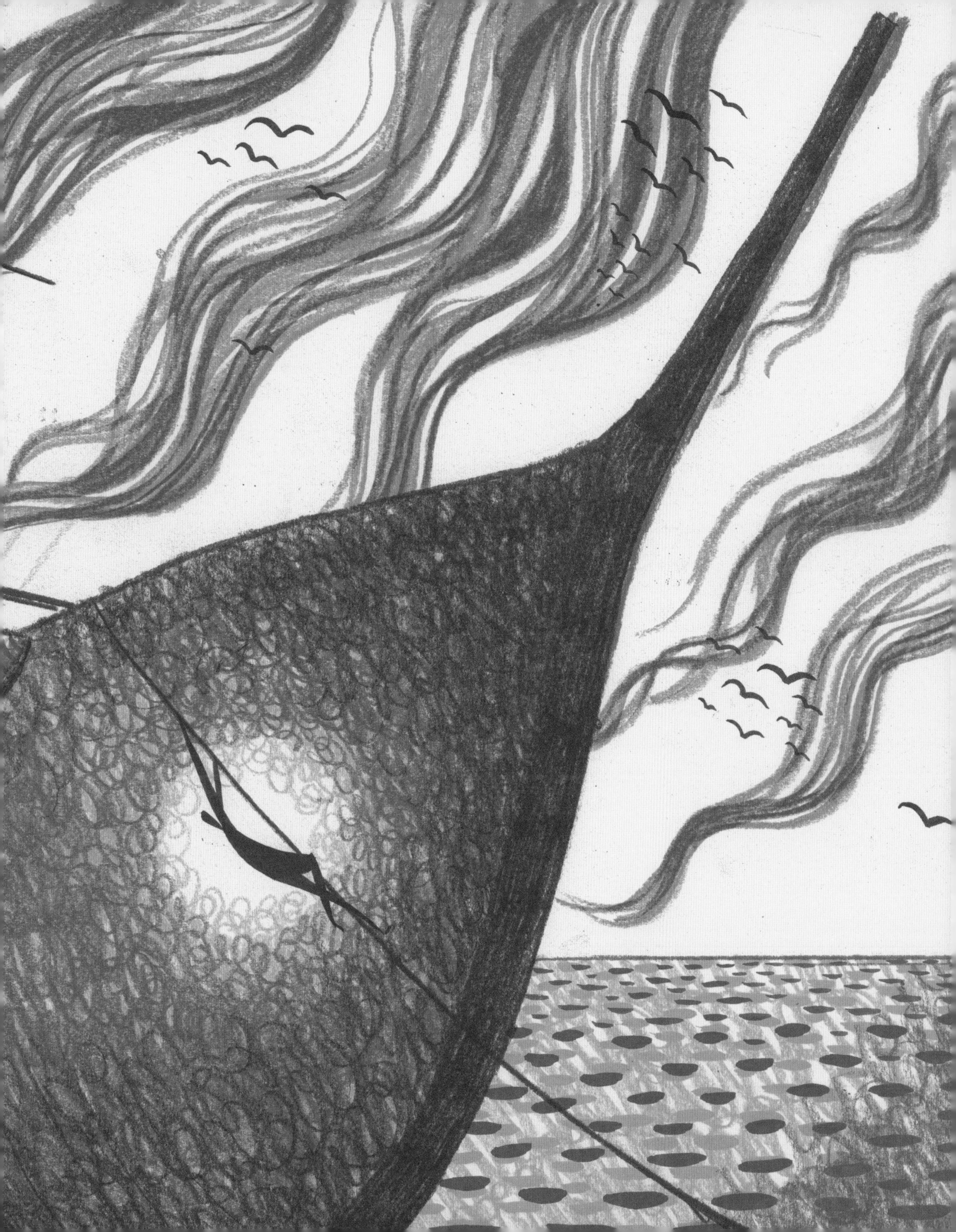

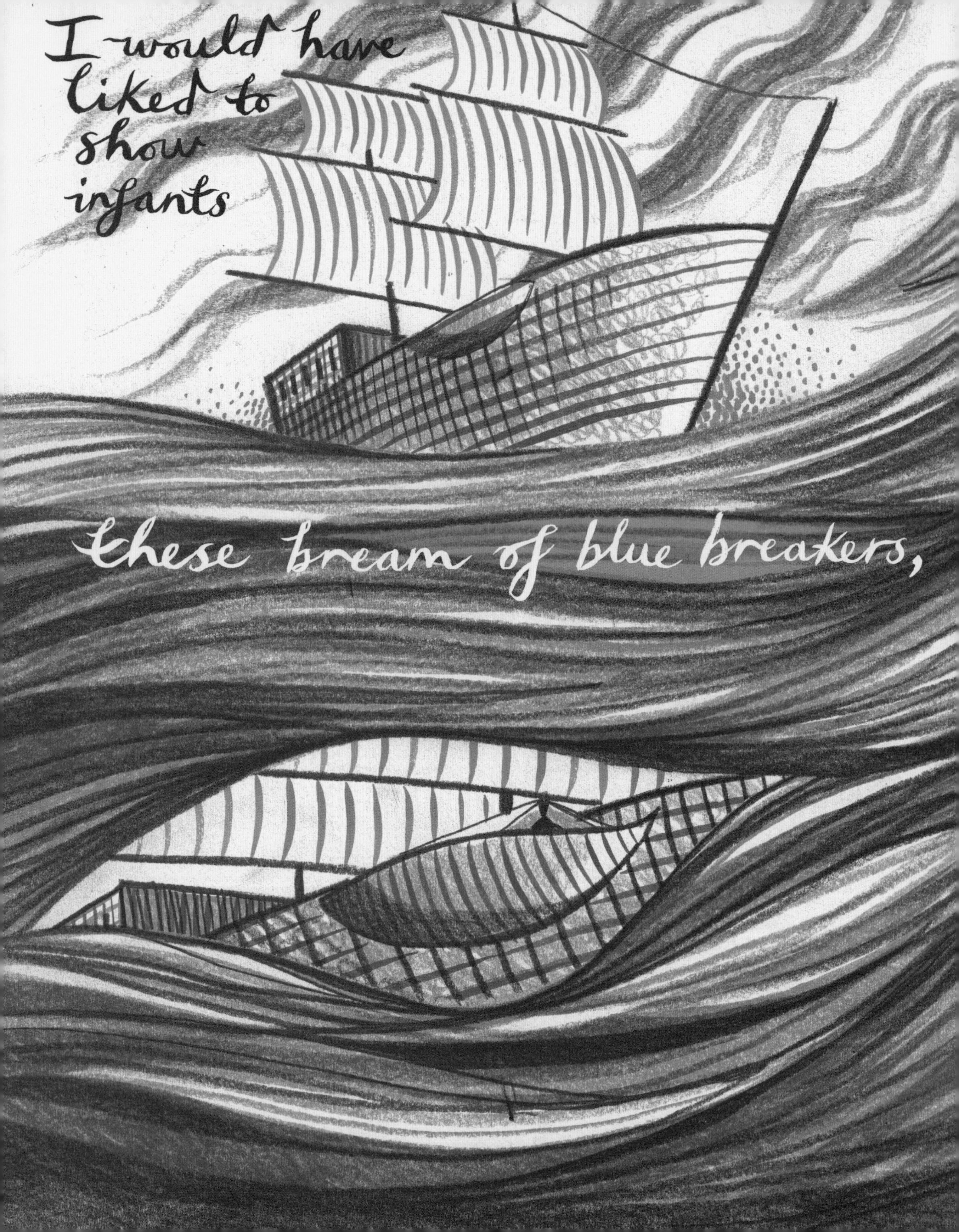
I would have liked to show infants
these bream of blue breakers,

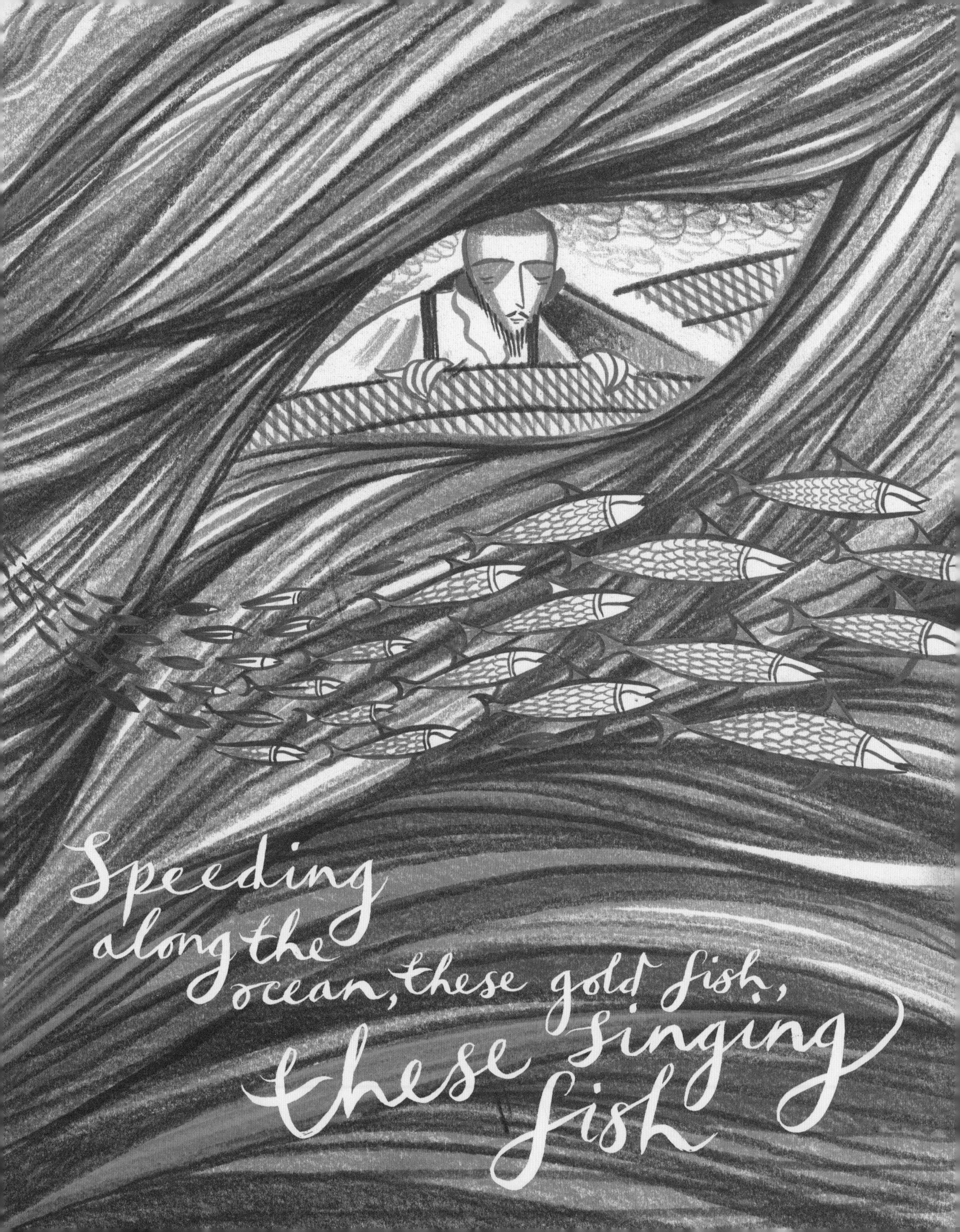

Speeding along the ocean, these gold fish, these singing fish

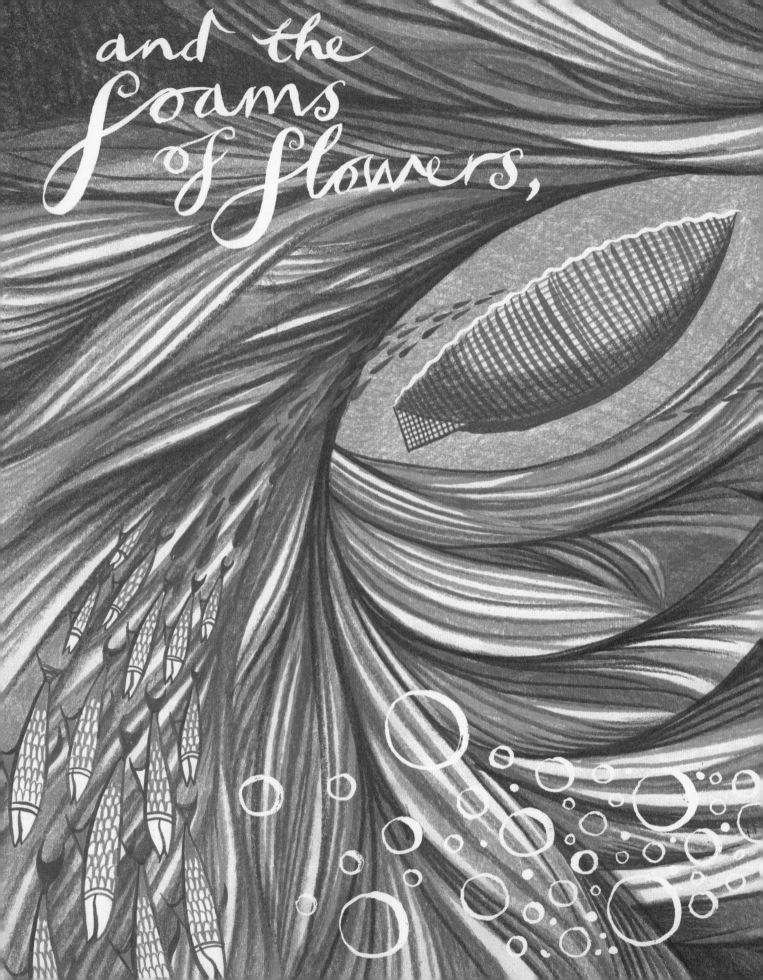

and the foams of flowers,

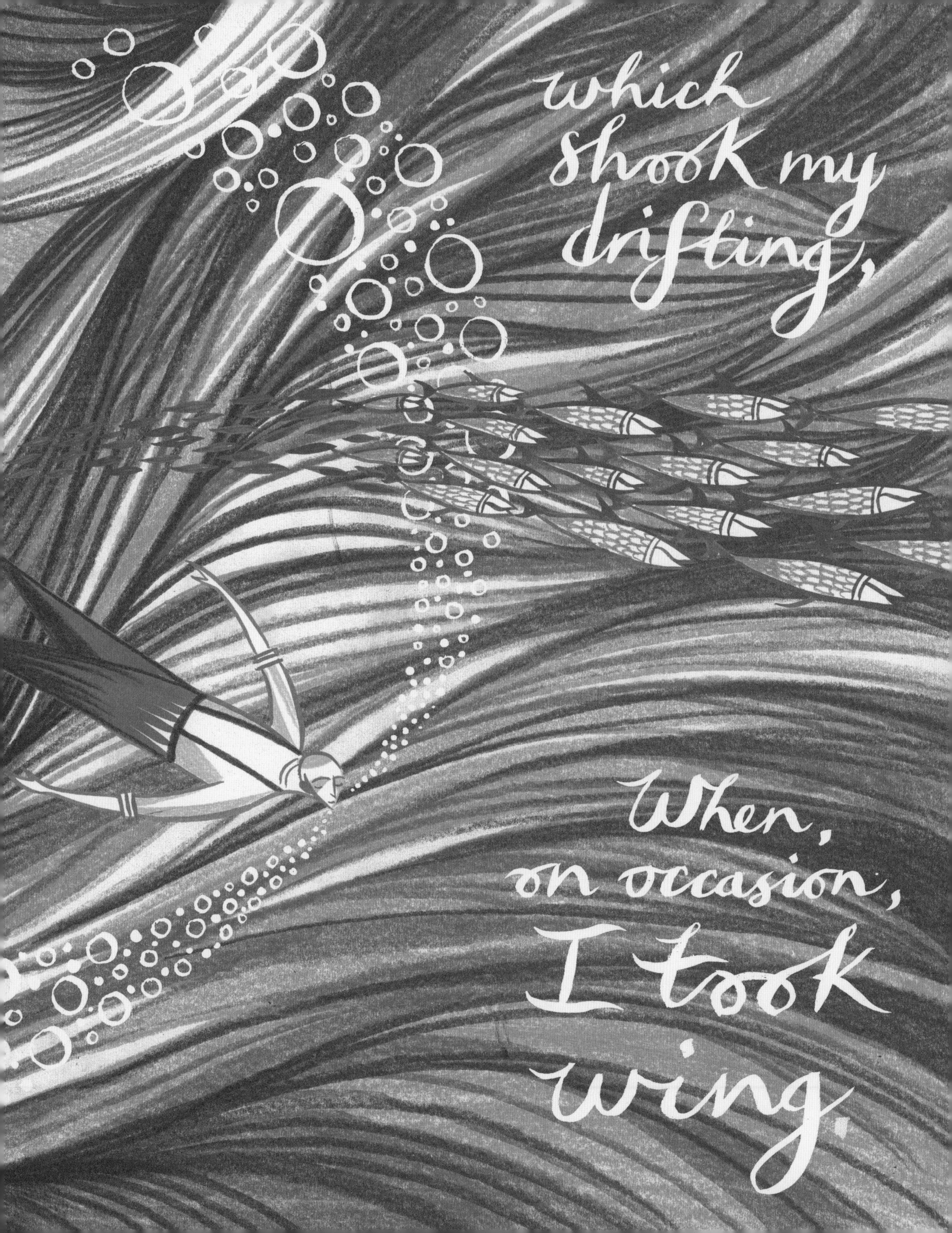
which shook my drifting,
When, on occasion, I took wing.

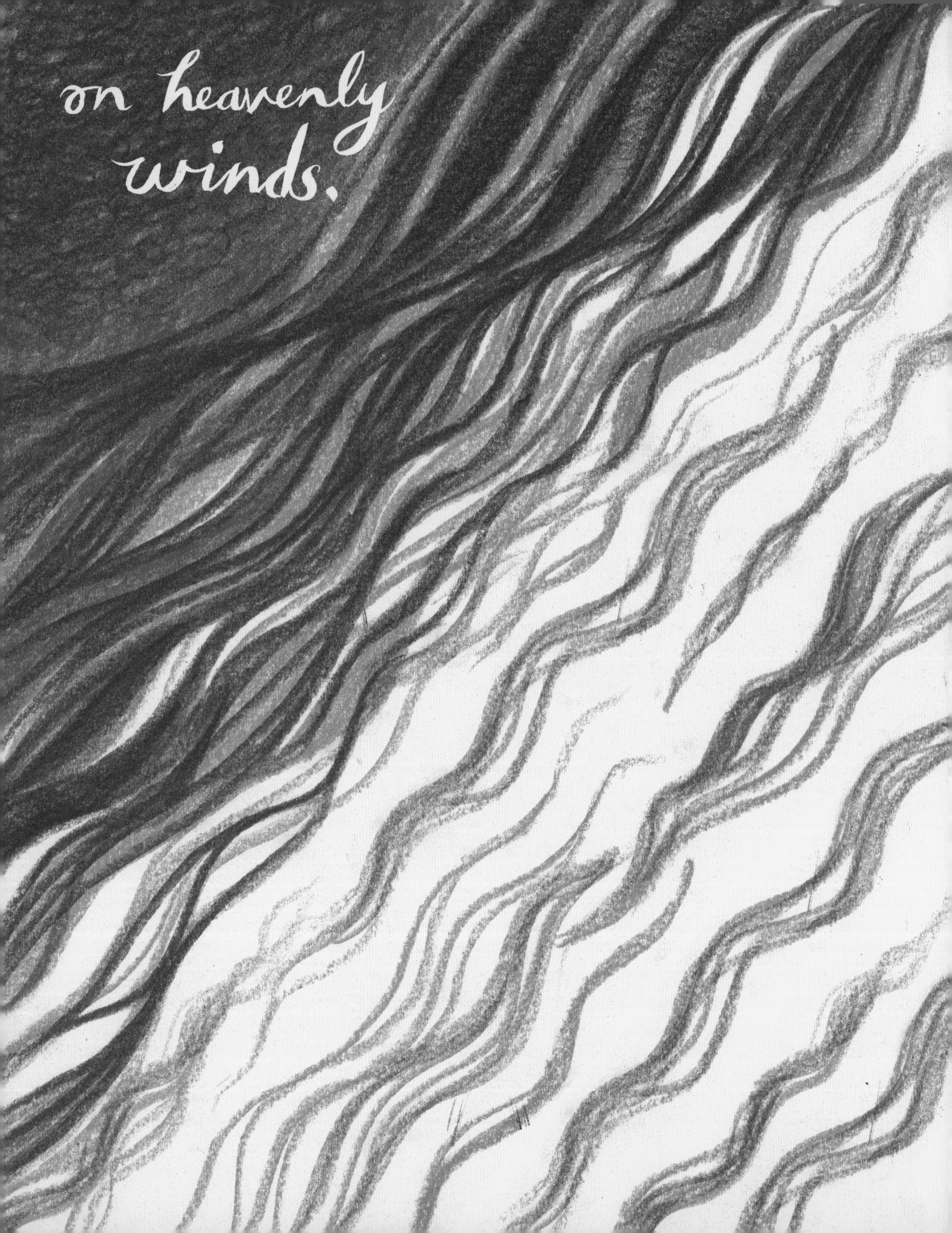
on heavenly
winds.

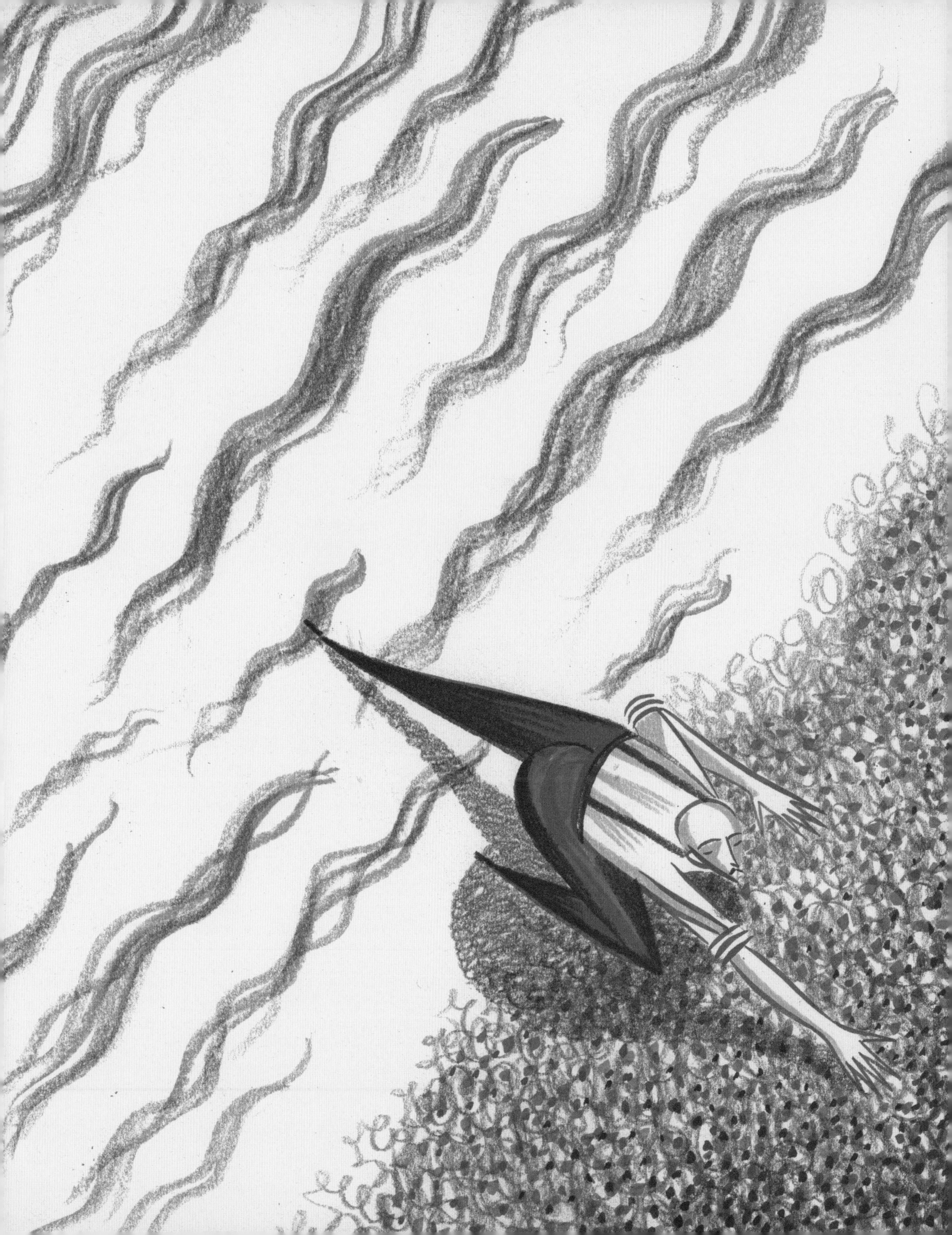

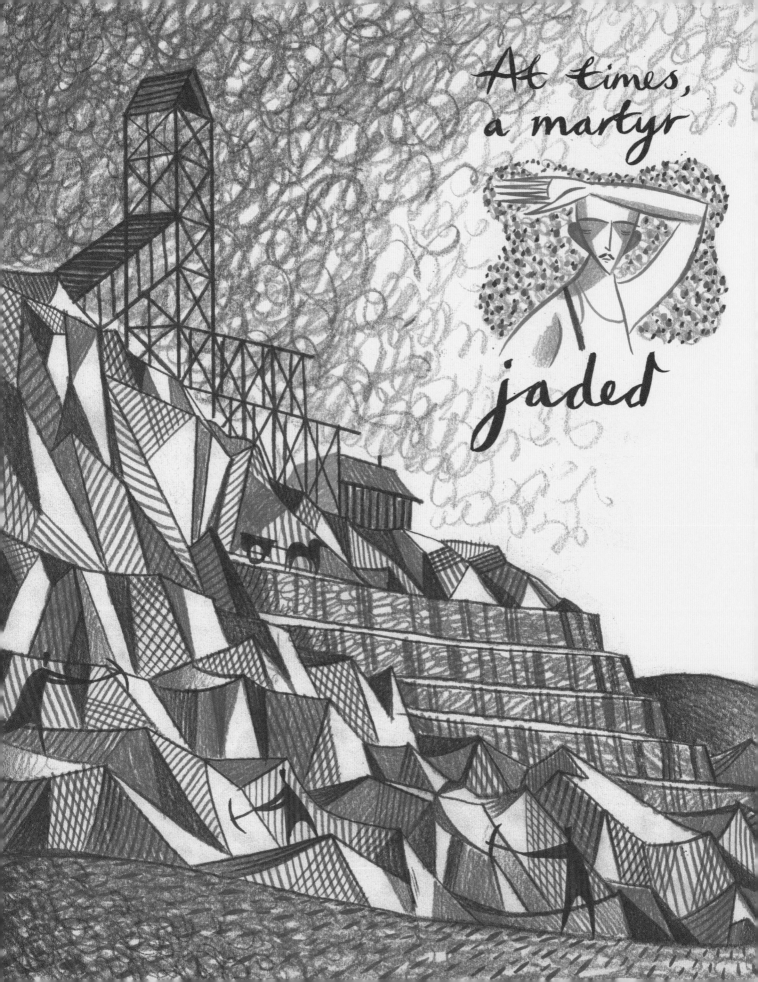

At times,
a martyr

jaded

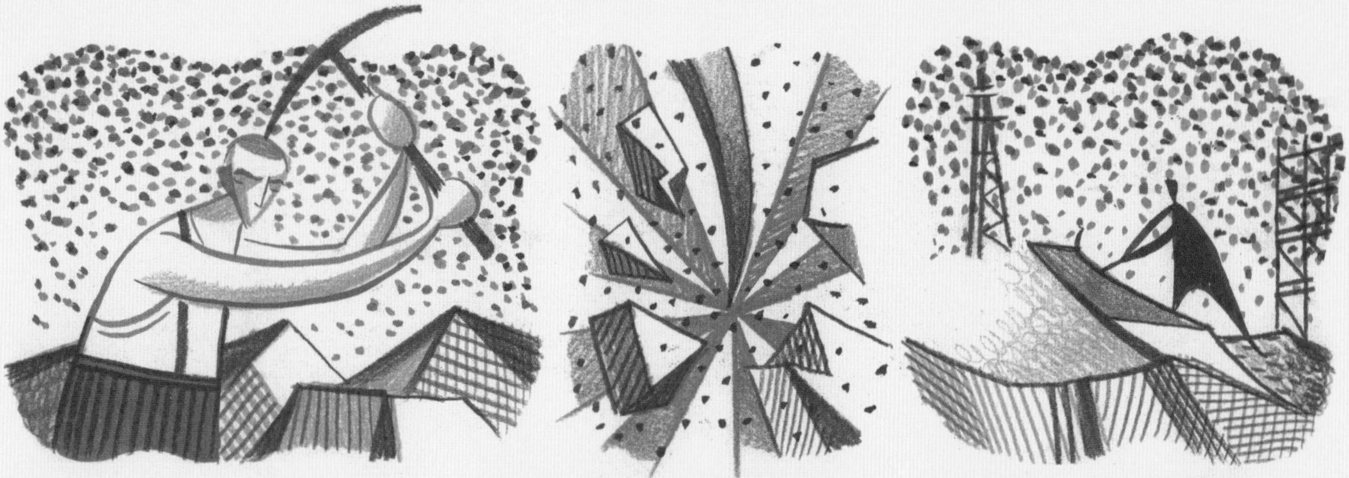

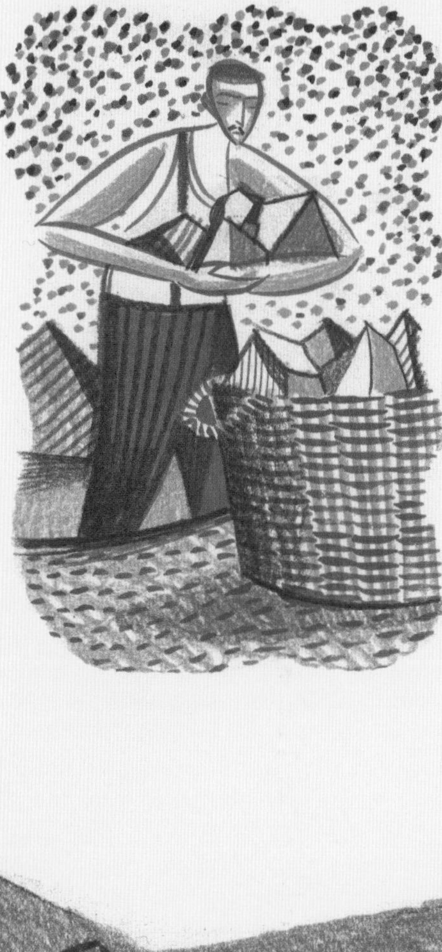

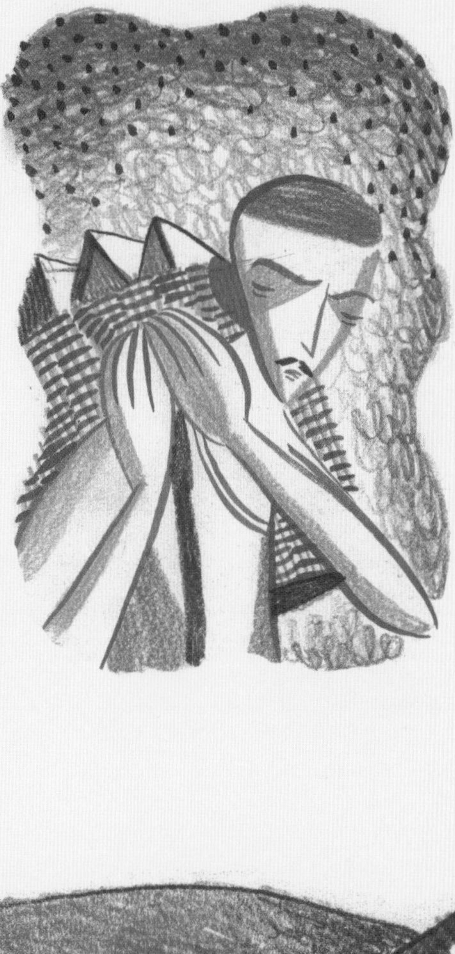

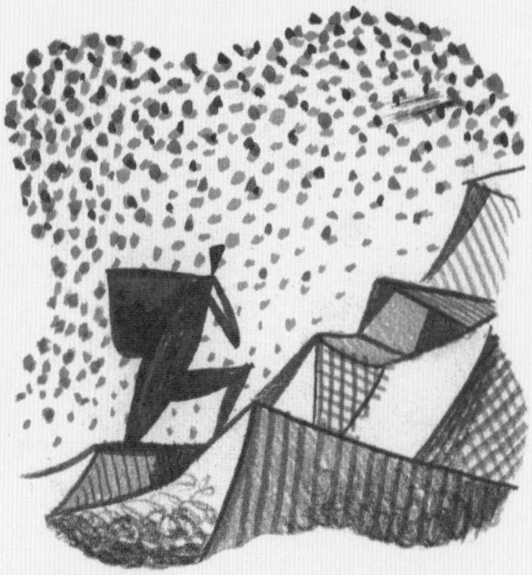

by poles
and zones,

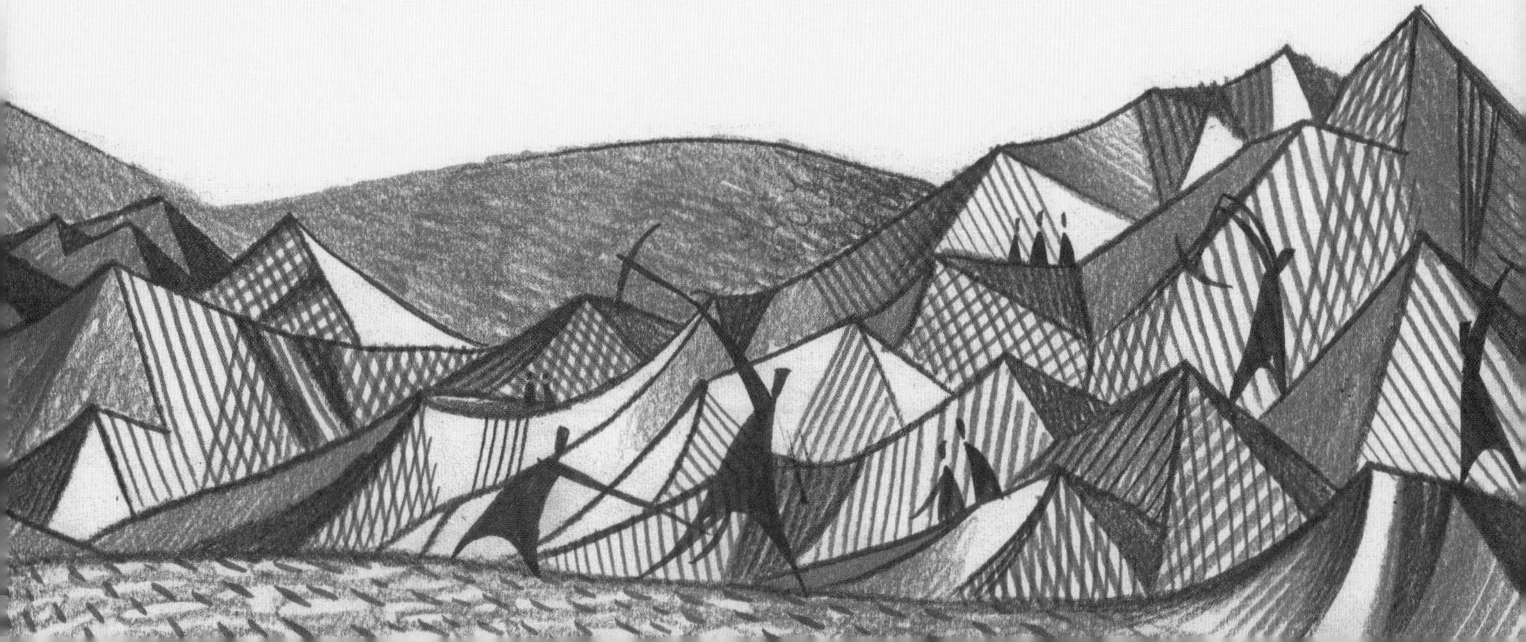

the sea,

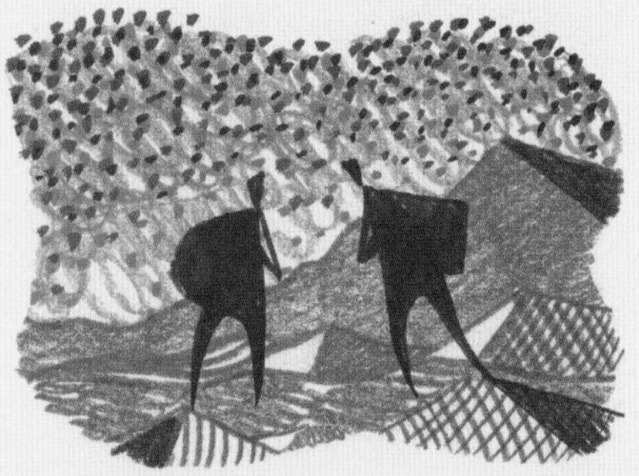

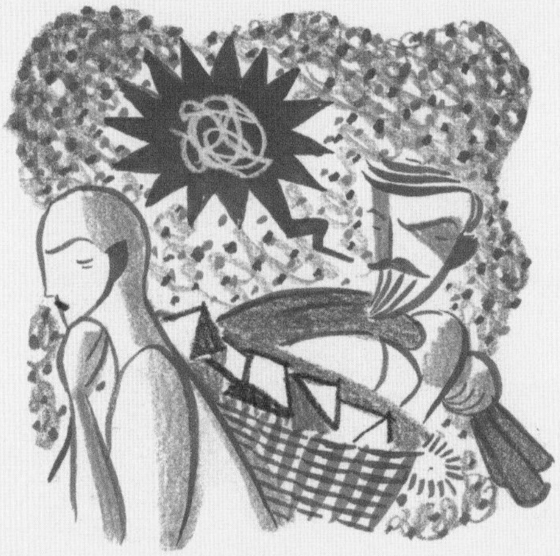

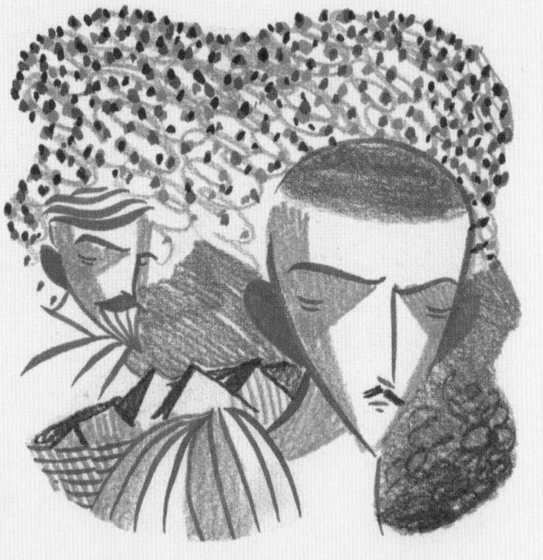

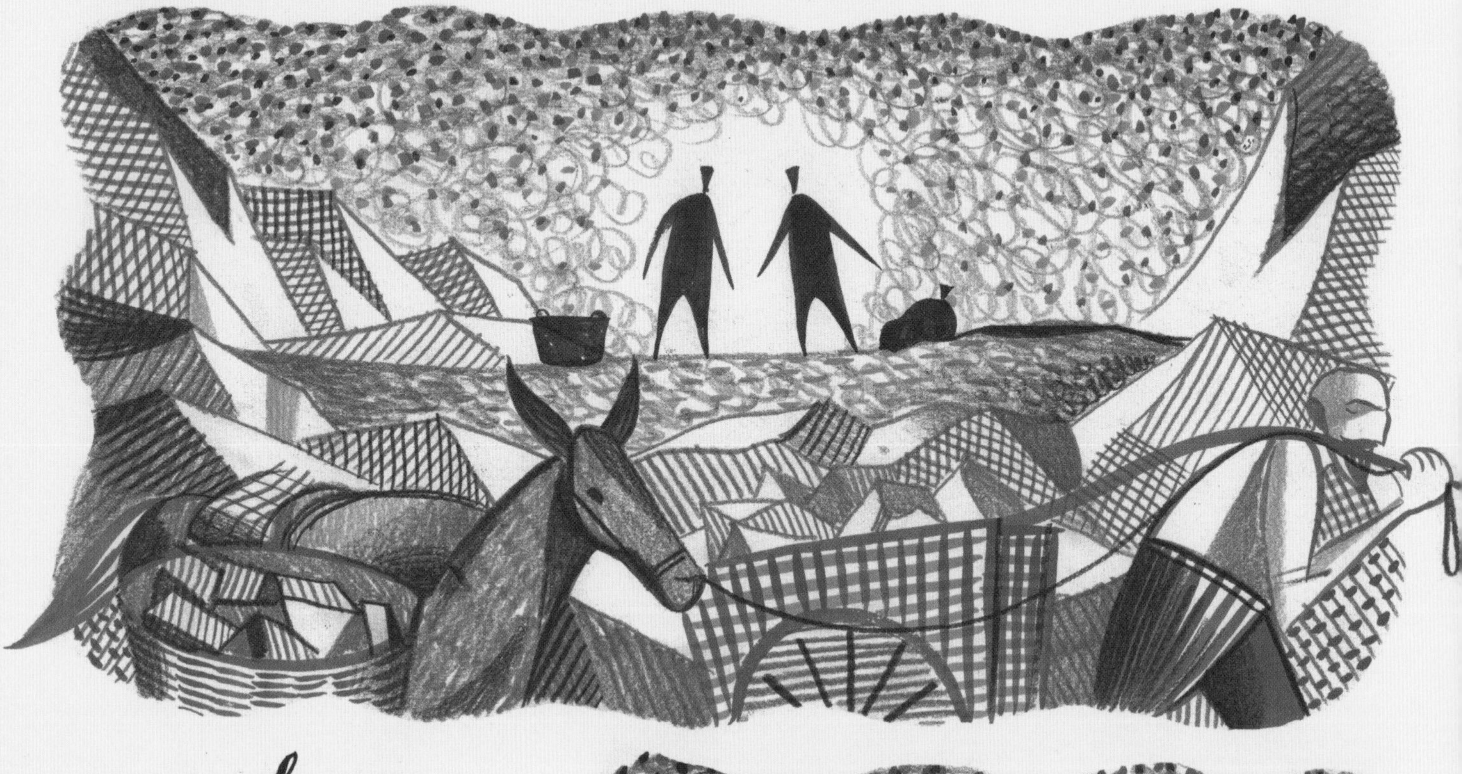

whose
SIGH
sweetened
my circuit,

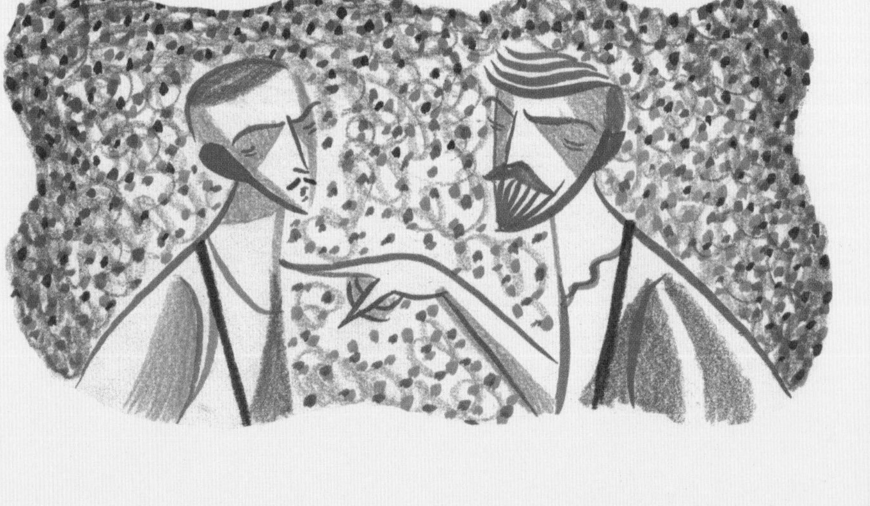

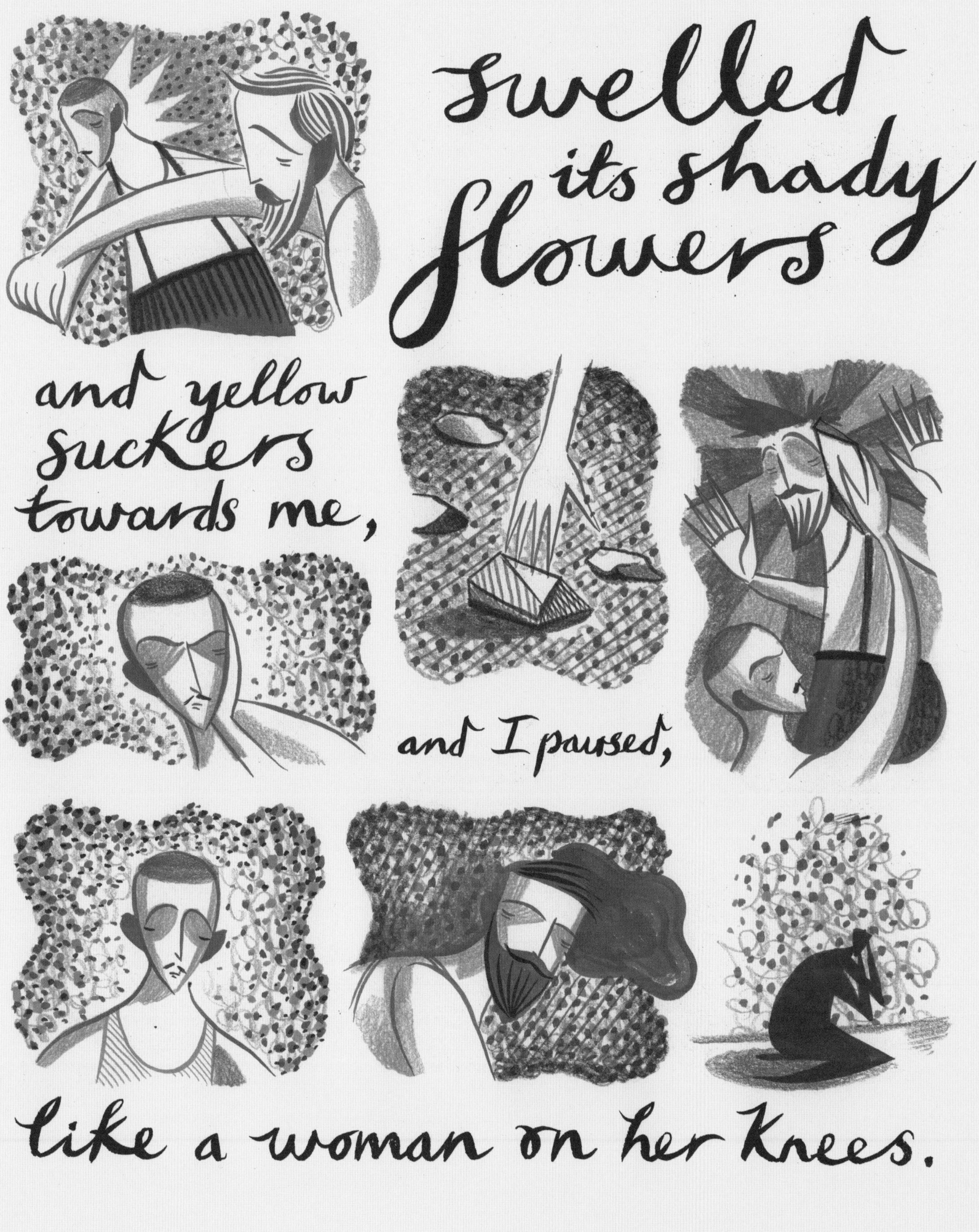
Swelled its shady flowers
and yellow suckers towards me,
and I paused,
like a woman on her knees.

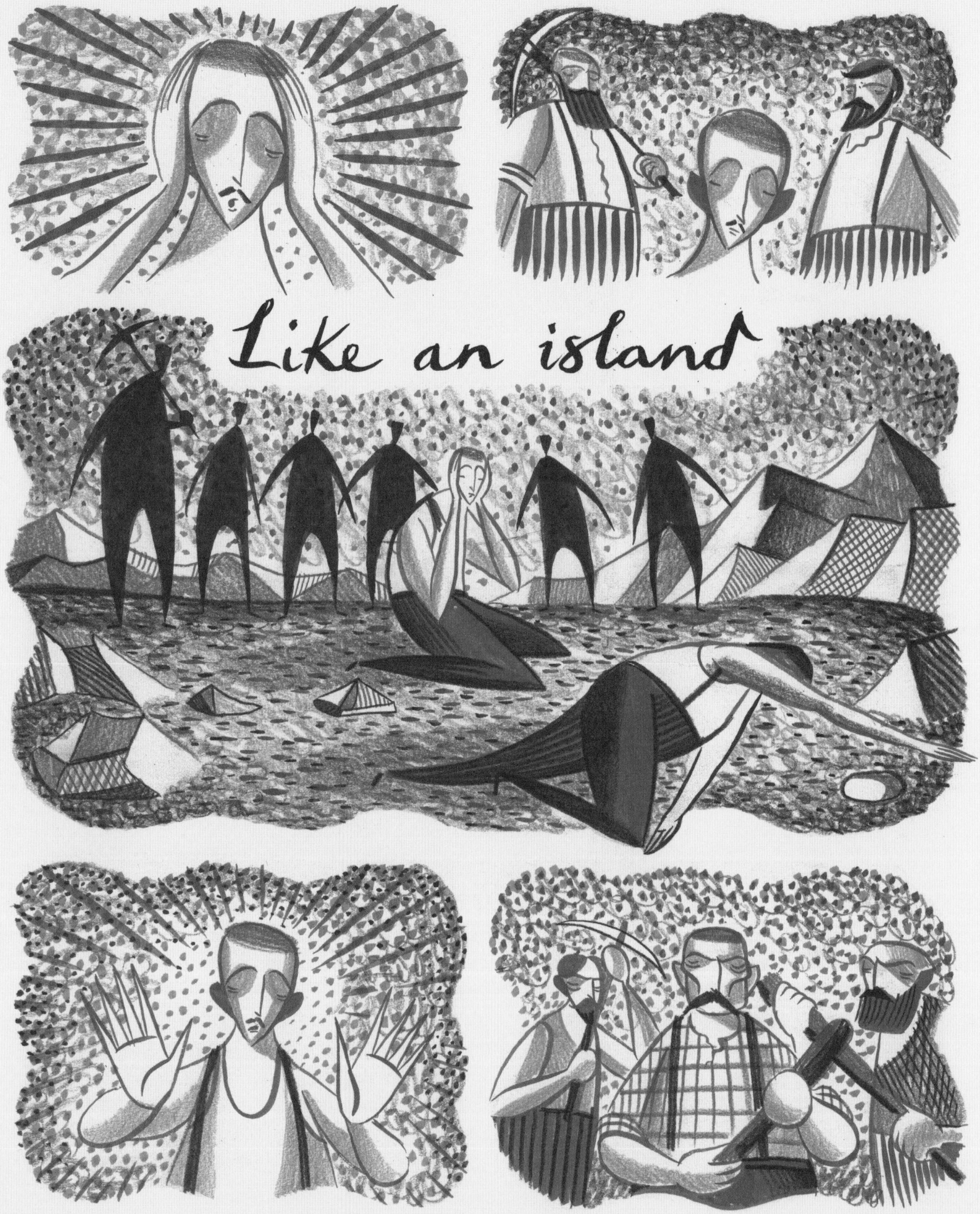
Like an island

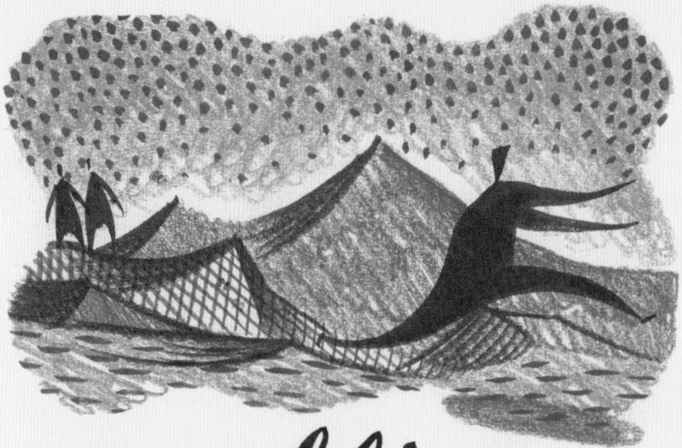

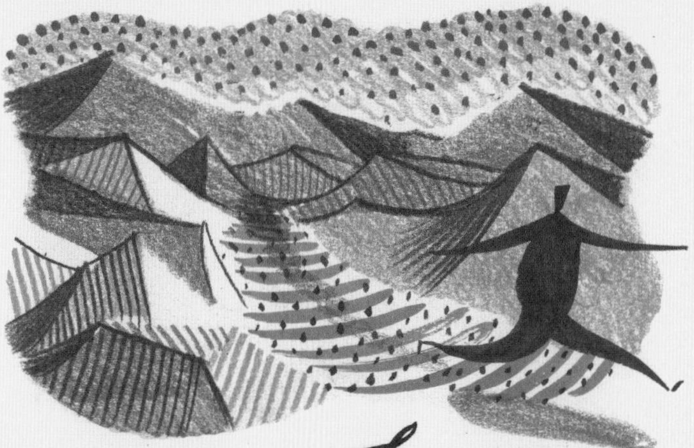

Swilling on my shores

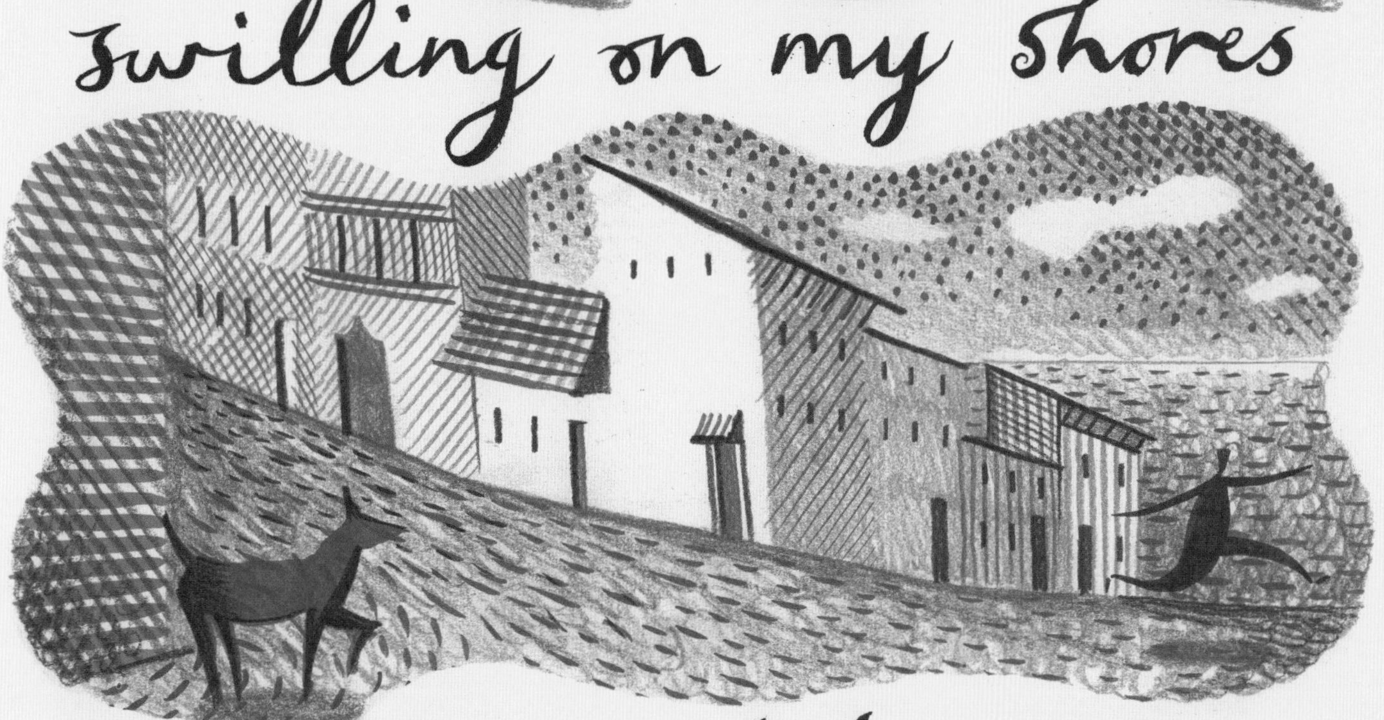

the strife and droppings

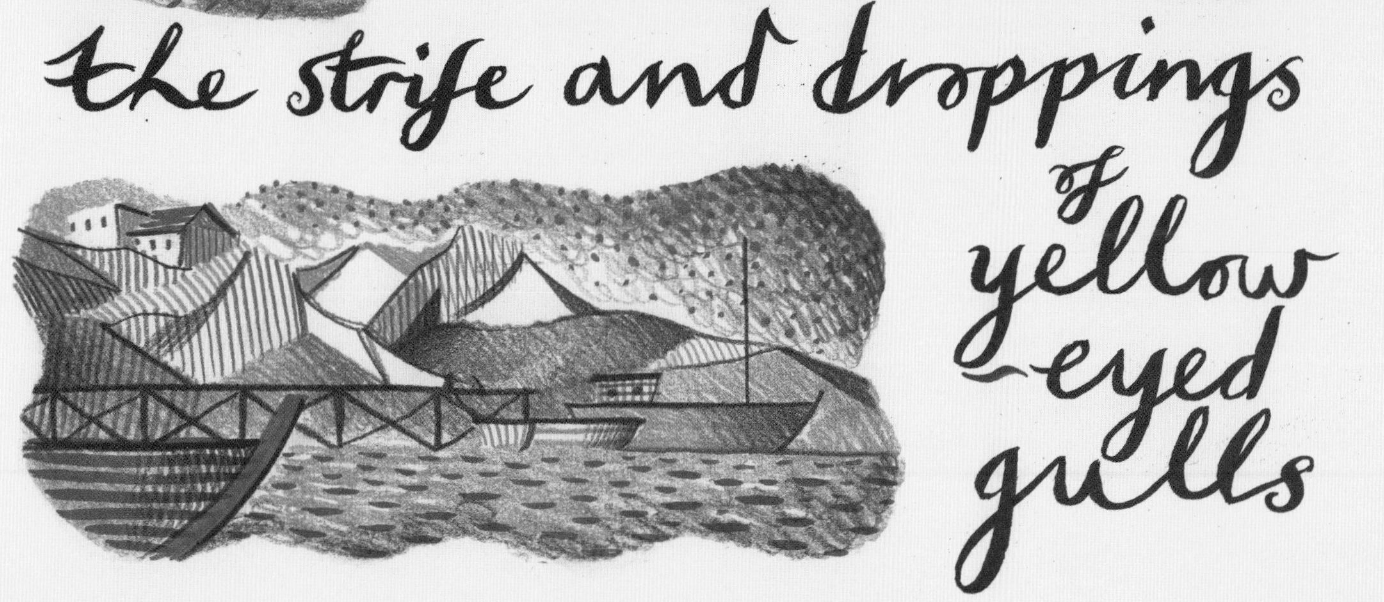

of yellow-eyed gulls

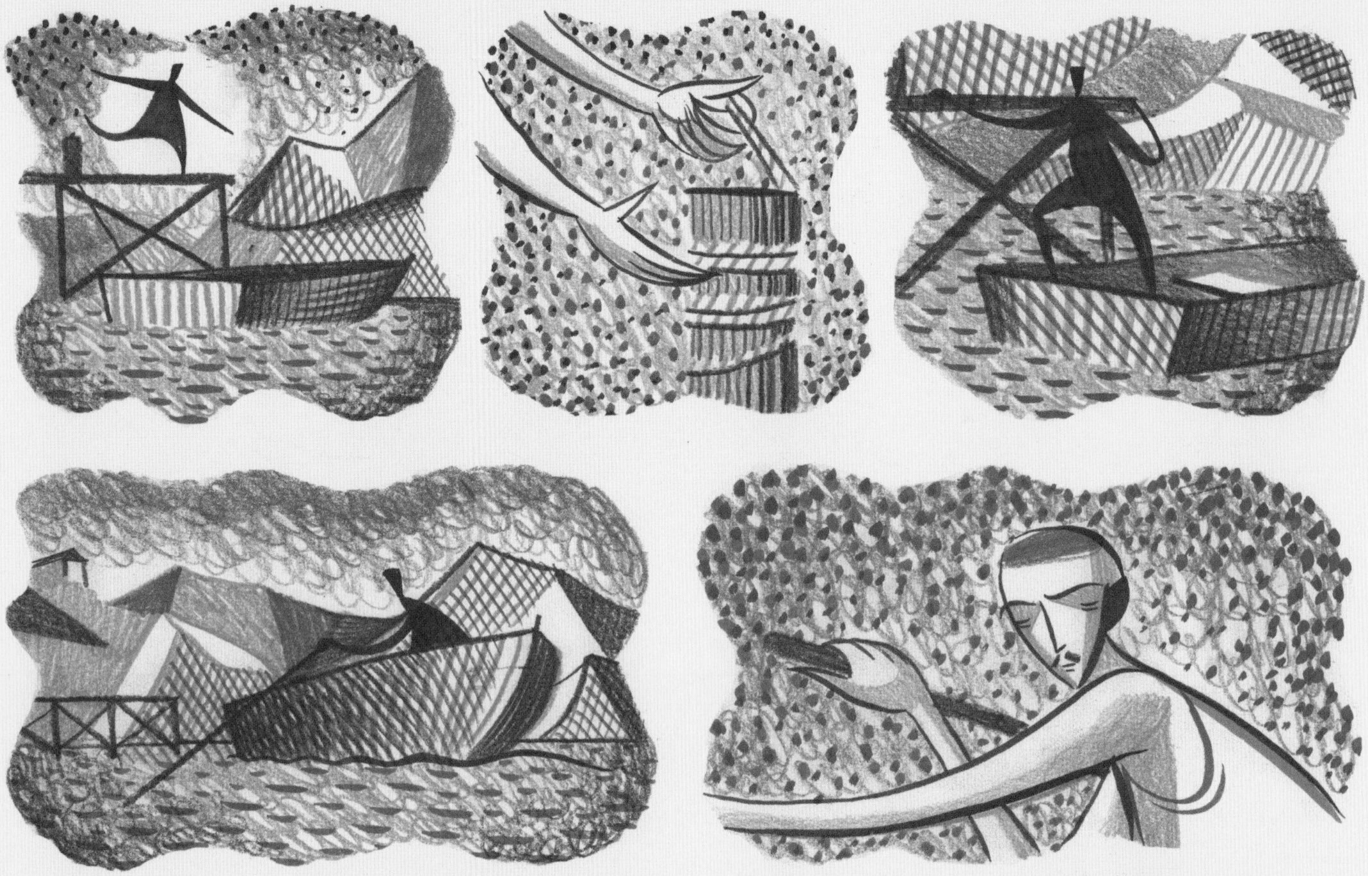

I voyaged on,

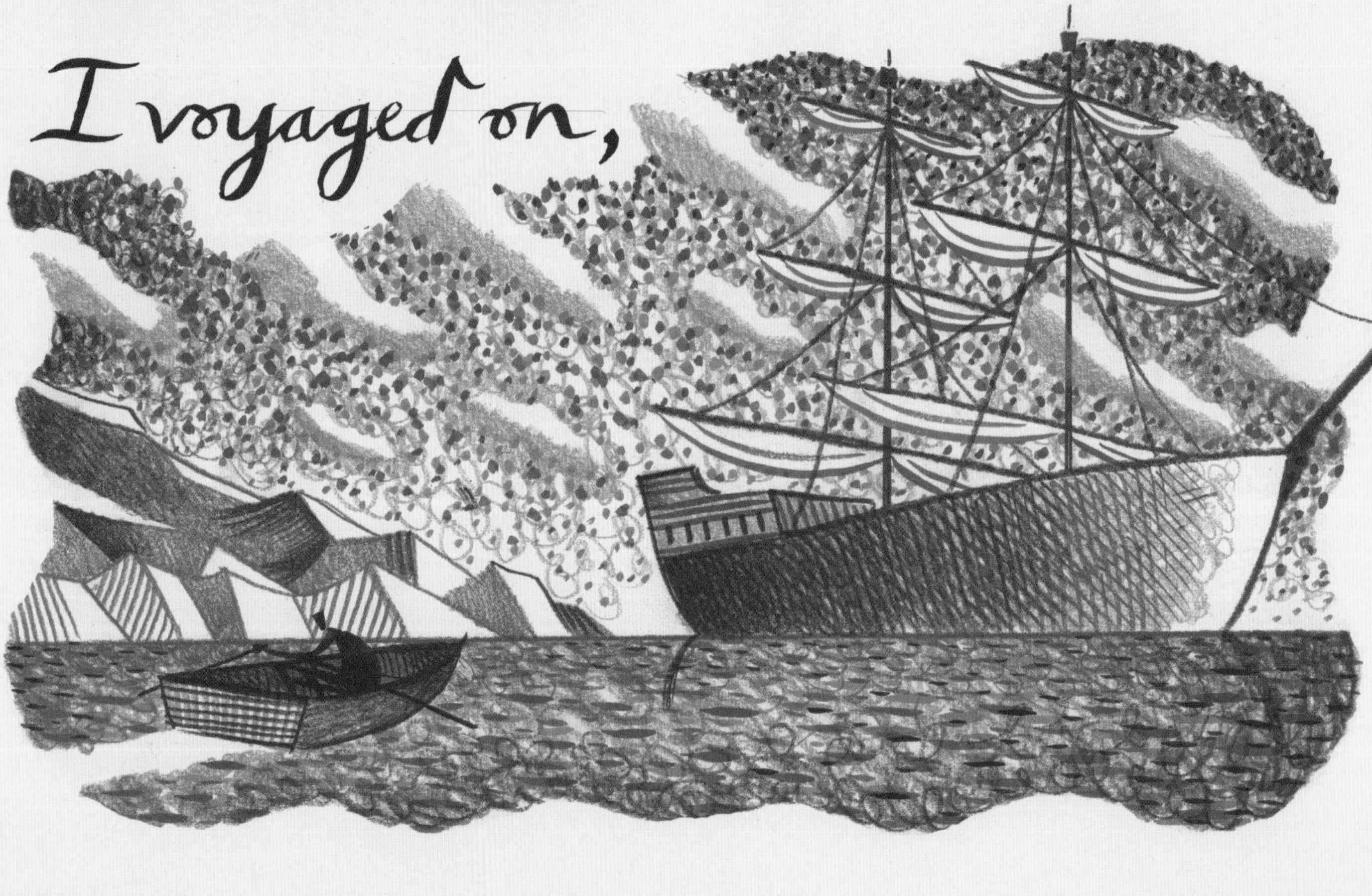

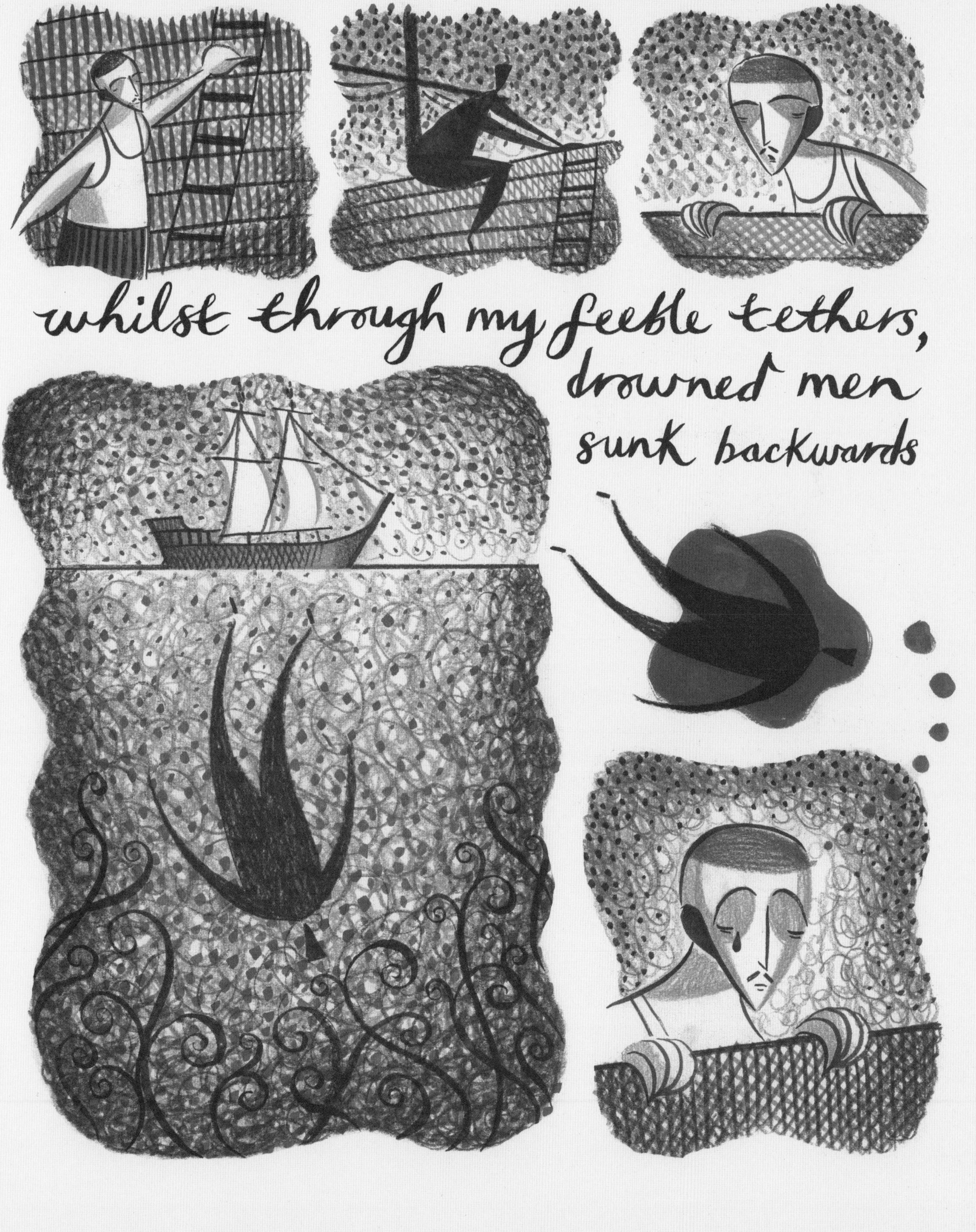
whilst through my feeble tethers,
drowned men
sunk backwards

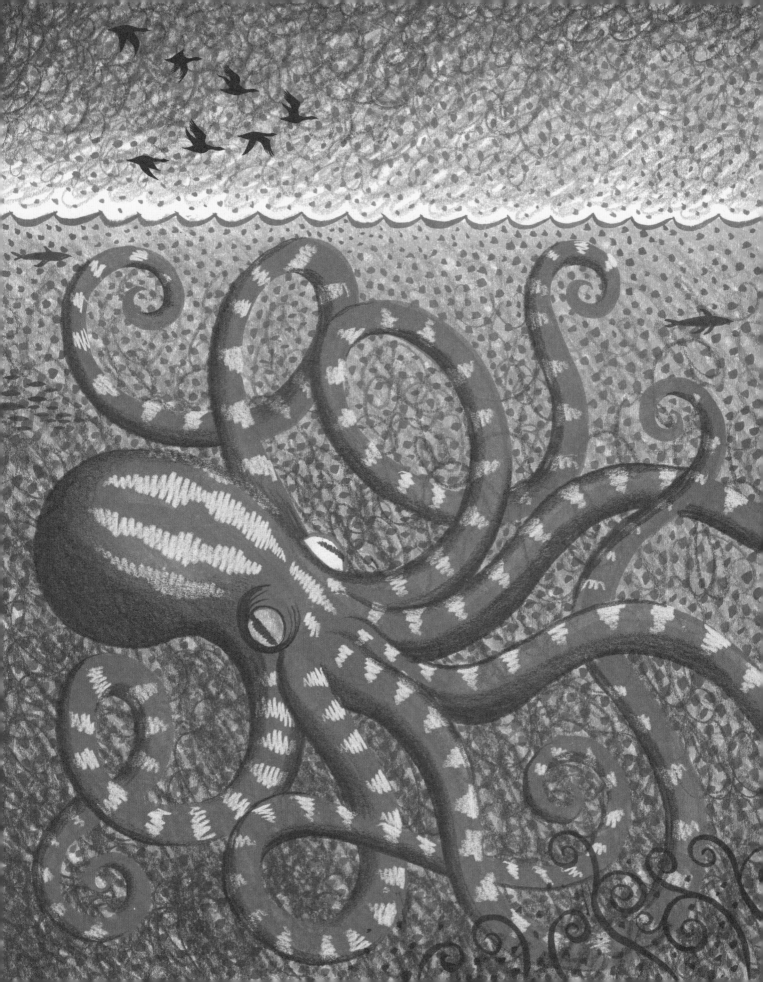

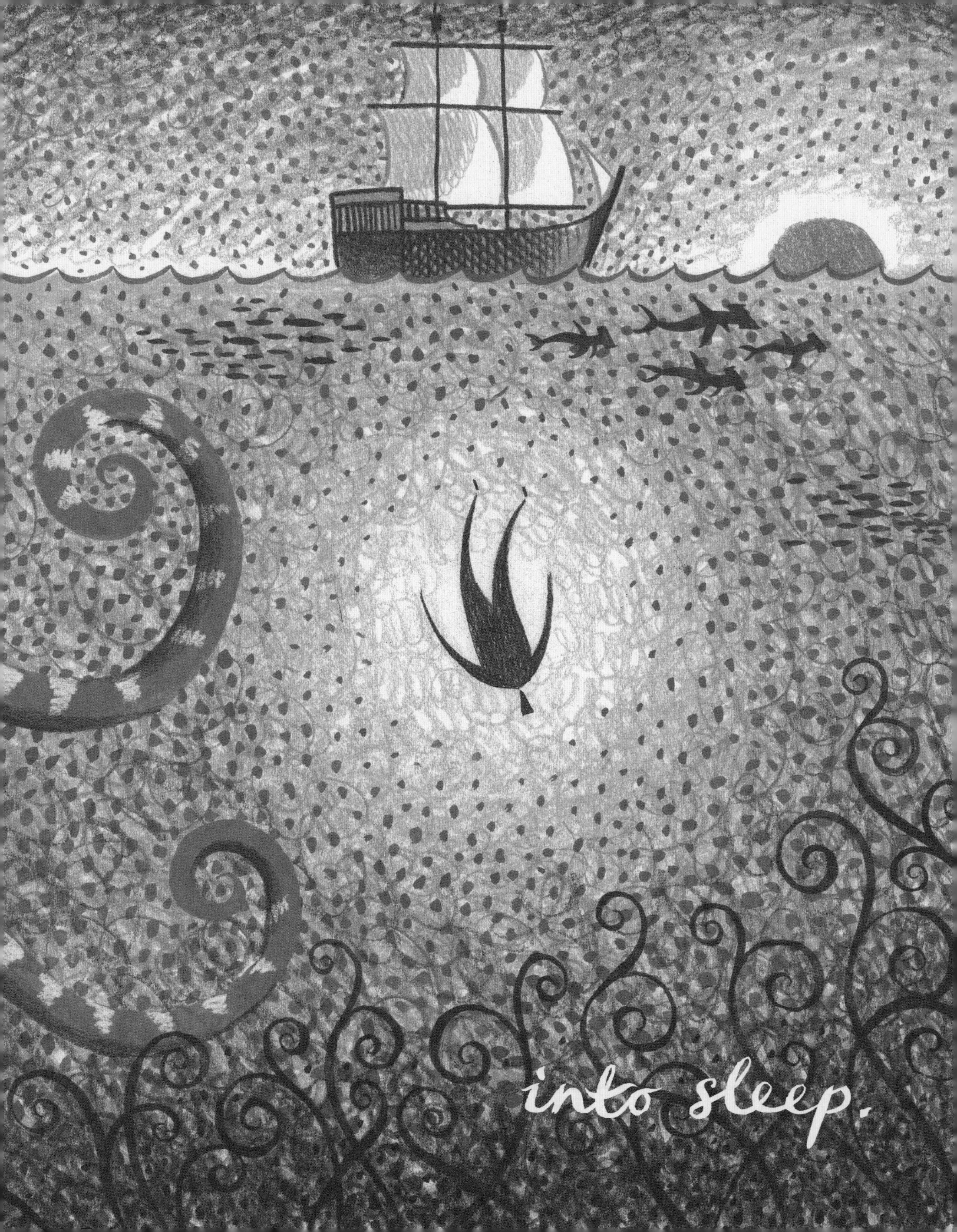
into sleep.

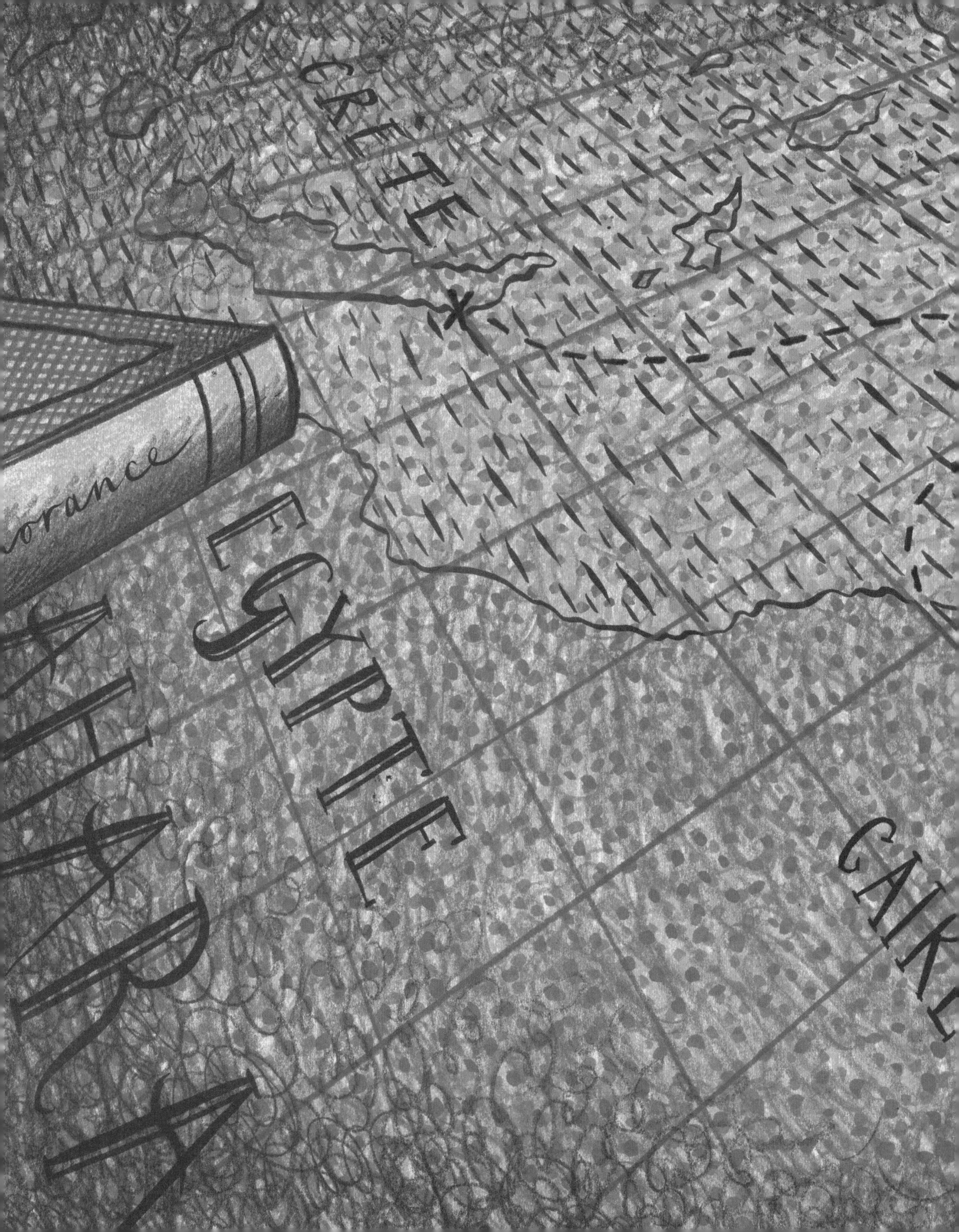
CRETE
EGYPT
SAHARA

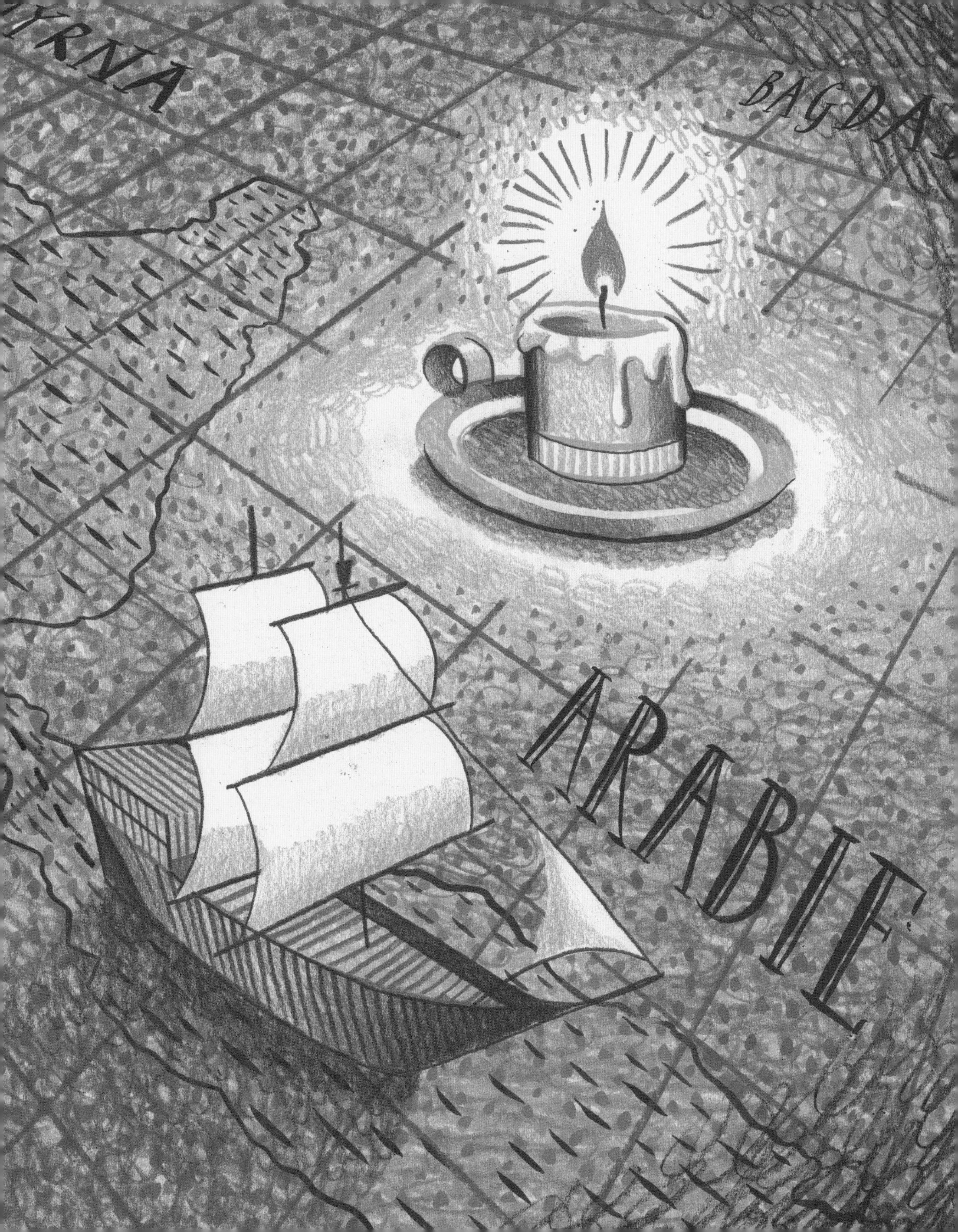
ARABIE

And now I,

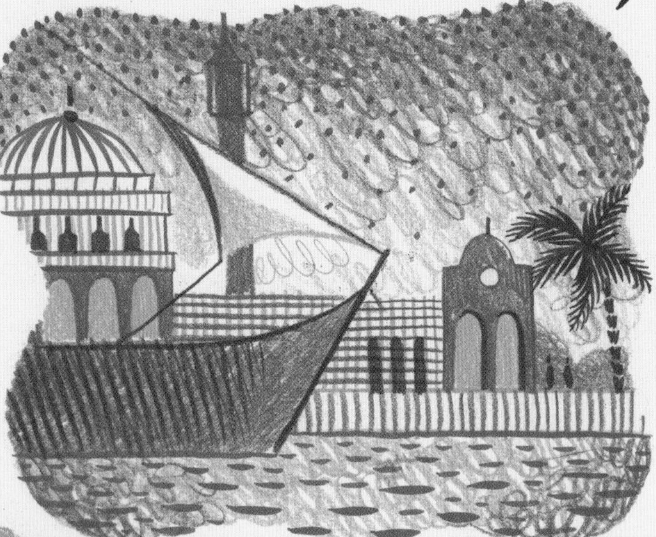

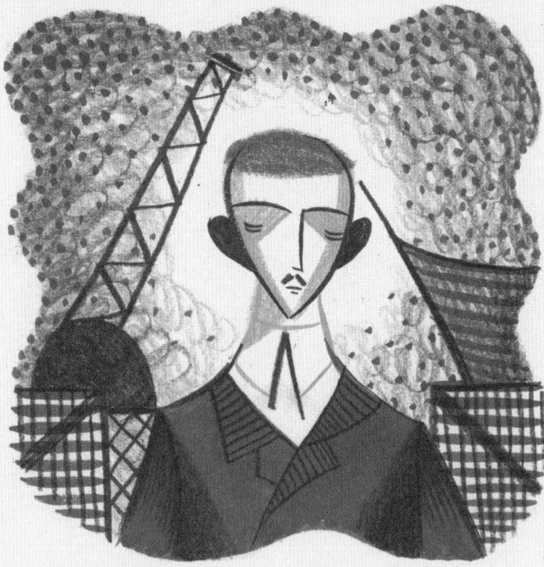

this boat,

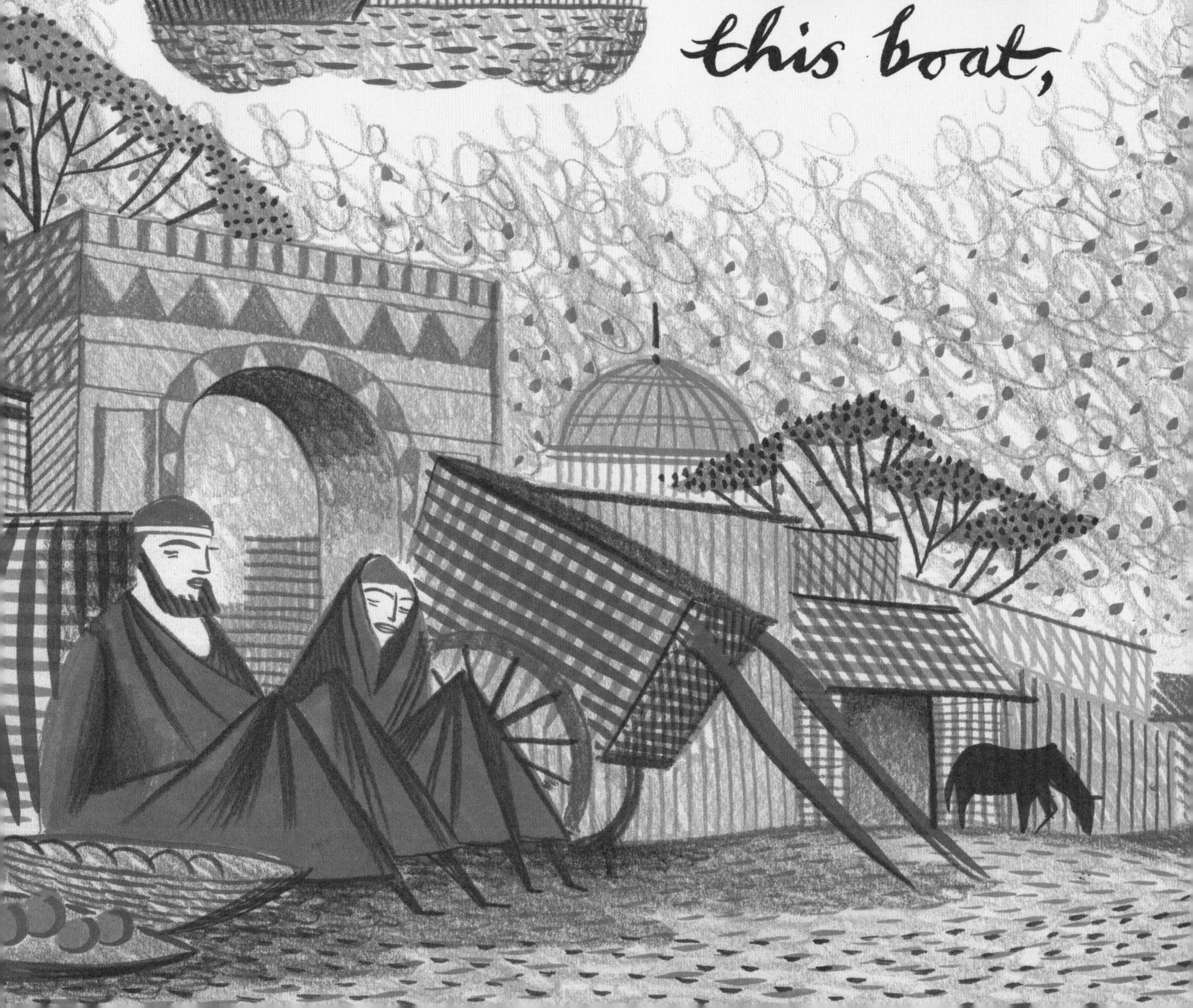

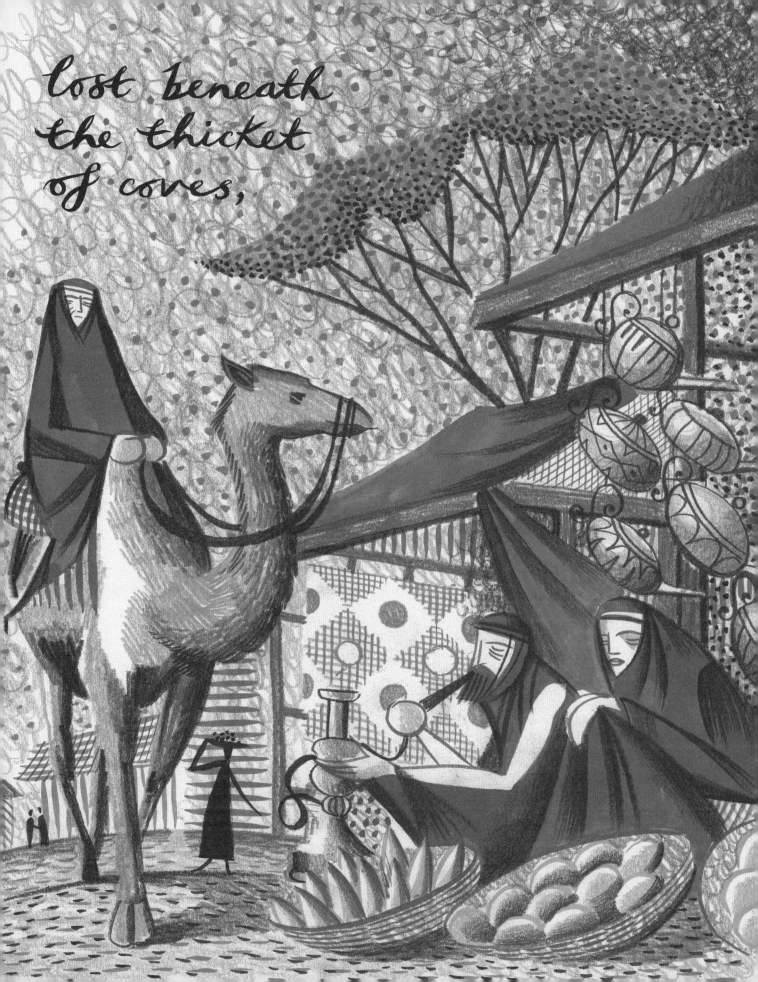

lost beneath
the thicket
of coves,

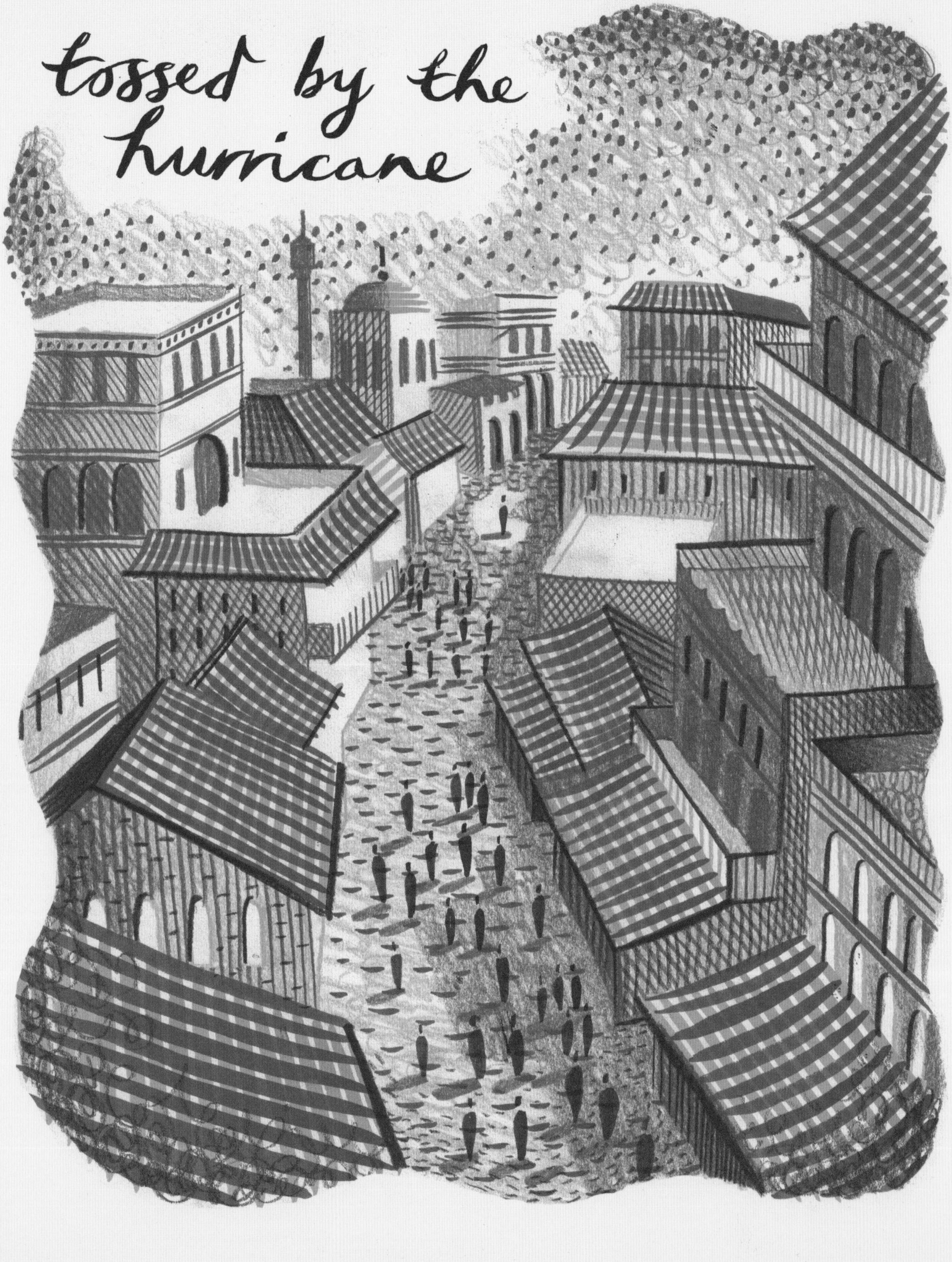
tossed by the
hurricane

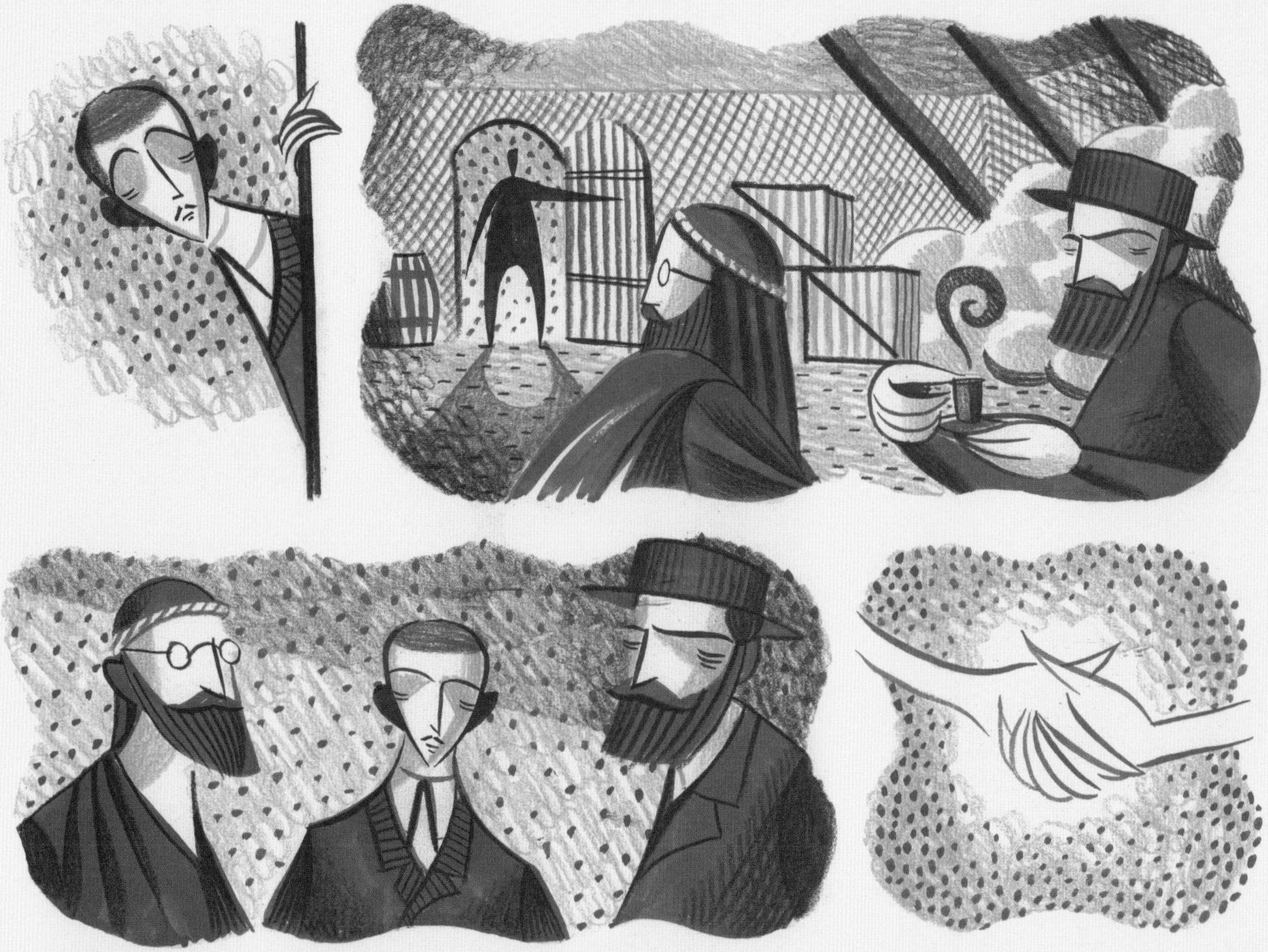

into the birdless SKY

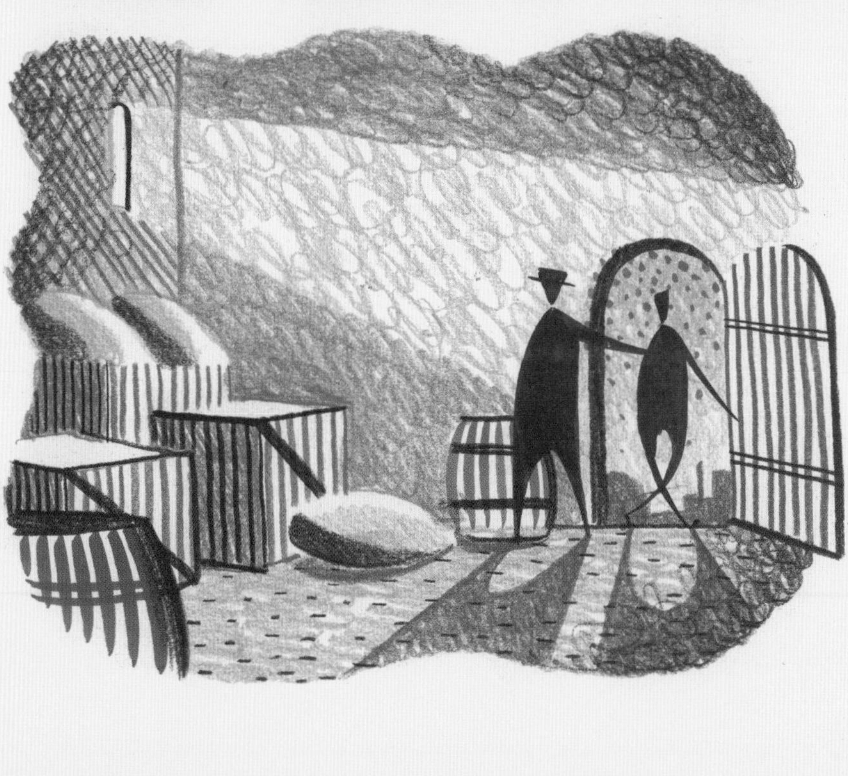

I

whose
carcass

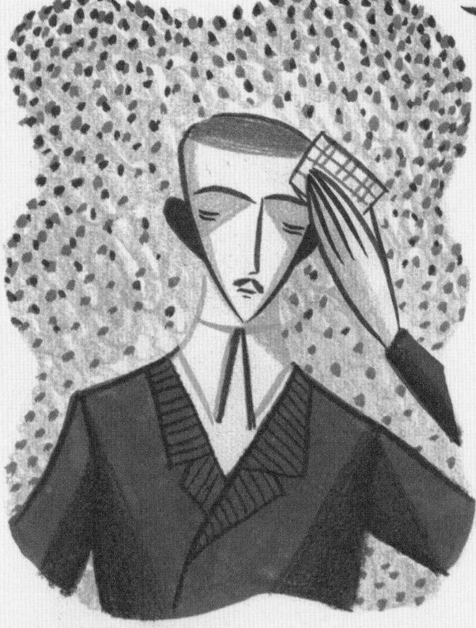

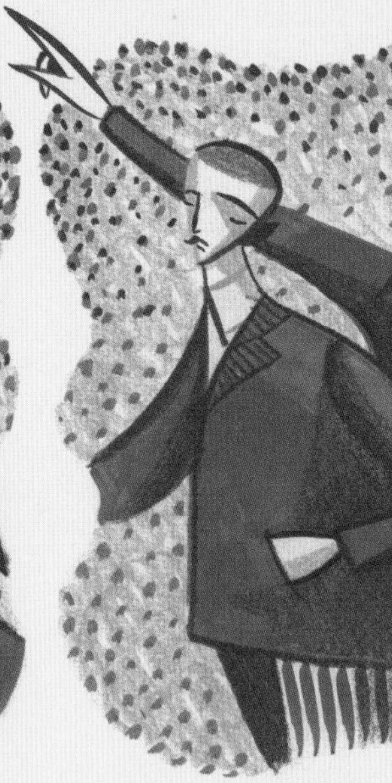

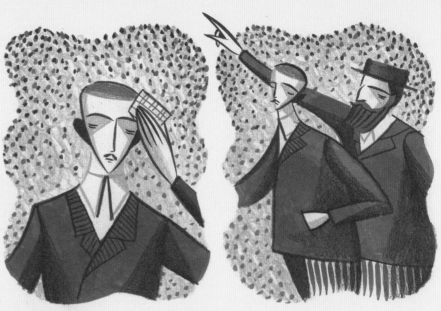

binged
in water

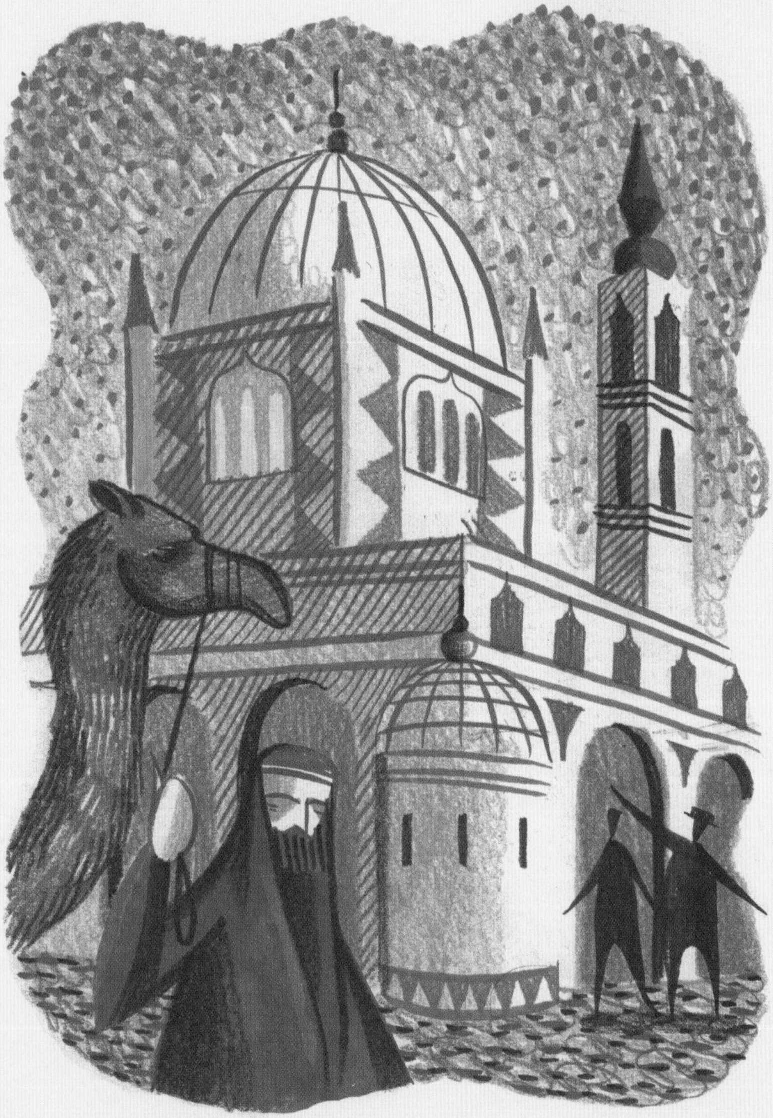

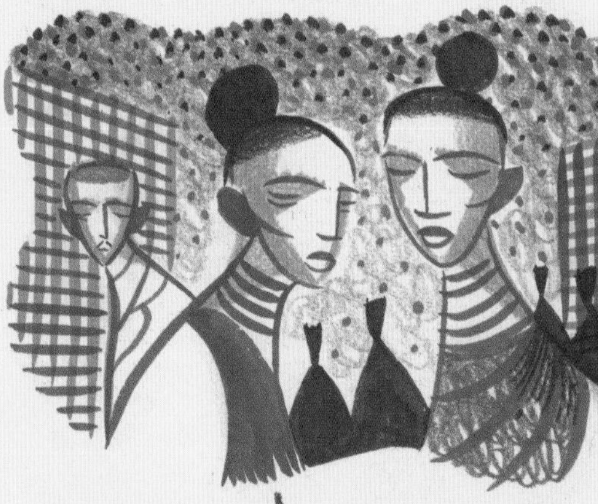

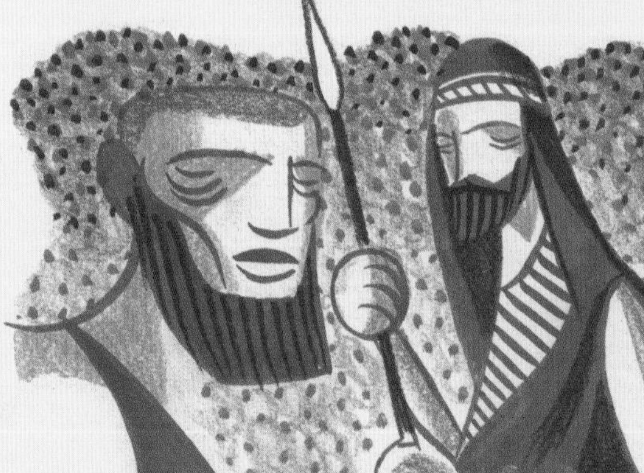

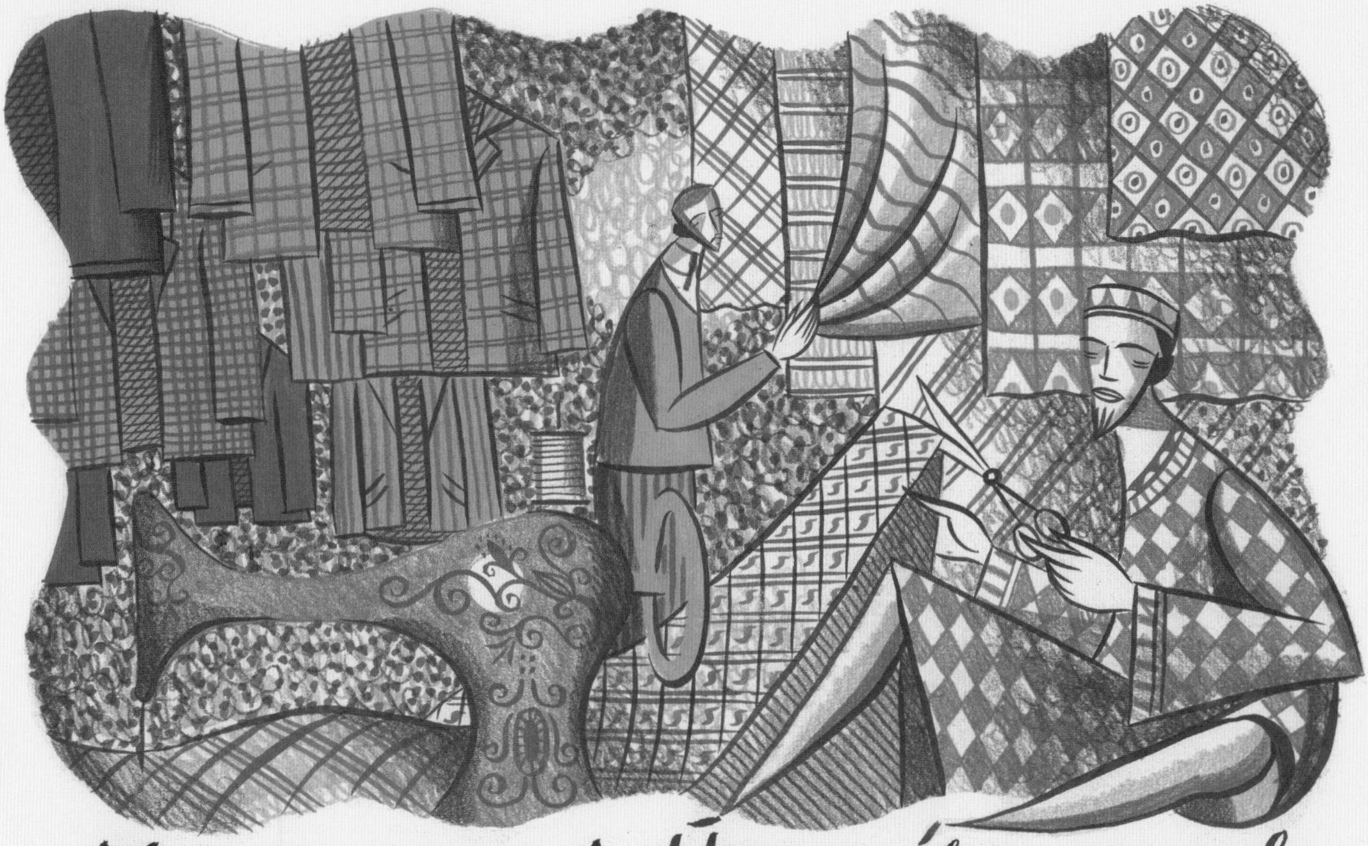

Monitors and Hanseatic vessels

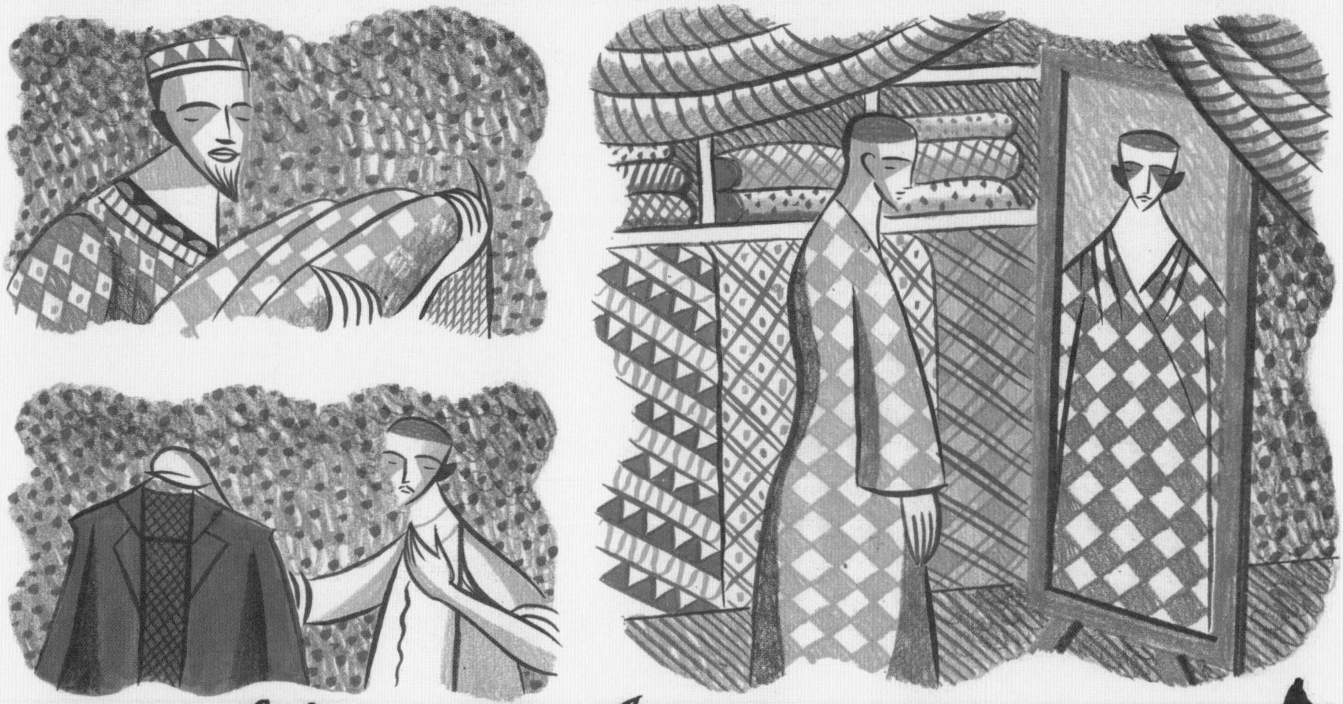

could not have recovered.

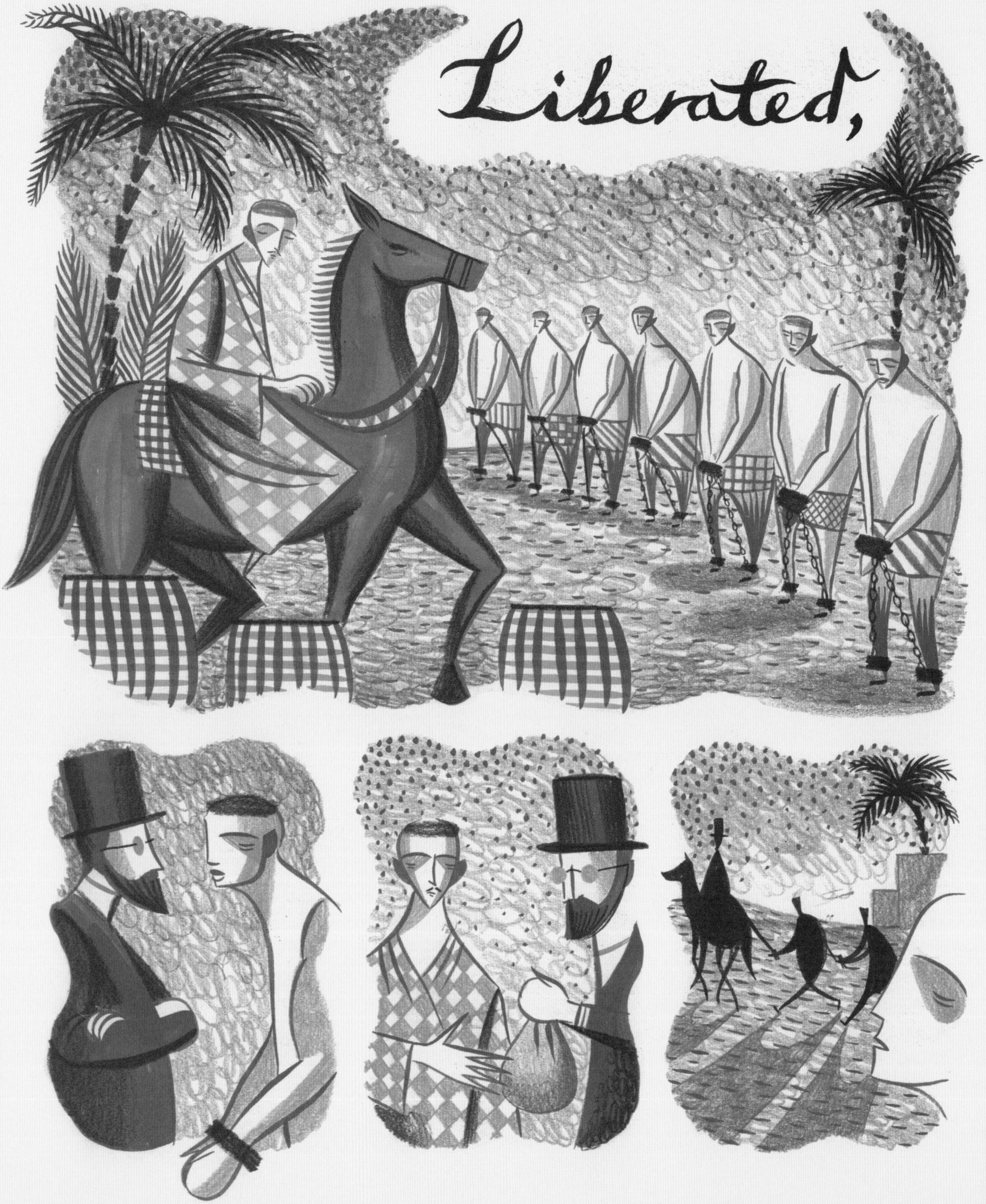
Liberated,

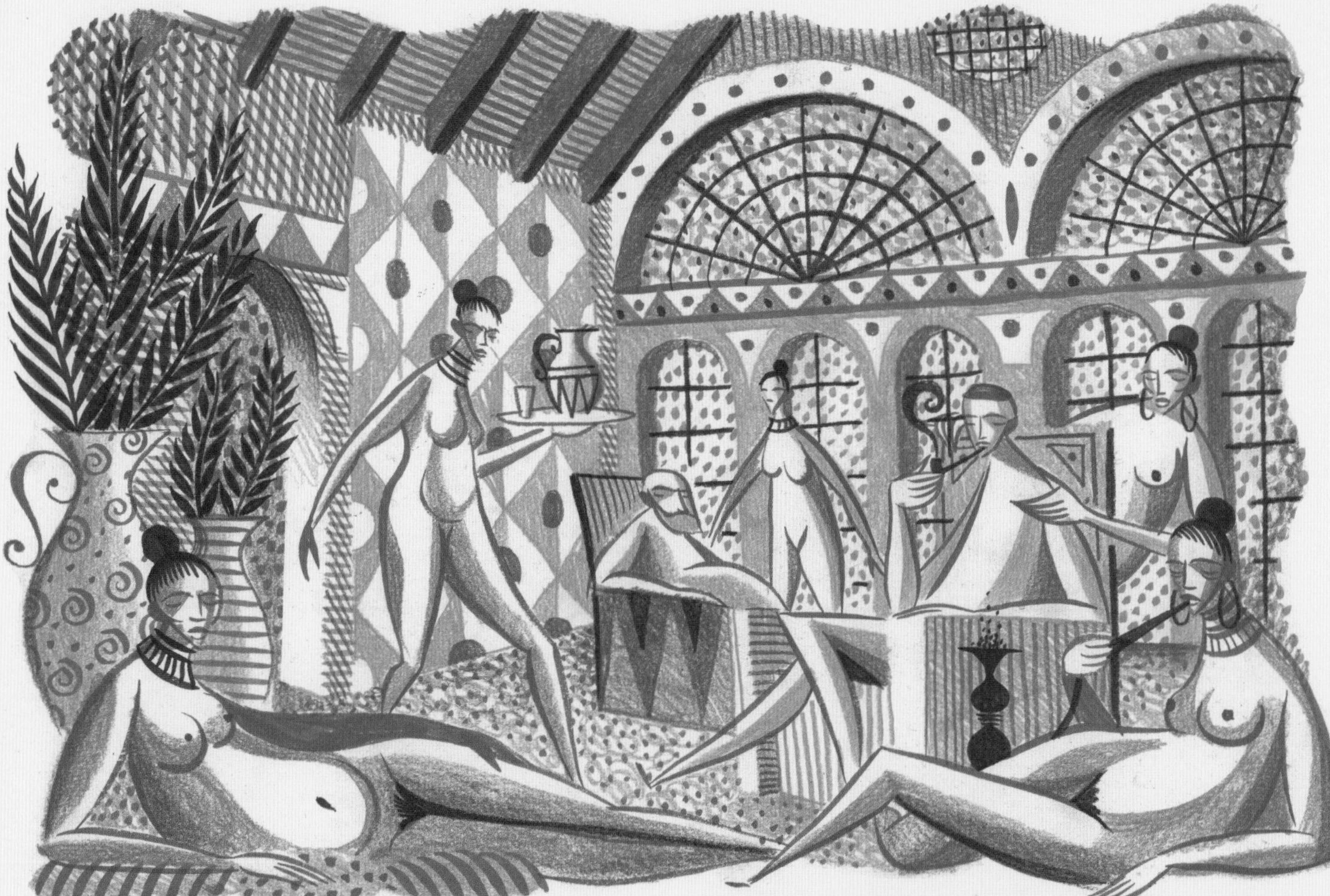

smouldering,

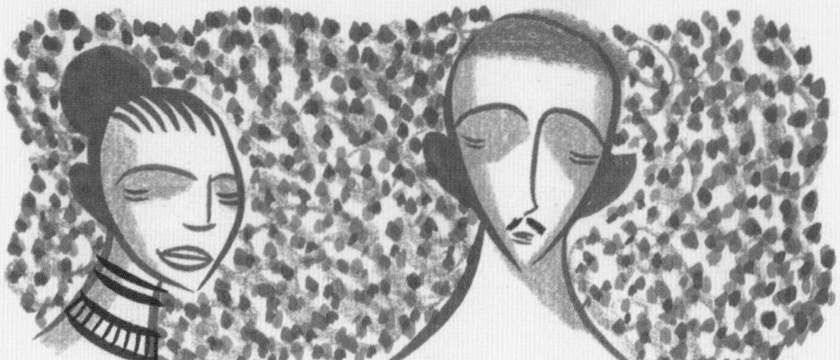

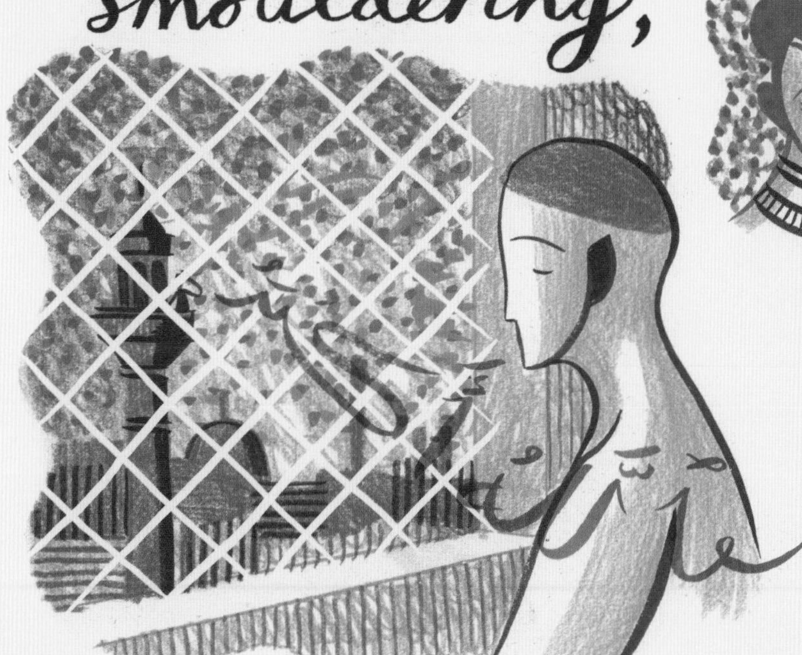

risen on
VIOLET
haze,

I who smashed through the brick-red wall of sky

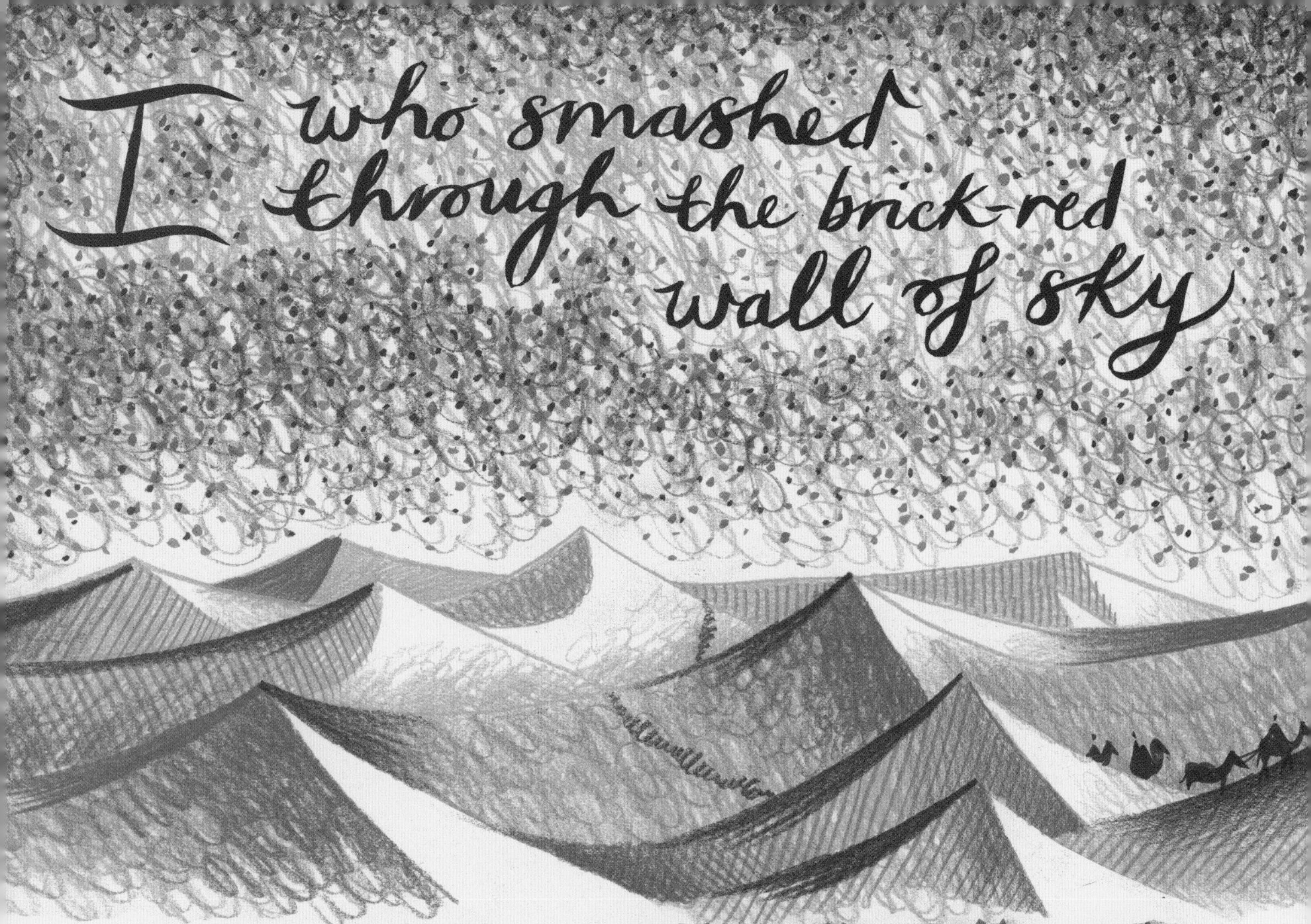

Who brought delicious jam for good poets,

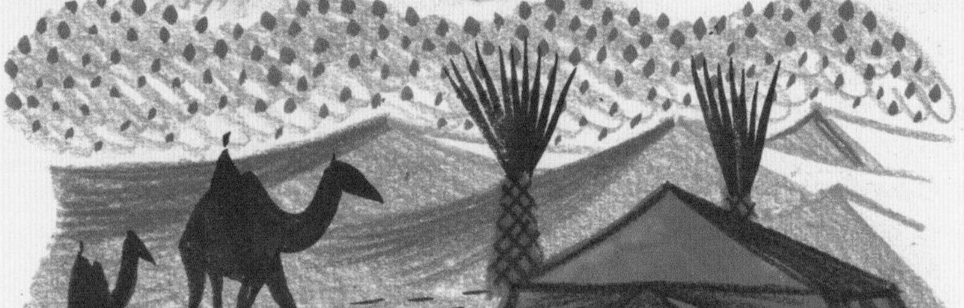

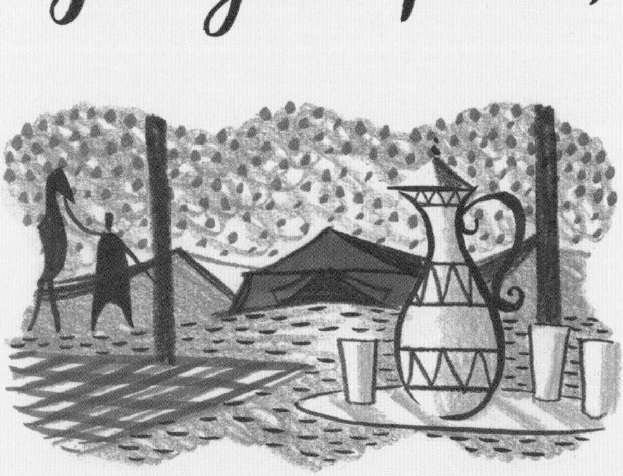

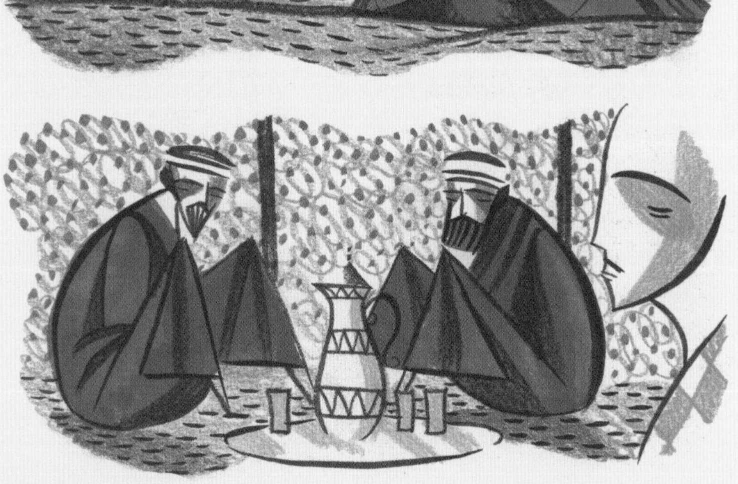

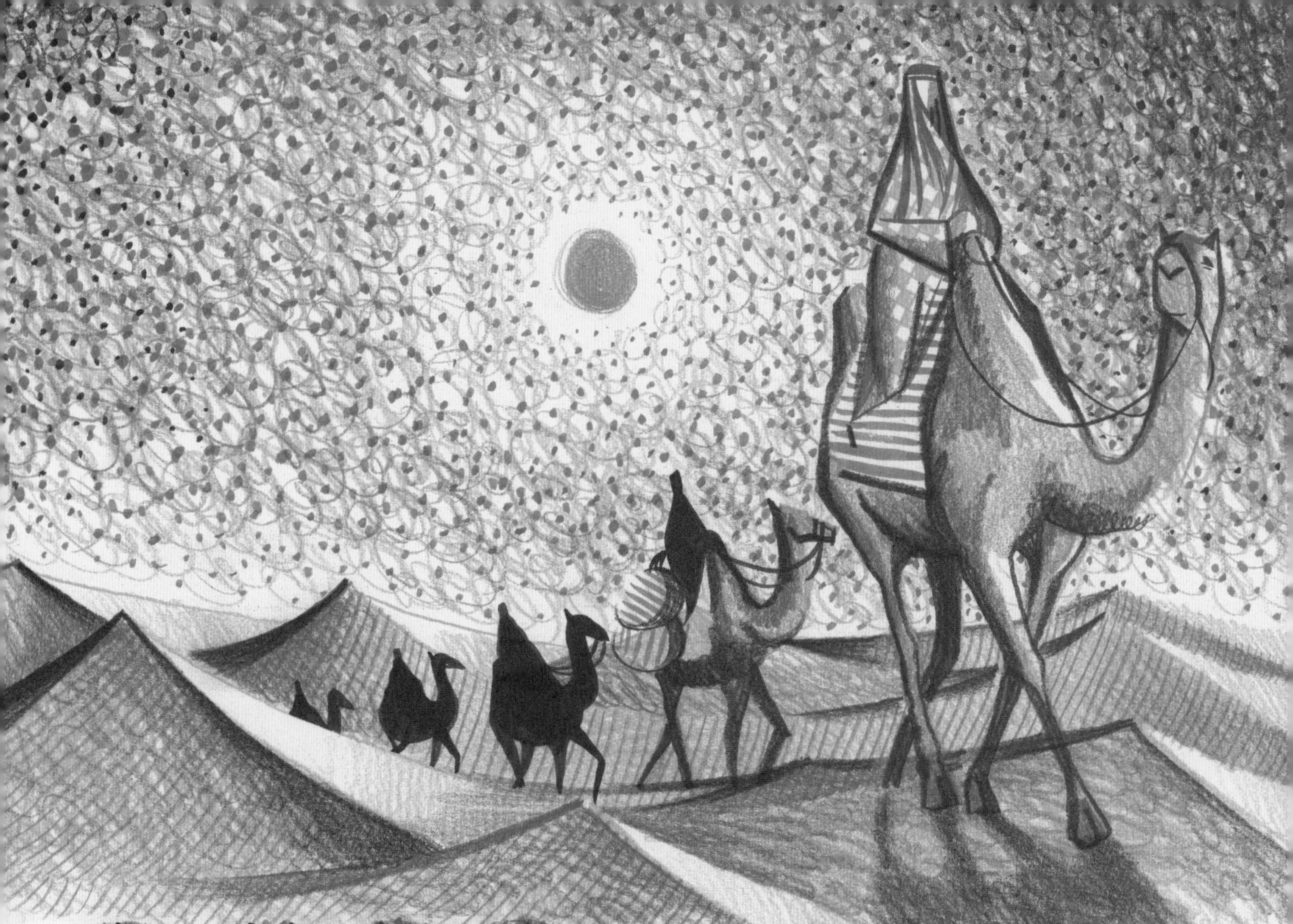

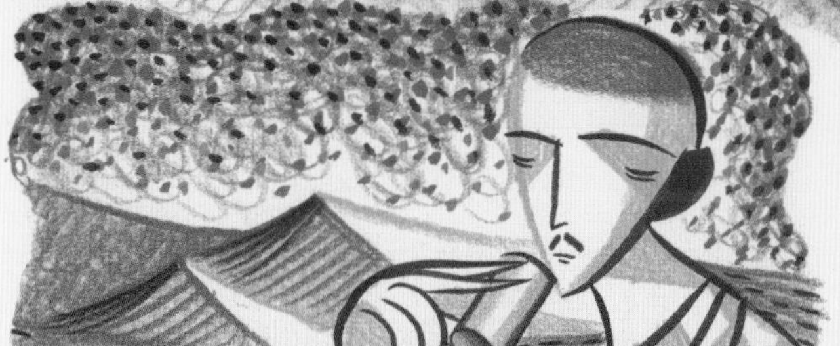

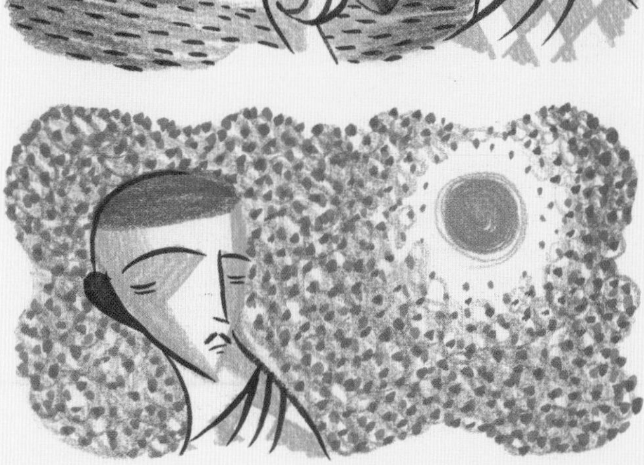

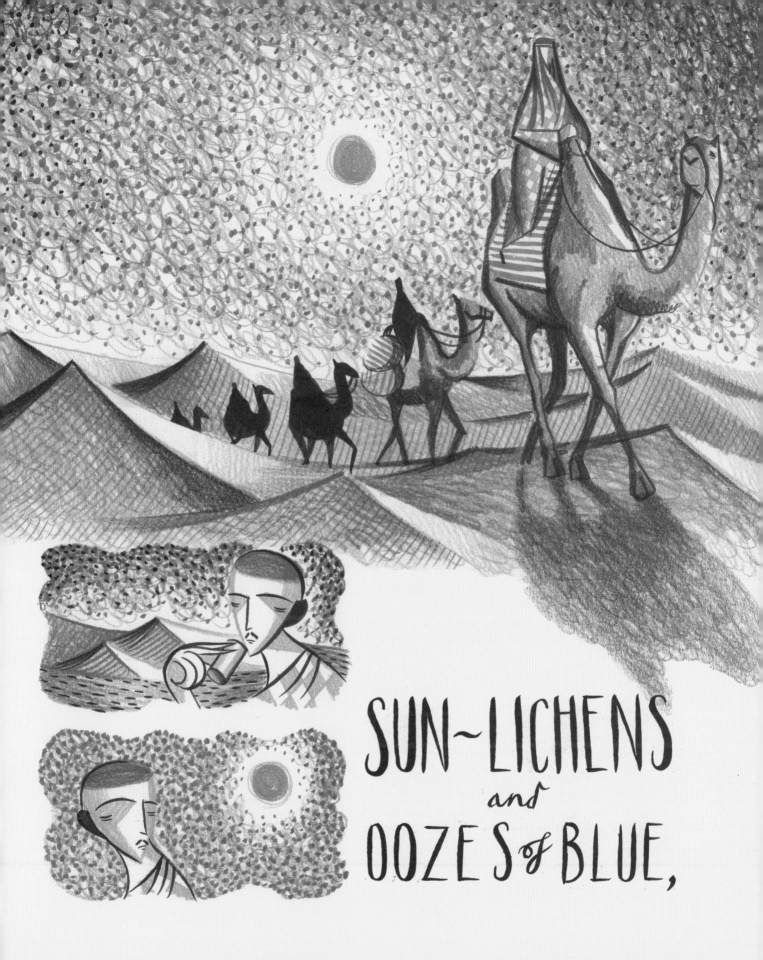

SUN-LICHENS and OOZES of BLUE,

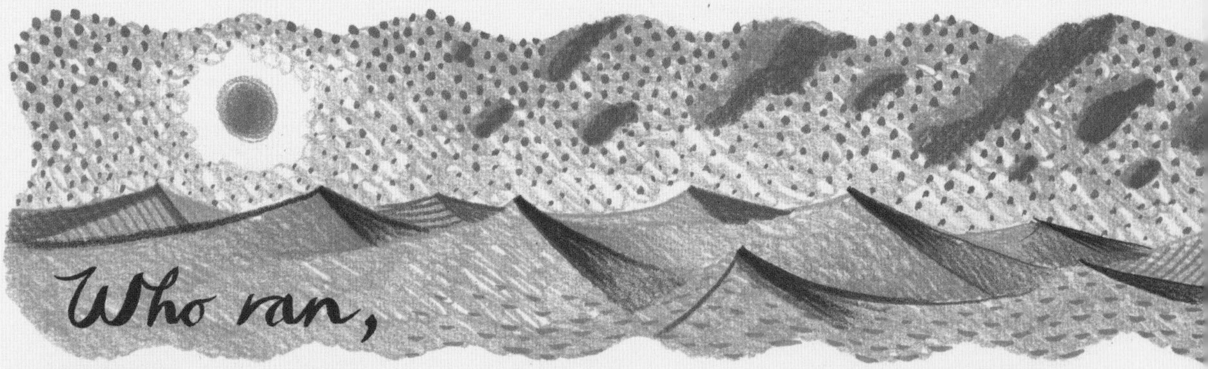
Who ran,

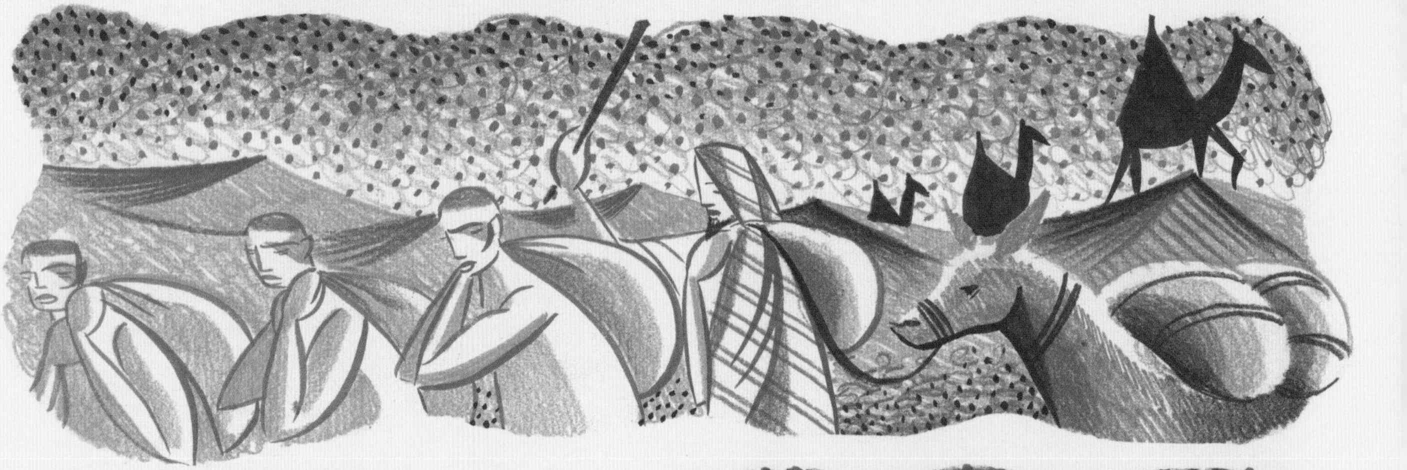

SPECKLED
with
electric orbs

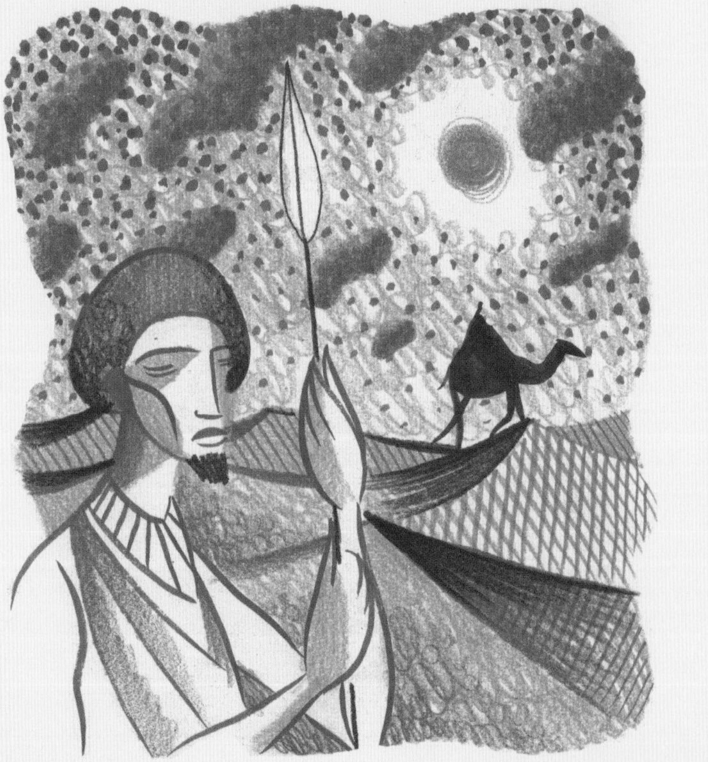

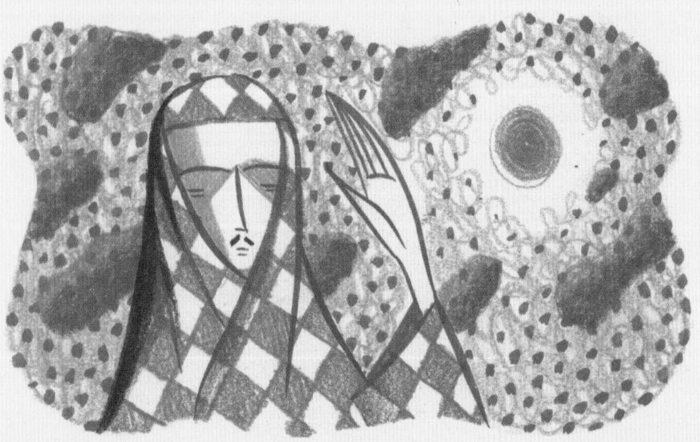

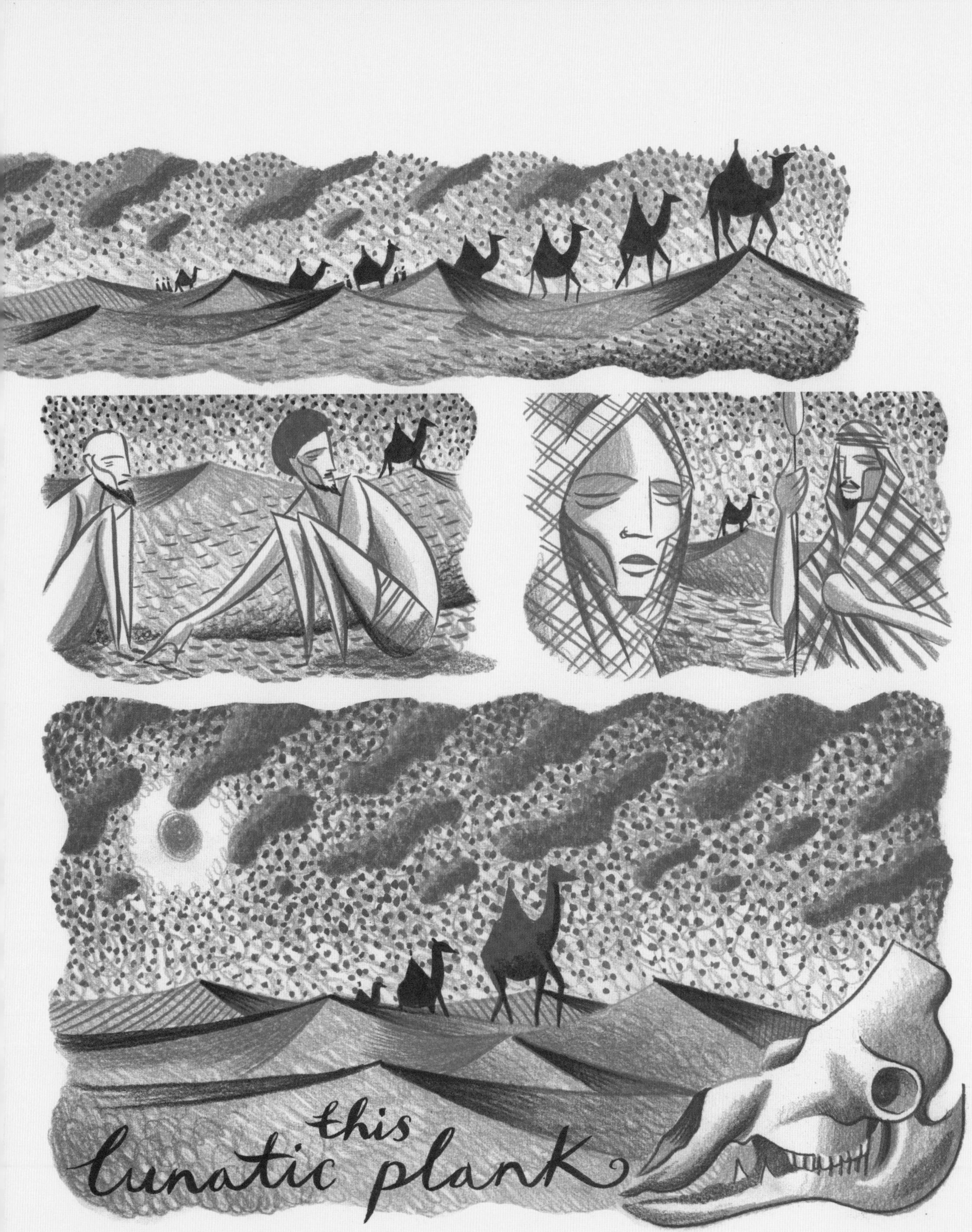
this
lunatic plank

With a convoy of
black seahorses

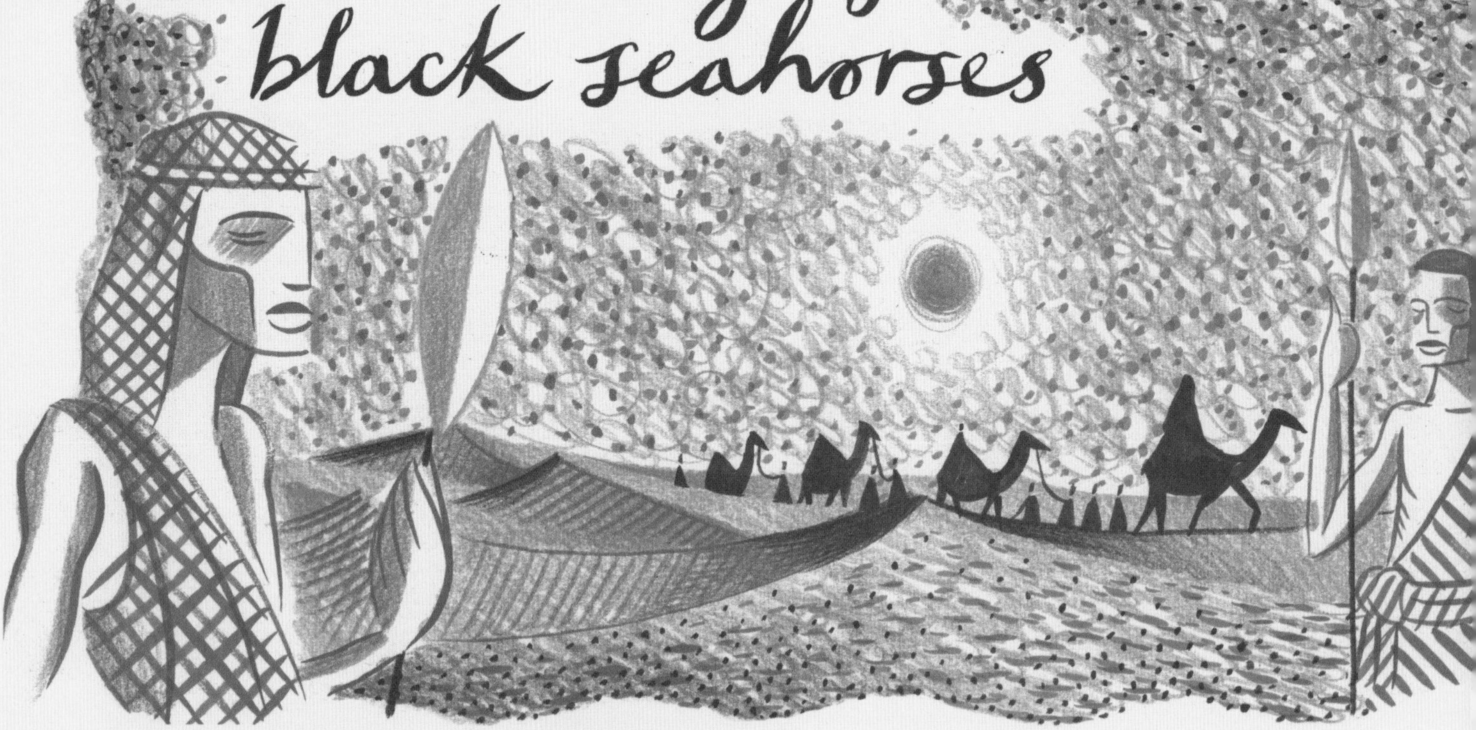

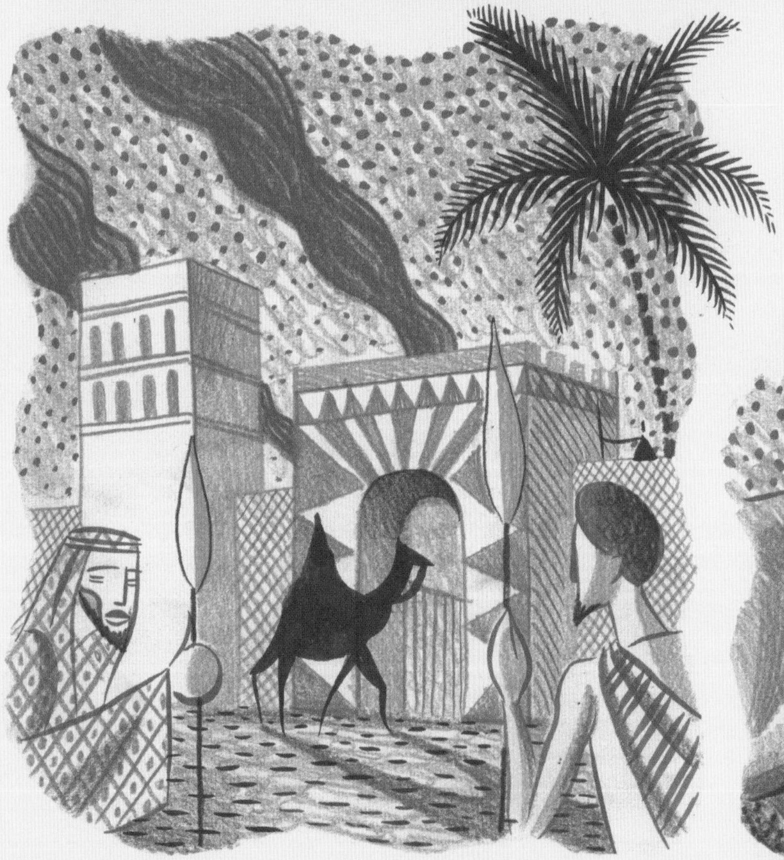

When
sea-blue
skies

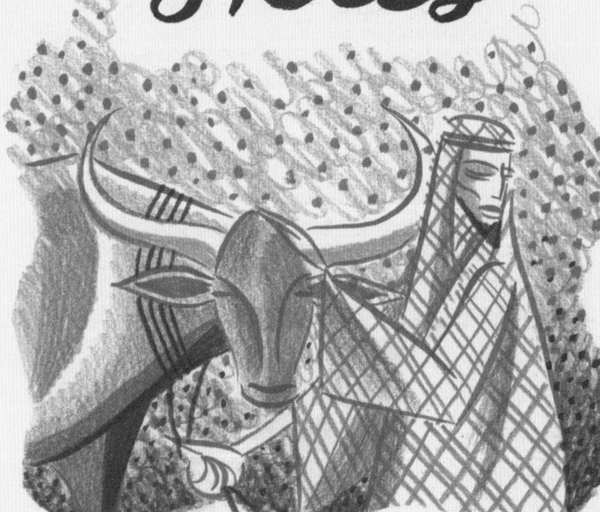

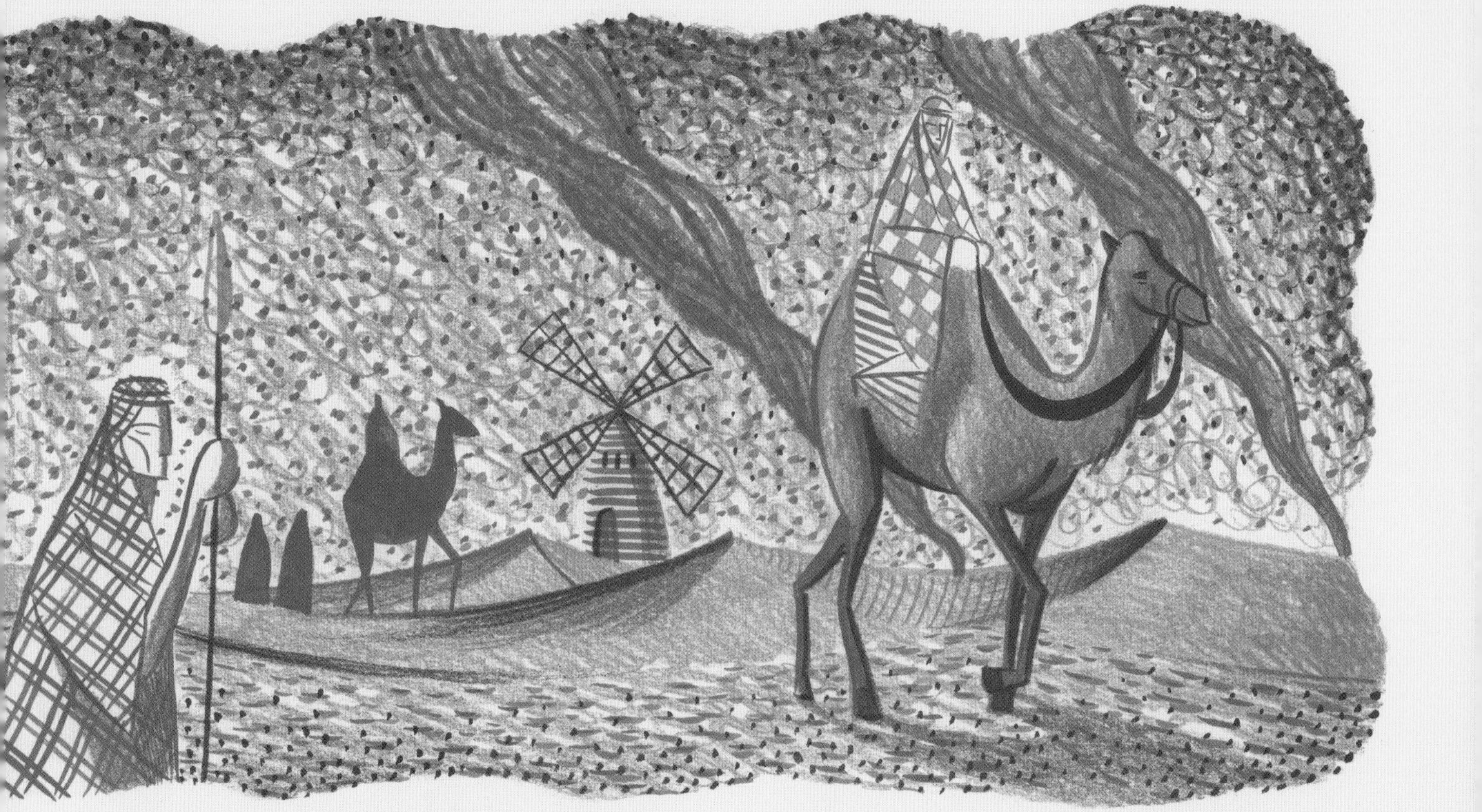

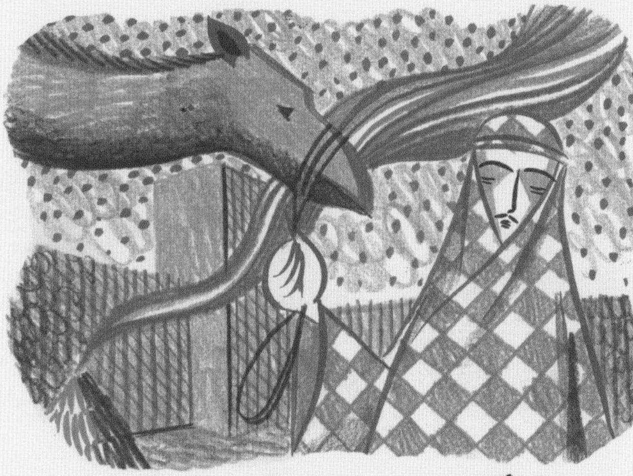

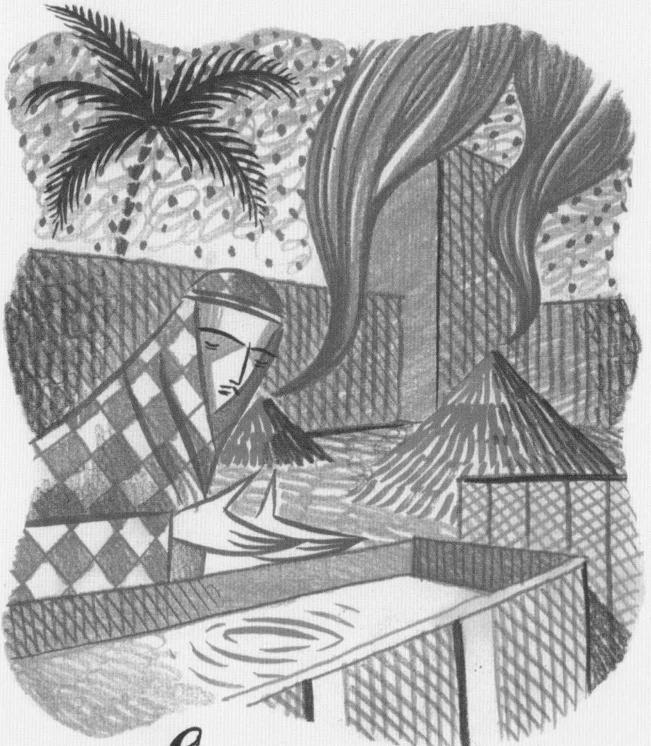

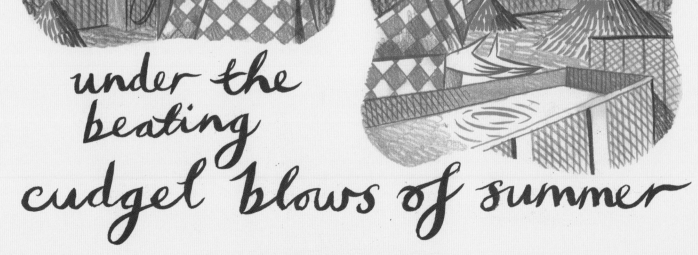

under the beating
cudgel blows of summer

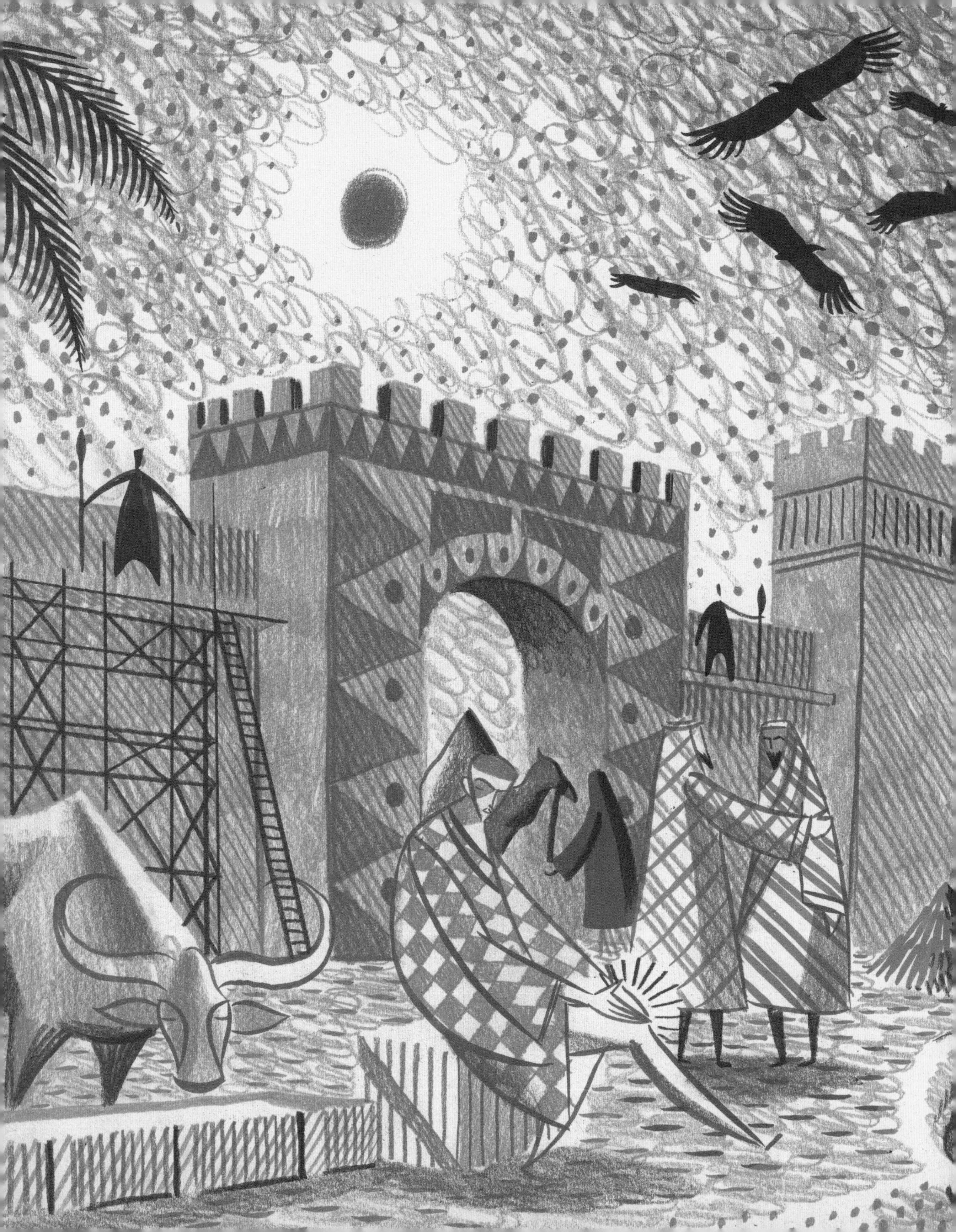

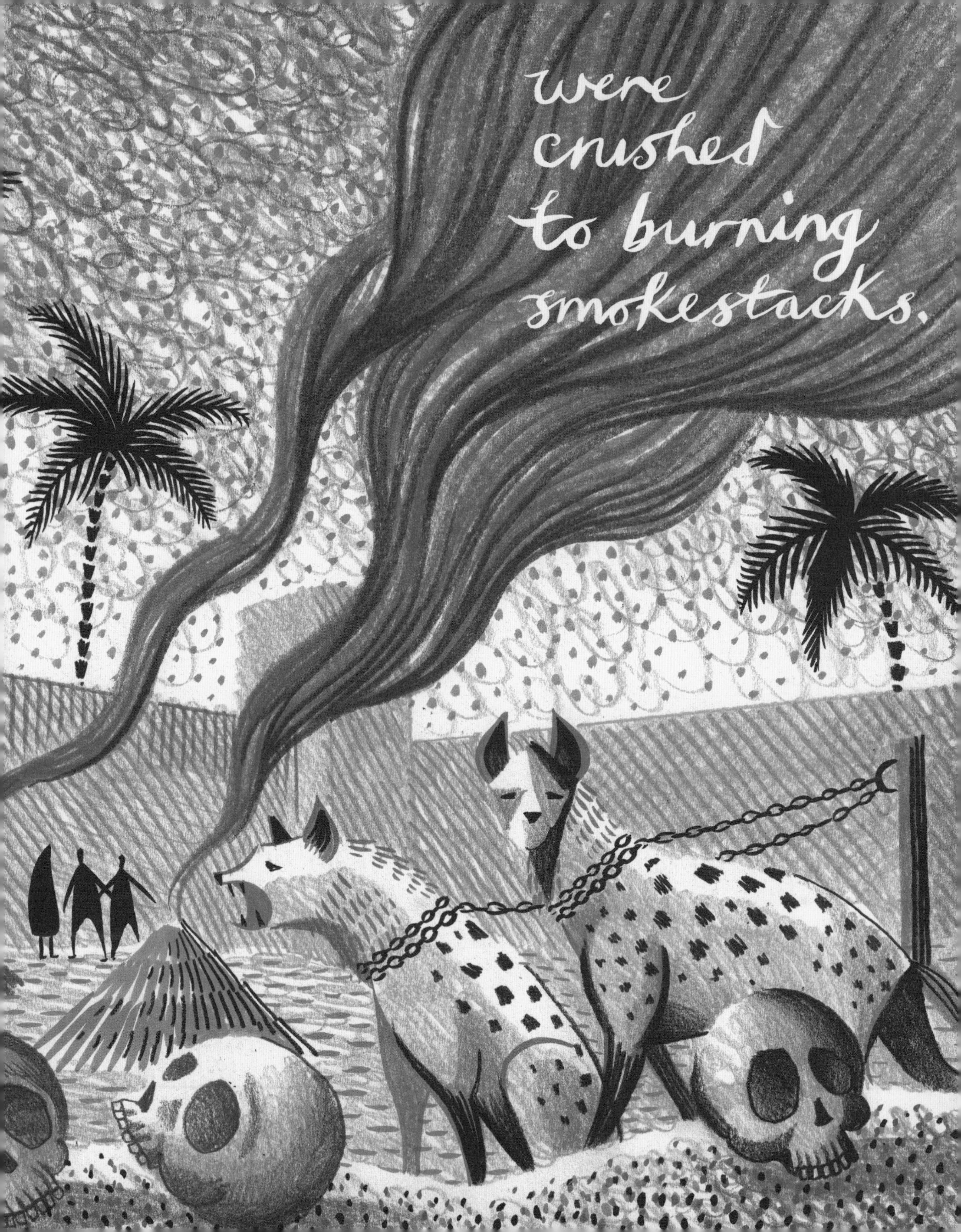
were crushed to burning smokestacks.

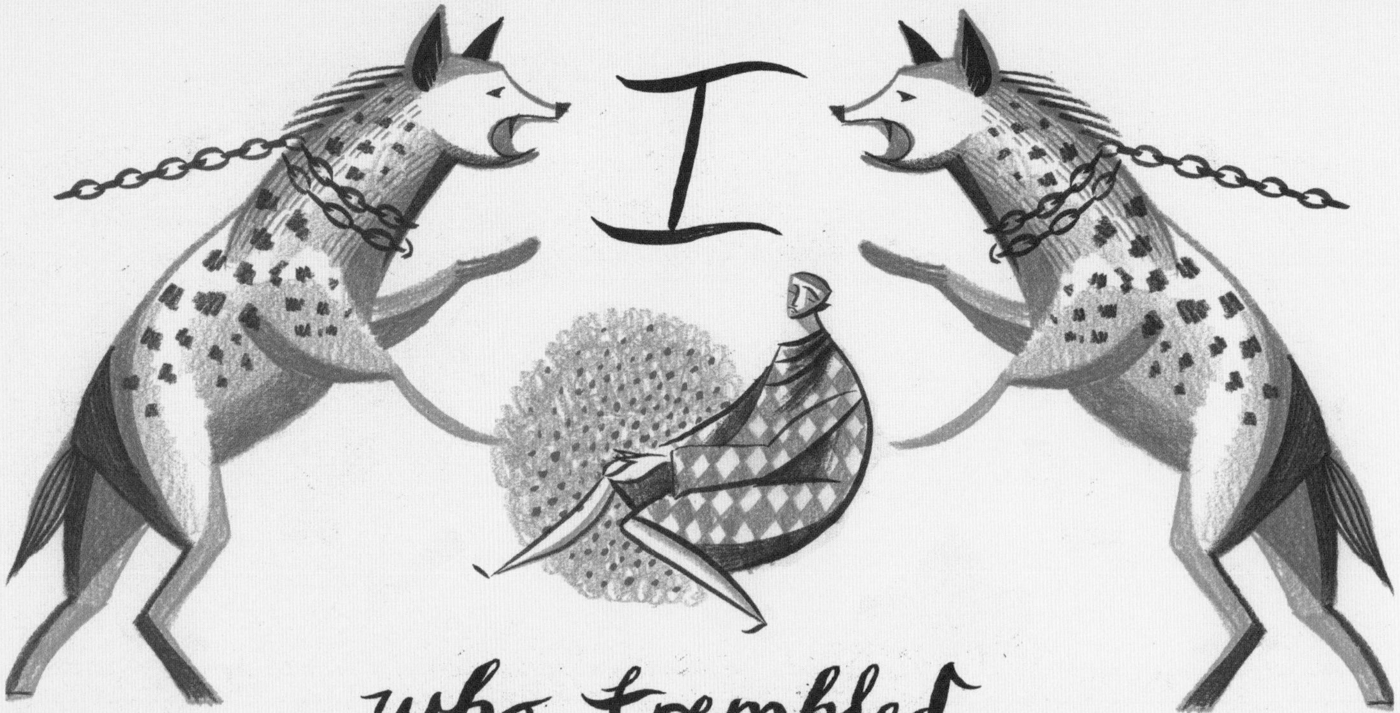

I

who trembled

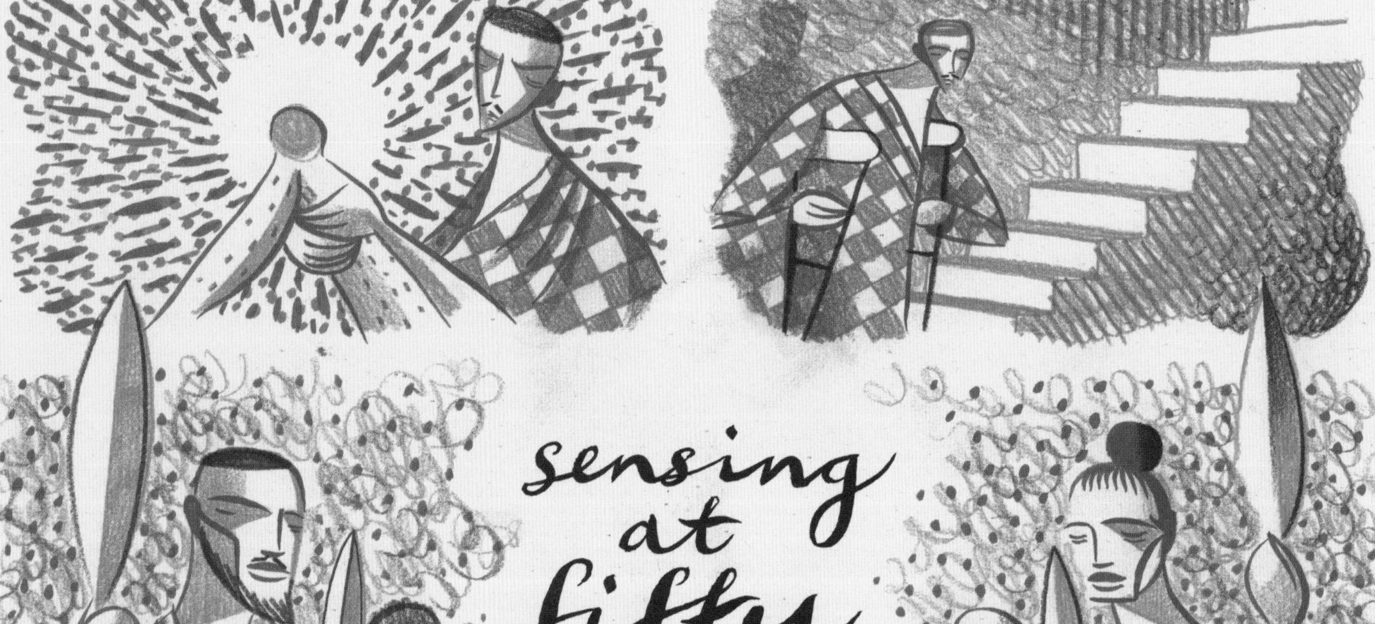

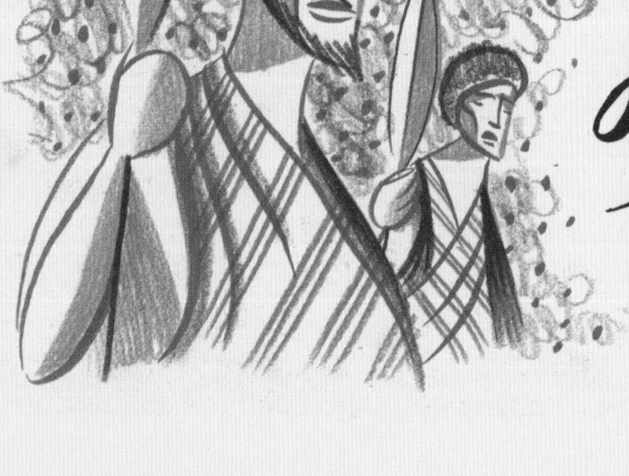

sensing
at
fifty
leagues

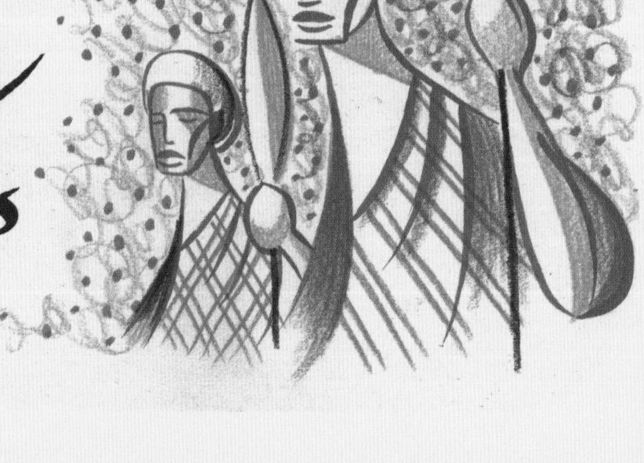

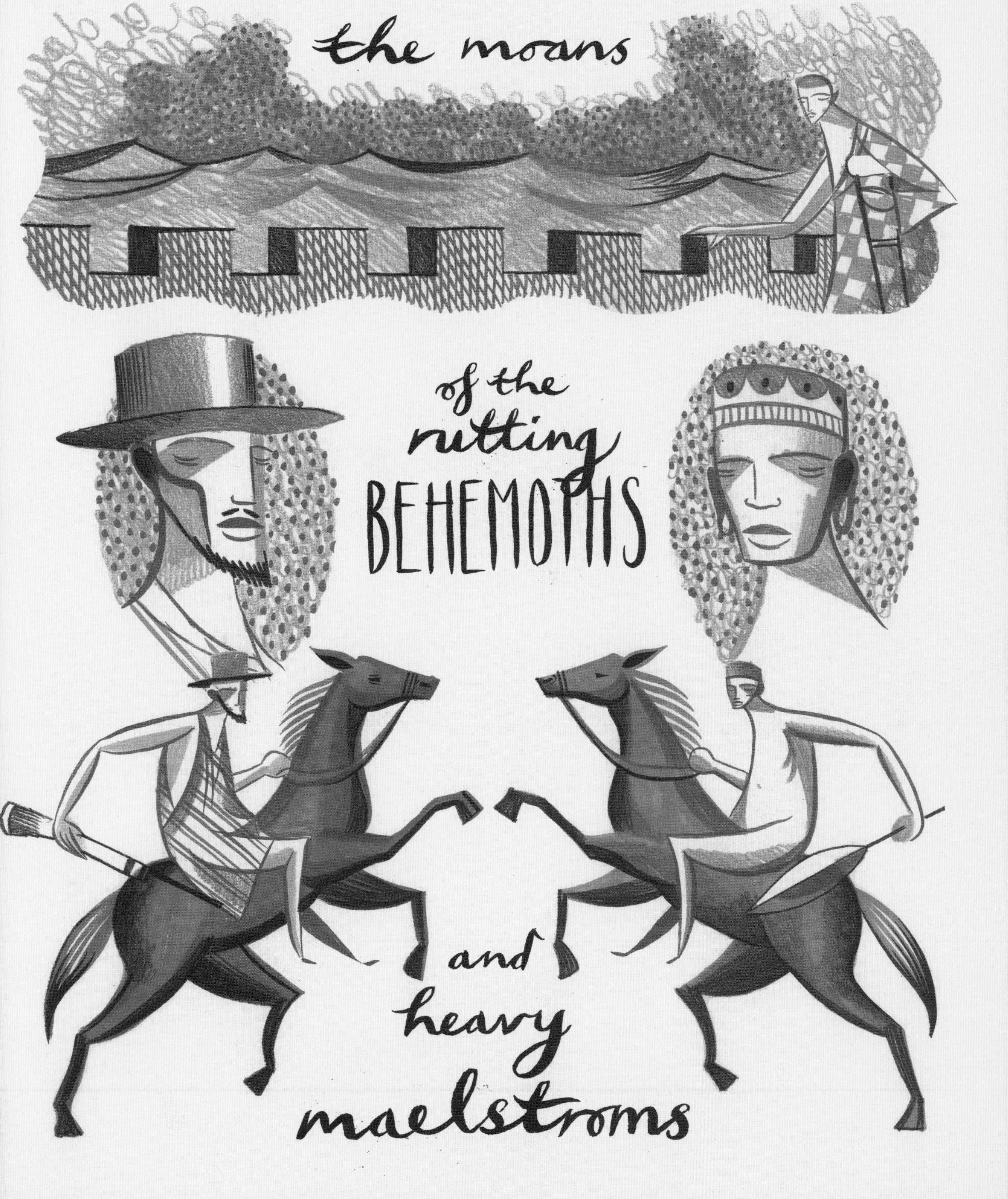
the moans
of the
rutting
BEHEMOTHS
and
heavy
maelstroms

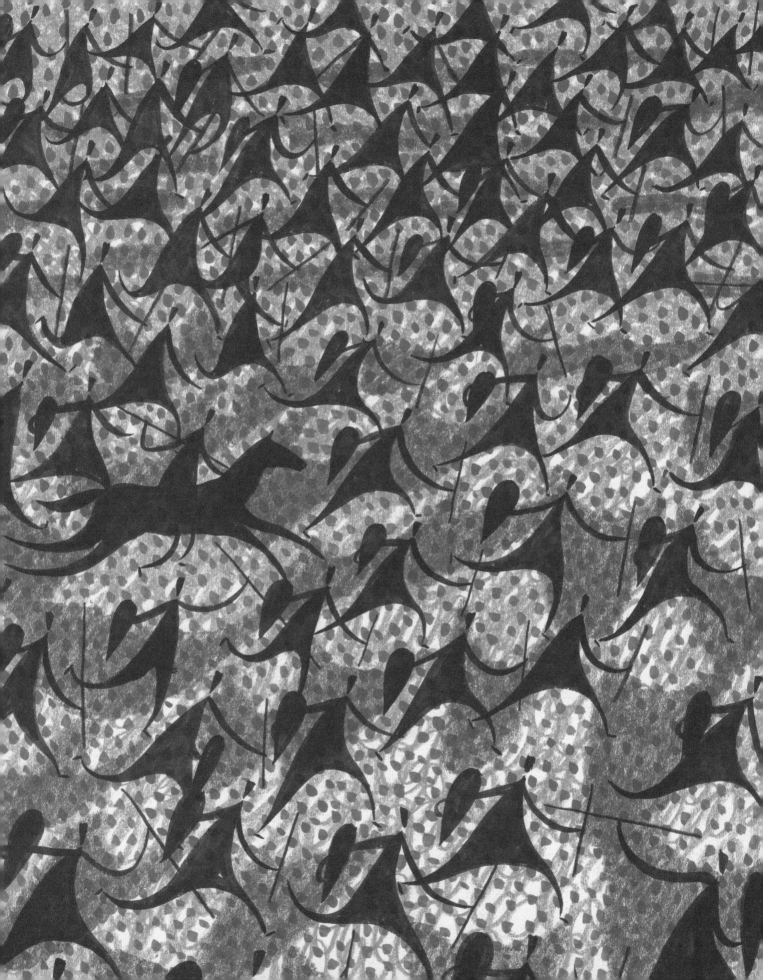

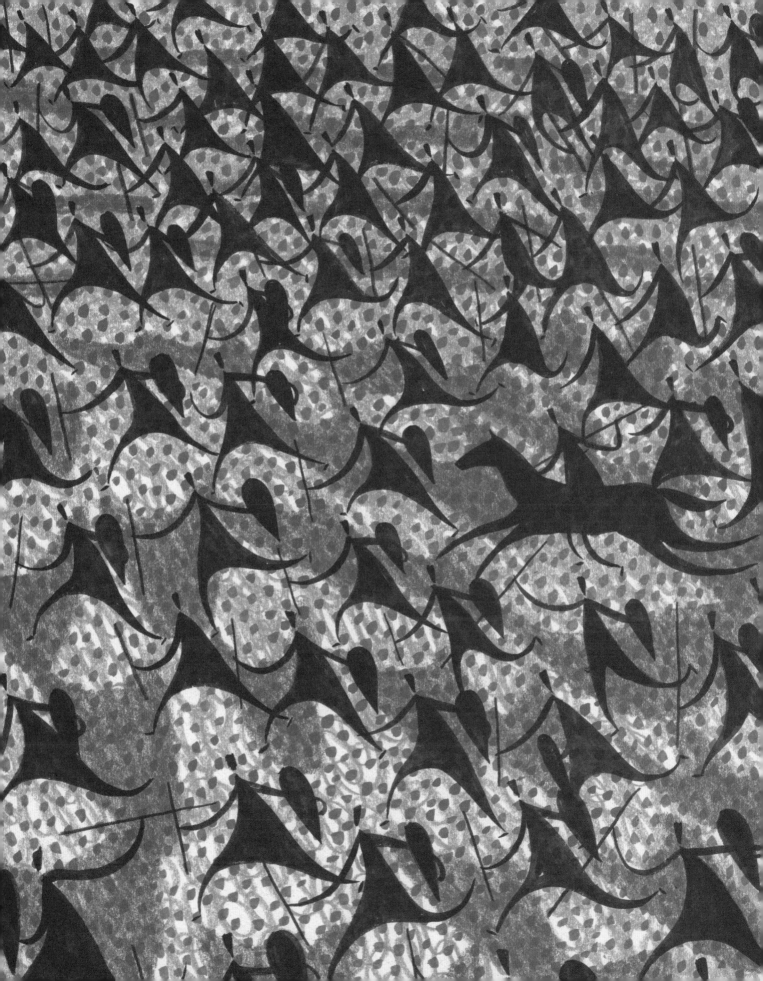

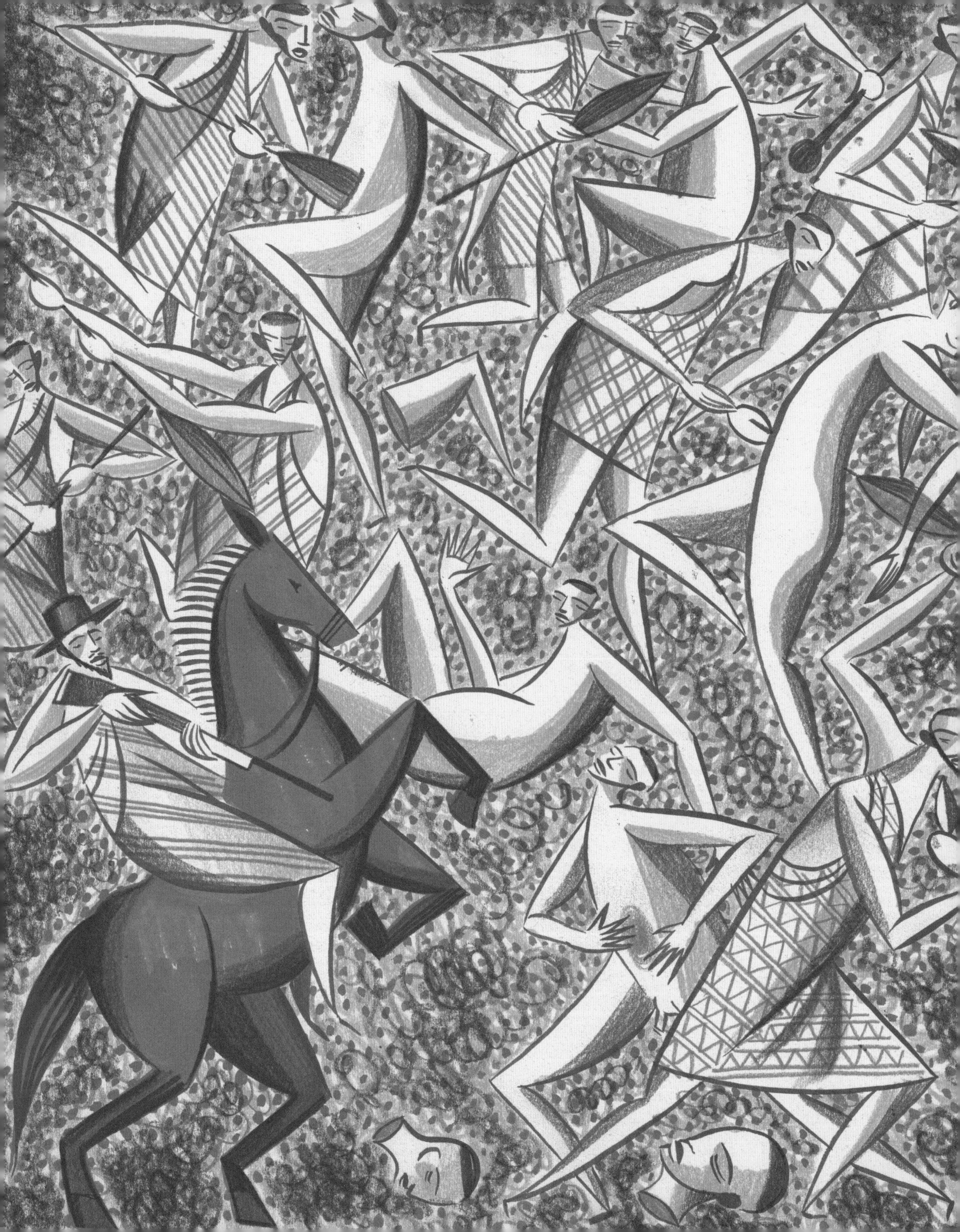

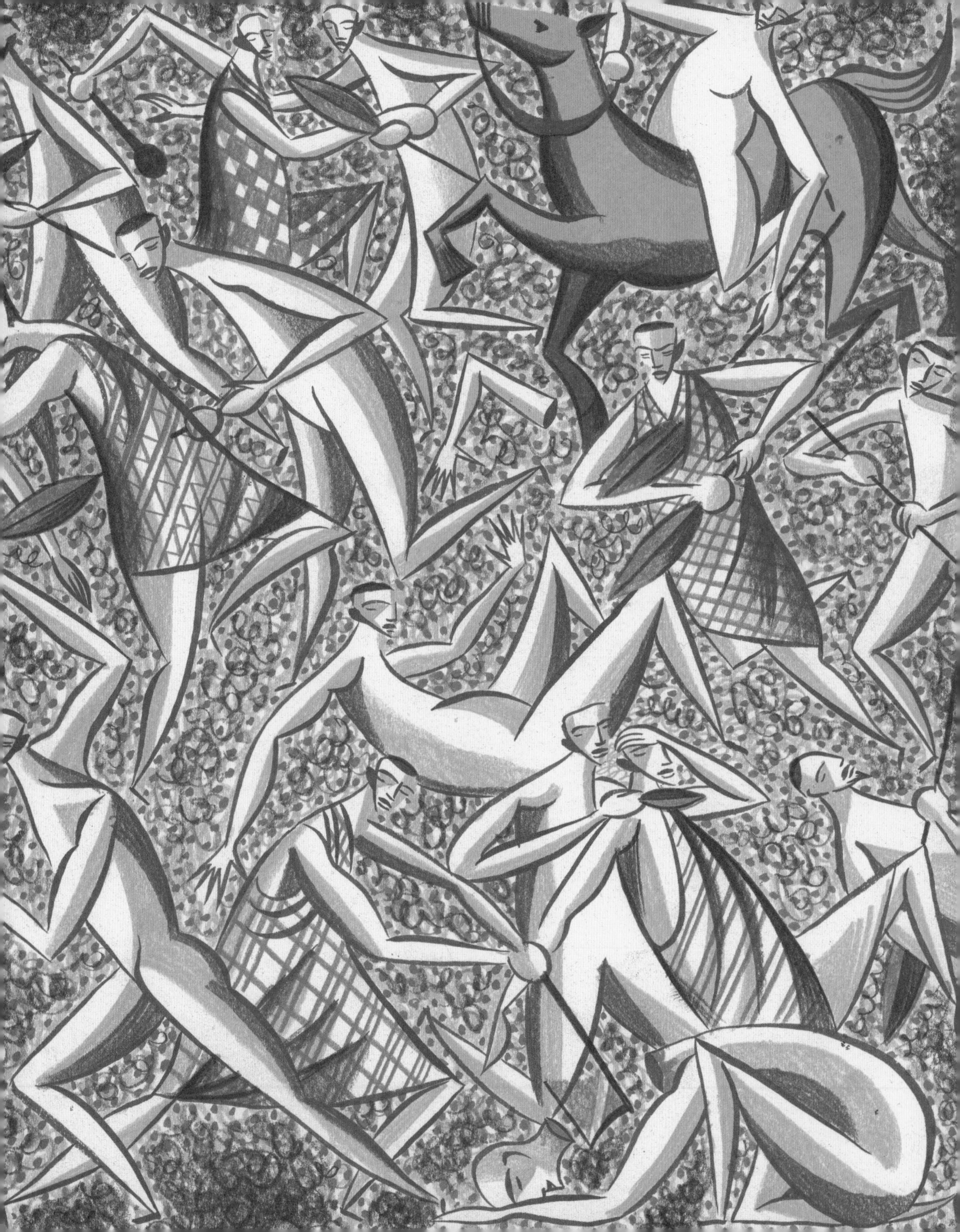

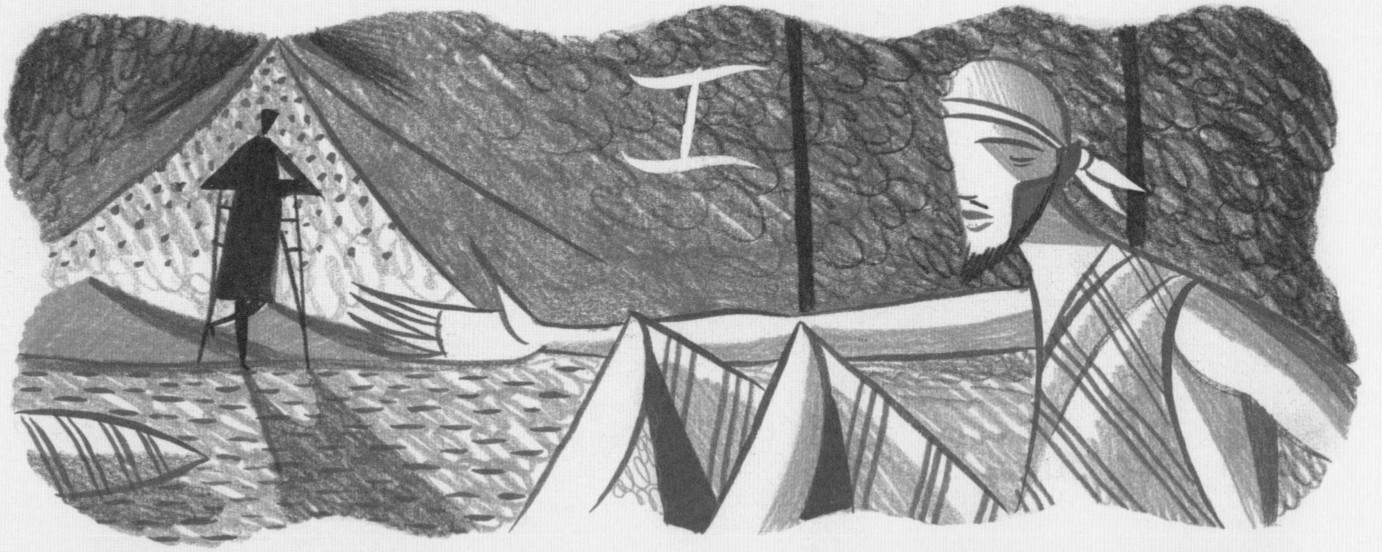
I

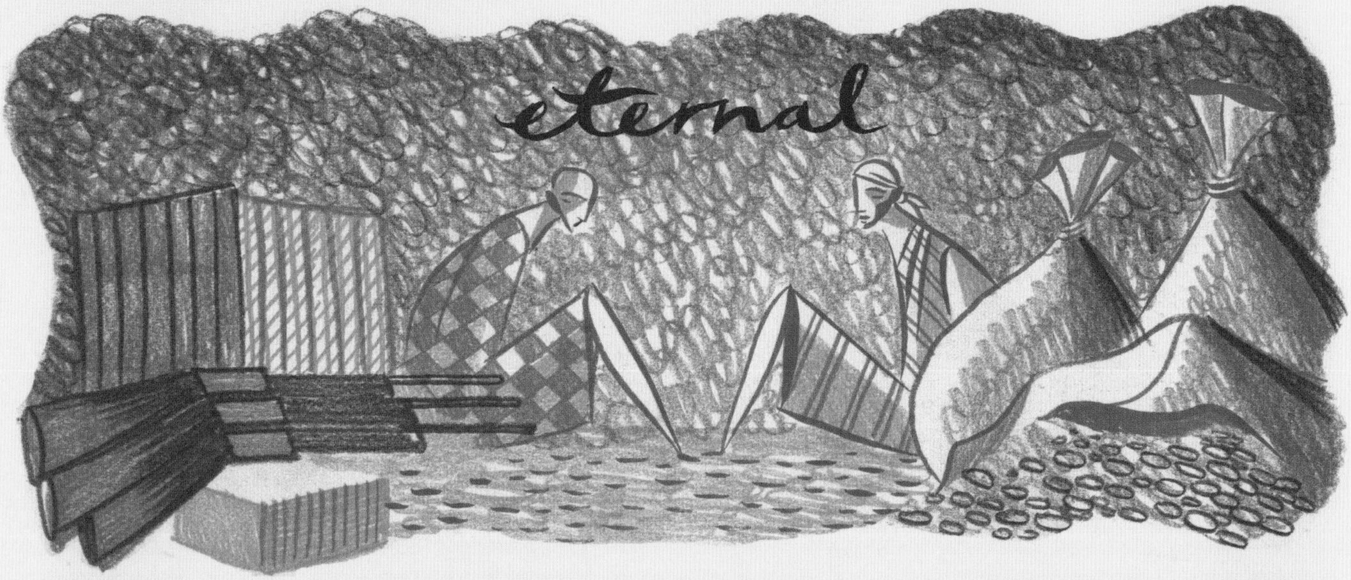
eternal

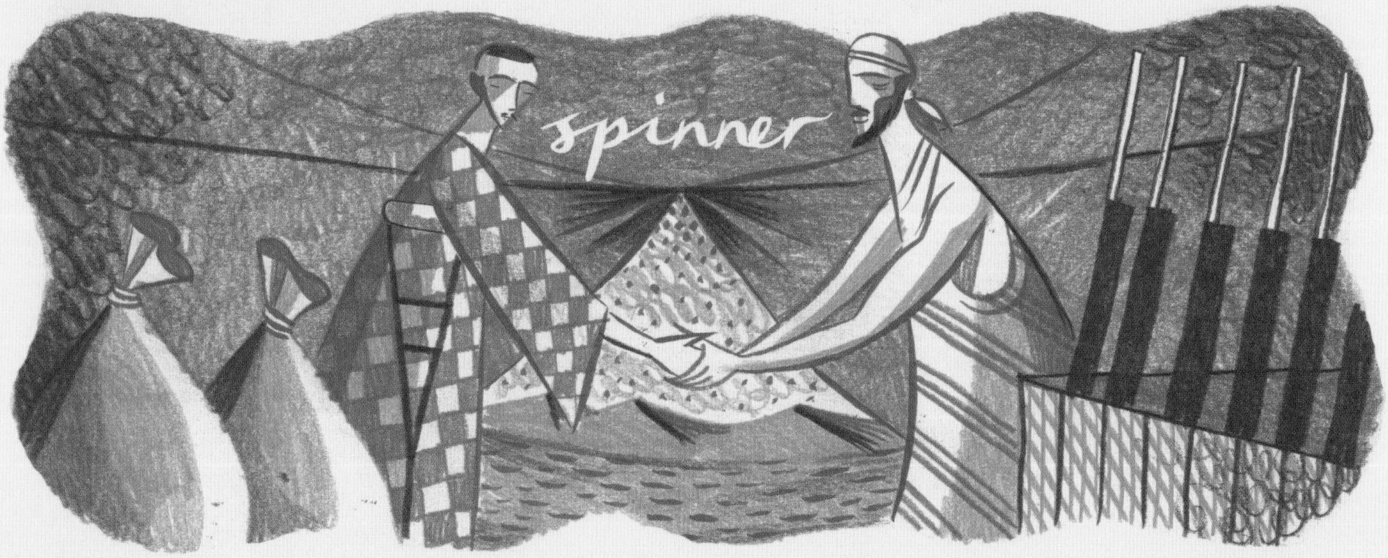
spinner

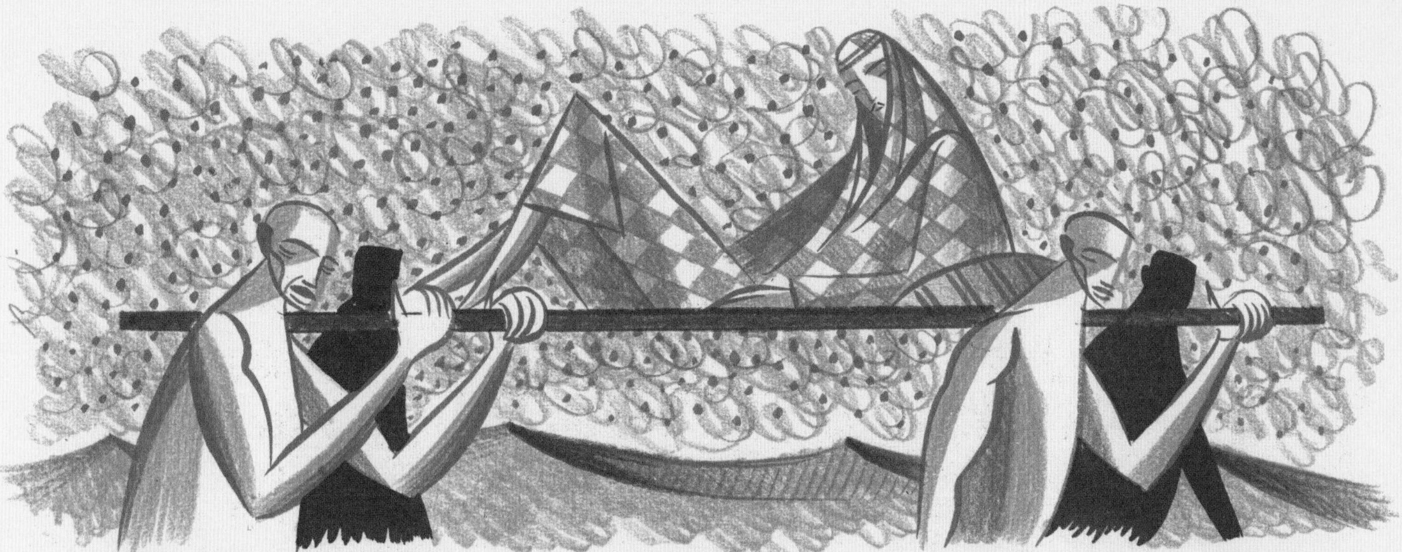

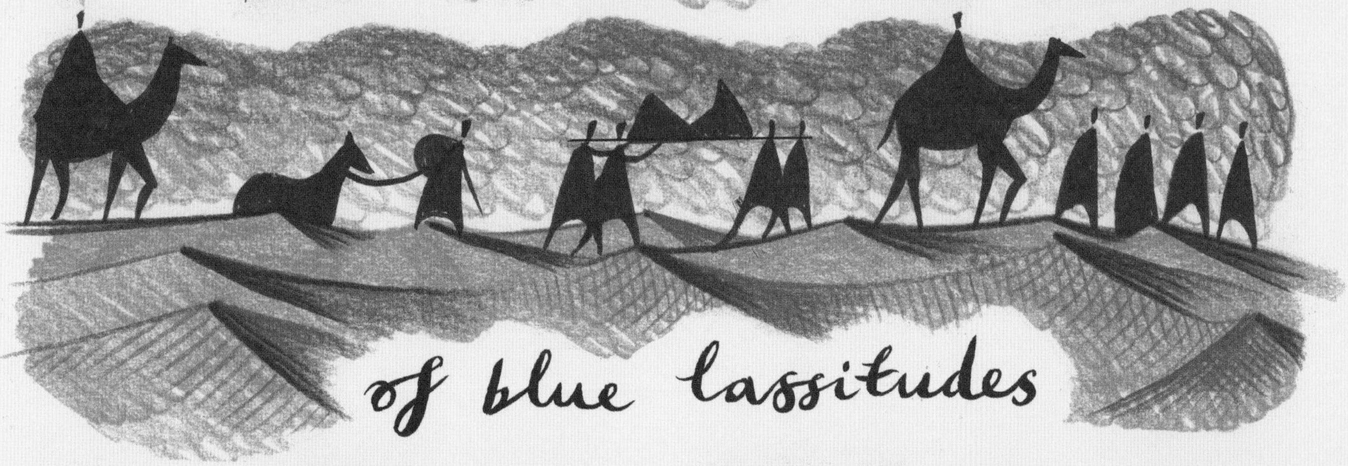
of blue lassitudes

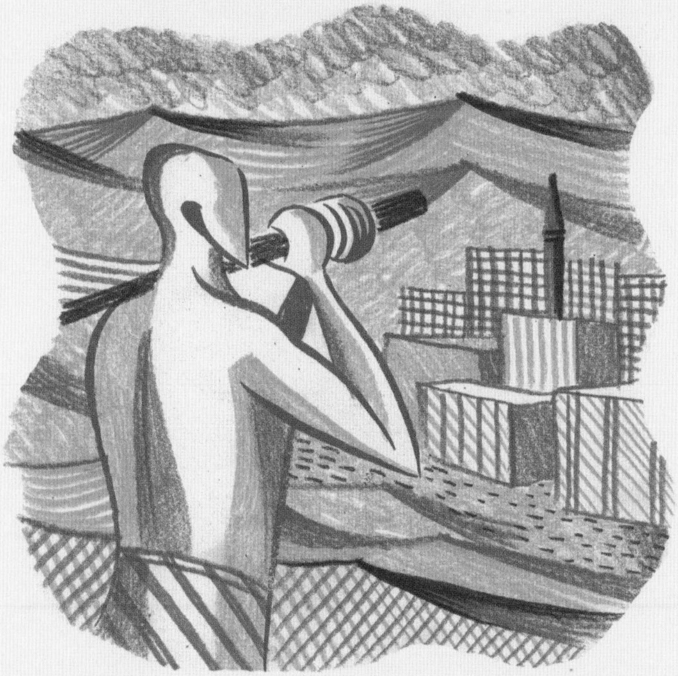

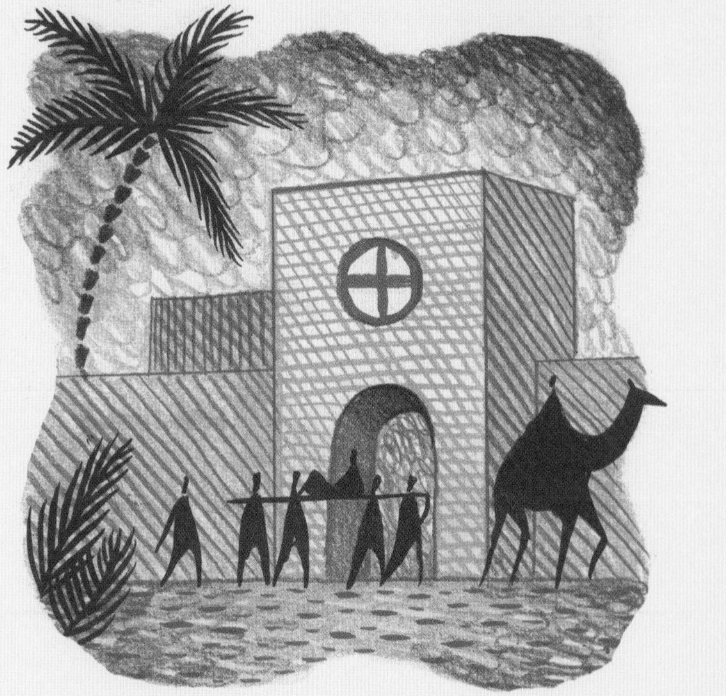

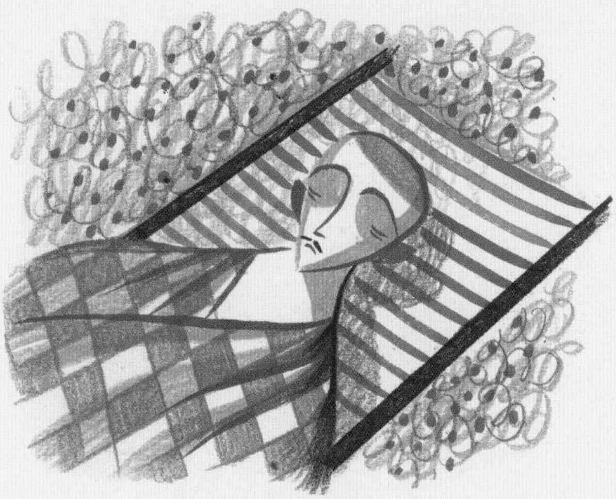

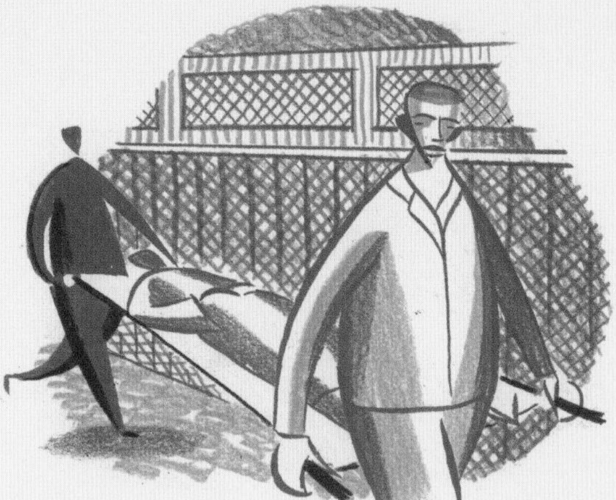

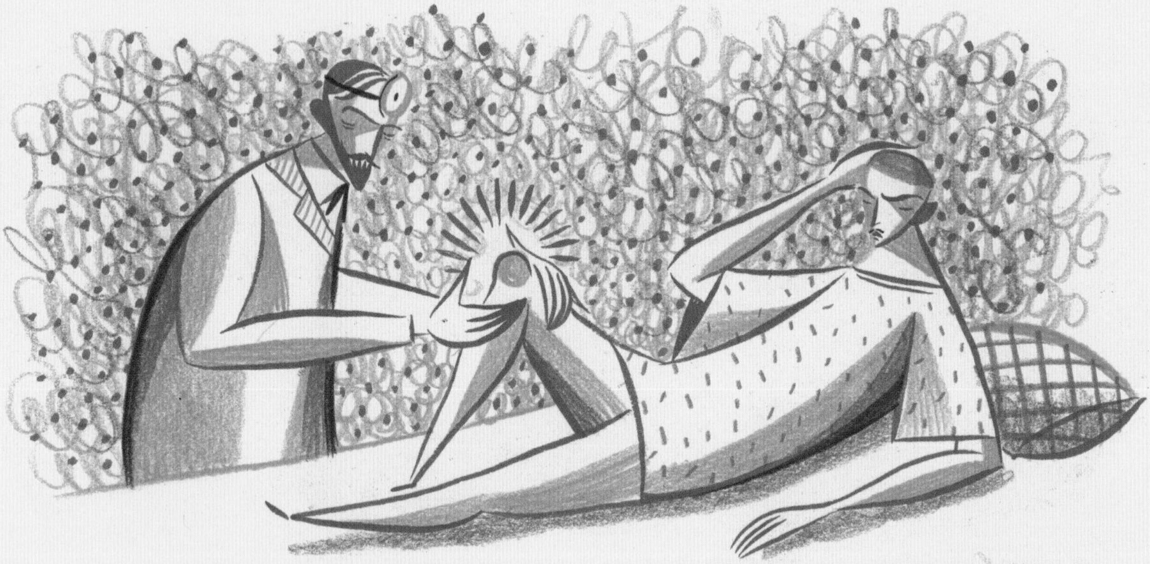

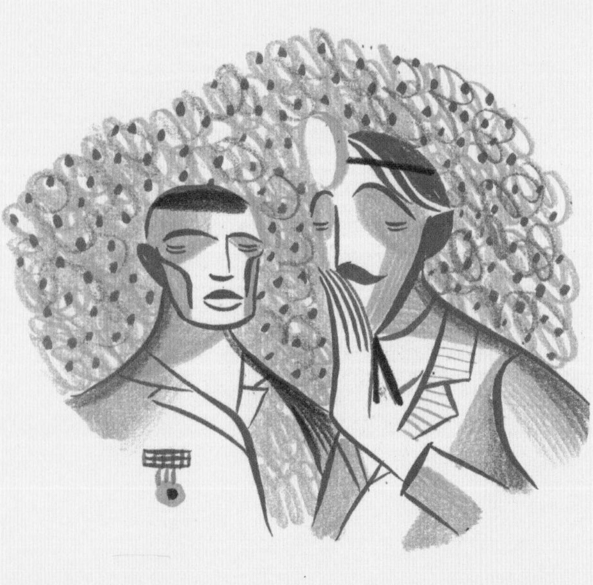

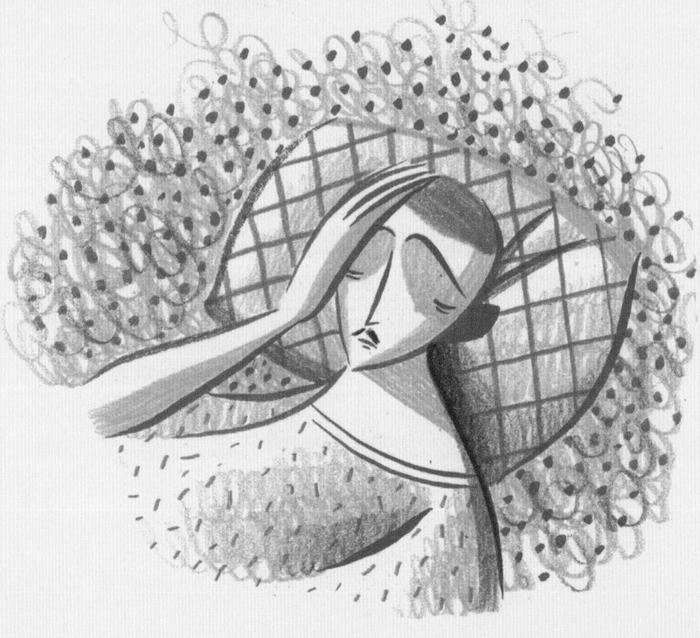

...I miss that Europe of antique parapets.

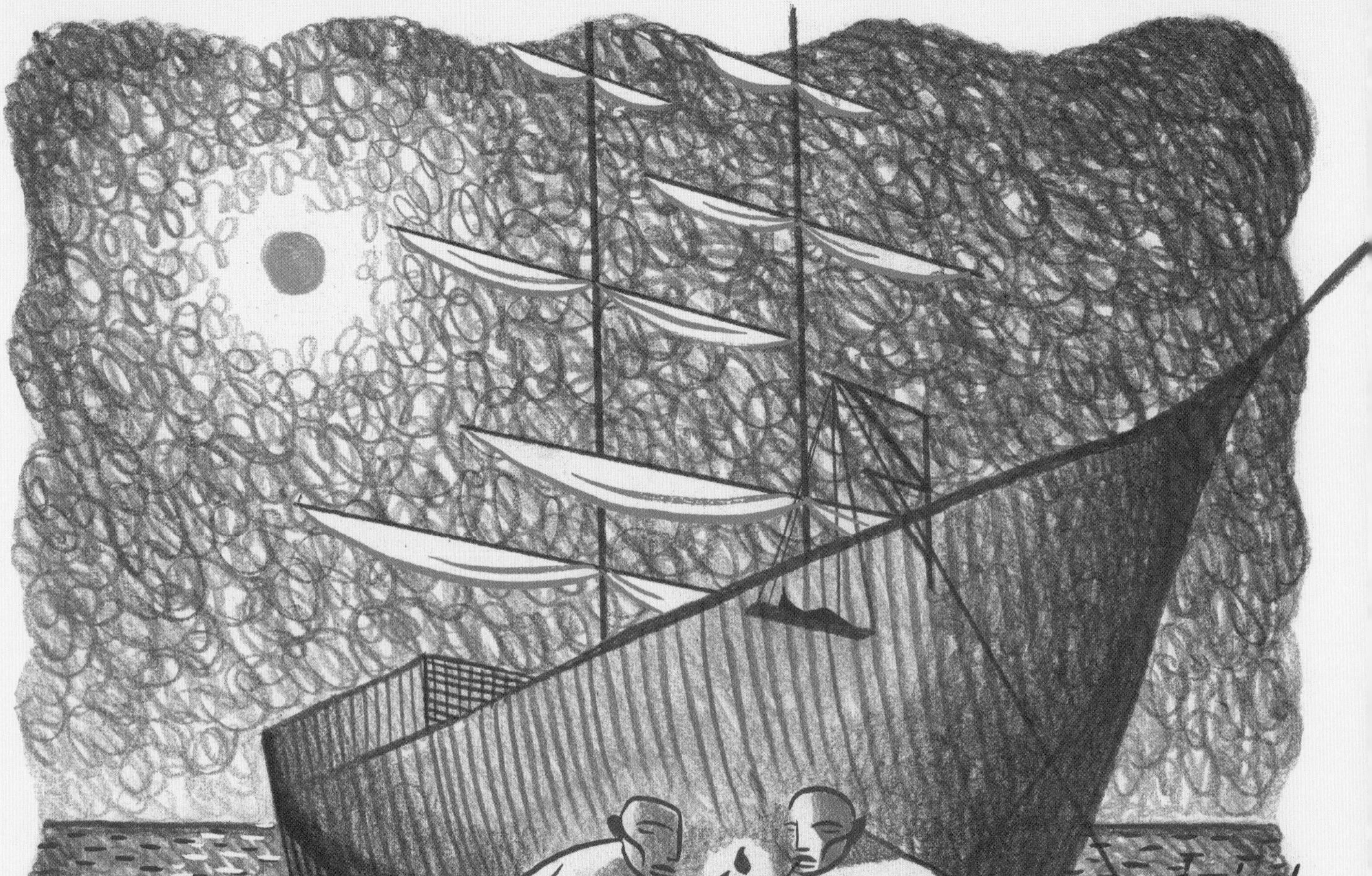

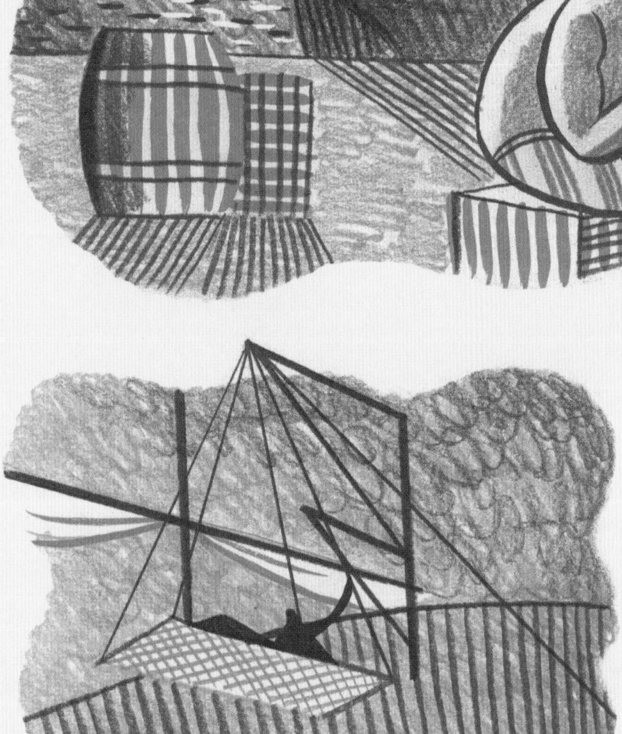

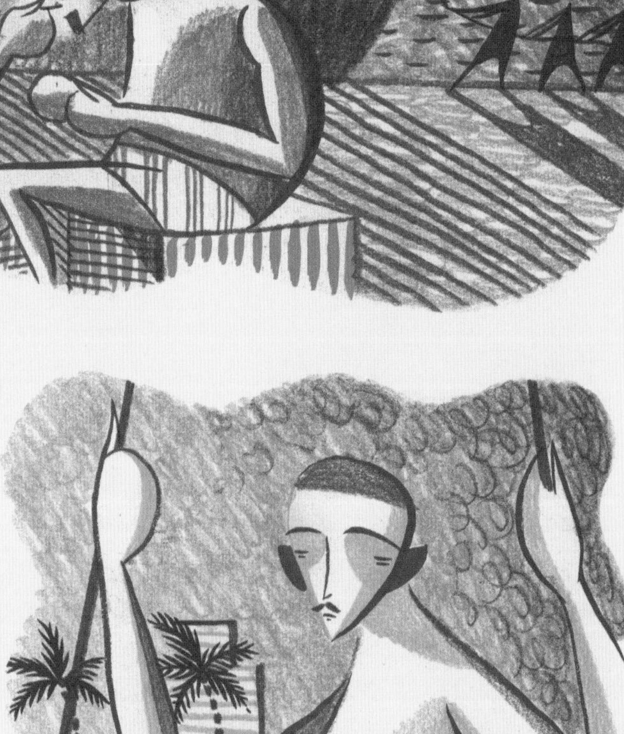

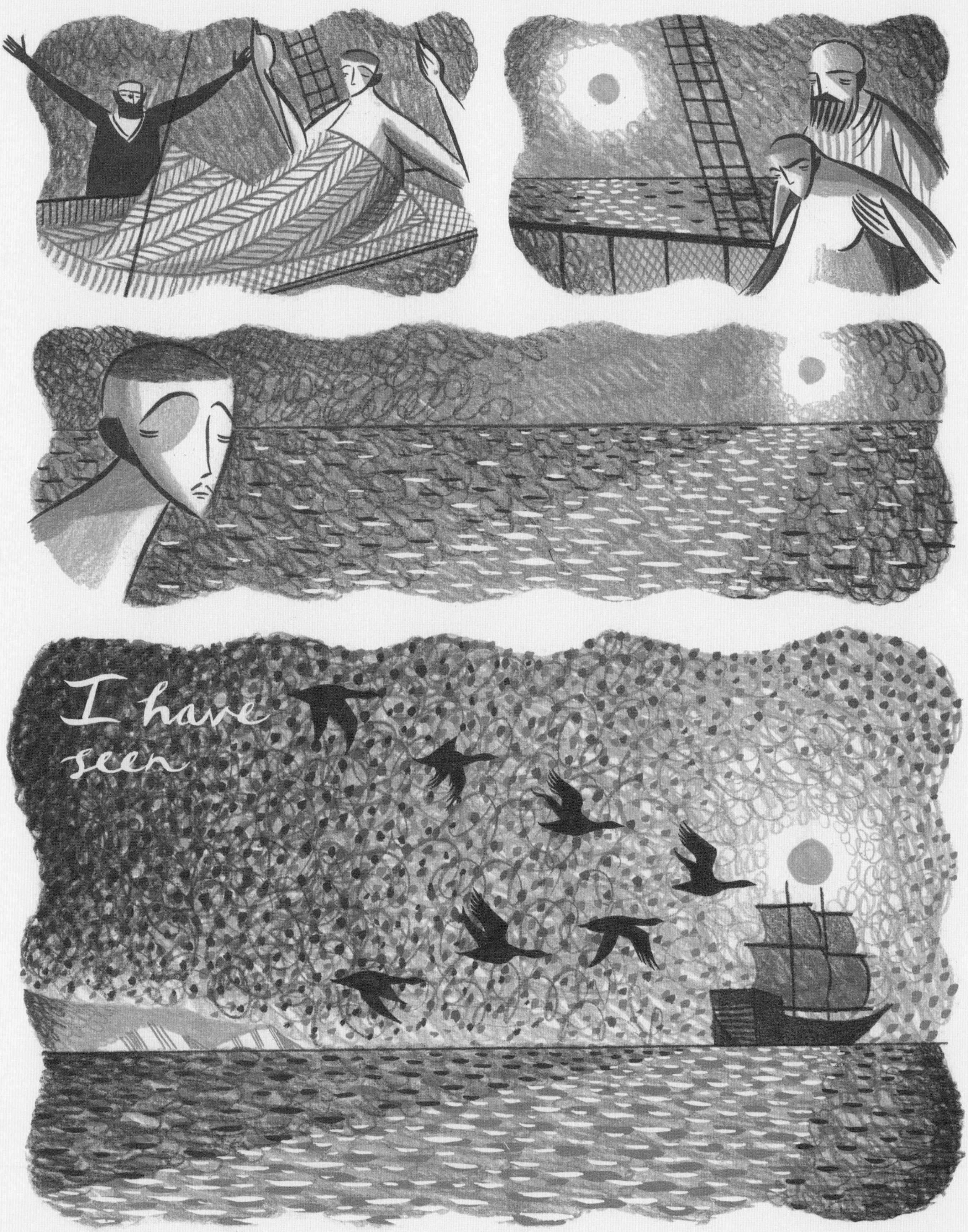
I have seen

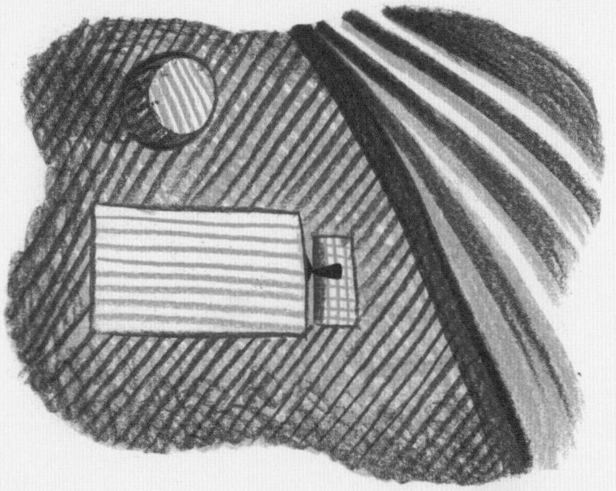 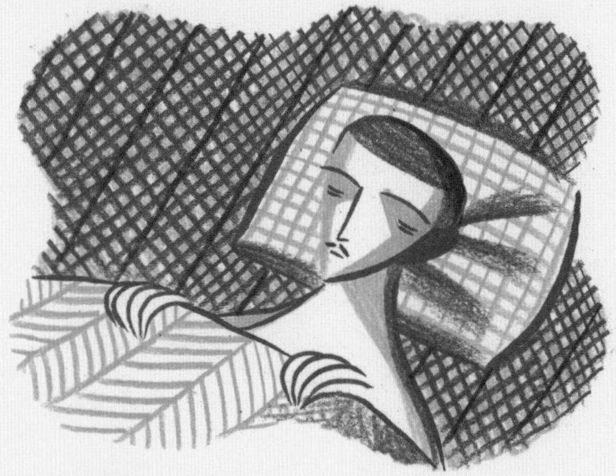

archipelagos
of stars,

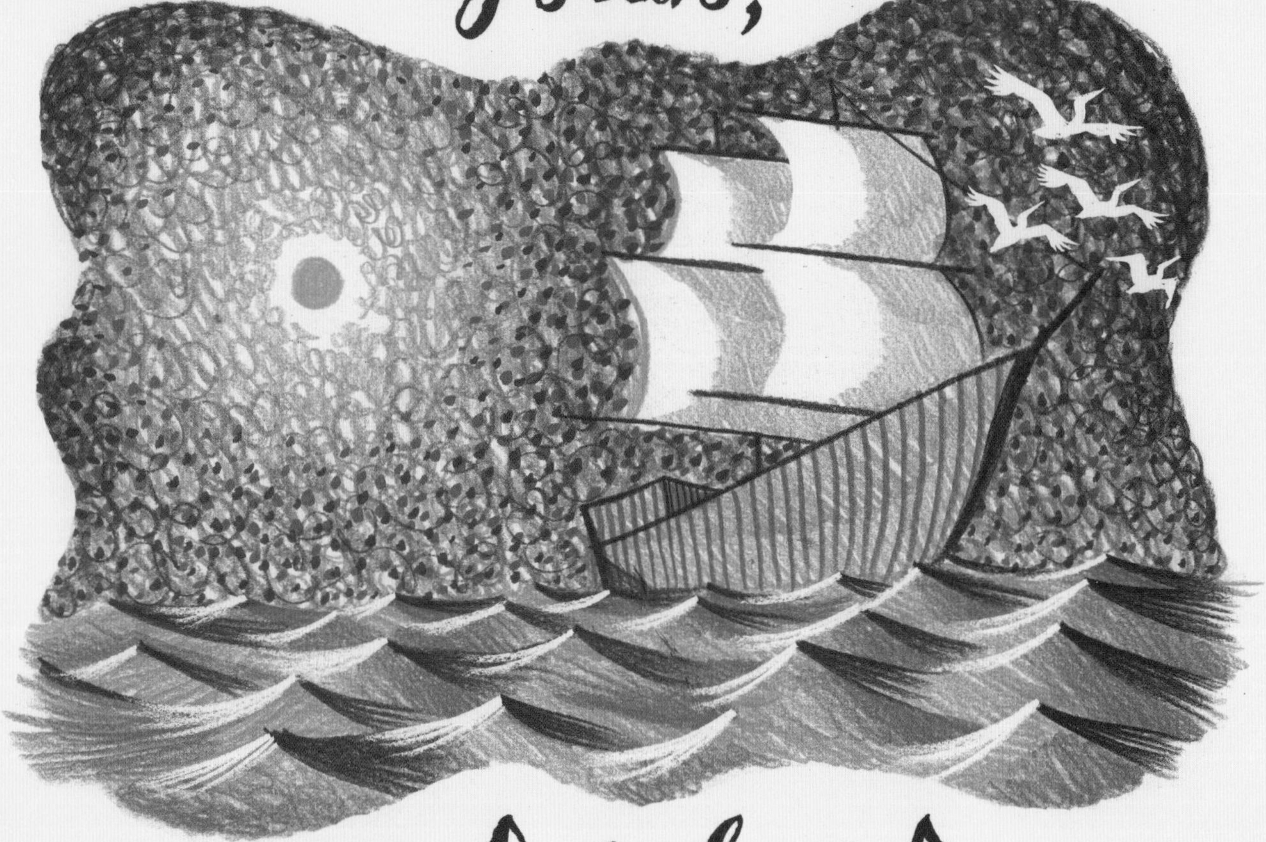

and islands

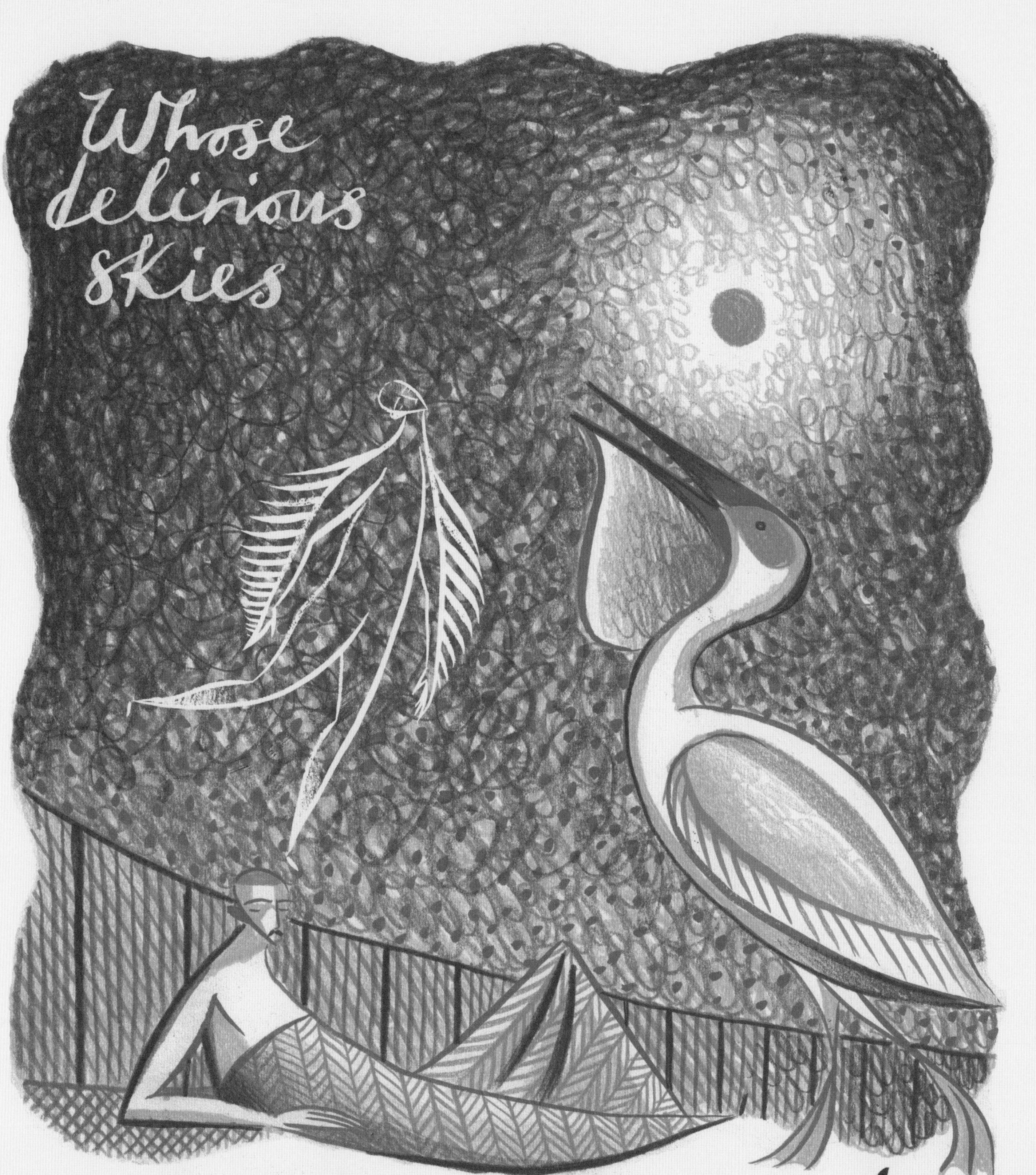
Whose
delirious
skies

beckon the seadog.

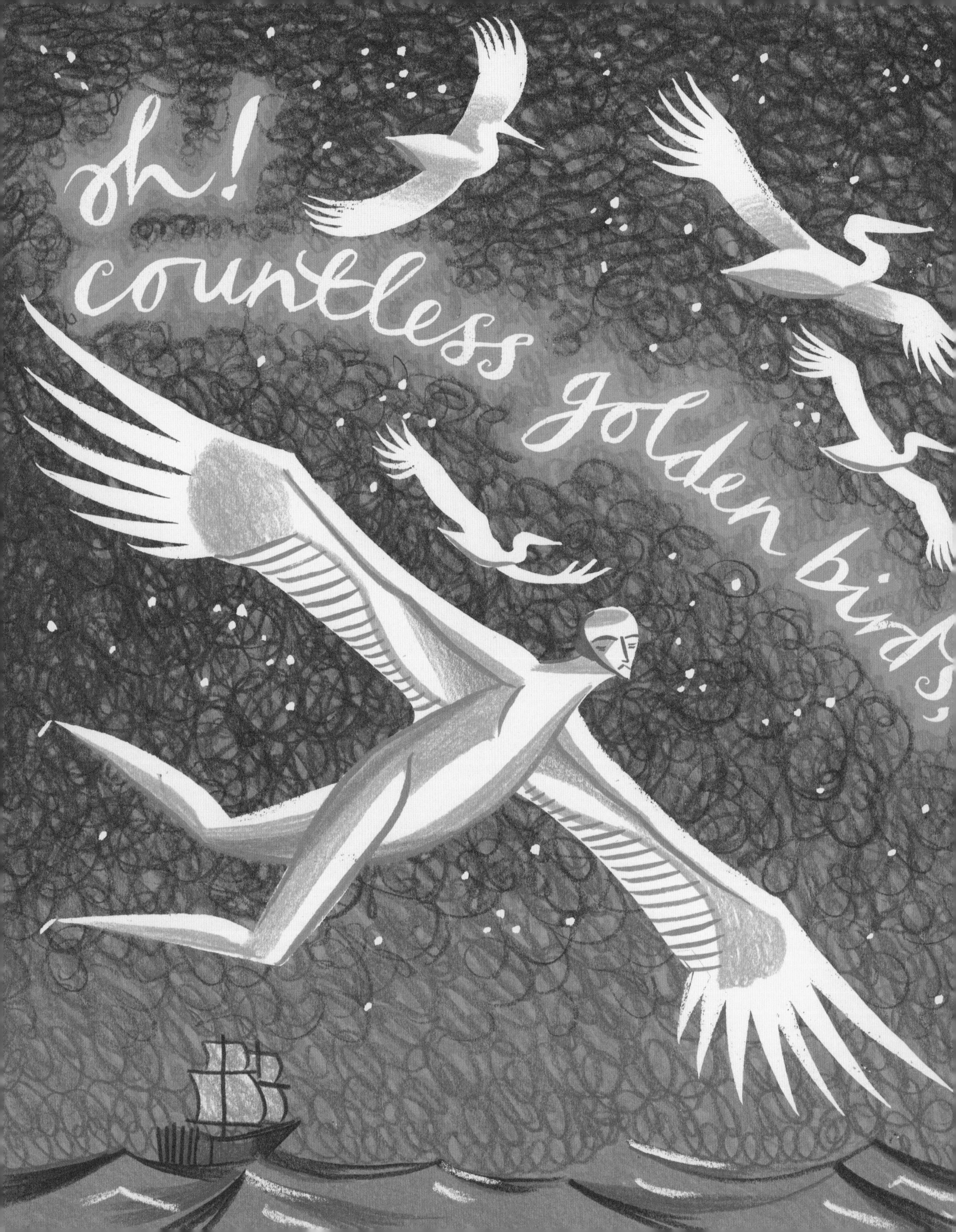
oh!
countless golden birds,

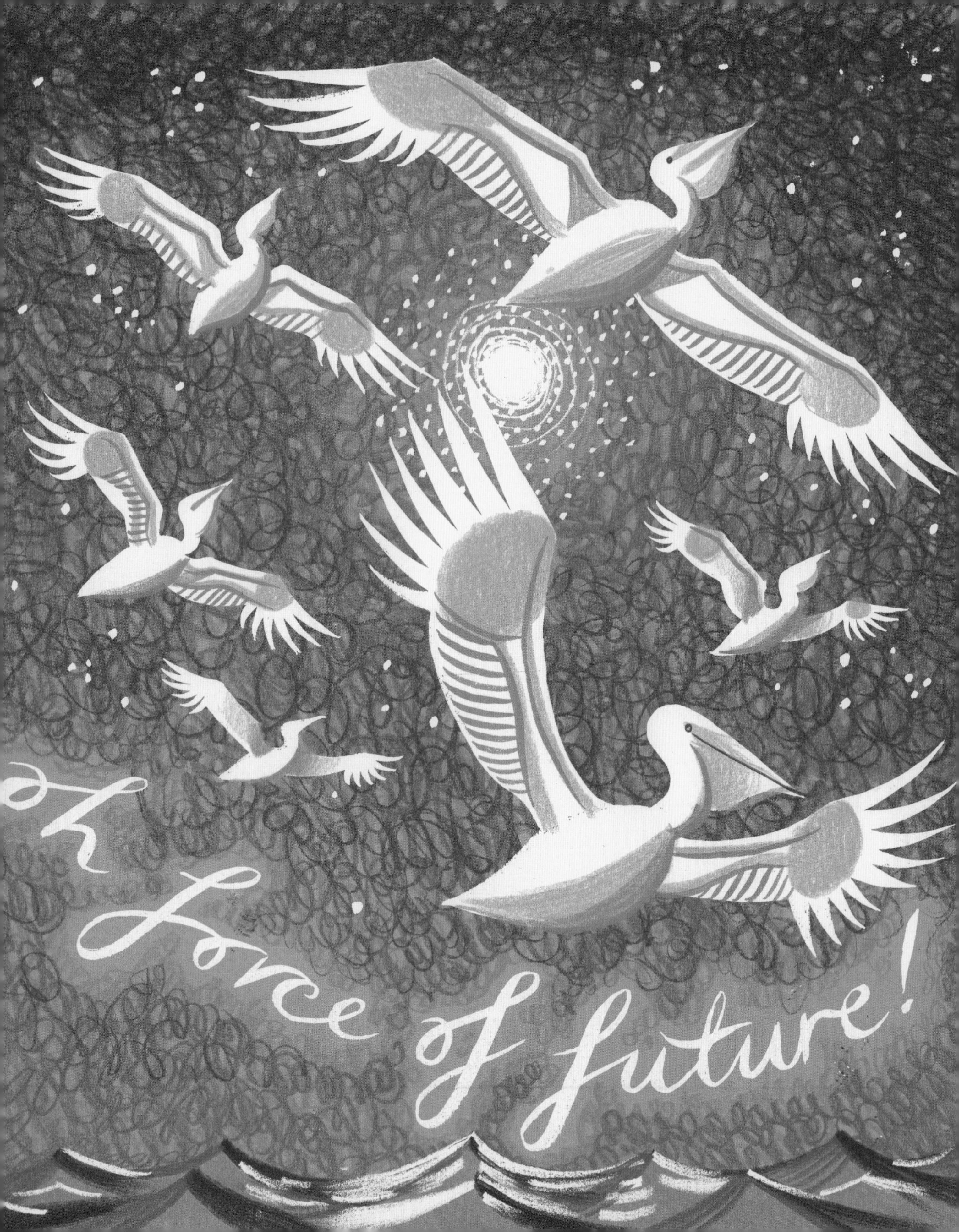
oh force of future!

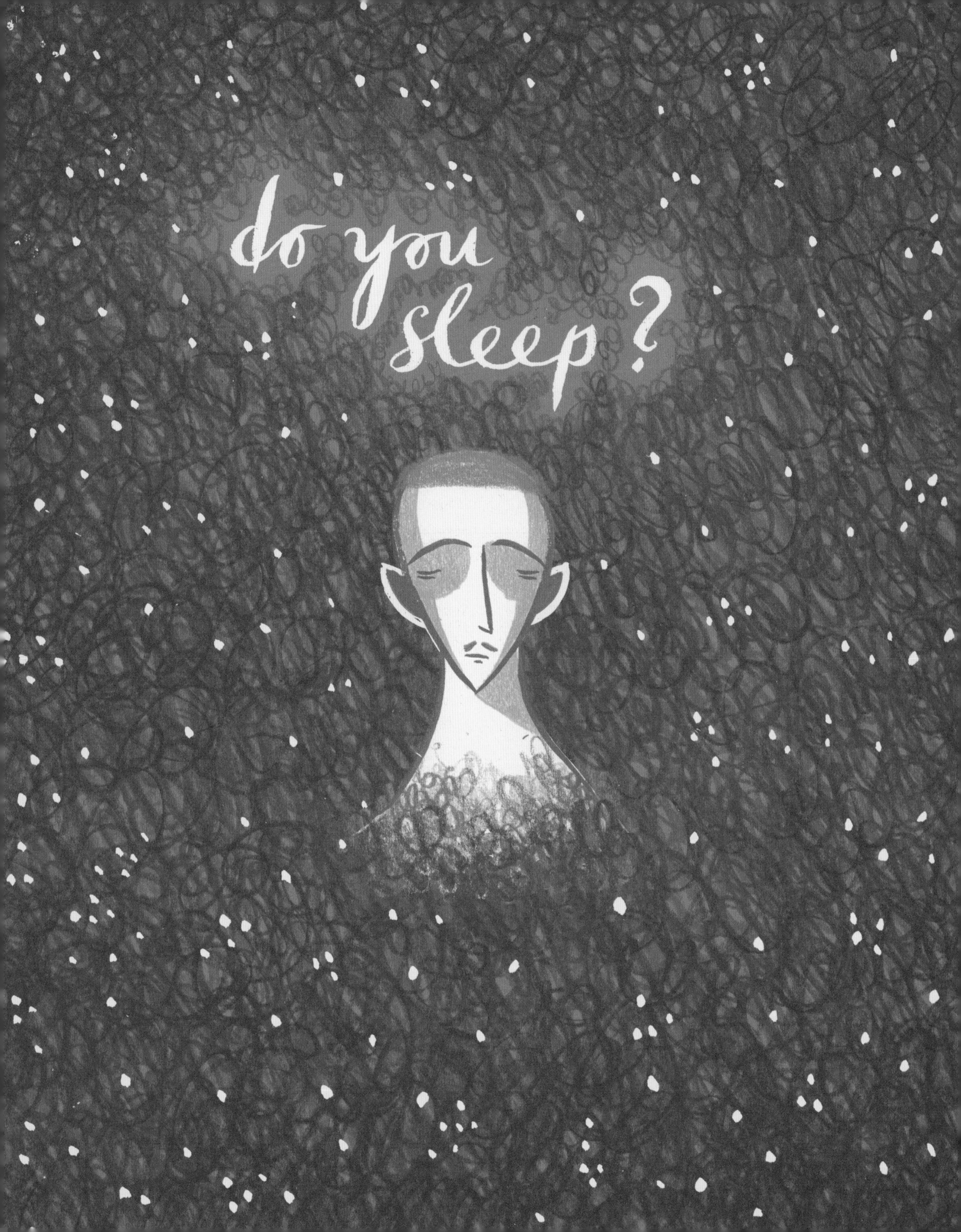
do you
sleep?

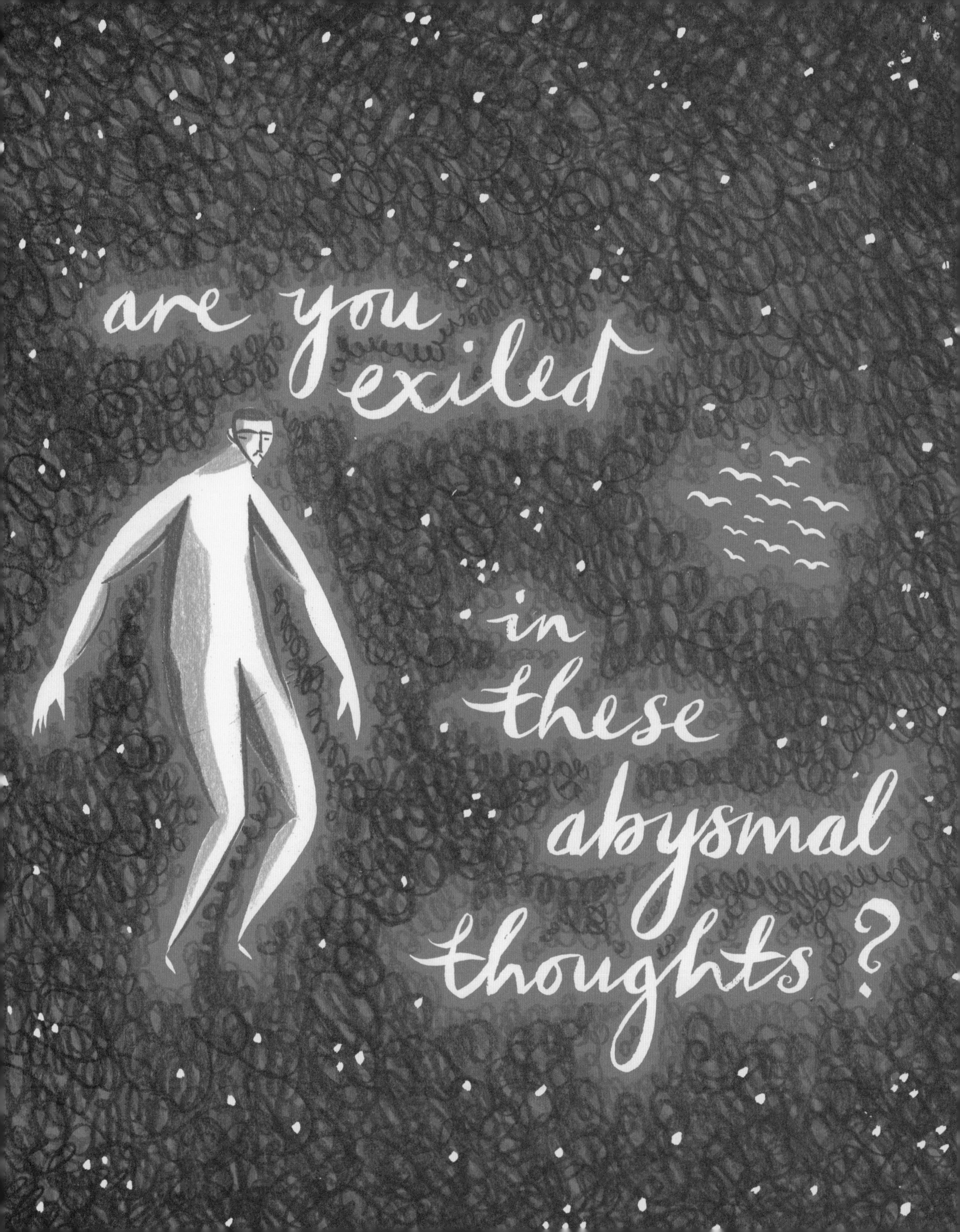
are you exiled
in these abysmal thoughts?

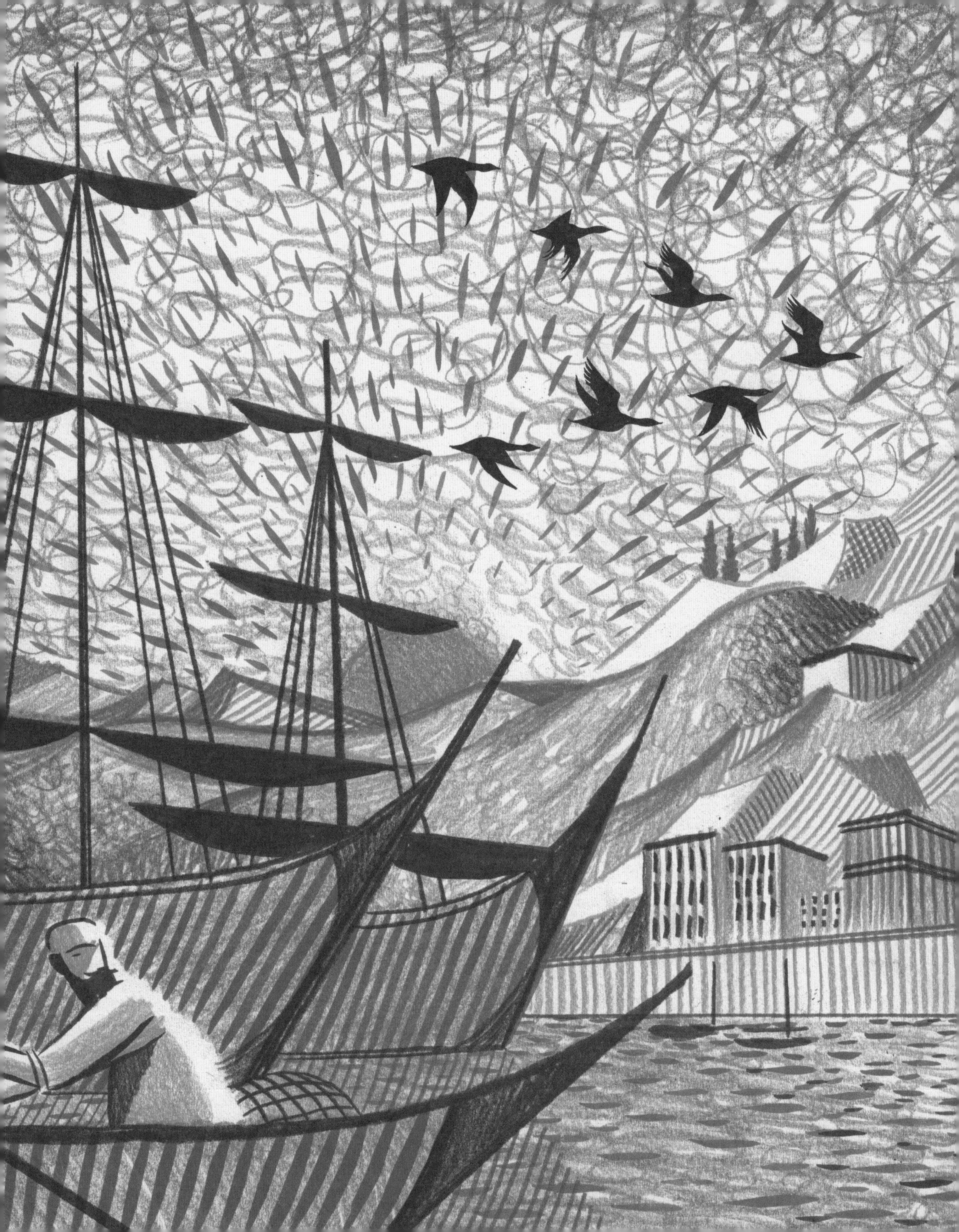

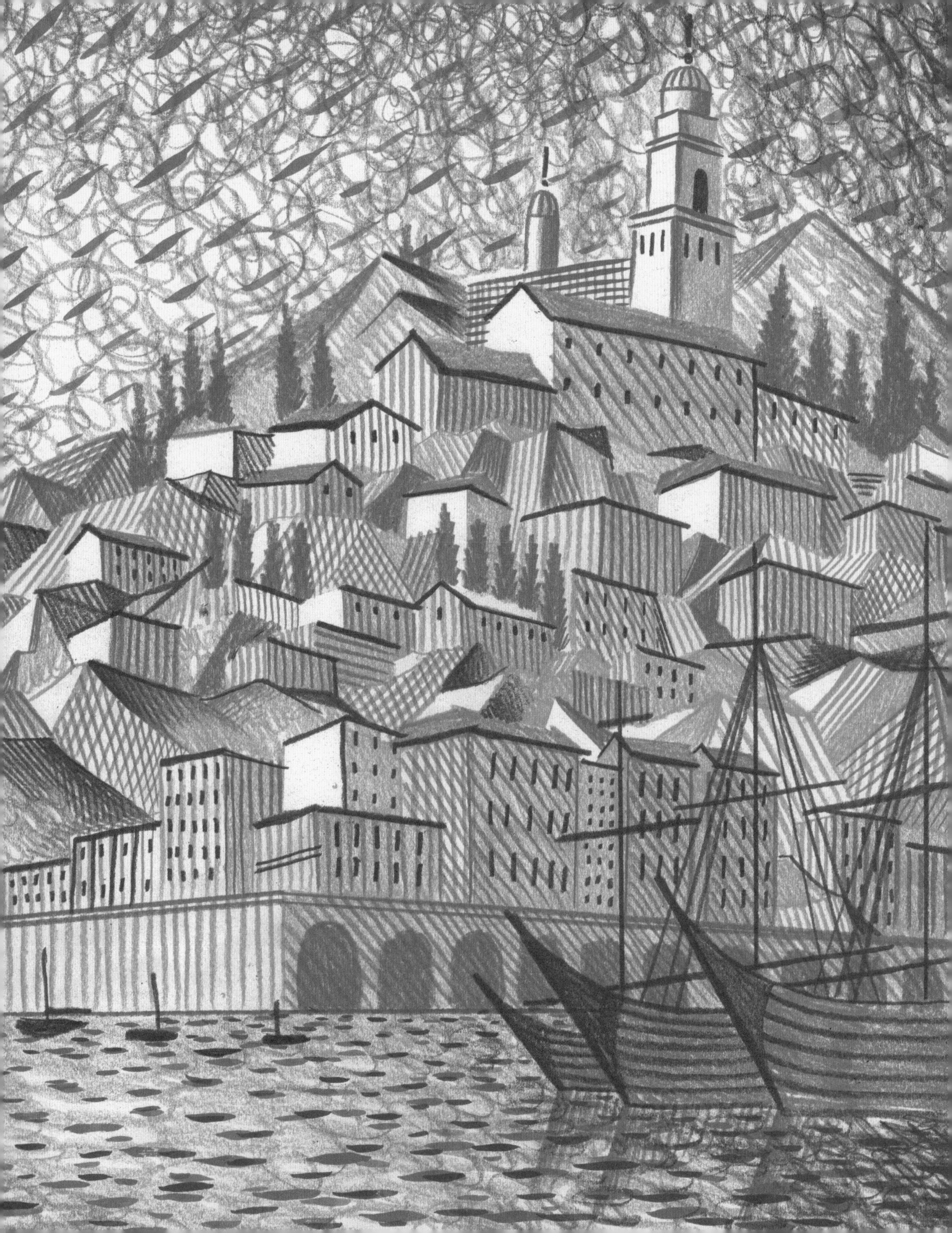

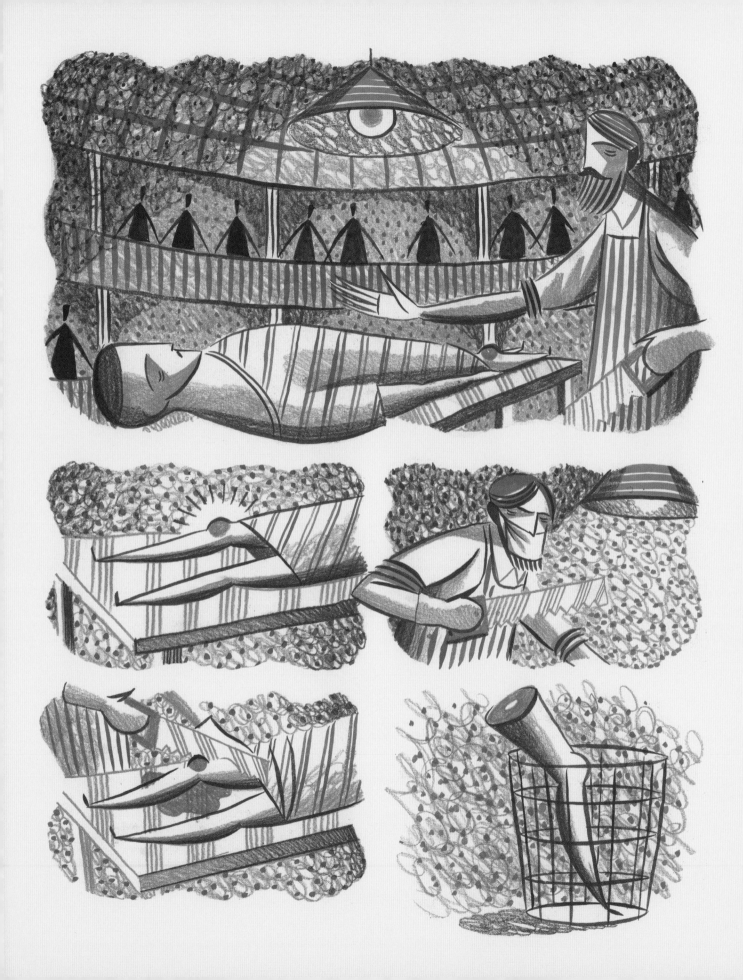

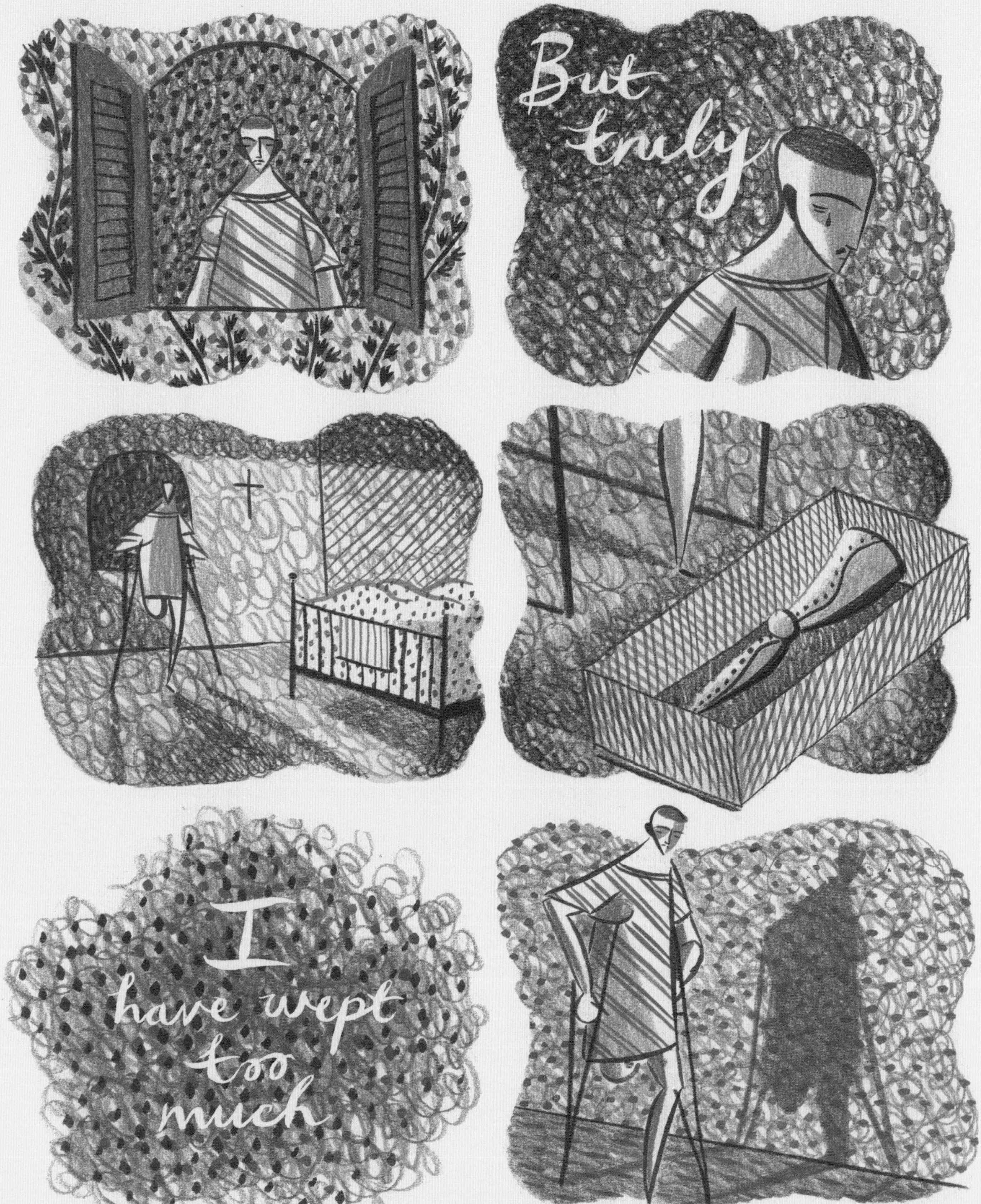
But truly
I have wept too much

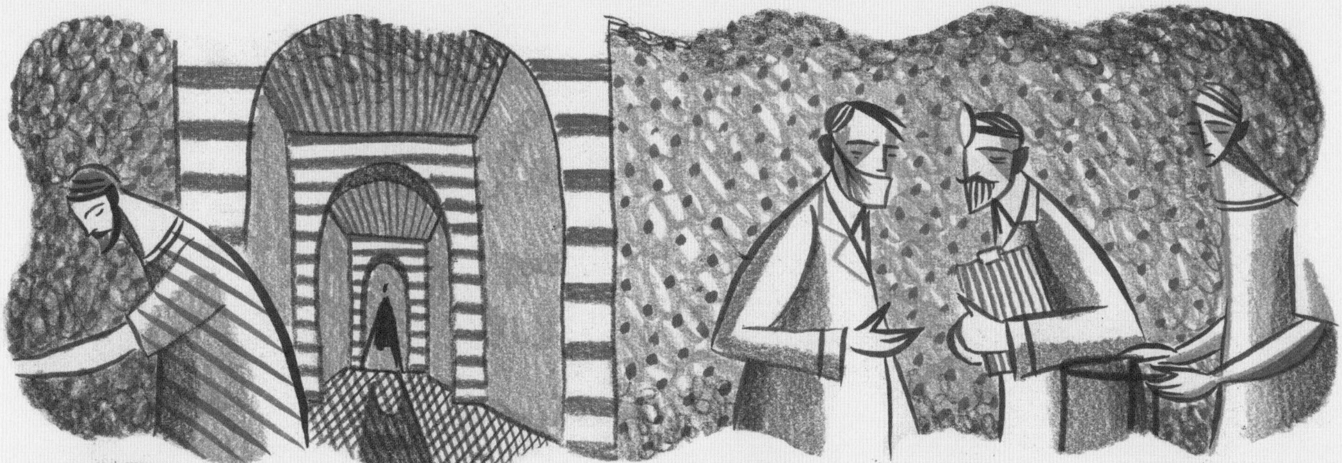

The dawns are heartbreaking,

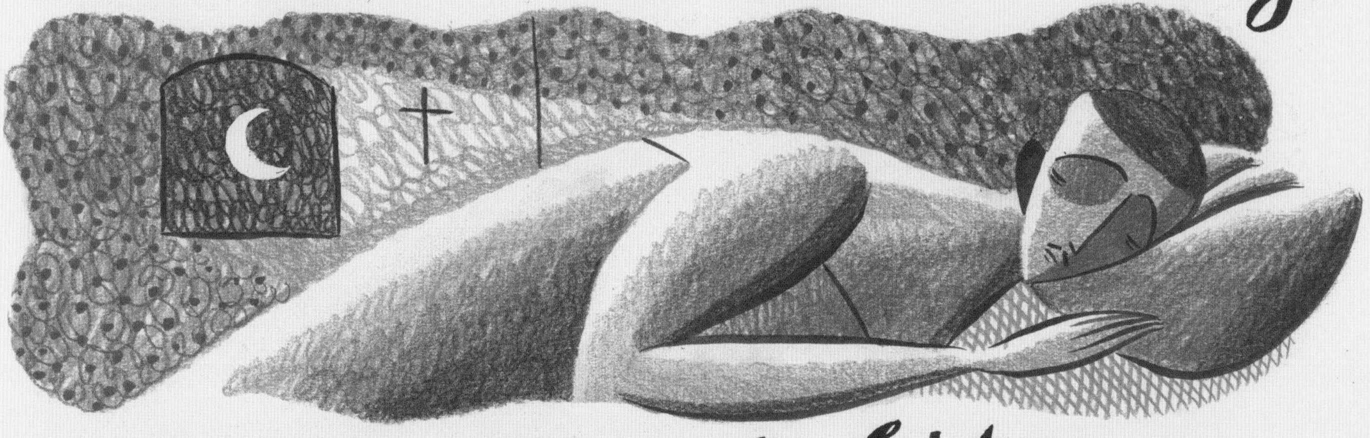

every moon is hideous,

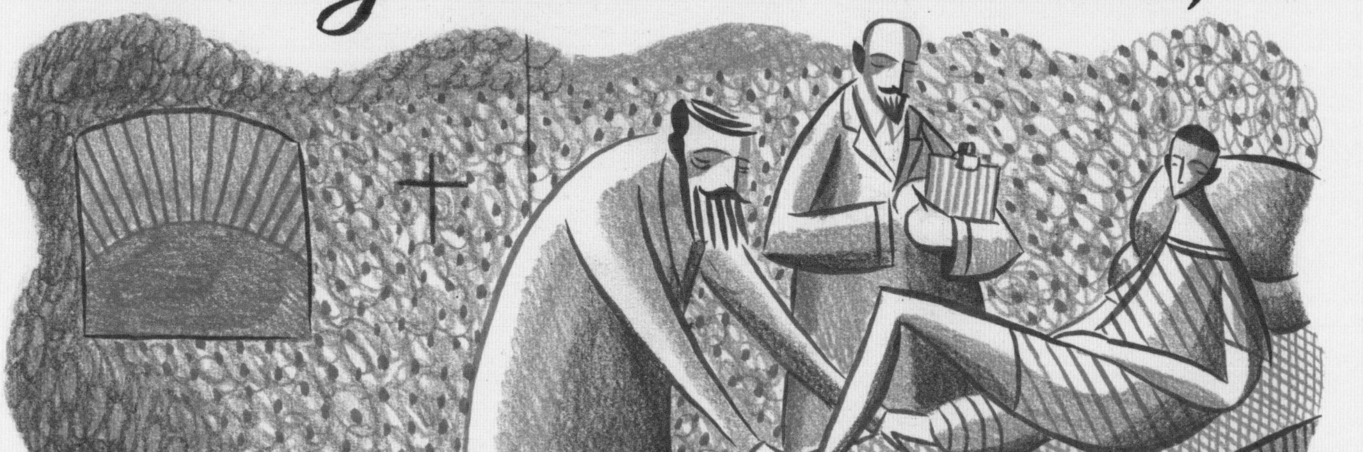

and every sun diabolic.

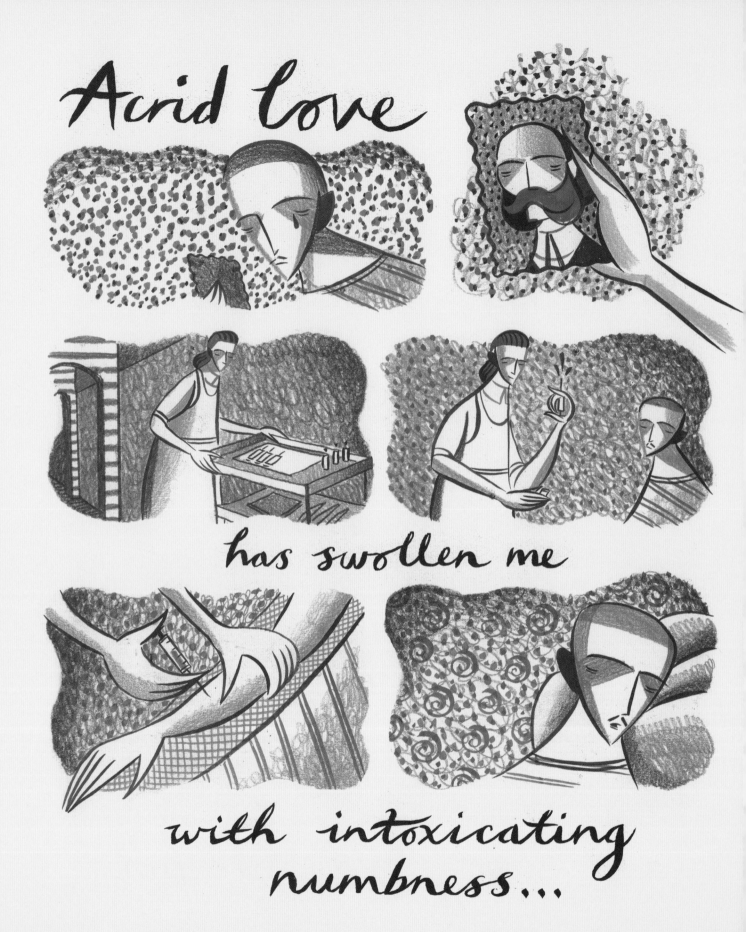

Acrid love

has swollen me

with intoxicating
numbness...

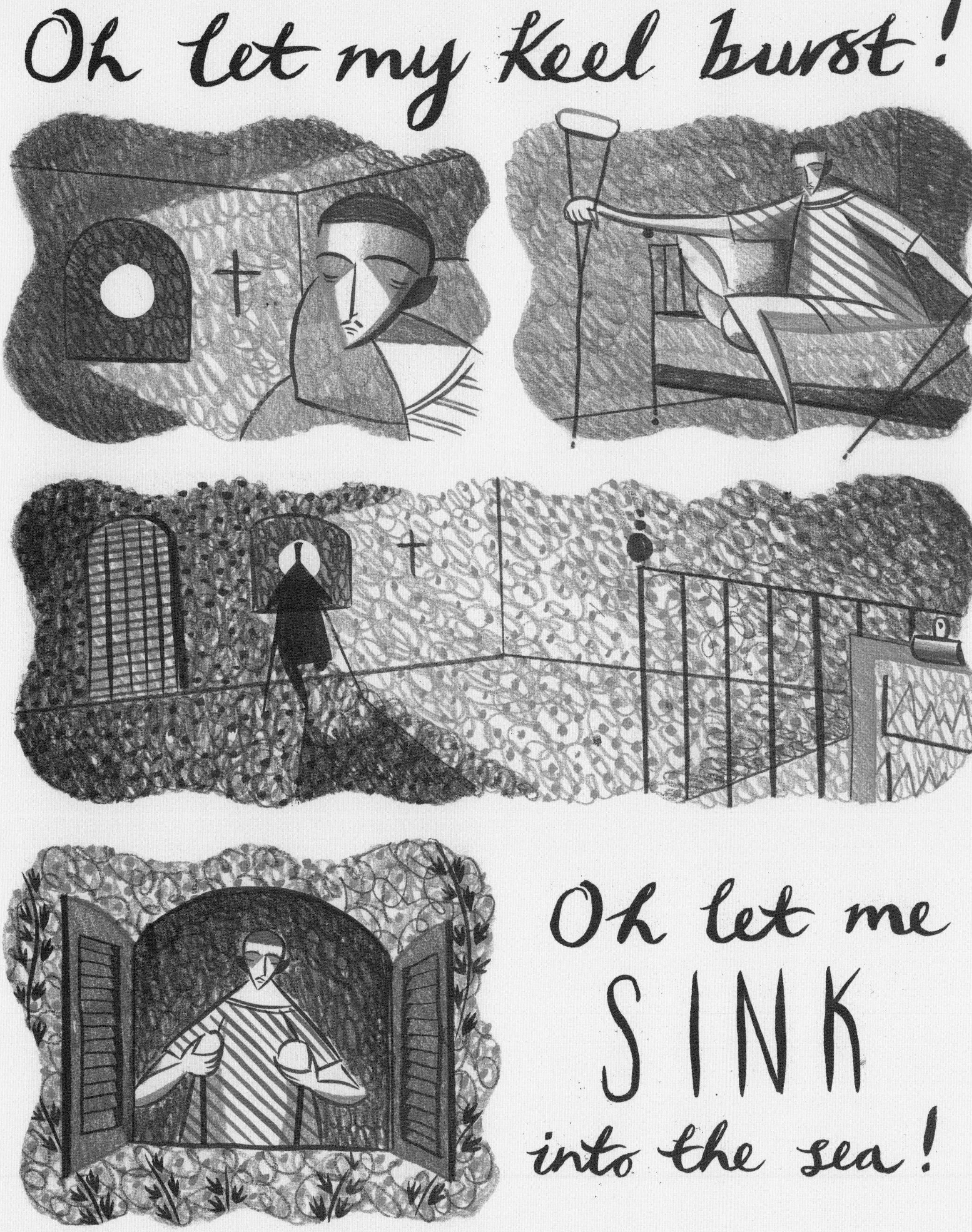
Oh let my keel burst!
Oh let me
SINK
into the sea!

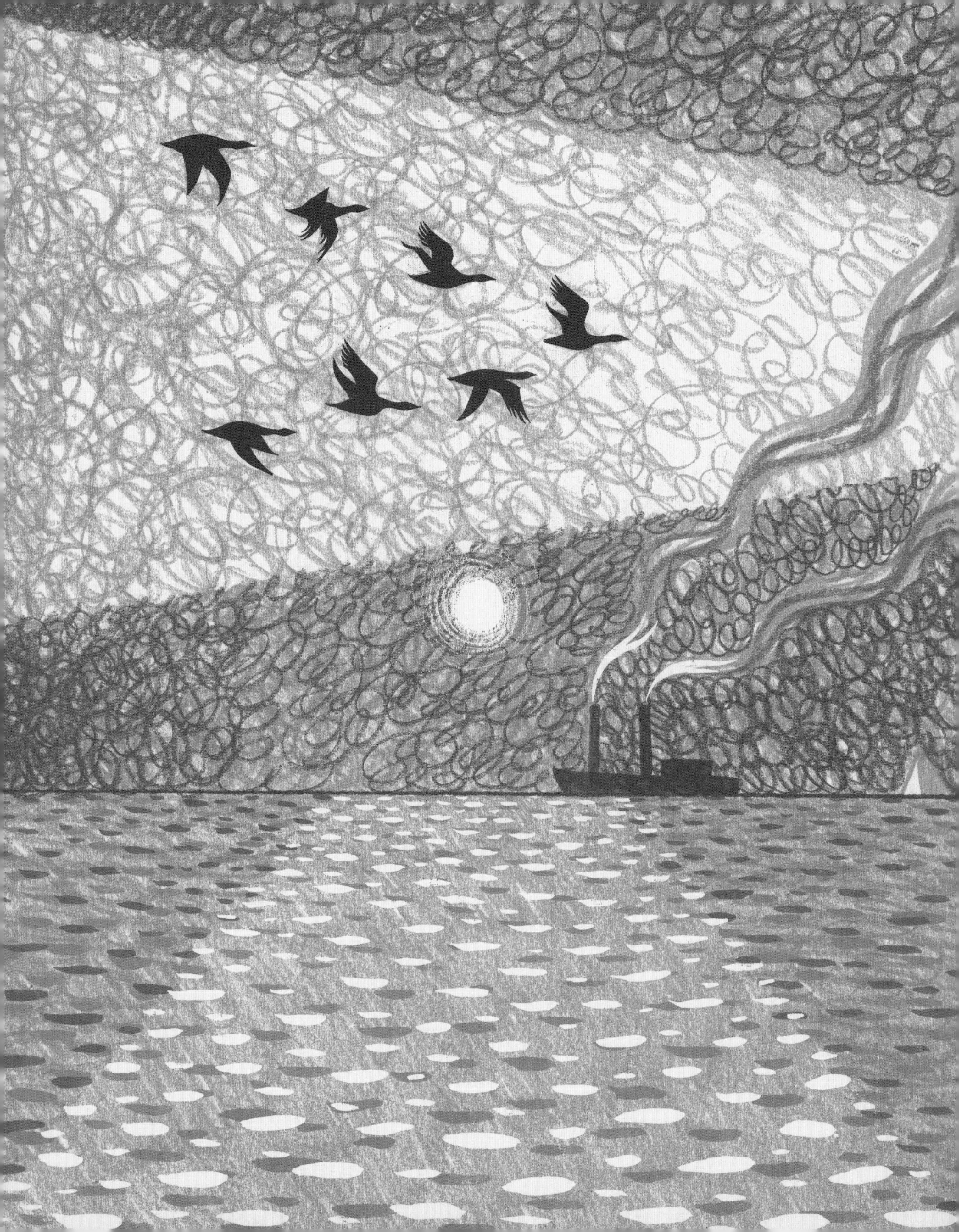

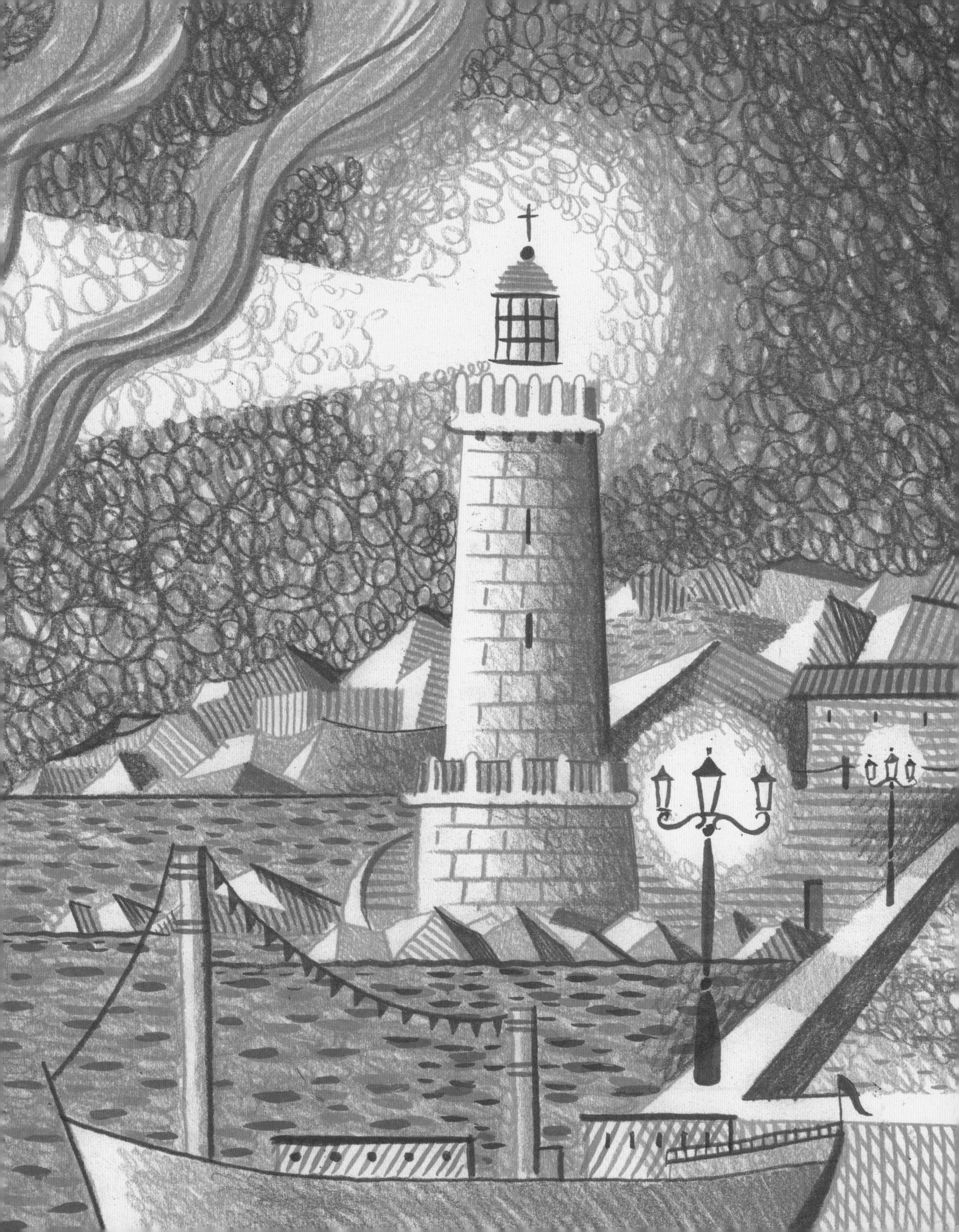

If I yearn

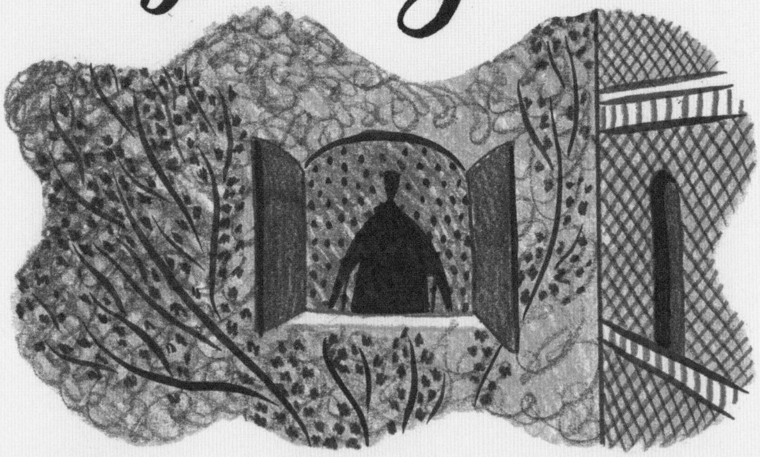

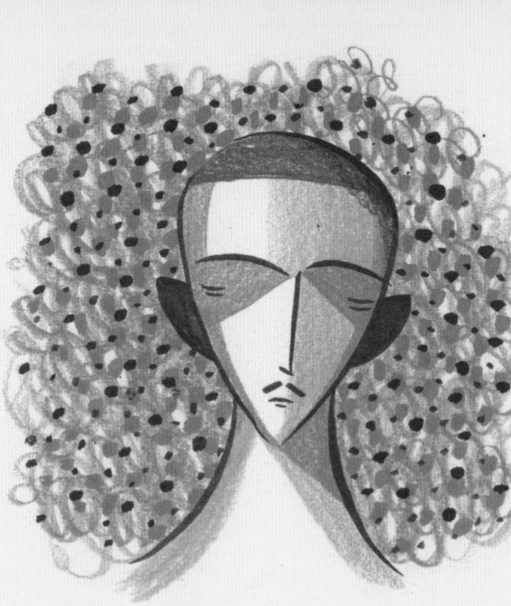

for just one

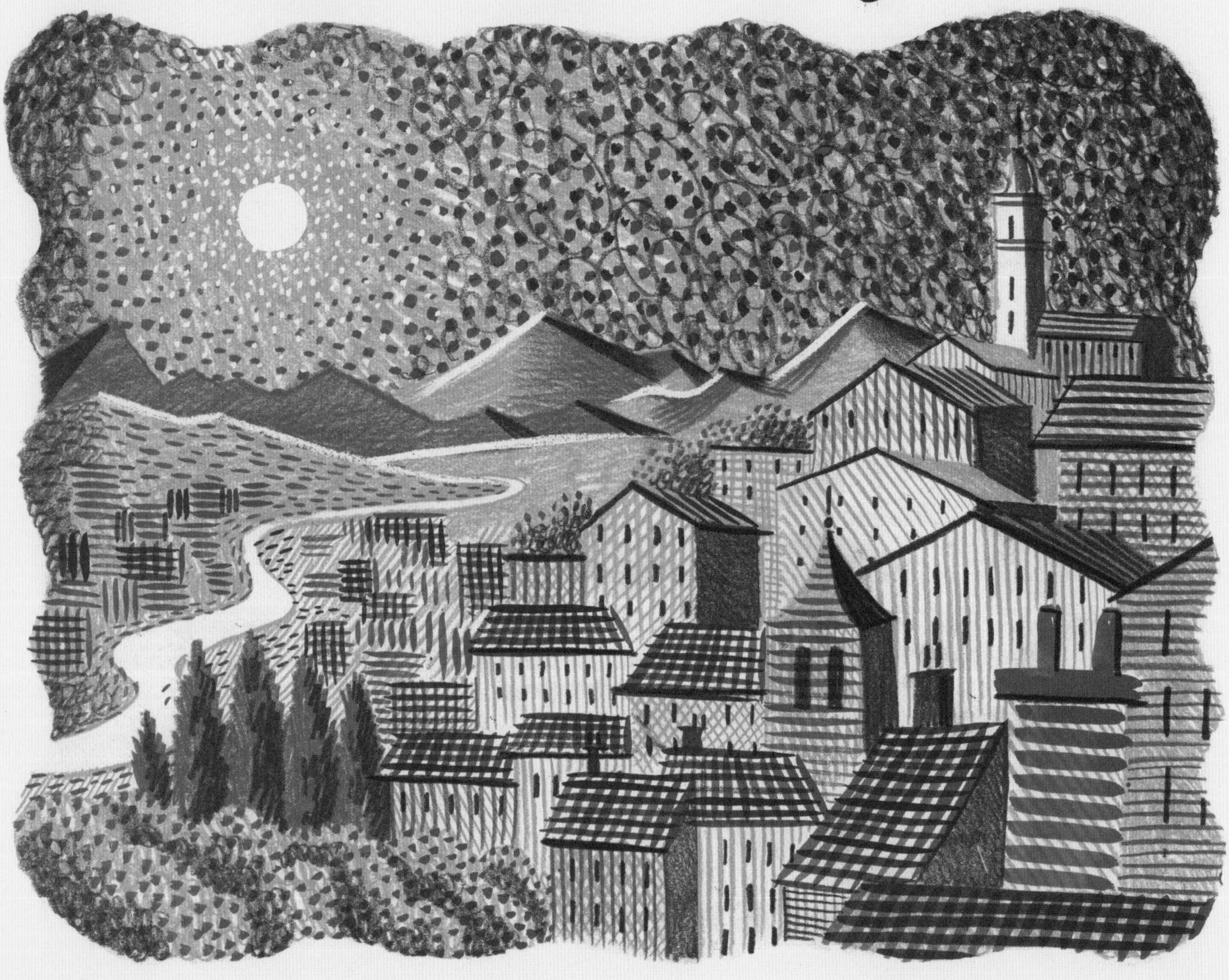

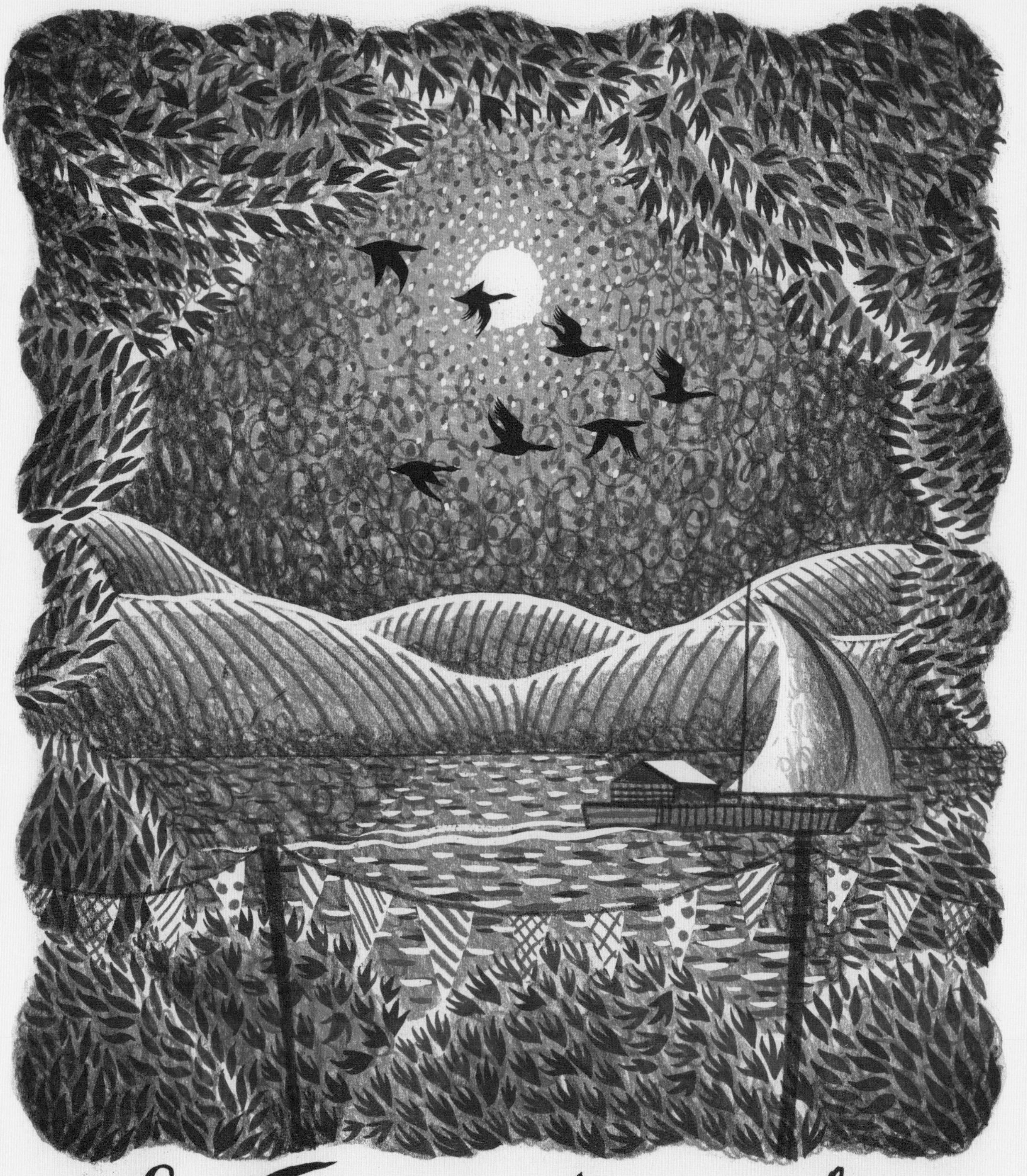

of Europe's waters,

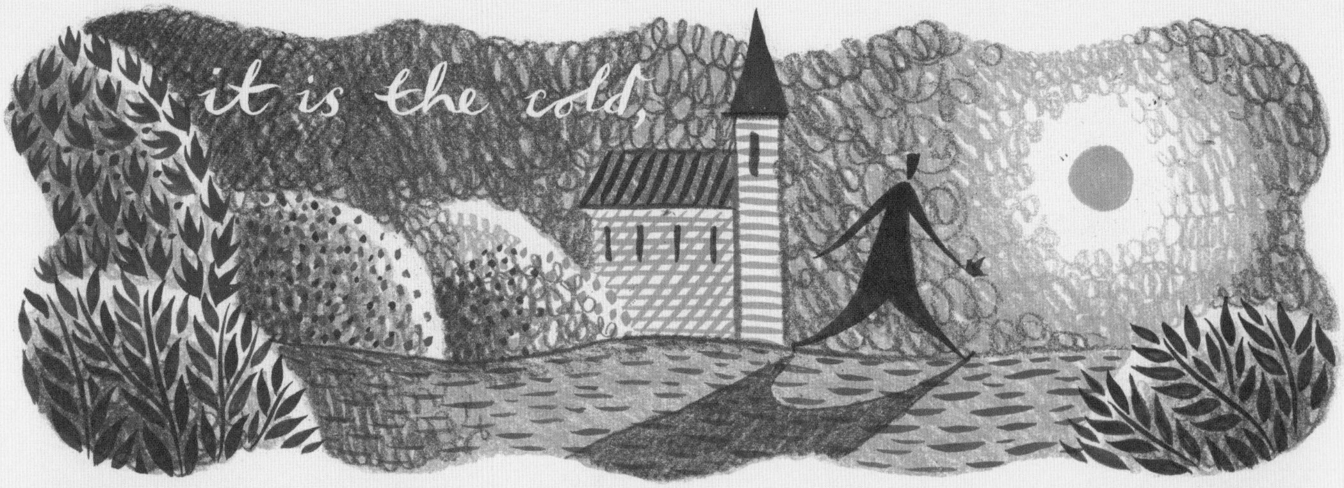
it is the cold,

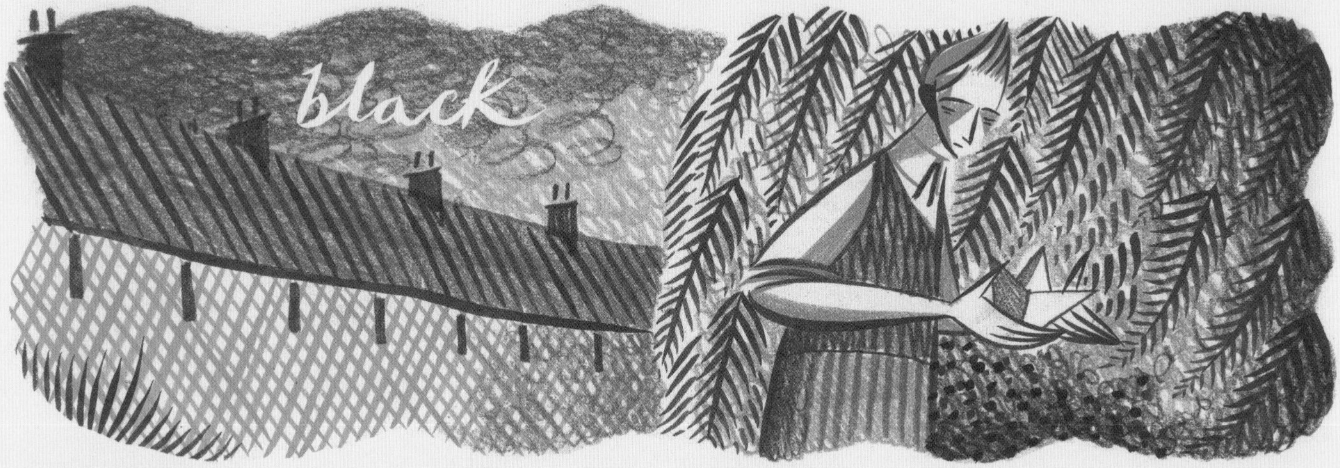
black

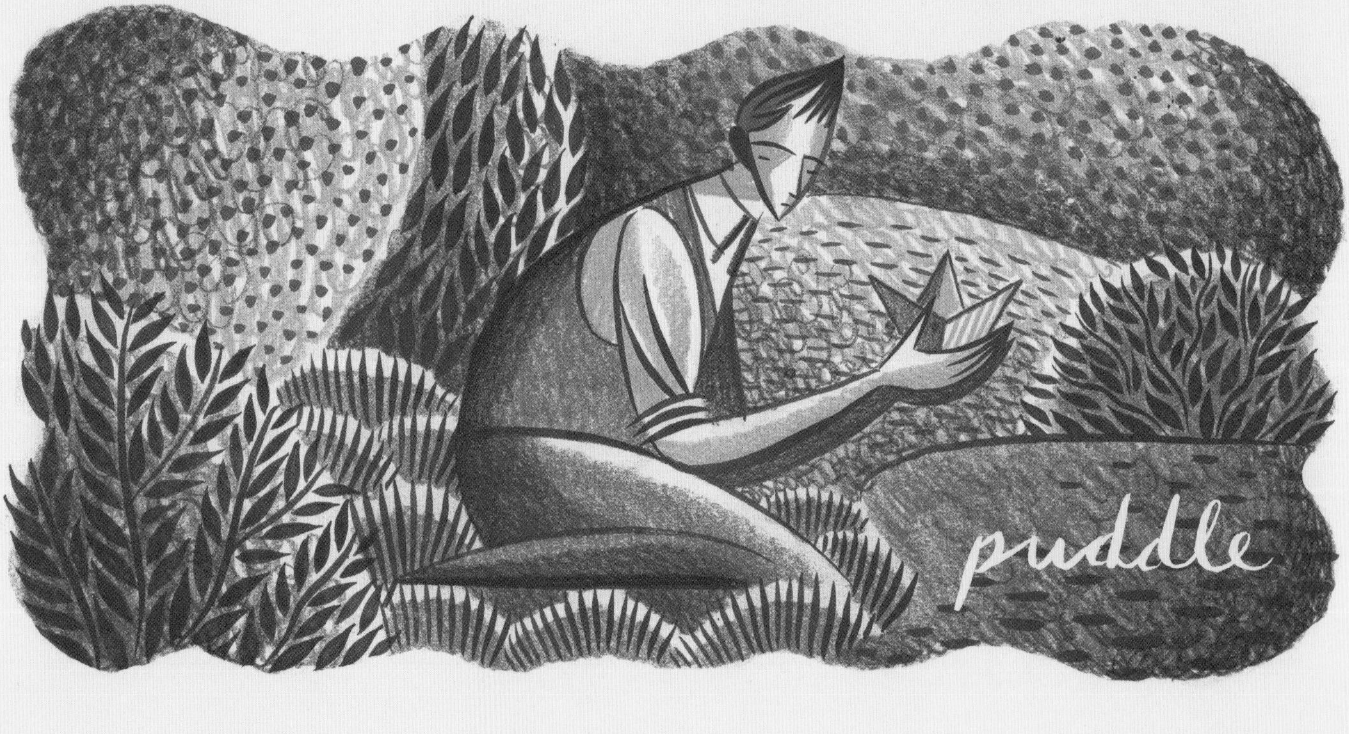
puddle

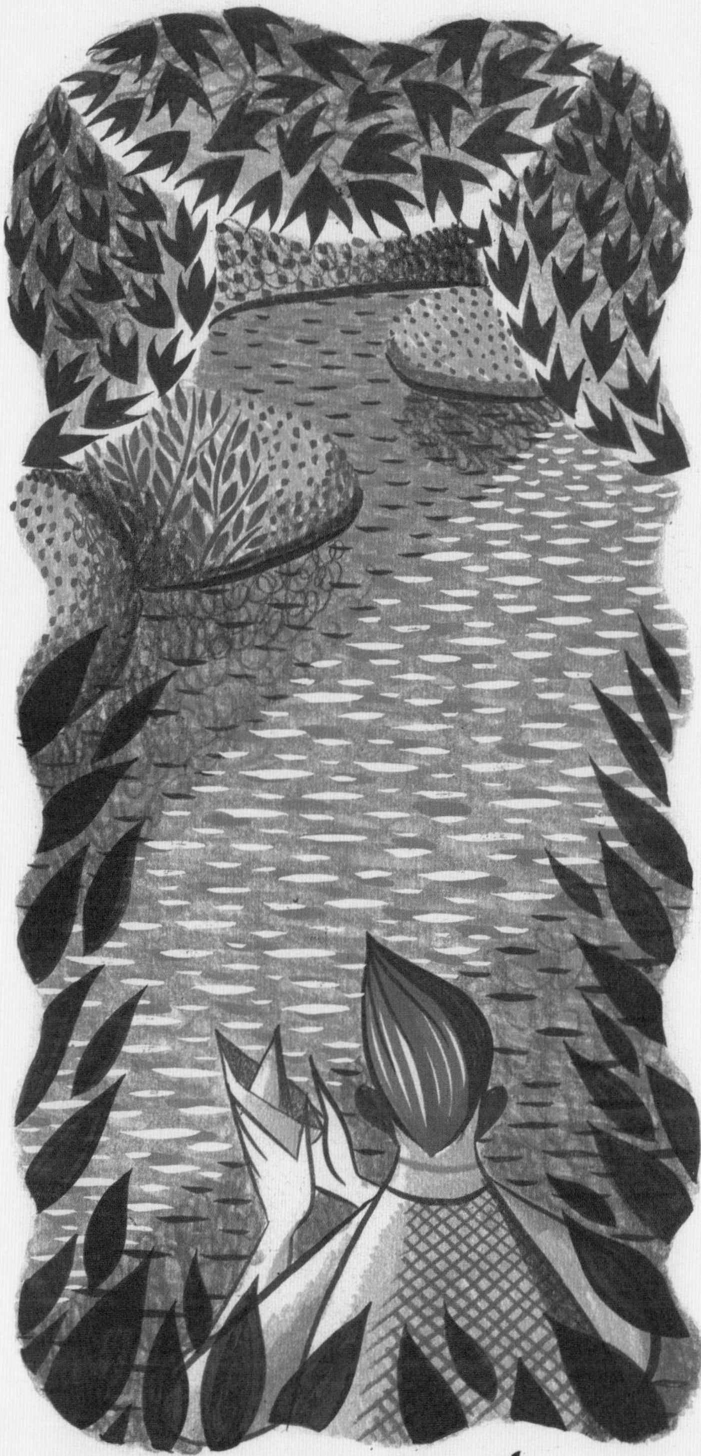

Where a child

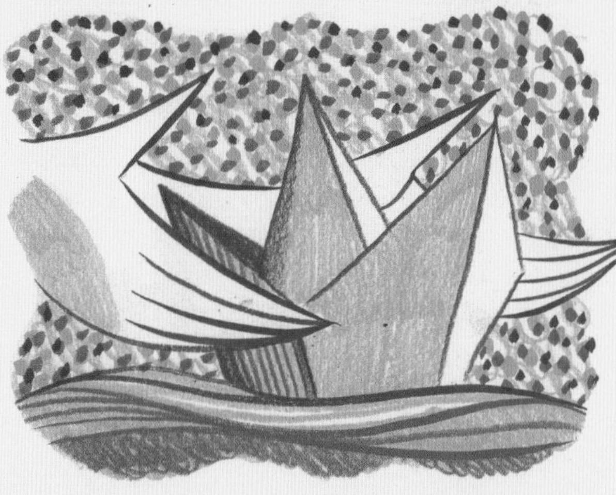

Squats

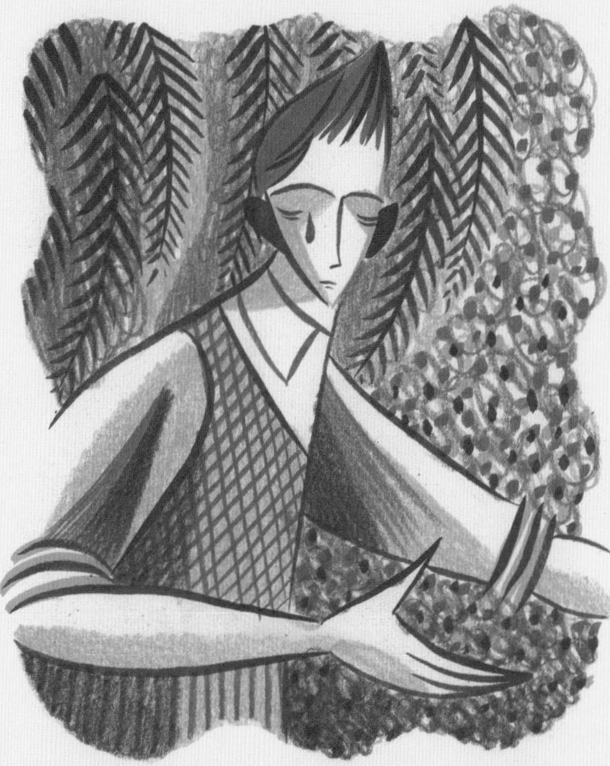

full of sadness
in the scented dusk

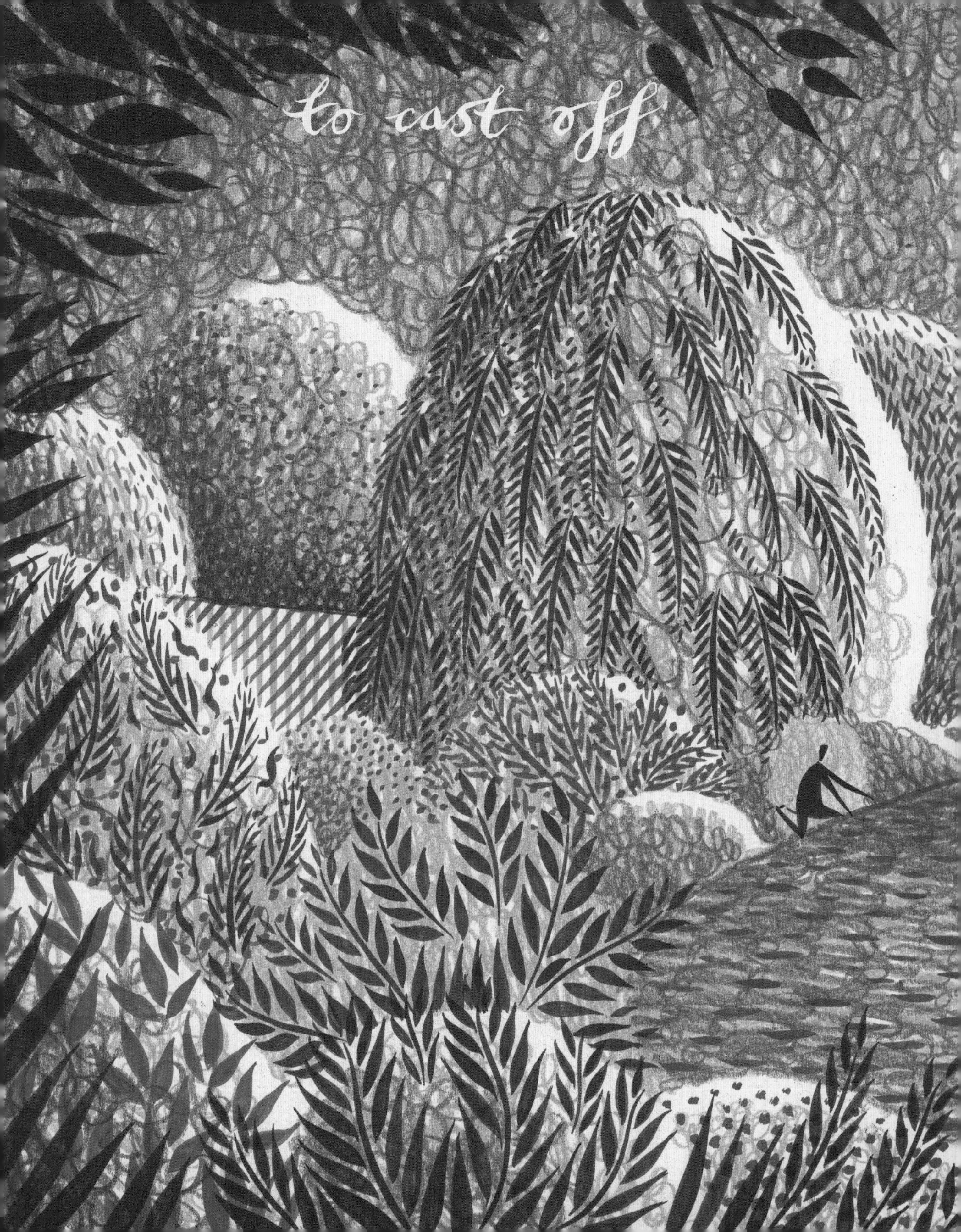
to cast off

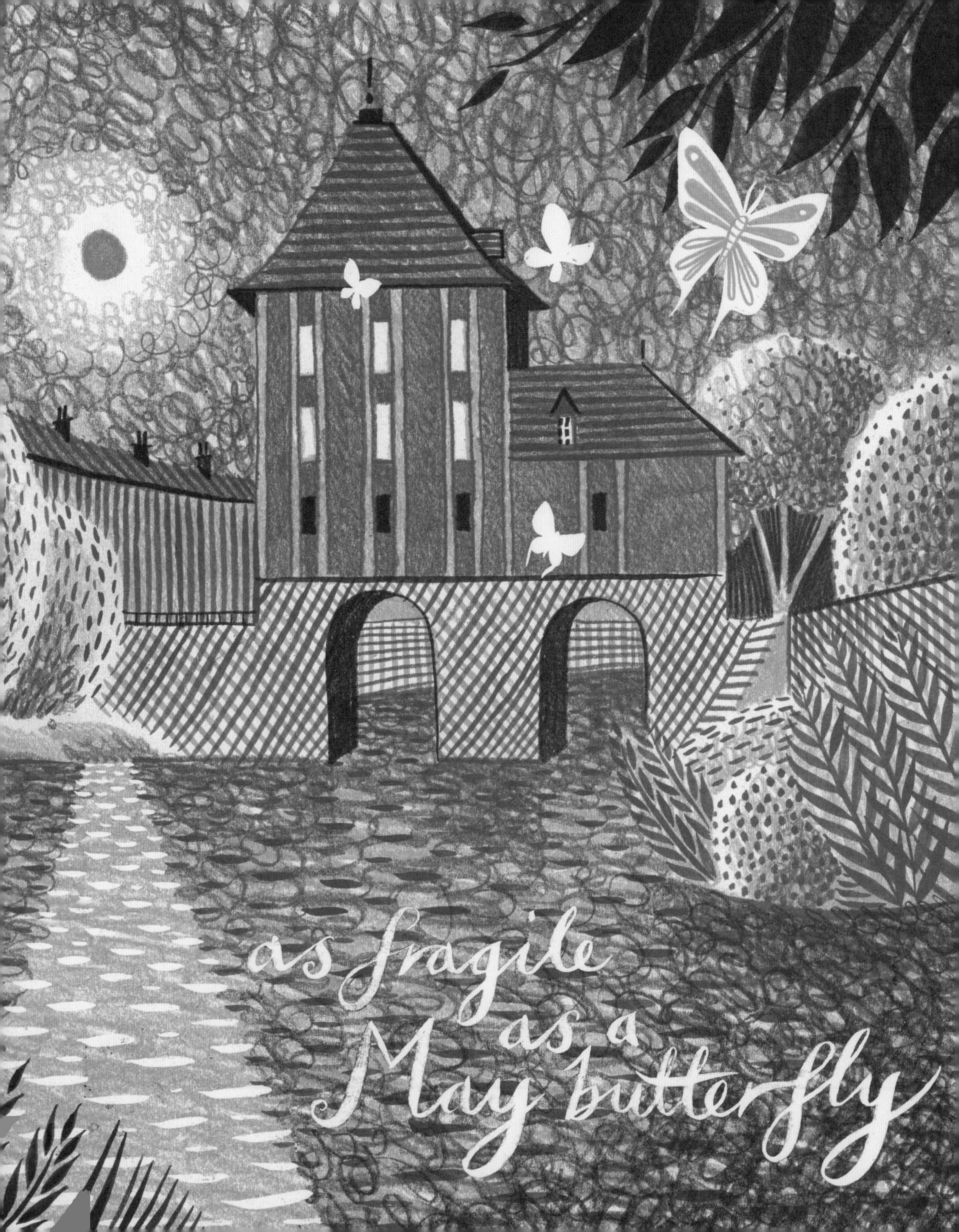
as fragile
as a
May butterfly

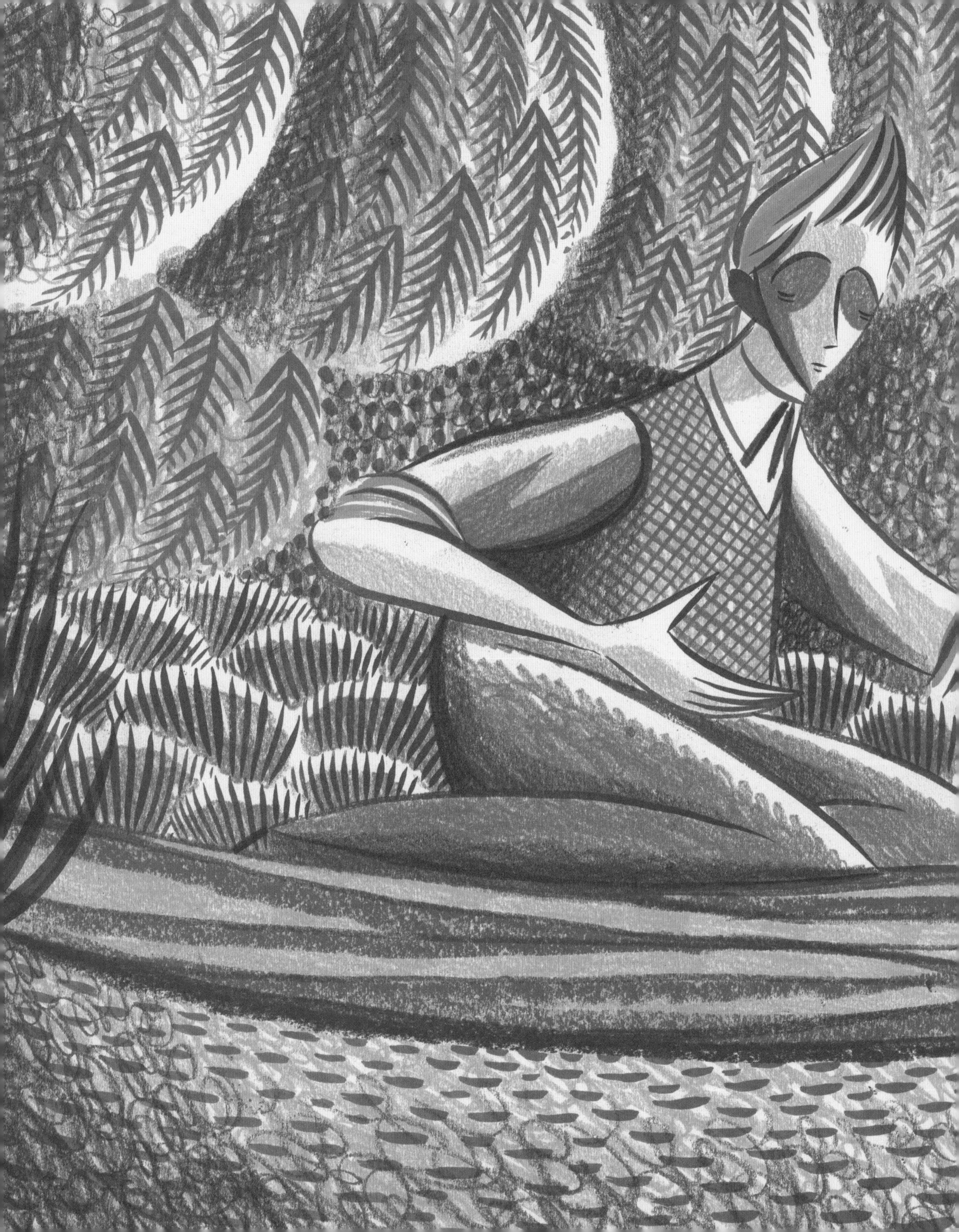

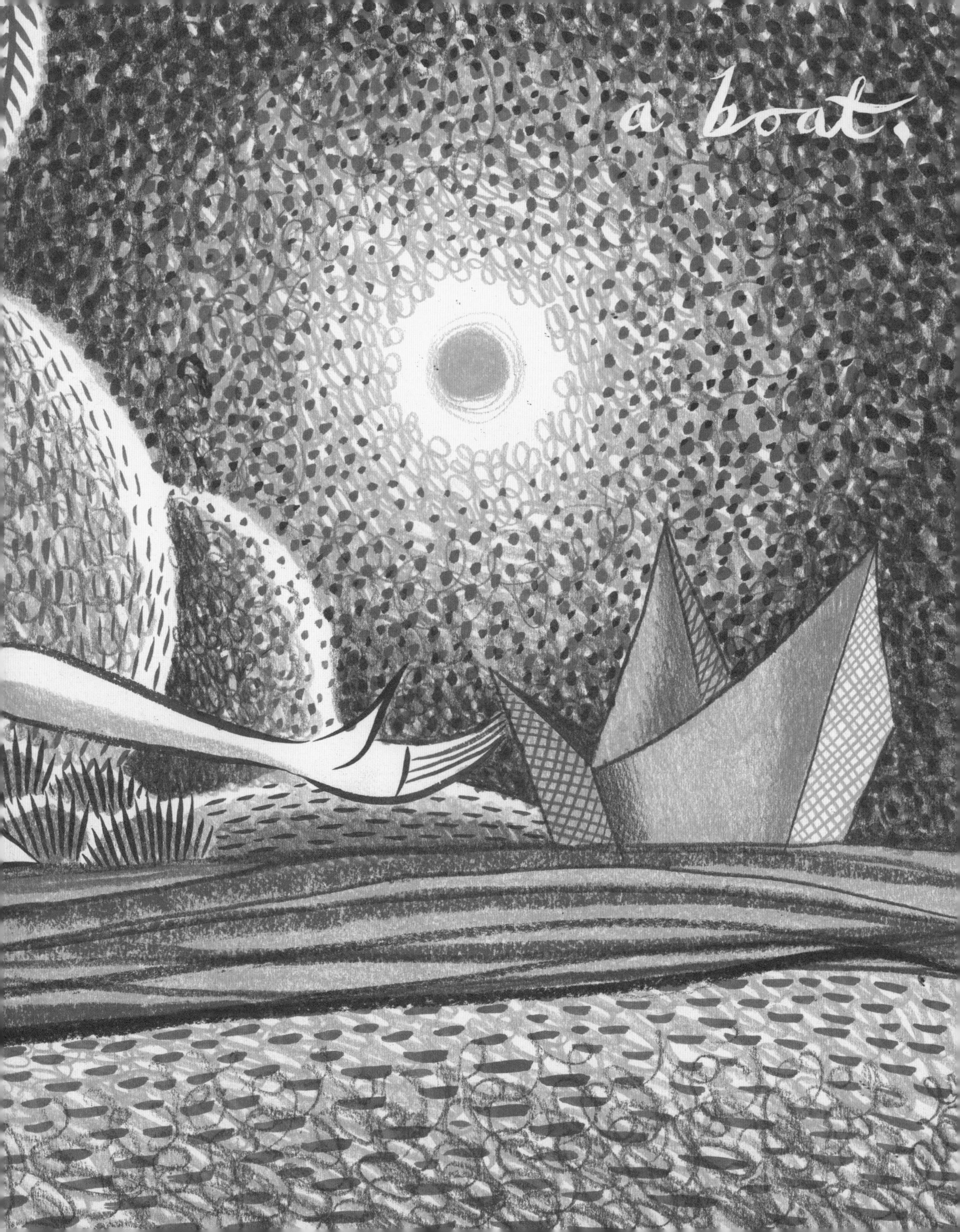
a boat.

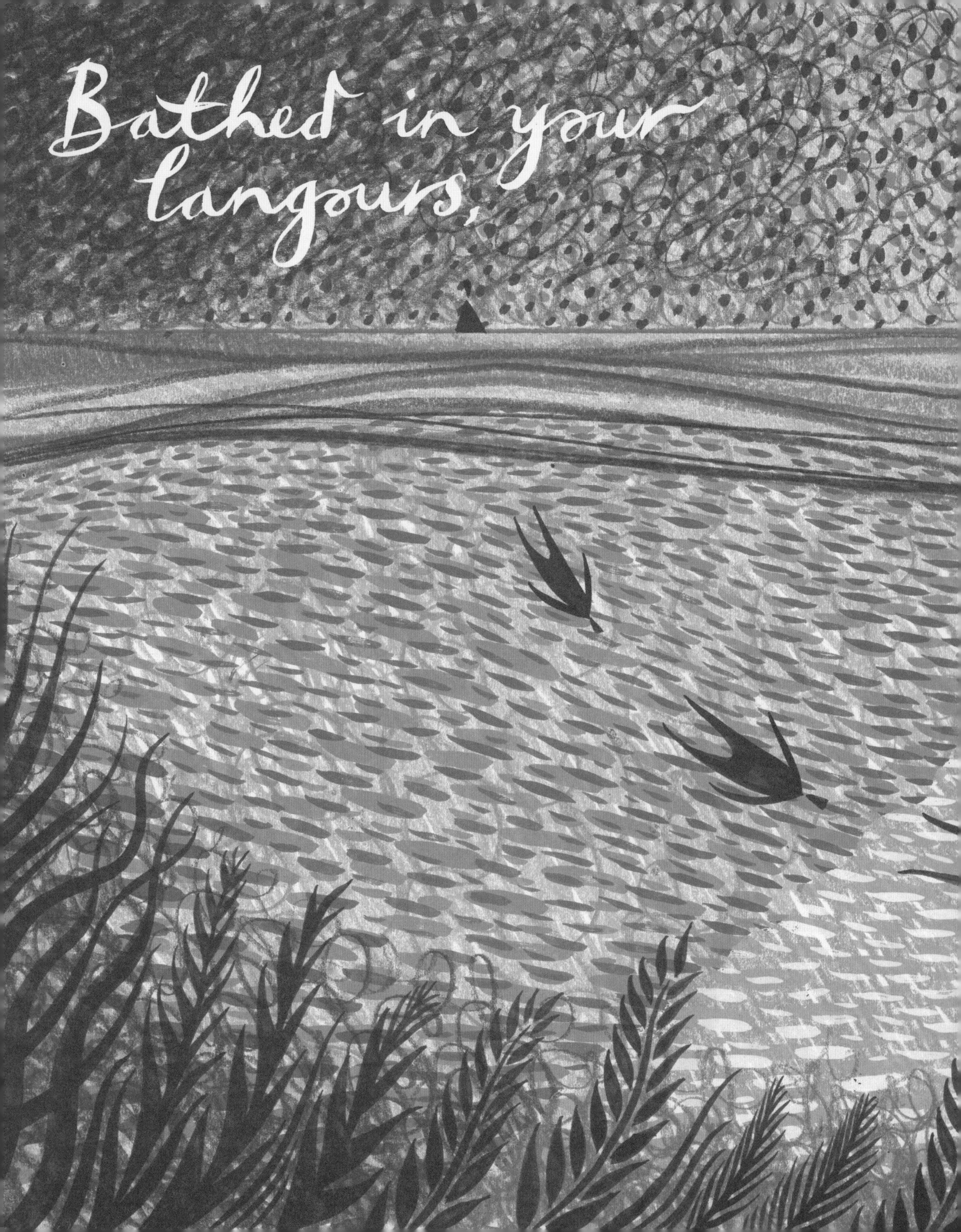
Bathed in your langours,

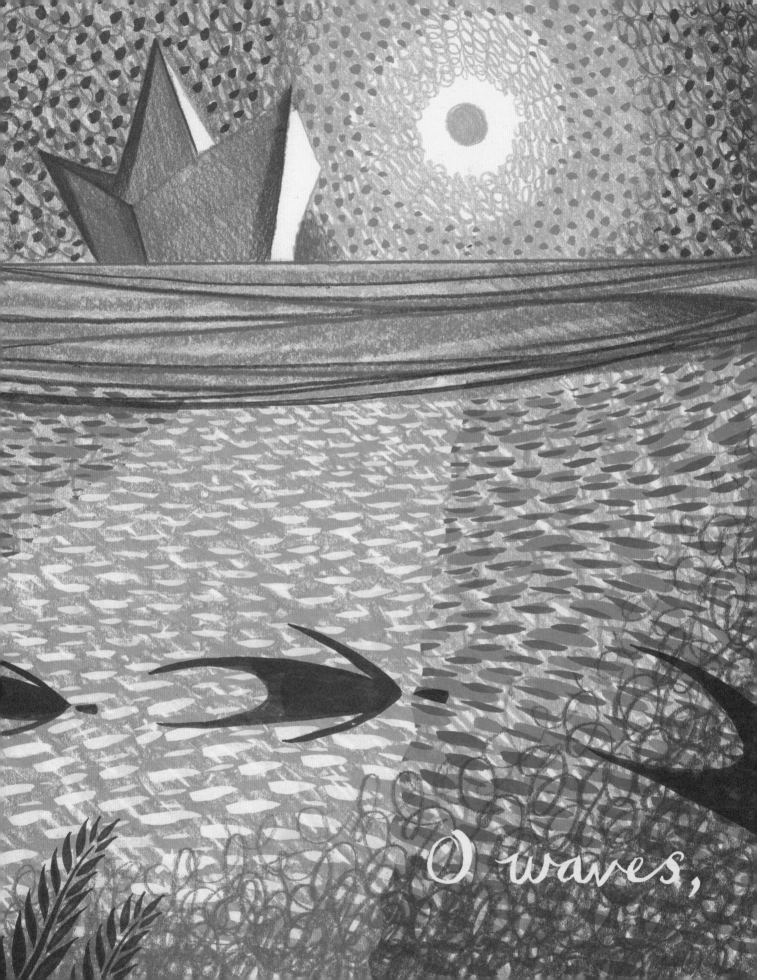

O waves,

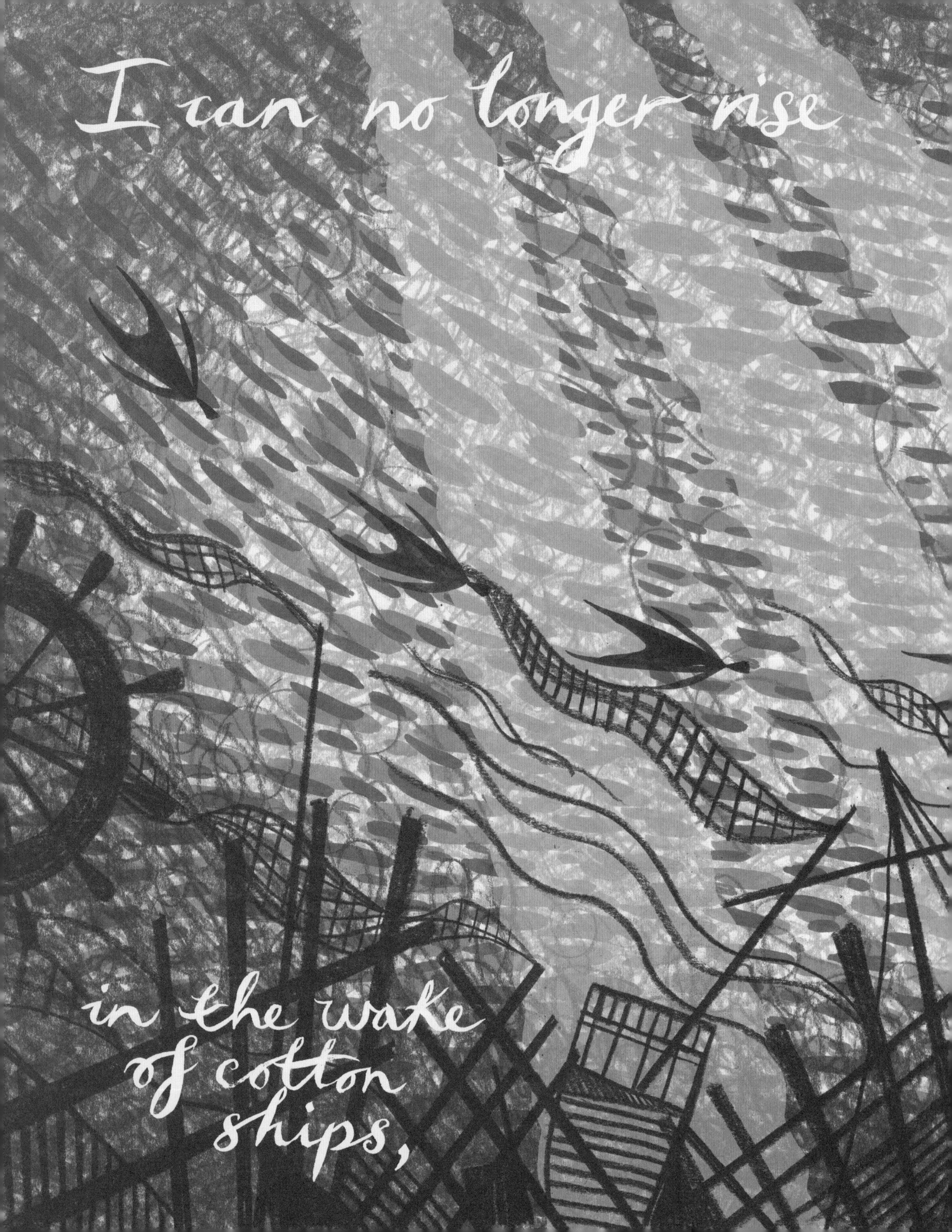
I can no longer rise
in the wake of cotton ships,

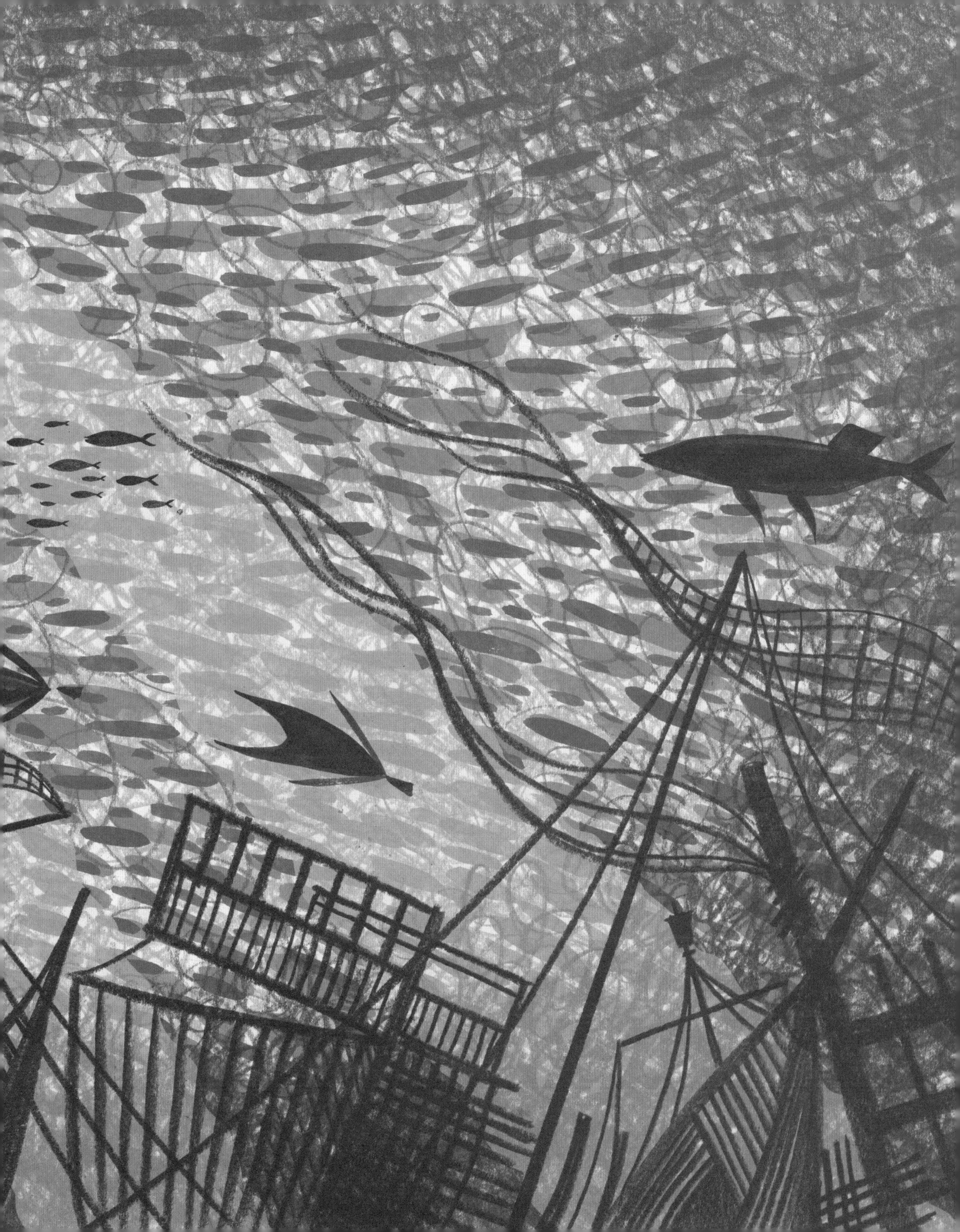

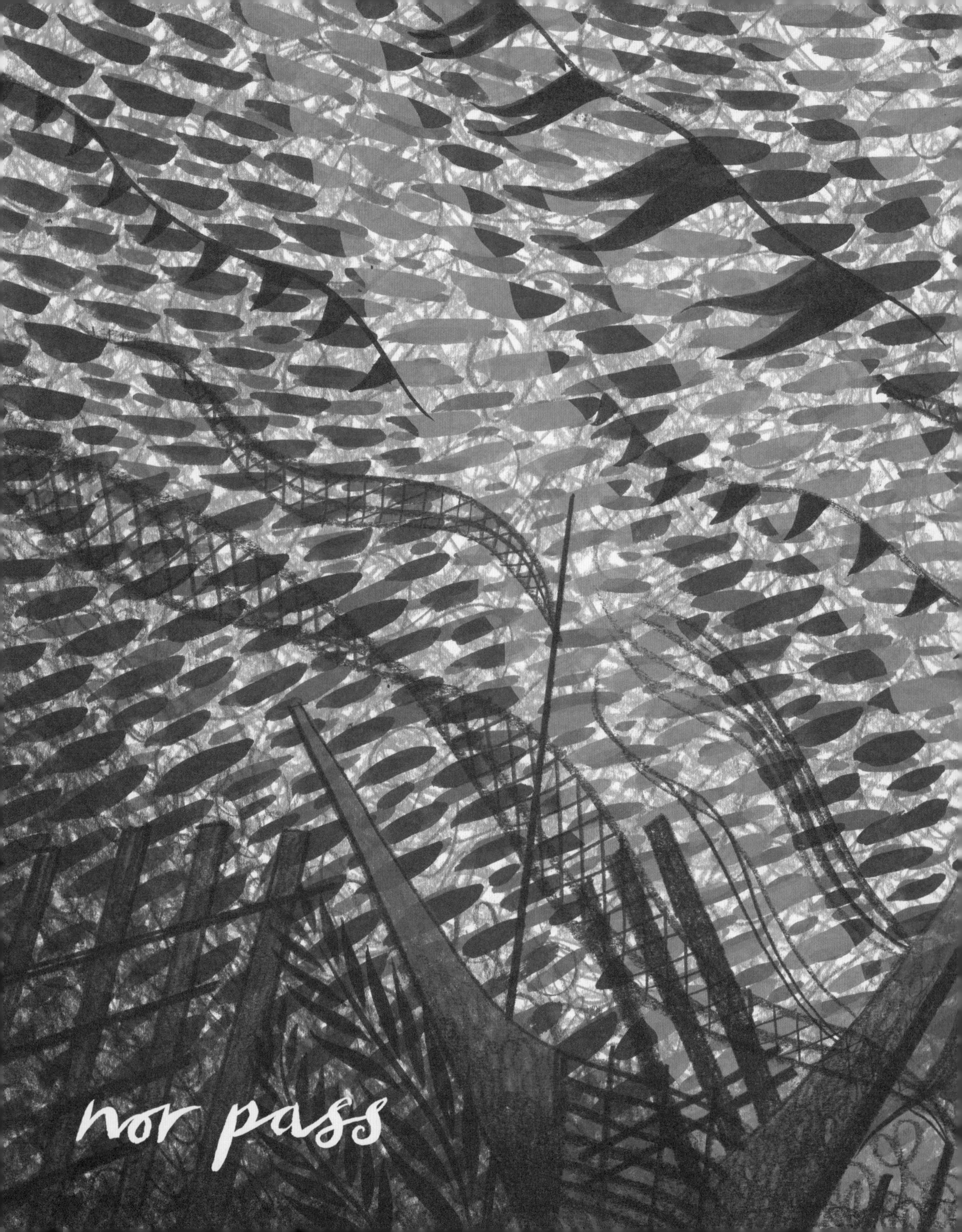
nor pass

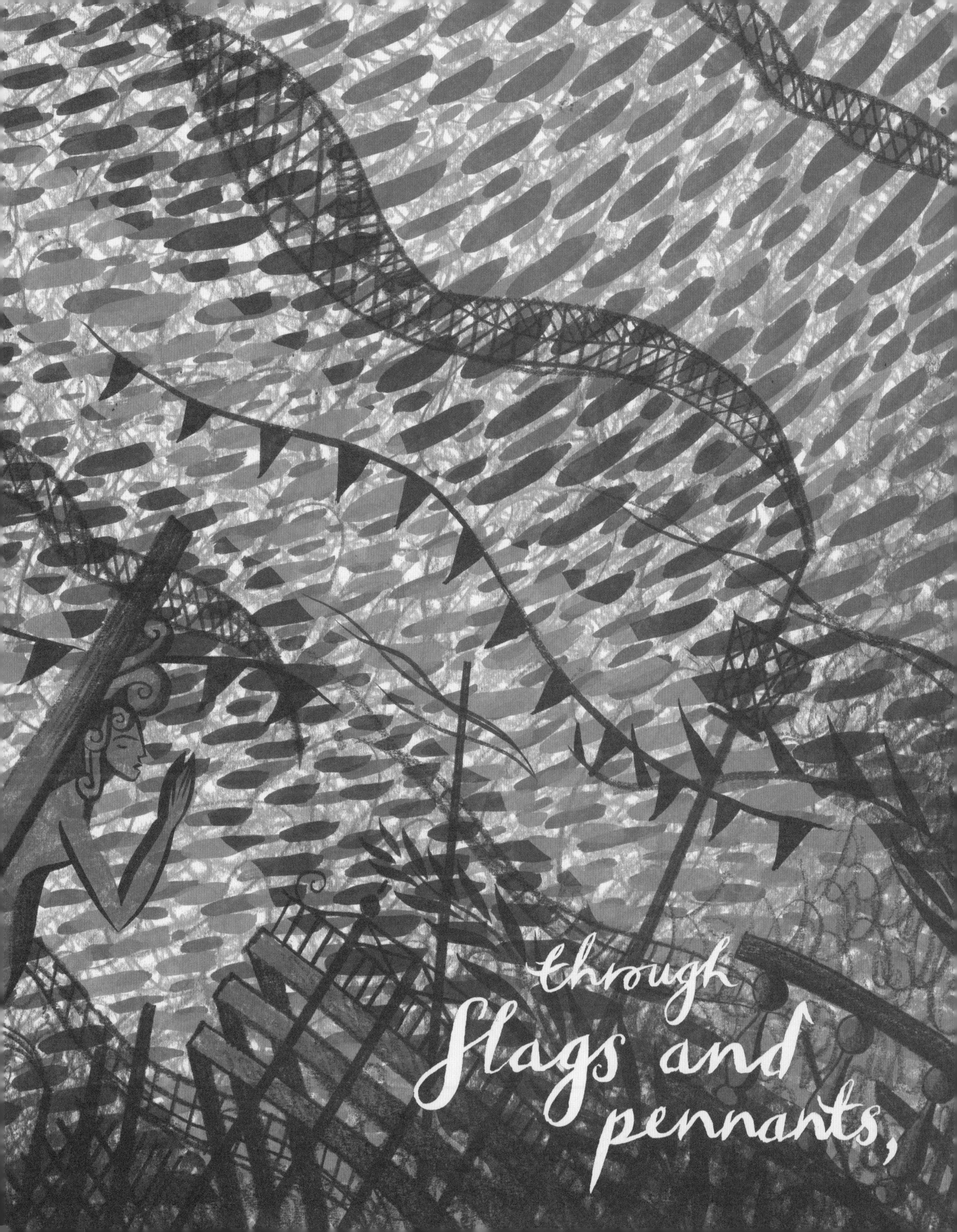
through
flags and
pennants,

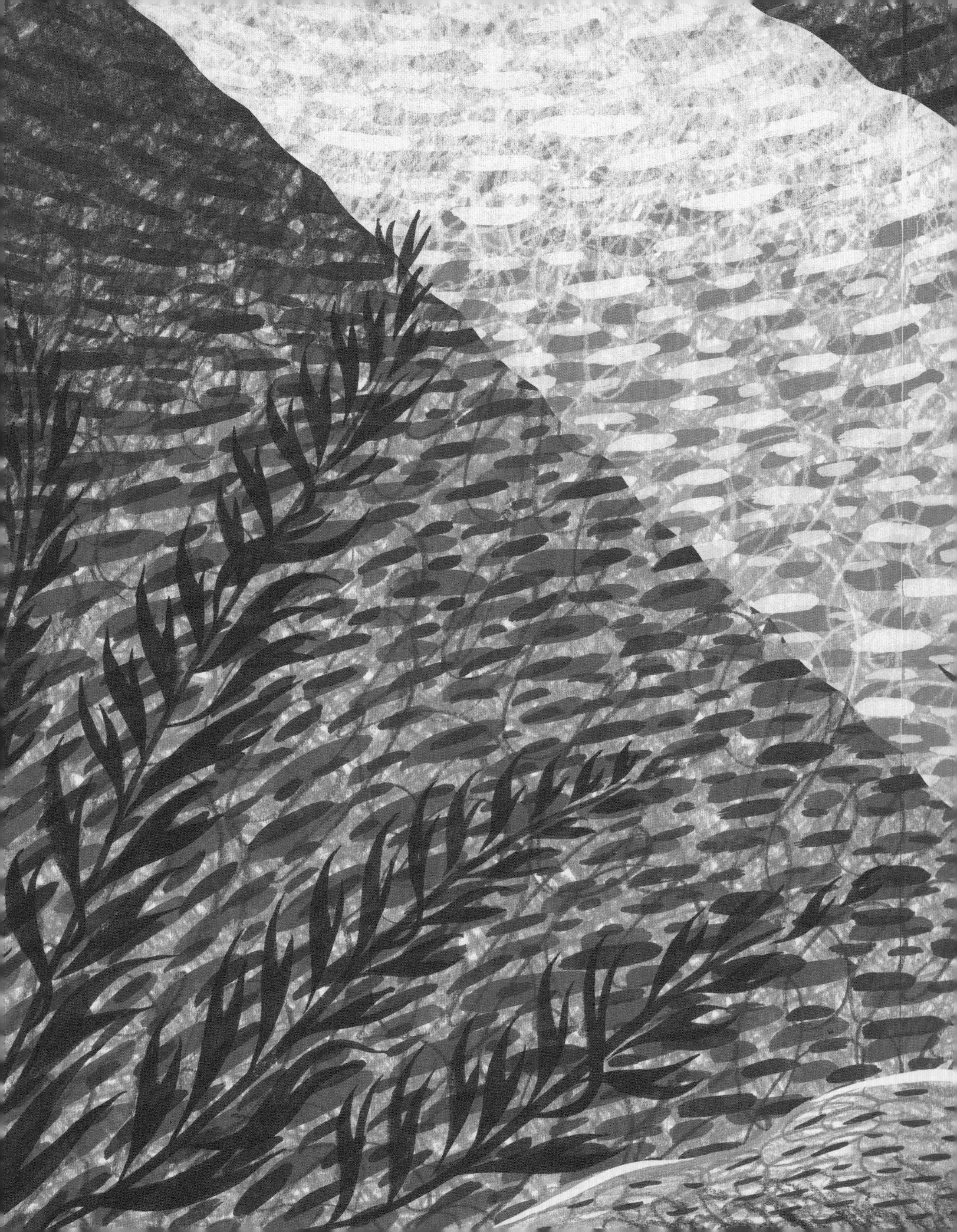

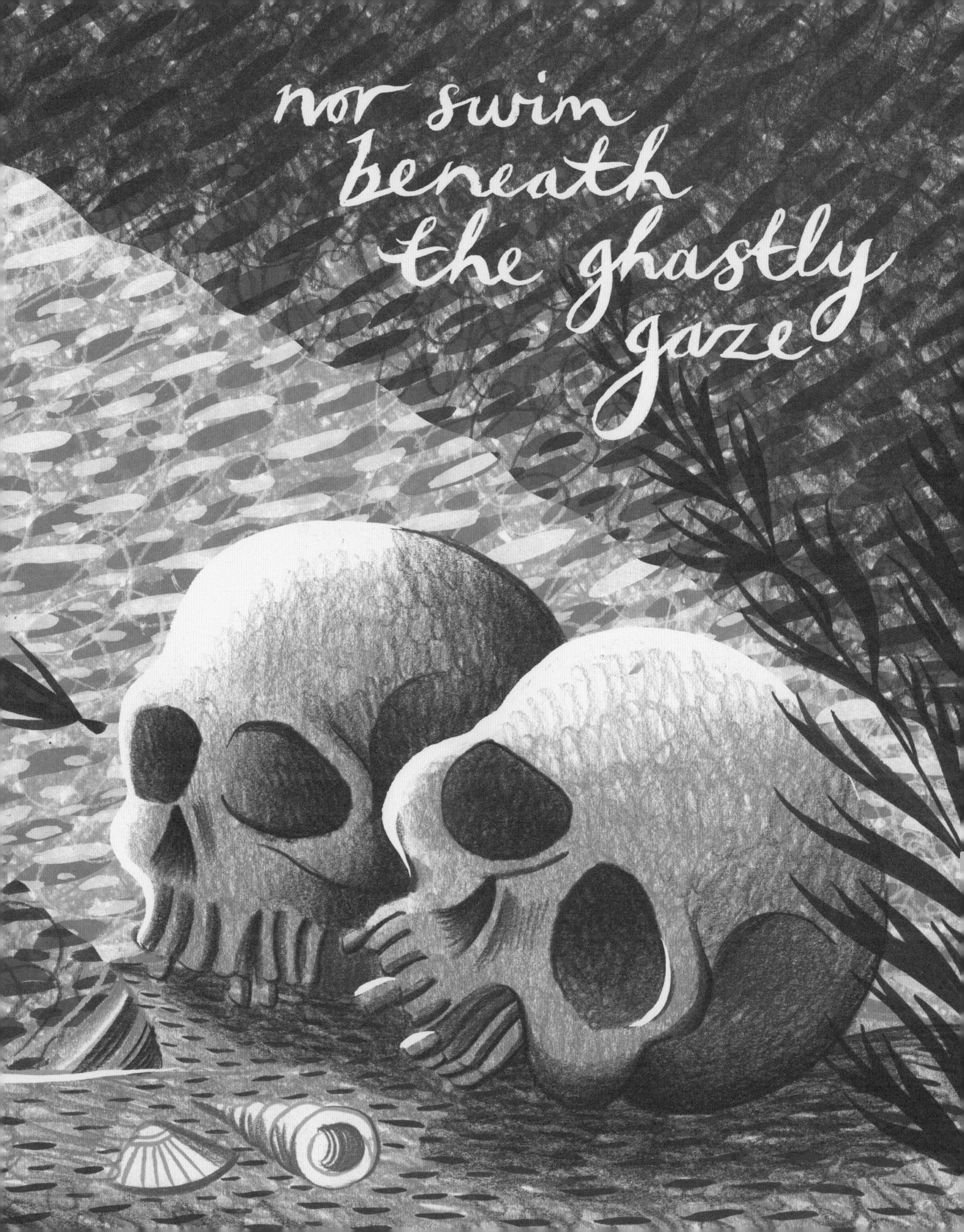
nor swim
beneath
the ghastly
gaze

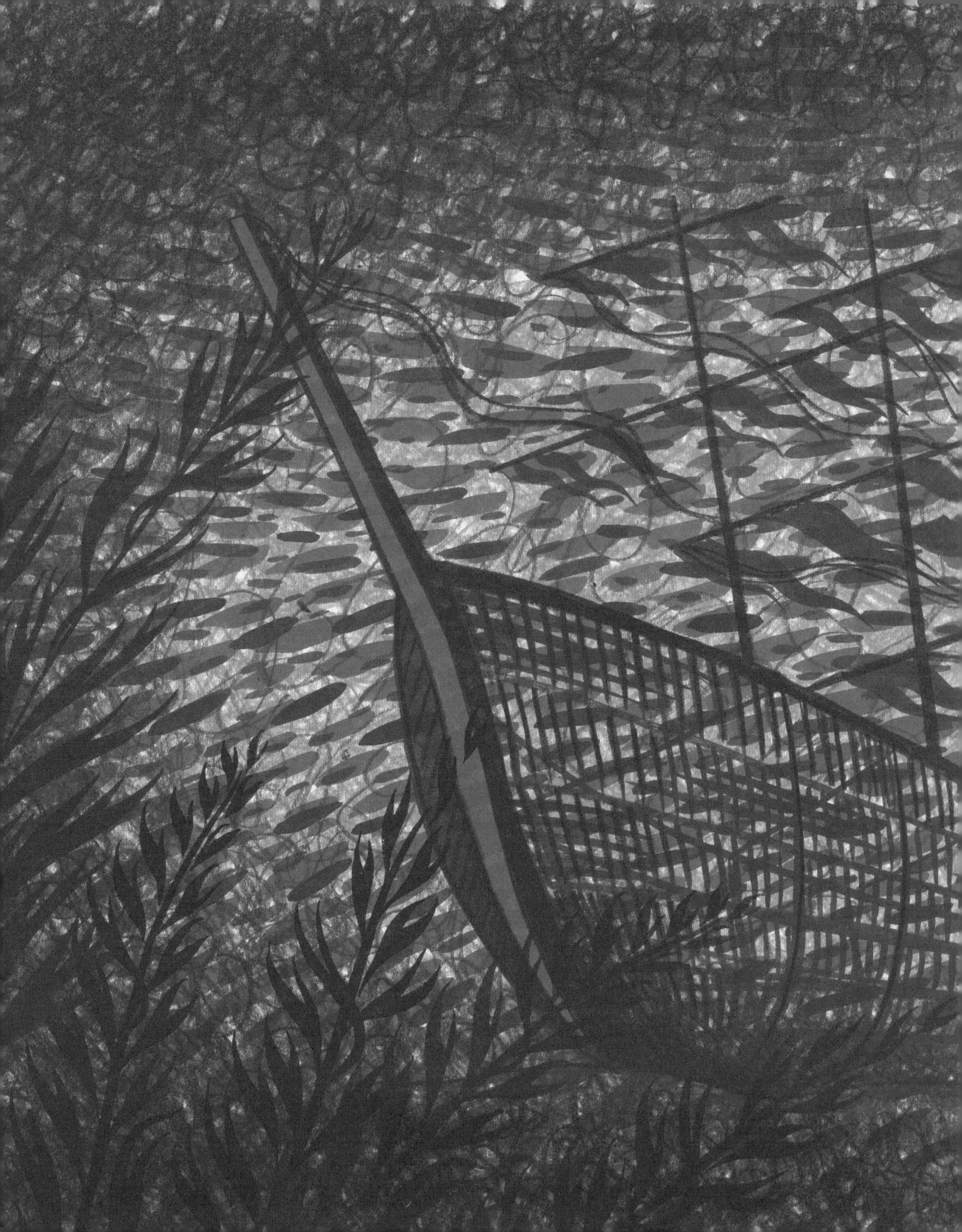

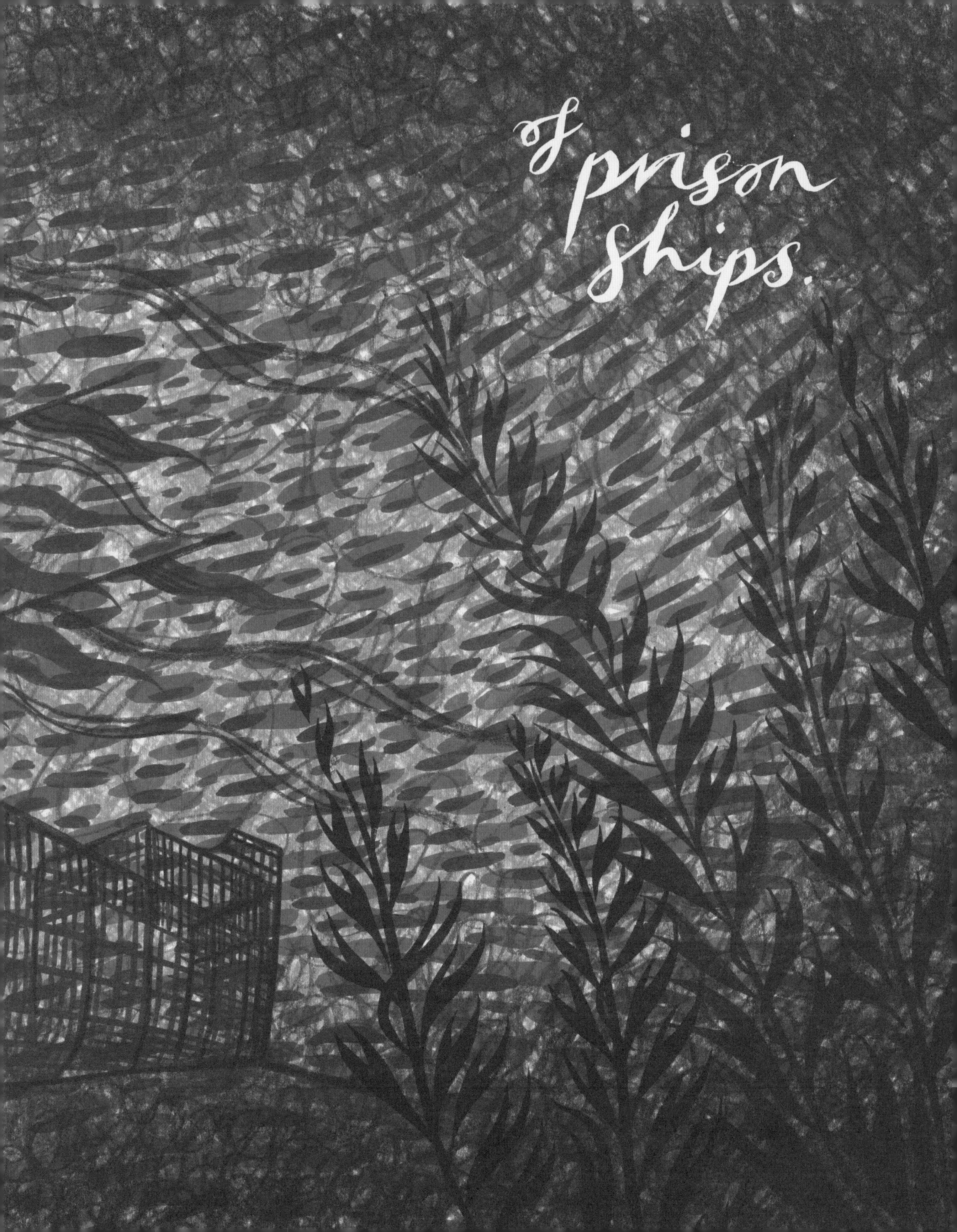
of prison ships.

Galleons of thanks to

Mr Leo Thaddeus Kay, for his friendship
and crow's nest, without which the
last two books would not have been
possible. To Brother Sam, for lunch.
To Neil Bradford, Alex Bowler and
Clare Bullock for all their help and
to Folio Art and Jessica Woollard for
reprazentin'. And to Lydia.